*For A.W. and R.Y.*
*Thanks for the trip*

Praise for *Tenement Kid*

'An obsessive music fan who fulfilled his wildest rock star dreams, Gillespie has found an authentic voice to describe his often hair-raising experiences, and the result is a rock 'n' roll epic'     *Daily Telegraph*

'*Tenement Kid* is a thrilling read laced with copious laugh out loud moments. This is a riveting account of how a tenement child of the Cold War era, and his friends, created a soundtrack for the hopes and dreams of a generation'     *Irish Times*

'I can't recommend this book highly enough . . . the best music-related book I've read this year, and essential reading for anyone who loves and cares about alternative music'     *Louder Than War*

'Readers will be astonished by the detail in his memoir, the extraordinary rolling energy of his prose, and his warmth, gratitude and performerly wisdom . . . The way Gillespie writes about music's intoxicating buzz is inspirational . . . T*enement Kid's* joy is in its undeviating belief in rock iconography'     *Mojo*

'This, as his enjoyable memoir *Tenement Kid* confirms, is a true believer steeped in politics and pop culture . . . The most arresting passages are those in which he captures the febrile, incestuous activity of Scotland's underground music scene in the Eighties/early Nineties . . . He also strikes an unforced yet tangible note of melancholy: we will never be so young and free again'     *Big Issue*

'Bobby Gillespie is a believer. A true disciple who, in his autobiography *Tenement Kid*, is going to take you on a spiritual journey through poverty and the struggles of a city at the end of time, in a country being dismantled by an evil overlord with all the might of the state behind her, and into the light and triumph of a band finding their identity. This is a tale of love; it is a tale of salvation . . . It does what you expect from a rock and roll memoir but also achieves something rare for the genre: it gives the sense that Gillespie is still one of us'     *Concrete Islands*

# Tenement Kid

# Bobby Gillespie

**WHITE
RABBIT**

First published in Great Britain in 2021 by White Rabbit,
This paperback edition published in 2022 by White Rabbit,
an imprint of The Orion Publishing Group Ltd
Carmelite House, 50 Victoria Embankment
London EC4Y 0DZ

An Hachette UK Company

1 3 5 7 9 10 8 6 4 2

A CIP catalogue record for this book is
available from the British Library.

ISBN (Mass Market Paperback) 978 1 4746 2208 0
ISBN (eBook) 978 1 4746 2209 7
ISBN (Audio) 978 1 4746 2210 3

Printed and bound in Great Britain by
Clays, Ltd, Elcograf, S.p.A

www.whiterabbitbooks.co.uk
www.orionbooks.co.uk

'When we go onstage, man, it's a war between us and the audience'

**– Robert Young**


'I do not want the world to change, I want to be against it'

**– Jean Genet**

# Contents

## Part Four (1986–1991)

# Part One
## (1961–1977)

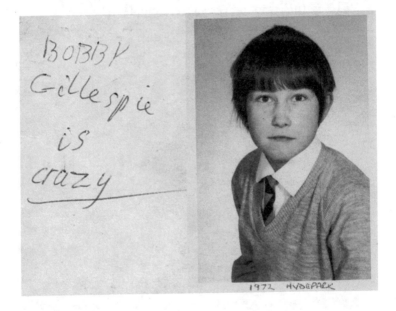

BOBBY
Gillespie
is
crazy

1972 HYDEPARK

# 1.

# A Springburn Boy and Proud of It

I grew up in spectral places. My playgrounds were an abandoned locomotive factory, a sprawling graveyard and ghostly streets of evacuated tenements. Springburn was torn down during Edward Heath's Conservative Government's 'slum clearance' programme of the late sixties; street by street the houses were evacuated, until the district resembled the photographs of German cities bombed by the allies in a World War Two history book my dad owned. It was scary but exciting. It became a wilderness. An older boy would help us break into the boarded-up flats and houses on Vulcan Street. Where once had lived the families of the hated 'Vulcies' (our street gang enemies) was now a void. Some people had left behind tables, chairs, beds, there were plates in the filthy sinks, and curtains were left hanging, collecting dust and dirt that would never be cleaned again. It had the feeling of flight and abandonment, as if the former tenants had fled an enemy army. In some ways they had. What had been a thriving working-class community was destroyed and replaced by a motorway.

Whatever happened to those people? What became of them? Where did they go? Here's what happened to me.

I was born on 22 June 1961 in Rottenrow Maternity Hospital, Townhead, Glasgow, in the heart of the old medieval city. It's a couple of streets away from Provand's Lordship, the oldest house in the city, built in 1471, overlooked by the twelfth-century cathedral where the city's patron saint St Mungo originally built his church. Nearby is the Necropolis cemetery – Glasgow's Père Lachaise – where the city's Victorian-era industrialists, sugar merchants and tobacco barons, some of whom made their vast fortunes from slavery, are interred. On top of the highest hill of the Necropolis stands the statue of the father of Scottish Presbyterianism, John Knox; his cold, pious, concrete gaze ever-vigilant, passing judgement on the wanton sinners below. There, also, on Cathedral Square, stands the statue of King William of Orange. My gran told me that drunken Catholics would come to throw bottles at King Billy on the anniversary of the Battle of the Boyne every summer. Religion, violence and alcohol are inextricable in Glasgow.

The Gaelic translation of Rottenrow is 'Road of Kings'. It is also traditionally an old English and Scottish street name given to a place where rows of rat-infested cottages once stood. You could say that I was born on a rat-infested road of kings.

I was born a year before the Cuban Missile Crisis, the year the Berlin Wall went up. My mother, Wilma Getty Gemmell Gillespie, was young when she had me. She told me that she was terrified Russia and America were going to annihilate the entire planet in an apocalyptic nuclear war when I was a baby. I was a child of the Cold War. The paranoia of imminent nuclear annihilation was ever-present in those days. She was twenty-one, and my father, Robert Pollock Gillespie, was twenty-three. They met when they were both working for Collins, the book publishers. Dad was a print labourer and member of the National Union of Printing, Bookbinding and Paper Workers; they were both members of Springburn Young Socialists. Dad was involved in a strike in the late fifties to reduce working hours from forty-five to forty hours per week, essentially introducing the five day week. Until the unions won that dispute employees were expected to work on Saturday mornings as part of the working week. Experiencing the power of class solidarity and the change it could bring politicised Dad. He had joined the army at seventeen – the usual story of a largely uneducated working-class kid with no real prospects being lured into the armed services by the promise of travel and adventure. He was a Lance Bombardier in the Royal Artillery and was stationed in Hong Kong during the Cold War, taking part in reconnaissance missions, positioned high on a mountaintop waiting for Mao Tse-tung's Red Army to come storming over the mountains. He told me that the army made a man out of him. It also gave him insight into the workings of the British class system. He would entertain my brother Graham and me with tales of his army days: huge barroom brawls with American GIs who the British lads thought were so soft and spoiled they couldn't fight a war without a Coca-Cola machine on the front line. Dad has the words 'HONG KONG' tattooed on his knuckles. He also has a black panther on his upper right arm (imagine my surprise when I saw the same panther tattooed on the upper *left* arm of my future wife, Katy, in the Hudson Hotel in New York in 2000), a Chinese lady on his upper right arm looking coy behind a fan, and the name 'Jim Surrey', his best mate in the army, on his lower left forearm. Back in the fifties, way before the current fashion for tattoos, only soldiers, sailors, Hells Angels, gangsters, criminals, felons and gypsies had their skin pierced by the tattooist's needle. Tattoos were strictly for outlaws and outcasts, not straights. Tattoos were taboo.

We lived on the third floor of a tenement building in a one-room flat bought for £100 at 35 Palermo Street in the district of Springburn. These flats were known in Glasgow as a 'single-end'. Ours consisted of one room, with a sink and a cooker. We shared an outside toilet on the landing with two other families. The only vivid memory I have of the single-end was when, still a toddler, I threw a full tin of Heinz baked beans out of the window. My mum was freaked out and rushed over to see if the can had hit anyone, but luckily it was daytime and everyone was at work or school. I just had an overwhelming urge to do it. I think I enjoyed the feeling of being bad. I also noticed the effect it had on my mother. My first ever transgressive act.

My brother Graham was born in 1964, just after we had moved to a slightly larger flat which cost £150 to buy on the landing directly below us, a 'room and kitchen'. There was a small hall adjoining both rooms. For the first decade of my life I shared a bedroom with my mum, dad and brother. Our parents bedded down together in a recess space, and Graham and I each had a single bed. There was a wardrobe, a tallboy and a wooden box which held our toys and cowboy and fireman outfits. God knows how much extra strain this arrangement put on their marriage. It must have been tough.

In the kitchen–living room there were two abstract water-colours, both painted by an artist friend of my parents, John Taylor. There was also a huge black and white poster of heroic Cuban revolutionary Che Guevara, based on that great Alberto Korda photograph, with Che looking totally heroic and hip in his zipped-up army flight jacket, beard and black beret with a star on it, looking to the future with a Christlike gaze. Che was our Jesus, a rockstar revolutionary. Dennis Hopper's whole sixties image was based on Che, Fidel, and the other bearded Cuban revolutionaries who had successfully expelled the US government and Mafia-backed dictator Batista. They say the Beatles kicked off the sixties but Fidel, Che and the boys beat them to it by three years. We also had a black and white photograph of US Olympic gold medallists Tommie Smith and John Carlos doing the Black Panther raised-arm clenched-fist salute on the winners' rostrum at the Mexico 1968 Olympics. I remember asking Dad what the guys were doing. Why did they have black gloves on, and why were their fists in the air? He explained to his seven-year-old kid that in the United States those men could not attend the same schools as white people, nor eat in the same restaurants, nor even drink from the same water fountain or sit on the same park bench. Dad also told me the story of how Cassius Clay, later Muhammad Ali, had refused to fight in Vietnam by saying, 'No Viet Cong ever called me nigger.' My first sporting heroes were Black: Muhammad Ali and Pelé. Sport is an incredible way of breaking down racial prejudice.

The room was sparsely furnished, with only a small couch and one other chair to sit on. There was a desk with Mum's typewriter sitting on top. She was a shorthand typist and there were always sheets of white A4 paper with the logo of the Campaign Against Racial Discrimination in the top right corner – a kite-shaped logo with a quartered black and white harlequin design – an organisation that helped bring members of the Asian community in Glasgow into left-wing politics as a pathway to power and influence. Dad was the driving force behind setting this up; the only person in Scotland to do so. We had no bath so Mum would bathe us in the sink. Like in the single-end we shared an outside toilet with two other families. There was a contraption called a 'pulley', made of four long pieces of wood held together at each end in a metal frame suspended from the ceiling by ropes on a mechanism. Mum would hang the wet, handwashed clothes up there. There was a bookcase along the length of the wall crammed with Dad's books. I remember a North Vietnamese flag on display somewhere. We also had a chirpy green and yellow budgie named Jackie.

Music was always playing in our house. Dad ran a folk club called the Midden where people like Matt McGinn and Hamish Imlach started out. I believe Billy Connolly actually *paid* my dad to play there; by which I mean he came along to watch and asked if he could get up and sing before the main act. Whenever Dad sees Billy at a funeral for an old pal Billy will say, 'Hey Geggie, remember I sang at your folk club?' and Dad will say, 'No, Billy, *you paid me to play.*'

Radical politics and folk music were intertwined back then, as the centuries-old songs often told stories of proletarian struggle. When you read history you understand that not a lot – in terms of class power and inequality – has changed since the eighteenth century. Dad was a working-class autodidact. His family circumstances meant he hardly went to school. During World War Two he was evacuated to the countryside in Ayrshire, near to where his mother worked in a plutonium factory, part of Britain's race to create an atomic weapon before the Nazis. His own father was away at war, an infantryman trapped on the beach at Dunkirk with the British Expeditionary Force, bombed by Göring's Luftwaffe and pounded by Rommel's Panzers. Dad's older sister Rosemary more or less brought him up whilst their mother worked. They never had their own place, always renting floor space in the flat of another family. Dad was born into and grew up in real poverty. At one point he became malnourished and was sent to a hospital to be properly fed and built back up to strength again. He told me that he never wanted to see any other kid experience the hunger, pain and humiliating deprivation he'd gone through as a young boy. That's why he has dedicated most of his adult life to changing society – he truly believes in socialism.

My first memory of recorded sound was on a Philips reel-to-reel tape recorder my parents owned. Dad would record performances at the Midden and he would also borrow records from friends and tape them. Muddy Waters was a favourite of his. He loved to sing 'Got My Mojo Working'. There is a tape of me somewhere, aged four, recorded on the Philips singing 'She Loves You' by the Beatles. My very first recording session. The most-played record in our flat in the sixties was Diana Ross & the Supremes' *Greatest Hits* on Motown. It had a purple cover with a painting of Diana, Flo and Mary. There was also Ray Charles' *Greatest Hits Volume 2* on the Stateside label with a cool photo of Ray. Dad would play this record *a lot*. Songs like 'Take These Chains from My

Heart', 'Busted', 'The Cincinnati Kid' (from the movie starring Steve McQueen), 'In the Heat of the Night' (from a Sidney Poitier movie) and the sad and beautiful 'Crying Time'. The blues seeped into my soul at an early age and made a deep impression on me. There was a lot of Bob Dylan played in the house. We had the *Greatest Hits* and Dad loved his *The Times They Are A-Changin'* LP with all the protest songs on it. There was Joan Baez, June Tabor and Irish rebel songs by the Dubliners. Mum owned a ten-inch album with a blue cover by Hank Williams titled *Moanin' the Blues* which she played a lot. Hank's voice was like no other. It was hard, serious, pained, and although I was too young to understand what he was singing about, I paid attention when he was on. Mum loved Doris Day. She also had an Elvis single with a picture sleeve that I used to gaze at for ages thinking how beautiful he looked. I later found out it was *Suspicious Minds*. I would read all the information on those sleeves. I remember a Smokey Robinson live album which had a quote from Bob Dylan proclaiming Smokey to be 'America's greatest living poet'.

There were no Beatles records in the house. Mum later told me she never liked them; she preferred the Stones.

My dad had a bookcase which ran the length of the hall stacked with books. He worked at Collins so he could easily source literature. He had Charles Dickens, Jane Austen, Daniel Defoe, Robert Louis Stevenson – all kinds of classics housed in a uniform green livery, the size of a pocket paperback. They sat on the top shelf of the bookcase. There were radical classics such as Robert Noonan's *The Ragged-Trousered Philanthropists* (published under the pseudonym Robert Tressell) and *Rights of Man* by Thomas Paine, the eighteenth-century English radical whose ideas were taken up by both the French and American revolutionaries who also helped to write up the French Constitution. Dad loved both these books and encouraged me to read them when I was a teenager. I never did. I was too busy reading *Sounds* and *NME*.

He had a couple of Victorian-era boys' adventure novels by controversial author G. A. Henty set in Afghanistan, Africa and India during the days of the British Empire. They were published by Blackie & Son and had these cool gold-embossed covers illustrated with tribal warriors. One was called *With Clive in India*. I guess Dad thought this might be the kind of thing two young boys might want to read. There were photographic military history books and Marxist literature. He had Henry Miller's *Tropic of Cancer* and *Tropic of Capricorn*, Mark Twain, Jack London, a biography of Guru Nanak, the founder of Sikhism, and other political books. One book which fascinated me was *The Book of American Folk Songs*. Here I found 'The Ballad of Jesse James' and Joe Hill. The records and books gave me some kind of early cultural reference points. My mind was curious.

We were surrounded by streets of tenements. They were constructed like impregnable medieval forts in a rectangular shape. Our block consisted of four streets: Springburn Road at the top, Palermo Street and Vulcan Street opposite each other and Ayr Street at the bottom.

Each tenement was three storeys high. There was a space outside the flats known as 'the back' where the dustbins were kept in the middens. The little brick washhouses where the women used to wash clothes had been boarded up by the time I was born. If you got inside these buildings you would find rusted antique mangles with huge winding handles to wring wet clothes on. There were filthy, cracked sinks too. These were foreboding, forbidden places and we hardly ever dared enter. Dead spaces with strange energy; spirits of the past were trapped there. As a kid I could feel unseen forces in abandoned places.

There was a brick wall that ran the length of the street which divided Vulcan Street from us, with a lane that could be accessed from Ayr Street. The ground was all black dirt with cracked and broken paving stones which would be pulled up and used in fights between a few scattered gangs in rival streets. There was no grass to be seen anywhere, and washing lines full of drying laundry held up by big wooden poles traversed the backs in every street. On a sunny day, women from the upper flats would hang their washing out on V-shaped poles from their back windows. The kids playing out would shout up to their ma for a piece and sugar, two slices of white bread spread with butter or margarine coated in sugar. That kept you going on those long summer days in the sixties.

The flats were accessed by 'the close', an open doorway at street level which led into a hallway that went straight through the building into the back. The doors to each flat were on the left and right side of the close and the stairs to the upper levels were broken by a small landing between each floor with an outside toilet.

Springburn was a really vibrant place. I remember the kids hanging outside the pub at the top of the street waiting for the dads to come out at teatime, because the men would finish work knackered and go for a quick drink and a blather with their mates before going home, when the wives would have their tea cooked and ready for them. There'd be men selling the evening *Times* newspaper, or the pink on a Saturday, which had the football results. I vividly remember coming home from visiting my grandparents in London Road, Bridgeton with Mum and Graham in 1971 and seeing the newspaper vendor on Springburn Road outside the pub at the top of our street selling the pink with the headline IBROX DISASTER – 66 RANGERS FANS CRUSHED TO DEATH. Celtic were winning by one goal to nil in the Old Firm derby and the Rangers fans, having given up hope, were leaving in droves. Then, in the very last minute of the game, Rangers centre forward Colin Stein equalised. Those leaving heard a huge roar from inside and tried to get back into the stadium, causing the flimsy metal safety barriers to collapse. Sixty-six people were tragically crushed to death. It had an effect on me, a feeling of dissociation (although I wouldn't have known to describe it as such at that age). Boys at my school would have been at the match with their dads. Death was real and close; not just something that happened to bad guys in the movies.

The Aberfan mining disaster in Wales had happened a few years earlier; a whole school full of kids the same age as me crushed to death underneath a mountain of coal spoil from the pit nearby. It had been all over the news. This tragedy entered my childhood imagination in a big way. Sometimes when I looked out the classroom window of my school, which was overlooked by a big hill on Hyde Park, I would wonder if a similar thing was going to happen to us.

Springburn Road had lots of shops and it was always very busy. There was a big department store called Hoey's and a cinema called the Princes on Gourlay Street, and every Saturday morning my mum would take me over there and leave me to watch films. They would have matinees – *Batman*, *The Magnificent Seven*, and *One Million Years B.C.* with Raquel Welch (my first crush, along with Catwoman). It was a magical place always packed with hysterical, screaming kids hopped up on sweets, teenage girls parading around the stalls with trays holding tubs of ice cream. We would all chant 'COME ON BATMAN! Watch your back!' like it was a football match and there would be a GOAL!-like cheer whenever he or Robin the Boy Wonder would punch out the Joker or the Riddler. In 1936 the world-famous escapologist Harry Houdini visited the Princes Cinema and did a show there, which would have been a mind-blowing experience for the Depression-battered and culture-starved proletariat of Springburn.

For my sixth birthday I received a Rangers strip from my grandparents. I didn't even know what football was. I wanted a cowboy or cavalryman outfit. I went up to their flat in London Road (ironically very close to Celtic Park) and they dressed me in this Rangers shirt and I didn't know what it was. It was the classic

1960s Jim Baxter-era strip – blue jersey with white V-neck, white shorts, black socks with red tops.

Later I knew about football alright.

I was friends with the boys on my street – on *my side* of the street. Even down to which side of the street you lived on there was territorialism. I never hung out with the guys on the other side. In the next close to me lived a kid called Alex Donnelly, and three closes up lived two brothers, David and Charles. Alex and David were the same age as me, Charles a year or two younger. They were all Celtic supporters, so I became a Celtic supporter because they were my mates. They all had Celtic strips; the 1960s green and white hoops and white shorts with green numbers on (a classic detail) and white socks. I thought it was *the coolest* strip ever, so fresh, clean and beautiful. Celtic were the best team in the world. This was the era of the legendary Lisbon Lions; the team had recently won the European Cup in Portugal, beating Inter Milan by two goals to one. Jock Stein was the manager and our captain was Billy McNeill. The fans had a nickname for (King) Billy: Caesar. If you look at photographs of him on that glorious May night in Lisbon 1967, holding aloft the European Cup as he stands on the winners' rostrum in the Stadium of Light, he looks imperious as a Roman Emperor. Hail Caesar!

That Celtic team captured the imagination of street kids like us. The mythology is genius. The whole squad came from within a ten-mile radius of Glasgow except Bobby Lennox, who came from Saltcoats, thirty miles away. In these days of globalised football it could never happen again. Jock Stein believed in a modern, fast, attacking style of football; that when the game was played in the right way it could be a thing of true beauty, a transcendent experience for those watching. Football in the sixties was a very working-class game, and often the only entertainment or culture in the lives of the (mostly) men and boys who attended the matches each week. Jock came from a village in Ayrshire, from a long line of miners, and shared a philosophy with his great friend and fellow shamanic manager, Liverpool's Bill Shankly, that football was really a form of socialism in action, an example of how eleven individuals can come together and achieve something bigger and more beautiful and powerful as a team, the sum of the parts being bigger than the whole, very much like a rock and roll band. Capitalism is predicated upon the potential gains and riches that await the (extremely lucky) 'sovereign' individual. Socialism is about the power of the collective.

There was a battle of light and darkness at play in that Lisbon final. Inter Milan were managed by Helenio Herrera, an exponent of the catenaccio system of football developed in Italy: a defensive style in which you wear your opponent down slowly over the course of the match, blocking and frustrating their every move, ten men behind the ball at all times. It was a negative, almost nihilistic vision of sport as a war of attrition, but the outcome was justified by the success this tactic had brought the great Italian clubs.

Later, in Primal Scream, Jock Stein's game philosophy played a huge part in how we shaped our attitude to playing and presenting our live shows. We believe that a live rock and roll show should be an assault on the senses, a commando-raid on the soul, a high-energy attack. You've gotta come out all guns blazing. Take it to the stage. Lift the people. Take them with you. Make it beautiful and entertaining and deadly all at the same time. Give one hundred per cent every time you play. The fans are rooting for you, and in return you have to give them your all. As Robert Young once said to me, 'When we go onstage, man, it's a *war* between us and the audience.'

We played football in the street, two tin cans from the midden in the back for goalposts. We all wanted to be Jimmy Johnstone or Stevie Chalmers or Bobby Lennox. The first Celtic match I ever saw was the 1970 European Cup final against Feyenoord. I watched it on our black and white telly in the kitchen. The image was washed out, almost distorted. In those days worldwide sporting events like Muhammad Ali's boxing matches and football finals in foreign countries would be beamed into British homes via satellite; the quality was always poor, flickering in and out of focus, which gave it a kind of ghostly quality. Everyone had black and white TVs in those days. No one had colour on our street. We had two channels: BBC and STV (Scottish Television). My friend in the next close had BBC2 which showed a Western programme that I loved called *The High Chaparral*. I pleaded with Mum to get BBC2 but it cost extra on the TV licence.

One day in the summer holidays I went out to play with my friends David and Charlie on the street. Everything was cool, then things got out of hand and they both started beating me up. I was shocked and traumatised, because these guys were my friends, and I totally trusted them. This was the first time anything like this had ever happened to me. I went home in tears. My mum asked me what had happened and when I told her she grabbed me and marched me up the street. She said, 'Right, you're gonna fight both of them.' I was screaming in fear all the way. She took me up to their close where they were sat on their doorstep. I was crying, and she said, 'Fight him first. Fight him! Fight him! Or else you're getting it.'

I was terrified. Terrified of both him *and* my mum. I didn't want another 'doing' (Glaswegian for a beating). I was still crying with fear, rage and skin-stripping, nerves-exposed humiliation from my earlier street encounter with them but I had no choice. It was either fight them of face the fury of my mum. I launched myself at David, the older brother, aiming a flurry of weak punches at his head until it banged against his front door. He didn't put up a fight, just stood there and took my blows without any retaliation. His little brother, Charles, was freaking out in silent terror, his eyes grown large and frozen with the dread of imminent violence as my mum stood guard on the tenement landing. Revenge had to be taken. There was no escape for any of us.

It wasn't a fair fight by any means because the presence of

my mum meant that David hardly fought back. Then it was Charles's turn to get hit around the head to salvage my family's wounded pride. Once both had been reduced to tears Mum was satisfied and dragged me away back down the stairs of the close, down the street and back up to our flat. It was a traumatising experience for me and I'm sure it was for them. They never bullied me again.

Now, I have never been a great fighter, physically speaking. I'm a coward when it comes to real hand-to-hand violence, I'd rather run than fight ... leave that stuff to the total bams and the headcases. I'm a skinny guy, there's not much muscle on me, and I'm a 'lover, not a fighter' as the old cliché goes. Instead I learned to defend myself with words, ideas and humour, not fists and boots. Still, my mum taught me a very important lesson that day: to stand up for myself and not be afraid of confrontation. It's stood me in good stead all down the years. Thanks, Mum.

I remember my mum leaving me on my first day of primary school. It was bewildering to be in a playground and classroom with a load of strangers. What unsettled me most was the fact that none of my friends from Palermo Street were there. When I came back home that first day I asked my dad why Alex, David and Charles weren't at school. My dad explained to me that they went to a different school, that I went to a Protestant school (though it was actually non-denominational, because Sikhs, Muslims and Jews could go there too) and the Breslin brothers and Donnelly went to a Catholic school. That was my first experience of the poison of Scottish sectarianism. It was bitter. 'Why is it like this?' I said to him. I felt the wrongness of it. And he said, 'Yes, it *is* wrong.' He explained in simple terms the stupidity and injustice of the situation, so that I as a five-year-old kid could understand. He could see that I was deeply upset.

Up until that day I had no idea what religion was. My parents were both socialists and although later on I found out that my grandparents, uncles and aunties on my mother's side had all been members of the Grand Orange Lodge of Scotland back in the thirties – an organisation that promotes Protestantism, Unionism and loyalty to the British Crown – it never had any influence in our house. My mum had been a member when she was younger but gave it up when she met my dad.

When I think about it now it's funny. Round Alex Donnelly's they had a framed picture of Pope Paul VI hanging on the wall above the fireplace. I'd go into other kids' houses and their parents would have a picture of HRH Queen Elizabeth II. We had Che Guevara and the Black Panthers. Thank fuck.

After that first day, I used to go to school on my own. I walked there and back, even in the winter, when you'd go to school in the dark and come home in the dark. When it snowed the contrast of walking on a carpet of pure white, untrodden fresh snow, against the deep, dark velvet shades of the bluish-black, low Scottish sky was beautiful. I remember feeling excited. The school was only a couple of streets away, a fifteen-minute walk. Still, at age five it's quite wild, an adventure in the snow.

There was a huge abandoned factory at the bottom of my street, the Cowlairs Works. At one point in the early twentieth century a quarter of all locomotive steam trains in the world were manufactured in Springburn. During the days of Empire there had been a lot of train industry, the factories and workshops providing valuable work for the people of the district. By the time I came along the area was well into the first stages of post-industrial decline. The factory ran alongside the length of the tracks coming out of Springburn railway station where we would play chicken on the lines. We'd stand there on the sleeper in the middle of the tracks and we'd see who'd jump off first when the train was coming, last guy being the winner. I always won. I loved it.

Springburn Engineering College was on Flemington Street and beside the college there was a whisky-bottling factory, and another factory next door to that which had been recently demolished. It looked like it had been hit in a bombing raid, exactly like the photos you see now of the buildings in Aleppo after Assad's and Putin's boys have dropped their murderous hellfire. Huge slabs of concrete converging at strange angles, as if a motorway flyover had collapsed at rush hour. There were rusted red spears of metal protruding from the slabs that had held up the floors where people had once worked. These spears jutted out of the collapsed concrete slabs here and there in twisted agony, as if held vainly by warriors in an ancient battle.

That's the kind of place we used to play in. It was dangerous and exciting and there were never any adults about, just you and your imagination. It was reminiscent of the Charlton Heston movie *The Omega Man*, a science fiction story set in the future in which Charlton is one of the only people still alive in in a city that has been destroyed in a nuclear war. He spends the whole movie fighting for his life against legions of rabid, zombie-like, bomb-damaged street survivors. A dystopian classic for a little kid to enjoy.

One summer day when I was eight or nine I was on my own in the demolished factory. My dad was on nightshifts, so he was sleeping, and my mum was out working. I was playing, possibly imagining I was Clint Eastwood in *Where Eagles Dare*, and I slipped. My right leg was trapped between two huge slabs of broken concrete. As I tried to pull my leg out I ripped the flesh on my upper thigh wide open on one of the rusted metal spears jutting out of the concrete. I thought I was gonna die. I'd never seen that much blood before for real (only in war movies), nor felt such searing pain. The sanctity of my body had been violated for the first time and I had no way to deal with the shock.

I managed to pull my leg out and started walking home, bleeding badly. I kept thinking I was going to die. Luckily, some friends found me limping down the street, and carried me the rest of the way home. I woke my dad up by banging at the door, and he took me to the hospital where I had thirteen stitches. The doctor was this very calm and handsome guy, he looked like Sidney Poitier. He could see I was in a state so he calmed me down and stitched me up real good and that was that. Thirteen stitches when you're that age is a big deal. For one thing, your legs are tiny so the stiches look enormous. There's a psychic scar from the trauma as well as a scar on your skin. Both are there forever. A couple of weeks later we went back to get the stitches out and it was a different doctor. I remember saying, 'I want the Black doctor, I want the Black doctor! I like that guy!'

Not long after, I had another accident. I fell off some pallets at the whisky-bottling factory. I used to climb over the perimeter fence and get up onto these disused pallets stacked twenty feet high. I'd jump between the pallets, on my own, thinking I was Steve McQueen in *The Great Escape*. I fell off and had five stitches in the left side of my head.

When I was eight or nine, I got run over by a car in Flemington Street. A girl from my class teased me about something. I got angry and she started laughing at me, so I chased after her, past the lollipop man who marshalled the busy street, and as she reached the pavement on the other side I was hit by a white Mini Cooper, went flying up in the air and lost consciousness. I woke up to a scene from a film where I was surrounded by ambulance men and a circle of nosy schoolkids (and the lollipop man) plus the worried student from the tech college who'd been driving the Mini. I was driven up to Stobhill Hospital in the ambulance. My leg had been badly bruised and I was concussed from banging my head on the road. It could have been worse. I was very lucky. That was an augury of things to come. I was to find out that chasing girls can be a dangerous and life-changing thing.

Consensual reality can be boring and growing up where I did there were not a lot of amenities available to us. We had no football pitches, and the only playgrounds with swings and roundabouts were up in Springburn Park which was too far away to go on your own. Mostly we played in the street or in Hyde Park after school using coats for posts. I would break into the condemned locomotive works in Ayr Street and shin up the pipes on the wall at the side of the building and crawl along the girders high up beside the glass roof. The girders were about forty or fifty feet above the concrete floor and if I'd fallen there would have been no one to help me because I always went there on my own and never told anyone where I was going. Mum never asked and I didn't know myself ahead of time. I'd just go out for the afternoon and see where my walkabouts would take me. You never knew who you would bump into on the street. Each day was different. As kids we have no real sense of time; we are constantly living in the moment. That power of *The Now* was something I would seek out later in life. I enjoyed the fantasy world. I imagined I was starring in an adventure movie. Breaking into that factory I was a commando on a dangerous mission into enemy territory. It gave me a feeling of freedom.

Life was good. Those Springburn streets were golden. We owned them. I never saw the cracks in the concrete pavements. They were open prairies that cowboys and Indians and the US cavalry would ride and fight on, or they were the racetrack at Le Mans. I'd seen the trailer for the Steve McQueen film of the same name at the cinema and imagined I was Steve on my chopper bike (mine wasn't a Raleigh chopper but a cheap copy with an electric-blue spangly plastic seat, like those beautiful lurex Teddy Boy jackets that King's Road designer Kenny McDonald made for PiL that I would admire a few years later). I would ride a non-stop circuit up to the top of Palermo Street, turn the corner into Springburn Road then down Vulcan Street and across Ayr Street back to Palermo Street, imagining I was McQueen in Monaco in his racing car.

*

Towards the end of the sixties all my friends began to leave the street. It was the beginning of the dreaded slum clearance programme coming to Springburn. I was far too young to understand. All I knew was that one day you'd be out on the street and your friends would have gone, disappeared. Because there were no kids left to talk to or play with on the street, I moved into my head and stayed there. It felt good and it felt safe. I dared myself to do things, like jump off the walls in the backyard onto other adjoining walls or middens. These were all about eight foot high. I once climbed the scaffolding attached to Springburn Tech and attempted a Tarzan jump between metal poles which were about six feet off the ground and six feet apart. I fell and banged my head on the concrete a few times but I was determined to prove to myself that I could do it so kept at it, pumped up on adrenaline, until I successfully caught the opposing pole.

We used to play this game called 'Best Man Falls', where one kid would stand on top of a midden and the guy on the ground would say, 'How do you want to die?' The kid on the wall would either ask for a hand grenade, a bomb, a knife or machine gun and then the kids on the ground would mime the action of throwing a knife or firing a gun and the kid would have to fall as if he'd been shot or blown up from the dyke or midden onto either an old mattress we'd found dumped in the back or a few pieces of cardboard sourced from the bins. Sometimes the mattress or cardboard would be pulled away from under you just as you fell and you would hit the cold hard dirt. We also played a game called 'Borstal'. Ten kids would each get an individual letter which together made up a secret word. They would all disperse around the surrounding streets and one guy (the Borstal Governor, or Chief Screw) would go hunting the 'escaped' kids down. Each kid that was caught would take a beating until they gave up their letter. Then they would help the Governor to hunt down the rest until he had enough letters to guess what the secret word was. I always told them my letter. No point in taking a beating for a stupid game, I thought to myself.

We were all mostly latchkey kids with both parents working. I learned how to climb up drainpipes, and could climb into somebody's first-floor window and open the door. It felt really good. I dug the idea of being a cat burglar dressed in a black polo neck and looking cool like David McCallum's character in *The Man from U.N.C.L.E.*, Illya Kuryakin.

I put myself in danger a lot. I was always drawn to transgression. You don't know the word *transgressive* as a child but you do feel the compulsion to do dangerous things. Looking for kicks. Cheap thrills. Sometimes I fantasised about being a stuntman. How cool would that be? You get to drive fast cars over cliffs and bridges, get into fights and always win! I remember flying off a midden wall when I was twelve, during the summer holidays, headfirst into the concrete, at the back of the tenement. I broke both my wrists. I had stitches in my head. I couldn't even wipe my own arse. It was at the start of the summer so I had to go the whole of the holidays with both wrists in plaster.

Other times, I wanted to be an astronaut. I was born in 1961, the same year Russian cosmonaut Yuri Gagarin became the first man in space. I loved that fact: me and Yuri sharing a moment in history. Mum gave me a stamp album with a lot of real Soviet-issue stamps featuring Yuri's face and a rocket in different colours, like a Warhol. Later in life, with the help of psychotropic drugs, I would become a cosmonaut of inner space.

My dad took me to the cinema most weekends, to the Odeon in Renfield Street, or Eglinton Toll in the Gorbals which had the biggest cinema screen in Europe. Years later Primal Scream played down the road from there, at the Bedford Cinema, now the Carling Academy, and Shane McGowan joined us to sing 'Born to Lose' by Johnny Thunders and the Heartbreakers. I remember my dad and Shane sharing jokes in the dressing room after the show.

As well as movies like *The Great Escape* and *Where Eagles Dare*, Dad would take me to see historical dramas like *Waterloo* with Christopher Plummer, *Young Winston* starring Simon Ward, and *Cromwell*, a film about the English Civil War starring Richard Harris and Alec Guinness as Charles I. I loved *The Magnificent Seven*. We all wanted to be Yul Brynner, the leader of the Seven, a cool, calm, cold and calculated gunman, dressed from head to toe in black. I remember Dad taking me to see *2001: A Space Odyssey*, and *Shalako*, a Western starring Sean Connery, Brigitte Bardot and Honor Blackman. A scene in this film burned itself into my pre-pubescent mind: the stagecoach carrying Blackman and the other rich white colonists is held up by the Apaches, and they choke Blackman to death by forcing her to swallow handfuls of sand and the string of pearls she is wearing. The image of Blackman lying on her back on the desert sand, her hair tumbling down in a mess after being proudly stacked up high in a bouffant and her breasts bursting out of her white bustier stayed with me.

On Gourlay Street there was a shop selling comics and toys. I used to buy DC and Marvel comics there, the first things I read passionately. Spider-Man, Superman, Batman, the Incredible Hulk, the Thing, Fantastic Four, Thor. Stan Lee was a god. That guy brought happiness into the lives of countless kids like myself and helped us imagine ourselves out of our humdrum working-class lives and into other universes. I used to buy these other comics about Lord Carnarvon the Victorian explorer, the guy who went to the pyramids and ransacked the graves of kings and queens, the mummies and other treasures of Ancient Egypt, bringing back the booty from conquered, non-white, pagan, so-called primitive civilisations. The British upper classes and their lower-class foot soldiers raped, plundered and pillaged every place on the map of the world that they conquered. Dad said he remembers his teacher pointing out all the countries coloured in pink on a map of the world and proudly announcing, 'See that little island here?' (pointing to the UK with his teaching stick) 'We rule all of these countries.'

\*

The first time my dad saw me on stage was at the Church of Pentecost up the top of our street. Mum used to leave me there sometimes; she had attended Sunday school when she was young, and thought it was the correct thing to do. It's weird when I think about it now, because they were both atheists and socialists, but at the church there was this thing for children called the Band of Hope, a Christian charity set up in Victorian times to educate working-class children about drug and alcohol abuse. I guess it was like free childcare. Dad said one day he was out in the street looking for me, it must've been teatime, and when he asked around the kids told him I was up the Band of Hope. When Dad walked in the first thing he saw was me up on stage singing the hymn 'My Cup is Full and Runneth Over'. That was my first gig. Aged five. At church. A temperance society. Singing the gospels. Oh, the irony! I got the blues. Fuck you.

The people who ran the Band of Hope were nice. They gave you a cup of tea and a biscuit. It was somewhere for us kids to hang out when there was nothing else happening on the street. Another place we would go was the Springburn Library on Ayr Street. Dad always encouraged me to read. He had experienced next to no education but he had enjoyed reading Mark Twain, Robert Louis Stevenson and Daniel Defoe when he was a kid and he wanted me to experience the stimulation of imagination that literature brings. There was an adult section which was quite serious, people would be in there reading and it was very well-kept. The librarians weren't to be messed with. I guess I just went in and looked at kids' books. Sometimes it was just a place to escape to that was not the street.

Just around the corner from the library on Vulcan Street there was a storefront church at ground level. Next door to that was a bookies, like a hole in the wall with no signage above it – a working-class bookies, not a bright, multicoloured, modern-style Ladbrokes or anything. We'd always see tired and beaten old men hanging out near the dark doorway, betting away their wages or dole money on fading dreams of winning horses. It's a fixed game and they all knew it, but that didn't stop them going back every other day to try it all over again. Addiction. Compulsion. Boredom. The storefront church had a Hammond organ in it, with all the stops and stuff to change the sound. A prim middle-aged lady would play it. I loved the sound she got out of the organ. There was something calming about it. Sometimes during school holidays we would go in and listen to the people singing their hymns. I always dug that and I was always respectful of other people's faith. I remember finding it fascinating – all these strangers singing hymns, standing together with a commonly held belief in something bigger and more powerful than themselves, a belief in a god. My family never attended church. Still, in the not-too-distant future I would find myself again singing hymns, but not as a believer.

Eventually, when I was nine or ten, I had to go to church for real because my school didn't have a football team and I was desperate to play. I joined the Boys' Brigade just so I could get in the team. But to get in, you had to go to church every Sunday, to Bible class. I had to learn the New Testament – a kids' version of the New Testament – and pass a test. I did really well at it. But all of this was just to get in the football team. My dad was cool with it even though he was a Marxist.

My parents were members of the International Socialists, or the 'IS' as it was known. They had meetings in a hall not far from our flat in Springburn. I was going to demonstrations from day one. There's a photo of me as a baby in Dad's arms on a May Day march in Queen's Park in 1962. My mother made the banner for the Springburn Young Socialists to take on marches. It was red with their name in white writing on it. Mum and a friend knocked it up on her sewing machine in our single-end flat on Palermo Street.

One of the members of Springburn YS in the picture with Dad was a teenager named Stuart Christie who had heard my dad speak on a street corner. Dad told him about the weekly YS meetings and invited him along. Stuart left the YS after a while because they were not revolutionary enough for him, so he joined an anarchist group. He believed that only direct action (not parliamentary politics) would lead to true, revolutionary change in society. Stuart was arrested in Madrid in July of 1964 in possession of explosives, with the intention of blowing up the fascist dictator General Franco. He faced the death penalty but in the end was sentenced to twenty years in prison. Dad and other friends protested outside the Spanish Embassy in Glasgow on Stuart's behalf – footage of them burning the Spanish flag was shown on local TV. Stuart was released after three years in Franco's prisons, during which time he made contact with Spanish anarchists. My parents remained in touch with him until he died in 2019.

Dad was always saying, 'You've gotta read, you've gotta read.' As I say, he never really went to school, because of the circumstances he grew up in. He was a feral kid on the streets, living in the Kingston district right next door to the Gorbals, close to the shipyards which had been bombed by the Germans during the war. Glasgow and Clydebank were bombed heavily by the Luftwaffe.

When he did go to school, my dad had a bad time of it. Teachers would humiliate him because he would be wearing rags, no underpants, holes in the arse of his trousers, and the teacher would parade him in front of the whole class, compare him to the best-dressed boy, point at the holes in his trousers then make him stand in the corner facing the wall and encourage the class to laugh at him. Making fun of an impoverished child. Imagine how that felt, for him. His sister Rosemary was responsible for looking after him and bringing him up. They had nowhere of their own to stay. They were staying in other people's tenement flats, paying for lodging and sleeping on the floor of somebody else's bedroom. When she was sixteen – quite a bit older than him – she got a job in another town, so he was left to his own devices and he lived on the streets for a while. He missed a lot of school. He told me that when he was evacuated to the countryside, he went and sat by the river in the woods, picked berries and felt like Tom Sawyer. He loved *Huckleberry Finn*. It helped him dream his way out of his disadvantaged situation. That's the power of art.

My dad didn't have much of an education, so he had to educate himself. He loved *Treasure Island* and *Robinson Crusoe*. I remember him saying to me when I was about eight or nine, 'Whatever you want to do, if you want to go to art school, study art or be a musician, I'll pay for lessons.' But at that age I didn't really know what the fuck he was talking about. I remember him taking me to a local art class and it was a bit dry. I just wanted to be outside playing with my mates, climbing, fighting, playing football.

Dad told me he'd go to the cinema when he was a kid, and they'd show two or three films – a matinée and then a main film. These films that he watched, the Marx Brothers or Buster Keaton, some of the big Hollywood films like *Casablanca* or *The Maltese Falcon* with stars such as Humphrey Bogart and Lauren Bacall and gangster movies starring Jimmy Cagney, Edward G. Robinson and George Raft, would take him away from the pain and squalor of living in poverty as a child, transport him to another world. He was trying to give me that same experience by taking me to the cinema every week. It was a really good thing to do, passing that culture on to me, and I'm grateful to him. He wasn't really into football. He liked it but couldn't take it seriously. Other kids' dads would take them to see Celtic and Rangers, but my dad wasn't into that.

One of the warmest memories of my childhood in Palermo Street was when my dad brought home a copy of Johnny Cash's 'A Boy Named Sue'. Graham and I both loved it whenever it came on the radio, both of us laughing at the story of a boy whose father had given him a girl's name. When you're a little kid, stuff like that is funny. In these days of 'intersectionality' anything goes, and so it should, but this was the mid-1960s.

Dad came home one day and said, 'I've got a surprise for you boys, close your eyes.' He then put on the seven-inch single with the burnt orange CBS label (I can still see it in all its glory in my mind's eye) on the family 'radiogram' and played it loud. When the music came through the speakers Graham and I were ecstatic, roaring with laughter as the Man in Black spun his tale of a sad and angry abandoned boy and his unfortunate childhood made hell by his hapless, wastrel father. Eventually the narrator gets to meet 'the son of a bitch who named me Sue' and they finally face each other down in the final verse of the song amid the throes of blood-splattered inter-familial violence. It's all told with Cash's genius talent for storytelling and humour and pathos mixed with vulnerability and toughness.

Dad then flipped the record and played the 'B' side, San Quentin, which Graham and I grew to love as much as 'A Boy Named Sue'. This was the very first rebel song I ever consciously listened to. Johnny assumes the character of an inmate at the legendary San Quentin prison. Cash's voice boomed out from the speakers filling up the space of our small living room with a low and threatening rumble. If God had a voice, I thought, it would sound like this: a dread rolling thunder old testament righteous sound, commanding us to listen to his story. We were held rapt under his spell; two little kids enjoying music with their dad is a deep bonding experience.

Graham and I loved it when Johnny sang, 'San Quentin may you rot and burn in hell.' I didn't know much about the world at the age of eight but I did understand that the message here was that Johnny Cash was taking the side of the prisoners – the unwanted and most despised people in society – and taking a stand against the prison wardens. Johnny was singing on behalf of society's downtrodden, the outcasts. When I became a teenager I realised that Johnny Cash was a bit of an outlaw himself. His show of empathy and solidarity with felons in San Quentin had been no hollow showbiz gesture but a real identification with men from the same background as him. We asked Dad to play us both sides of the record again that afternoon. Graham and I were both lost in music, captivated.

My dad also introduced us to the joys of the Marx Brothers movies and many a Saturday afternoon was spent with the three of us falling off the settee onto the carpet, our faces wet with tears of joy, our bodies convulsed in fits of hilarity, shaking so hard that I thought I was going to die of laughter as the anarchic antics of Groucho, Chico and Harpo exploded onto out little black and white TV screen, transforming our tiny tenement into a theatre of pleasure and mirth. Films such as *A Night at the Opera*, *A Day at the Races* and *Horse Feathers* poked fun at the absurdity of the world and made nonsense of consensual reality. Shane MacGowan once said to me, when I asked him about politics, that 'the world is just one big Marx Brothers movie'. Shane may well have been correct about that. If all the world is one big lunatic asylum and we are the inmates but most of us don't realise the fact that we are merely minor actors in a movie that someone else is directing to our misfortune and their benefit, then it takes a genius like Karl or Groucho Marx to point out the scam that has taken us for fools. In our house Groucho was equally as important as Karl. Without fun and dancing, what was the point of revolution?

In the early seventies we had this car, a beautiful dark green Vauxhall Viva. It had a cassette player too and Dad would play Simon & Garfunkel's *Bridge Over Troubled Water* and Glen Campbell's 'Where's the Playground Susie'. That's when I first heard the Rolling Stones, in that car. He also had Charley Pride, a Black country singer, and I remember hearing 'Streets of Baltimore'. When I got older, Gram Parsons did another version I love. It's a beautiful song. I heard a lot of music in that car. I thought it was really glamorous. Later, when we moved to Mount Florida,

Dad had a Ford Capri, the same colour as Man City's strip, sky blue. That was glamorous as well. I guess they were the British version of American muscle cars.

My parents knew a lot of musicians. They often had parties, and of course we could hear them because we were just in the next room. Sometimes I remember the parties ending in an argument, and a big scene.

There was a lot of arguing between my parents at this point. Really bad arguments. It accelerated when my dad got his job with the union when I was seven or eight. He wasn't much of a drinker before that, but when he became a union official, got out of the factory, and rose up through the ranks of the union h e started drinking. He eventually became Branch Secretary for the west of Scotland for the Society of Graphical and Allied Trades, or SOGAT. They were a very powerful union in the country, especially on Fleet Street at the time. With the better job came more pressure. He wouldn't finish at five o'clock. He gave his life to the struggle of the Labour movement and he sacrificed a lot of time he might otherwise have devoted to his family. It wasn't just a job, for him, it was a vocation, a cause, a struggle. He was a very well-respected man in the Labour movement. People like *Daily Mirror* journalist and *Private Eye* columnist Paul Foot would come and stay with us in the sixties when we lived in Palermo Street. He even kindly helped us with the loan of some money to buy the room-and-kitchen, according to Mum. Dad knew Arthur Scargill, leader of the NUM, and Mick McGahey, the Communist leader of Scottish Miners, was a close friend too. He knew future Chancellor and Prime Minister Gordon Brown; both were comrades in the Scottish Labour movement pre-New Labour. Socialism was what defined him; it gave him an identity and a sense of purpose in life, strength and pride, a sense of self-worth.

When I was a kid I worshipped my dad. Before the age of ten, I didn't really know the importance of his job. I remember he had the night shift, then day shift, then suddenly he was wearing suits. I thought he looked great. He would wear brightly coloured off-the-peg suits, probably from Burton the tailors, and always a white shirt with a wide, striped kipper tie. He was flash. When you see men in business suits they always choose dull, drab colours – dark greys or black, but Dad was rock and roll. He later told me with a sly smile on his face that when he went in to negotiate with an employer he was representing the working class and it was essential he looked sharper than the class enemy. He had an office on Hope Street, across from Glasgow Central Station. I remember visiting that office a few times. It felt very important. There were some lovely Victorian-era red sandstone buildings which had become blackened over time on Hope Street, right in the centre of Glasgow. The nearby Station Hotel is where Bob Dylan stayed on his '66 tour.

Unfortunately, some of my most vivid memories of that flat in 35 Palermo Street are the many late-night arguments between my mum and dad. There were times when he would come home near midnight, causing her to rise from bed and go into the living room-kitchenette, and the angry noise would begin. My little brother Graham and I would be woken up by the shouting and we would both hide under our blankets, scared in the dark. I asked Dad about this stuff in later life and he told me these incidents almost always happened after he'd put in a long day at work and had gone straight from his office to hosting the monthly SOGAT branch meeting at the trade union centre. It was a very boozy, macho culture and he said he would be so stressed and wired on adrenaline that he didn't want to go straight home, but needed to unwind first. I remember my mother threatening to leave and coming into our bedroom, turning on the light and demanding that my brother and I choose between them. Would we leave with her or stay with him? Dad would say that she shouldn't treat us like human tennis balls to be smashed back and forth over a metaphorical net between two sides, battling for our loyalty. That is not a choice to present to crying six- and nine-year-old children at midnight, or any time. Graham and I were torn. We didn't want to leave home with Mum, we wanted her to stay with us and Dad. We loved our parents and hated the idea of our family unit, the bedrock that gave us our identity and strength, breaking up. Even at that age I had a strong belief in family. It is all you know and when that is threatened, everything you believe in just shatters. It's as if your faith has been attacked, and you collapse. As a child you haven't yet built the necessary psychological and emotional defences to deal with such trauma. It's a powerful thing, the threat to the feeling of security in someone so young. You never really recover from it and you carry the feelings of upset and familial destruction with you throughout your life. It affects the life choices you make and every single relationship you ever have.

I fucking hated every second of these midnight arguments, and I quickly learned to dissociate in these situations; a therapist later said to me that when I did this my breaths were so short it was as if I wasn't breathing, as if I was already dead. This comes from not wanting to be noticed, not wanting to be in the line of fire. There are poisonous wells of anger and resentment buried deep in many people who on the surface seem really nice, pleasant and well-mannered when they are out in the world, but are revealed only to their closest family members and the ones they love. People can wear many masks. Even one's parents.

Though my parents' marriage was turbulent, Dad was generally a very laid-back character. He was never violent, and his way of disciplining us was to make us stay at home. It was a much more effective form of punishment – looking out the window and seeing the other kids playing in the street on a warm summer's day was torture. Mum had more of a temper and could be prone to an emotional outburst. They were deeply unhappy in their marriage but did their best for us.

I began to question the world and other people from a young

age. I suppose that gave me a sense of emotional distance, a lack of trust in future friendships and relationships; I would assume a friendly and open manner, a cloak of safety. The price you pay is a fear of commitment and all the loneliness that entails. I was quietly angry, always have been. I still feel it, but I'm working on it. If you're anything like me you have to recognise this well of poison that we carry, isolate the reason why we're always ready to spring up like a cobra and bite at any time, any place, anyone. Unless you deal with it you will always repeat the same disastrous mistakes. You've got to confront your demons. Those painful childhood memories we bury, that some of us try and drown out with sex, drugs, alcohol, gambling, all the usual crutches and distractions. These childhood experiences are going to be really painful to engage with, no one wants anyone else to be exposed to their deepest, darkest, most shameful secrets, but unless these issues are talked about they can never be defeated, and you will never be at peace with yourself or anyone else. You have one day got to face that shit head-on and defeat it. Believe me.

Anger at home, anger in the streets, anger in the classroom, anger on the football terraces, anger at work, anger at teenage discos, anger, anger, anger. Anger in me. Anger is an energy, as John Lydon says.

I think my mother wanted more out of life than being a house-wife, perhaps to be creative and make things. I remember her wearing an Indian sari to go to the Sikh Temple in the sixties. She was the one who would decorate the house, strip the walls, paint them, put up the new wallpaper, and she did that in every house we ever lived in. She was artistic. She would make clothes for me and for herself on the sewing machine. She made me a Spider-Man costume, an all-in-one bodysuit with a mask, somehow having managed to find this red fabric with a webbed print on it. She also made me a great Captain Scarlet outfit using duffle-coat toggles as epaulettes. I loved it. In my teenage years, as I was attempting to make sense of my family's emotional tensions, I came to realise she was frustrated with her situation and her marriage. Maybe they'd fallen out of love. Perhaps that happened early on, or maybe it was the pressures of life and the responsibility of bringing up a young family.

Before I was ten my mother could sometimes be hard on me. But her family history is complicated. Her mother had four children. Two of them died in infancy; the older sister Jessie died when she was twenty of TB, and her father left her mother and then came back. My mother was a result of the father coming back. For her whole life, and in the eyes of her own mother, my mum was never good enough, because she couldn't live up to her big sister Jessie, this sister who I don't think she ever knew. By all accounts she was a beautiful girl, very pretty, and my grandmother's favourite. My mum was brought up hard, as was the way with Glasgow's working class.

I knew Mum wasn't so happy, and something wasn't right between my parents. The arguing carried on, from Springburn, when I was a kid, all the way through to when I was a teenager living in Mount Florida. It just got worse. When I was a teenager I started to think about how dedicated Dad was to the struggle for working-class rights. He had devoted his life to the Labour cause fighting inequality and that's fucking great. I was proud of him. But what about women? He was out fighting the cause, and my mother was at home running the house. Where do women stand in the revolution? I'd seen Paine's *Rights of Man* on his bookshelf. I wondered to myself, what about the rights of women?

It sounds like I'm making excuses for him, but it was the seventies and feminism hadn't yet made a deep impact on the Labour movement. Dad was born in the thirties like most of his comrades, and they had all been brought up in an environment where the men went out to work and the women stayed at home and looked after the kids, cooked and cleaned the house. I kind of became a feminist from an early age, even though I wasn't aware of the feminist movement in any way. I admired my mum a lot. In her own quiet way she was a fighter. Dad was a charismatic guy, a big personality, a raconteur, so she would be overshadowed by him at times. He was also quite an imposing man physically: broad-shouldered, barrel-chested, striking and handsome with a great head of hair. Mum was a housewife during the day and went out to work at night. She took a job as a barmaid in a trade union club. I suspect my dad didn't like the fact she was working in the bar where he was a regular.

I carried a lot of shame because my parents were fighting. You think something is wrong with you because your parents don't get along. I think this darkness seeped into my consciousness. You don't talk about this stuff with anyone as a kid, you hold it in. You go to school and think everybody else's family is normal. You bear a lot of shame and pain, and you don't know what to do with it, you don't recognise it as such – you bury it deep, but it comes out later on in life in many different ways. It grows, like Blake's poison tree: 'And I water'd it in fears ...'

I had an anger from an early age. It comes from home, and it comes from Glasgow. It comes from having to be wary about what street you walked down, where you could go and where you couldn't go. Not very far from the cinema, maybe half a mile or less, there were places called Possilpark and Maryhill, and they were just scary. We travelled through them on the bus sometimes and they looked grim: bleak and unforgiving places where the kids – girls and boys – had a permanently hostile look on their faces, and the dogs, normally underfed, wolflike Alsatians never on a leash or collar, looked ready to sink their rabid, yellowy fangs into trespassing strangers. Springburn seemed a lot safer by comparison. Still, if somebody asked you to fight them, you'd have to fight them. If you didn't fight you'd get bullied. The older you were the more of a target you became.

In those days, if you stuck to your street and the street either side of you, you were OK, up to a point. If you went beyond that, you could get beaten up by kids your own age, or the teenagers in gangs. The local gang was called the Bison. I remember seeing the name written on the wall and this kid coming in the summer holidays saying, 'You'd better get off the street – the Bison are coming,' and thinking, 'Fuck, they're gonna kill me.' I'd seen black and white cowboy movies on TV with gigantic herds of buffalo covering the plains like an invading army. I imagined this gang as a herd of bison about to stampede anyone in its path. So, I hid under a car. I just lay there trying not to breathe, hoping that the Bison wouldn't find me. I must've lain under that car for an hour. Why didn't I just run home? What was I thinking? I remember playing in our back yard in Palermo Street, I must've been eight or nine, and a guy suddenly appeared on the midden wall and threw a whole brick at me. Random acts of violence were a regular occurrence in working-class lives. It was just accepted as normal behaviour.

One of the first gang slogans I ever saw, apart from the Bison, was near Sighthill Flats, giant brutalist fortresses bordered by British Rail works on one side and Springburn Cemetery on another. The territorial declarations were daubed on a wall in spidery silver spray paint:

**GEO IS 100% MENTAL**
**GEO IS A SPRINGBURN BOY AND PROUD OF IT**
**GEO IS 100% CRAZY**

Every time I passed that on the bus with my mum, going to visit my grandma in Bridgeton, I remember thinking, 'I do not want to meet Geo.' This is a guy who will just cut you up. My imagination was full of these psychotic gang members, unseen bogeymen. Life was determined by invisible borders, and if you crossed them, you could be in danger of your life. There were guys with axes and knives, you were told not by your parents but by kids in the streets. Though I do remember my dad saying to me in the summer holidays, 'You gotta be home before it's dark because when it gets dark, the man with the iron teeth walks the streets and he picks up little kids and he takes them away.'

Glasgow in the sixties and seventies was extremely violent, and it made me defensive, wary, and cautious of other people. I learned to dissociate. I took myself out of the scene. In later life, when I got into some kind of argument or something happened that would trigger this feeling, I would dissociate, become disengaged, absent; my body was there, but I'd be powerless. This stuff affected me deeply and I didn't realise it, I never understood the roots of the feeling until I undertook therapy for drug addiction in my forties.

When I was a teenager I had some kind of depression – a melancholia – that was maybe tied into this stuff. I remember when I was seventeen standing in front of the bathroom mirror with a razorblade and having an urge to cut up my unpimpled, perfect, baby-soft unshaven face. I inwardly cursed my parents for giving birth to me, I was consumed by an indescribable pain, both spiritual and psychic. I couldn't speak to anyone about it. I started to question love, and the people who said they loved me. I didn't trust other people: I was scared of relationships, of committing to people and saying 'I love you' (I still have a huge problem with this phrase). I was like, this is how life really is. There's no such thing as love, people don't love each other. All life is confrontation, compromise and violence.

So, when punk came along, I was just ready for it.

# 2.

# Arthur Black's and High-Waisters (School Daze in the Mount)

School was violent. The teachers were animals and would ritually humiliate kids in front of the rest of the class. They'd belt us – give us 'six of the best' – and this punishment was meted out daily to wrongdoers like myself for insolence and not submitting homework on time. I was in the bottom set for maths and our teacher was called Mr D, a tightly wound, wired-up skinny guy, always dressed in a brown checked tweed jacket with a black shock of tight curly corkscrew hair sticking upwards from his anaemic, skull-like face. I really liked this girl April H. One day she said something cheeky that made the whole class laugh. Mr D totally lost his shit. He shoved all the desks together from where he was standing near the blackboard until they crushed April hard up against the back wall. We were all in shock. He dragged her out of the classroom into the corridor, taking his taws (punishment belt) with him, and gave April six of the best whilst screaming 'Bitch! Bitch!' at her.

The everyday sadism at school was just something we accepted. Towards the end of my time at King's Park I stopped bothering with maths homework. Mr D ordered me to come out and stand in front of the class to be belted. I stuck my arms out towards him in the usual submissive manner but stared at him defiantly. Just before he brought his belt down on me in a first stroke I looked round at the class slyly and quickly pulled my hands away so that Mr D belted his own legs instead. The whole class roared with laughter, including April. He went apeshit. Then I just let him belt me and showed no pain, apology or contrition. I quietly sat down at my desk, continued with the lesson and kept my dignity, which is more than I can say for the teacher. Corporal punishment is no deterrent; only fascists and sadists enjoy that stuff and are convinced by it. It only breeds insolence, resentment and rebellion. You have to take someone's freedom away to really punish them. Violence is not the answer.

You had to find ways of negotiating your way through school. For some reason, tough guys liked me. I was good at football and I had some kind of attitude, so I managed to get through school without getting my head kicked in, which was quite a feat.

The slum clearances were like an evacuation after the war. Suddenly the streets were deserted. People were being rehoused and we were one of the last families left on the street. I guess my parents were holding out for a decent council house in a good area. I don't think they wanted to go to Blackhill, Easterhouse, Castlemilk, some of the really hard areas. In Springburn, the life expectancy for a man was in the mid-fifties. But to me it was still a magical place. We moved to a place called Mount Florida, a decent working-class area on the Southside of Glasgow. We got a brand-new council flat, where my brother and I had our own room, and even an inside toilet with a bath. There was a kitchen, a living room and a hallway. The building was only three storeys high and we were at the top. It was beautiful to me.

I thought from the name that Mount Florida was going to be a posh area full of rich people, though I wouldn't have recognised a rich person anyway. I just thought it was going to be soft. Springburn was my home, even though it was beginning to look like a scene straight out of a post-apocalyptic war film. It looked like Dresden after Bomber Harris had destroyed it.

In my early days at Mount Florida primary school, in 1972, I remember a kid saying to me at playtime, 'Did you hear about Skin from the Tiki? He got an axe in his back last night.' The Tiki were the local gang, their spray-painted name tags were proudly displayed everywhere in the Mount. So, it wasn't that posh after all. Everywhere you went in Glasgow there were gangs.

On my first day this kid came up to me in the playground and said, 'Who are you? Where'd you come from?' He was trying to get hard on me.

These three other kids saw what was happening so they came over and said 'leave him alone, he's alright'. It worked – the asshole who was trying to bully me fucked off and one of the kids said to me, 'What are you doing after school? Do you want to come up to my house? I live just a couple of streets away.' I went, 'OK, that'd be nice, thanks.' I thought I may as well try and make a friend.

He lived in the top floor of a tenement. We were sitting in his room and this kid said to me 'Do you like T. Rex?' and I said I did. They were always on the radio. My mum listened to the radio in the morning, so I knew Gary Glitter, Slade, the Sweet, other early glam stuff. He pulled the record out and put it on his record player. He gave me the album sleeve and said 'Listen to this, man, check out the words.' It was the *Electric Warrior* album; beautiful Bolan wielding his Les Paul guitar in front of a big Vamp amplifier stack, silhouetted in lustrous, luminous gold against an all-black background. A wonderful, dark, mysterious rock and roll image that burned itself into my still-forming consciousness. Then he put on 'Rip Off' which is a heavy rock track – very Zeppelin – and Bolan sang:

*Rocking in the nude*
*I'm feeling such a dude*
*It's a rip-off*

And I was like whoa, that's so good. I'd never heard music like this before: bluesy hard rock. This wasn't pop music, this was rock and roll. I loved it. I was eleven.

Later, that same kid passed me *Aladdin Sane* (A Lad Insane) in class with Bowie airbrushed full-length in the nude on the inside gatefold cover looking like a satyr, half-man, half-beast of indeterminate sex. It was a totally mind-blowing image. My mind was already sent spinning by the pun of the album title. WOW! That started me thinking in a way the teacher's lessons never could. And those lyrics to 'Time':

*Time, he flexes like a whore*
*Falls wanking to the floor*
*His trick is you and me, boy*

This was the first time I'd seen or heard sex openly referenced. I didn't know what sex was, to be honest, but the combination of this part-man, part-woman, part-mythical space creature referencing insanity and sex infected me with a cultural curiosity which would come to the surface five years later, in 1977, when punk exploded my consciousness forevermore. At home, I started to watch *Top of the Pops* every week and would see the Sweet, Roy Wood and Wizzard, Gary Glitter, Slade, Mott the Hoople, Bowie, Sparks and T. Rex performing their latest singles. Bowie and Bolan introduced me to androgyny and poetry. I thank them forever. I loved them both. They inspired my generation to challenge the constraints of masculinity, femininity and gender. They also made acting and looking like a rock and roll star fun.

At school, there was a lot of fighting. It was engineered like this: a kid would whisper in your ear in class that another kid had said something snide about you. The offending kid would be identified and at the same time you would be pointed out to the offending kid, him being informed of a similar slight. This would result in either the offending kid or yourself uttering the dreadful curse, 'Your fight's on at four', and that was it settled. There was to be a battle after school and you both had to defend your honour.

Normally this took place on the open waste ground outside Lesser Hampden, the corrugated iron fenced training ground beside the national stadium. The whole school would follow both boys over to the designated ring and watch the fight, all cheering and hurling insults at the two 'warriors'. Neither kid would ever really want to be involved in this awful, sadistic ritual but social conditioning meant you could never back down. The shame and humiliation would be too much and you knew that if you backed out of a fight you were then fair game for bullies. Once the fight started you would just go nervously at each other, throwing ineffectual punches that usually missed the target (the face) and then move onto kicking, scratching and pulling hair. My tactic was to pull the other kid's head down by the hair and kick him in the face. If that didn't work I'd get them on the ground and sit on top of them with my knees on their shoulders pinning them to the ground, then I'd grab their head and smash it into the concrete. It always worked and after a few head smashes the kid would surrender. Then the mob would walk away in silence. They'd had their entertainment. I remember saying sorry to one crying kid. By this time we'd fought our way up from Hampden Terrace outside the gates of the Rangers end up the lane to Sommerville Drive at the bottom of Brownlie Street.

When we were eleven we had to sit an exam to decide who would go on to a posh middle-class school like Glasgow High or Hutchesons' Grammar. These schools almost guaranteed a place at university. If you failed you would attend the local comprehensive, King's Park Secondary. I didn't revise for this test. I didn't know how you did that. We were never taught how to by the teachers at our school. They would just announce one day that this test was coming up. Off I went to King's Park. I remember feeling a bit of a failure.

On my first day there I looked around and clocked the sizes of the older boys who were all a lot bigger and stronger than I was and way more confident in the way they carried themselves. I knew right there and then that I was *not* gonna be tricked into any more fights after school. I needed a different strategy if I was gonna get through the next four years without getting my head totally kicked in.

The 1970 World Cup was the first tournament I'd ever watched and it truly captured the imaginations of myself and all my friends on the street. We *all* wanted to possess the black magic skills of the amazing winger Jairzinho. No one could stop him as he mesmerised opponent after opponent. Or the shamanic Pelé. We could all reel off the names of this magical team. Mum bought me a Brazil strip. Their style of beautiful attacking football allowed kids like me to dream our way out of the cold, grey Glasgow streets and imagine we were playing in the Maracanã stadium in Rio de Janeiro instead in front of 250,000 fanatical spectators. Watching a great team like Brazil 1970, Holland 1974 or Barca 2009 is as pleasurable and inspiring as watching footage of Jimi Hendrix in 1967, the Rolling Stones in 1969 or the Sex Pistols in 1977. It just hits you deep in your soul.

It was school summer holidays so myself, my brother Graham and some other kids from around Stanmore Road went down to Lesser Hampden to watch the world champions train. We hoped for autographs at best, but the gates were open and we were allowed in to watch Brazil do their training for the big match the following day. After they finished training the team came out and began making their way back down to the dressing room facilities at Hampden Park stadium. We got the autographs of Jairzinho, Rivelino, Gérson and Tostão. We'd brought our own balls along and I kicked mine to Jairzinho and he passed it back to me. I was in football heaven.

In the early seventies I was obsessed by football. Not just Celtic FC. I would buy *Shoot* magazine every week to find out all about the latest players. I dreamed of playing for Celtic and Scotland. I wanted to know as much about the stars who played it as I possibly could. I watched every match I could on TV, whether it was a Scottish league match commentated by Archie McPherson or the more glamorous international games. Celtic's team still consisted of a few remaining members of the legendary Lisbon Lions: Billy McNeill, Tommy Gemmell, Jimmy Johnstone, Bobby Lennox and Bobby Murdoch were on display each week at Paradise (Celtic Park) and the shamanic Jock Stein was manager. I watched the European Cup semi-final against Atlético Madrid live on TV and the deeply cynical tactics of the ultra-violent, murderous, hateful Atlético team brought me to tears. The mostly Argentinian Atlético squad were under orders from manager Juan Carlos Lorenzo to virtually assassinate wee Jimmy Johnstone from the get-go. It was like televised gang war, not a football match. When you're twelve years of age you're still (hopefully) innocent; you still believe that people should play fair and that sport is a noble endeavour. Violence is for the streets, not the pitch. This was a lesson in negation and intimidation, in organised violence and cynicism, in real life.

I would proudly wear my full Celtic strip in PE, which invited quite a few hard tackles from the majority Rangers-supporting boys. It never bothered me. I liked being different. Funnily enough, most of these aggressive incursions came from one particular guy who was a swot in the top maths class and a Boys' Brigade squad leader. He was on the surface a very well-behaved, clean living, grade-A student, but underneath the cloak of academic and church respectability there hid the poisonous soul of a West of Scotland Protestant sectarian bigot. Fuck him, I thought, as I dribbled the ball around him, always keeping my composure and never losing my head, quietly picking myself up and carrying on with the game, never allowing him to think he was rattling me. No fucking way.

I remember getting in free for the last twenty minutes of the

Celtic v Rangers Scottish Cup semi-final on a wet Wednesday night with the rain pouring down like a biblical storm. Some say there were 120,000 jammed into the terraces that night and Celtic won. Being children we had no money for tickets so we would ask the men outside the stadium, 'Can you give me a lift please, mister?' and they would haul you over the turnstile. Once inside the ground you were free to go and watch the match wherever you liked. This was the days before all seated grounds. Celtic v Rangers was fucking insane. I'd watch the after-match violence from the safety of a grassy bank beside the stairs on the Celtic end and there would be running battles in Sommerville Drive between grown men using broken beer bottles and any weapon they could fashion out of planks of wood and worse. The police would occasionally ride in on horses and attempt to disperse what was effectively a sectarian riot, but they would be pelted by a hail of bottles, beer cans and other missiles and would have to beat a retreat. And so the fighting would start all over again.

I would wait until the battle ended and slowly make my way home to Stanmore Road a couple of streets away, hiding my Celtic scarf in case I ran into a gang of angry Rangers fans. I'd go through tenement courts and people's back gardens, avoiding streets like Bolivar Terrace where I could be spotted and attacked. One time I spied a satin Celtic scarf that had been abandoned in a garden in Brownlie Street, close to the Rangers end, hanging off a thorn bush. I couldn't resist going into the garden and taking the scarf for myself. Then I heard an angry voice: 'Hey you, ya wee fenian bastard, gies that fucking piece a shite yur holding.' I looked up and it was a grown man, in his late thirties, about my dad's age. He was extremely drunk and wearing the red, white and blue scarf of Rangers. There was no one around, the streets were quiet, deserted. I honestly thought he was going to batter me. I was terrified. I handed him the scarf and he said, 'Fuck off now ya wee fenian prick,' and stumbled away, lost in his reverie.

\*

I never really knew what I was supposed to be doing at secondary school. The exam system is set up to disqualify anyone with any real imagination. As far as I could see it was a two-tier system designed to discriminate against anyone who didn't play by the established rules of 'learning'. The kids who obtained top grades on their O levels and Highers (what are now called A levels) would definitely be going onto further education at art school or university and most probably a well-paid professional job at the end of it, as a doctor or a teacher. The 'less educationally talented' ones were lucky to get an apprenticeship doing skilled or semi-skilled work in an industrial trade as a car mechanic, steelworker, joiner, electrician, or in my case a lithographic printer, and would attend a technical college suited to the need of their specific trade. The failed majority were destined for a lifetime as members of the lumpen proletariat in unskilled, low-paid work, or stranded on the scrapheap of the terminally unemployed, 'the dole'. I'd know all about that when I was older, in the early days of Primal Scream.

The exception was a great English teacher called Mr Hughes. He never raised his voice or belted us or humiliated us like some of the other teachers. One day we went into his class on the first floor and he said to us, 'Today, instead of reading and learning, we are going to watch a film.' I turned round to see that there was a big black metal movie projector set up at the back of the classroom. Mr Hughes then pulled down a white cinema screen contraption in front of the blackboard, pulled down the blinds, turned off the lights and up on the screen came the word 'IF ....' It was Lindsay Anderson's 1968 film about life in an elite English private boarding school starring Malcolm McDowell as Mick Travis. It's a revolutionary story and it resonated with the teenage malcontent that I was slowly becoming. What kid doesn't dream of an uprising in their school?

In the seventies some of the teachers were allowed to get away with acts of random violence, both physical and mental cruelty. *If....* is still one of my favourite movies. When I met the Jesus and Mary Chain guys later it was something that united us, because it was an important film for them too. Mr Hughes also showed us the funereal comedy *Harold and Maude* directed by Hal Ashby starring Bud Cort, a sort of sick comedy in which an eighteen-year-old kid gets his kicks from joining the mourners at funerals of people he doesn't know. He notices this old lady at every funeral he attends so they begin a relationship which is frowned upon by straight society. Bud Cort does stuff like staging a hanging, so his mother walks into his bedroom at home and finds him swinging from the ceiling with a noose around his neck. I loved the dark humour of that movie too.

When I was twelve Mum took me down to Mount Florida Church of Scotland and enrolled me in the 83rd Boys' Brigade. She had been a member of the Girl Guides in her younger days and felt that it would be a good place for me to express my love of sport. I was always out in the street or on any spare ground playing football. I was football crazy. The 83rd had better sporting equipment than school. They had a brand-new Olympic-size trampoline, table tennis tables, a vaulting horse, trampettes, volleyball, badminton, five-a-side football, all played on a Friday night in the church hall. The officers were all good guys, volunteers helping to keep us kids off the streets, and instilling a sense of discipline, organisation and self-respect.

The BB, as it was known, was a Christian organisation based on quasi-military principles. My main attraction was to get into the football team: the 83rd played to a high standard and the various age group teams had been successful in the Glasgow-wide BB football leagues. I wanted in. I really looked forward to coming home from school, eating my tea, and getting ready for the 7 p.m. start time. We had a uniform that consisted of smart trousers (no jeans), polished shoes, a blazer (school style), white shirt and a suitably coloured tie, tied tight, and a brown leather belt with a brass buckle, engraved with the BB logo, which was an anchor emblemising the 'Sure and Steadfast' motto of the organisation: pure Christian military imagery. We also wore a white sash which hung diagonally from the right shoulder to left hip and was held in place under the belt. To complete the army look we wore a navy-blue hat in the Glengarry style which was worn tilted slightly to the side of the head. There was a little red plastic 'BB' badge on the left side, near the front of the hat, also displaying the anchor logo.

We would assemble in groups of ten or eleven boys with our group commander to the right of us. There were ten groups in total, so maybe eighty to one hundred boys each session. The Brigade Commander would stand in front of us like a general addressing his army and lead us in prayer. I found all this unnecessary and boring, but I knew the deal; I would do anything to get in an organised football team playing in a proper league every Saturday morning. The drawback to all the sporting fun and camaraderie was that you had to attend Bible class in Church each Sunday morning. I had already accrued some biblical knowledge when I lived in Springburn, so I was able to bluff it, just sit there and feign interest. It was worth it to get a place in the BB football team.

One Saturday morning in July we assembled outside the church and drove to Berwick-upon-Tweed for summer camp on a tour bus full of excited boys. It was the first time I'd ever been anywhere outside of Glasgow without my parents. Each 'squad' had their own tent with eight boys in it. The officers had their own tents too. My tent commander was a great guy – he was maybe fifteen and captain of the football team.

Some of the older boys were allowed to attend a local teenage disco in Berwick-upon-Tweed, and the next day I asked him if he'd had a good time. 'Wee man, I was dancing with this beautiful girl with bright orange carrot-coloured hair cut in the style of David Bowie to "The Jean Genie",' he said. 'You should've seen her face, it was heaven.' He looked so pure, so true, so innocent, so young and handsome. I'll always remember the look of joy on his face when he told me about his disco adventure. *That's* the romance of rock and roll: dancing with a girl you fancy who looks like a boy pop star. Androgyny in action.

My family never went on holidays. In the sixties we'd only ever venture as far as Saltcoats or Ayr on a hot summer day and sit on the sand dunes, play with our red plastic buckets and spades that Mum would buy from the beachfront kiosk, eat our sandwiches (prepared earlier that morning by Mum) and look out at the Irish Sea. I once asked Dad why we weren't going to Spain like other kids' families I knew and he said that Spain was ruled by a fascist dictator and that Spanish workers were being tortured, imprisoned and killed by Franco's regime so we had to show solidarity with them by boycotting the tourist industry. I asked Mum about this recently and she said we never had enough money to travel abroad. Somewhere between these two stories lies the truth.

So, the BB summer camps were where my brother Graham and I went on holiday between the ages of twelve and fifteen. We camped in Oban and Fraserburgh on the west and east coasts of Scotland and also somewhere outside Torquay in Devon. These were good times. I was eventually promoted to squad leader then tent commander, and I have to say I enjoyed the responsibility of both positions. This was to be of great help to me later on in life when I formed my own band and started working with musicians and record producers, both in practice rooms and studio sessions. Someone's got to take charge and direct the troops, and if I was writing the songs and forming the band's image in my mind then it may as well be me.

One dark, rainy, cold, miserable winter-bound Glasgow Friday night, our Brigade Commander, Captain Wallace, led us in prayers. He muttered the phrase, 'and Lord, deliver us from the

Strikers, who are bringing the country to its knees.' This was the era of the three-day week and the power cuts, Britain's economy crippled by both international politics and strike after strike by militant Trade Unionists. There had been a power grab by the mainly Arab OPEC countries in 1973. They had come together and decided they were tired of being exploited in a post-colonial manner by the Western powers so they raised the price of oil and that, in turn, caused widespread economic chaos across the world. The Trade Union movement and in particular the National Union of Mine Workers was fighting hard against Edward Heath's Tory government for higher pay because they had issued a 'wage freeze' for all public sector workers, even as the cost of living sky-rocketed due to higher oil prices. People were asked to cut down on buying petrol, and also to conserve energy in the home. I remember whole nights when the power grid and streetlights were turned off and Glasgow was hidden beneath a cloak of total darkness. Mum lit the house up with candles. I thought it was really exciting. It had a wartime atmosphere, like how I imagined the Blitz would be (without the Nazi bombs, of course). I loved it. There were rumours that Heath was going to send the British Army in to transport the stockpiles of coal from the striking mines and to work in the power stations too. My dad's great friend, the Communist leader of the Scottish NUM Mick McGahey, asked for a thirty-five per cent wage increase and pleaded to the soldiers to disobey orders and join the striking miners on picket lines. Over one hundred right-wing Labour MPs signed a letter condemning McGahey's statement, to which he replied, 'You can't dig coal with bayonets.'

Because of Dad's involvement in Trade Union activism and politics, my sympathies were one hundred per cent with the striking miners, although the ins and outs of the dispute were clearly beyond my thirteen-year-old football-obsessed mind's comprehension. I loved the idea that just by simple, direct strike action, ordinary people – by sticking together and showing class solidarity for a common cause they all truly believed in – could stop the country, bring it to a halt, stop all state and commercial television stations from broadcasting, close the nation's harbours, keep ships full of goods unloaded, close the petrol stations by refusing to transport oil, stop cars from driving, making it impossible for scab labour class traitors from breaking the strike, stop newspapers from being printed, close the mines and so cut off the coal that generates the energy that the power stations produce to keep the country at work. It was glorious. They had the collective power to turn the fucking lights off in the country and no one could stop them. That felt like real power and I was proud my dad was involved as a Comrade of Mick's in this revolutionary activity.

So, when Captain Wallace uttered his reactionary prayer I remember feeling ill at ease. He was a churchgoing Christian conservative who loved Queen and Country, but that was alright by me, because I understood the ideals the organisation represented, and although we might have differed in political outlook, Wallace and the other officers were totally committed to providing an exciting, stimulating, safe space for us potentially wayward kids to keep us off the streets and out of trouble. They were never too heavy with the Bible stuff either. They knew that the main attraction for the majority of us teenagers was the great sporting facilities they provided. I really loved the camaraderie of the 83rd, and I look back fondly on those innocent, fun days.

One great thing I learned in the BB was the value of teamwork. In a football team you're only as good as your weakest member. You have to learn to work to a strategy, make a plan and stick with it, listen to the manager and take orders from the captain. The team also has to respect the character and judgement of the manager. You can't lead people into battle if they don't believe in the cause. If one guy thinks he's shit-hot and is playing too flash and showing off for his own glory rather than for the team then it just ain't gonna work. It's not about one- or two-star players;

it's about how well all eleven work together. We each play our part in the success of the team: the goalkeeper is as important as the striker, the back four and the central midfielders must communicate properly with the wingers and centre forward, just as the drummer is as important as the lead singer, and the bassist has to lock into a deep groove with the rhythm guitarist, and the lead guitar player and singer will both count for nothing unless the sound-bed created by the rhythm section is a solid foundation on which to build the sound of the group. As Jimi sang, 'Castles made of sand fall in the sea eventually.'

Like a football team, a great band is always more than the sum of its parts. With the right squad, or the right musicians, real magic can happen, but you have to work hard at creating it. If one person thinks they're more important than the other players then the magic won't happen. Everyone has to feel that their contribution is crucial. It's all for one and one for all. When you hit the stage you have to believe that you can count on every single band member to deliver. If there are any doubts in your mind about anyone in the squad or band then you cannot let go and feel free enough to live in the moment. The teamwork ethos I learned in the Boys' Brigade helped me later on when I started Primal Scream.

The one class I did enjoy at school was Art. We had this foxy teacher who was in her late twenties. She was tall and had dark-ish red hair which was sculpted into a perfect bowl-cut shape very much like Joanna Lumley's 'Purdey' character, and wore big, seventies Dory Previn glasses. She had a beautiful face, kind of rounded like the actress Ellen Burstyn's, with high cheek-bones, big hazel eyes and a wide, sensuous mouth. We named her 'Thunderthighs' (after Mott the Hoople's backing singers), because everyone was in love with her. I enjoyed drawing and painting and the relaxed, contemplative, clear-thinking mental space that being in art class brought to me.

I also enjoyed History, and for my O level exams I chose to study the Russian Revolution. It had all the drama and excitement of an adventure movie and I had more than a bit of anti-establishment radicalism running through my family so it seemed perfect. I loved the way the Bolsheviks took their chance and assumed power during the historical tumult which consumed Czarist rule in Imperial Russia. The idea of destroying the corrupt old order which represented aristocratic privilege and the godlike status of the Czars and replacing it with a socialist state devoted to the needs of the exploited peasants and workers deeply appealed to the teenage romantic socialist in me. The cultural symbolism of the Bolsheviks' assassination of the Romanov family, ending their tyrannical dynasty, seemed like an act of beauty to me: what a way to start the twentieth century! Imagine the shockwaves of fear and dread that the Communist regicide sent throughout the world? Every royal and aristocratic family in Europe must have been shaken. The Bolsheviks set up workers' councils to assume power and take over the management of farms and factories from the despised masters and bosses. Everyone would now share in the profits made from these miserable places of exploitation. There's a fantastic Karl Marx quote that describes this perfectly: 'Expropriate the expropriators'. I was inspired by the revolutionary phrase, 'All power to the Soviets'. This was anarchy in action, pure syndicalism. Workers' power. My ancestors suffered generations of indentured labour as serfs and tenant farmers and now I was of the age where I was just about to enter the world of industrial exploitation. Wage-slave blues! Pay it all back! Reparations now!

In my last year I was placed into what the teachers referred to as a 'remedial' class. This consisted of all of the most disruptive characters in the fourth form. Every single hooligan or gang member who wasn't truanting was in this class. I actually enjoyed being in remedial class. It was always a right laugh. Once, when the teacher had locked us up, some kids launched a desk and chairs out the window, and they went crashing down to the playground below. The whole class was in hysterics, everyone cheering and banging their desks with their fists in rebellious glee. The teacher always locked the door on us so we couldn't escape and the classroom was on the second floor of the school building, a big concrete brutalist structure. Now, imagine there had been a fire and in the chaos of evacuating the school the teacher hadn't come back to unlock the door for us?

That remedial class had kids like Peter Derrick, the best fighter in the school, a guy who always carried an edge of danger, and the glamorous April, a really cool girl who could have easily started in a 1960s kitchen-sink drama as a wayward but loveable working-class lass. Wild, larger than life characters who were actually fun to be around. I felt more in common with these educationally throwaway kids, those who were considered so useless that school deemed them (and me) unworthy of learning, than the 'swots' who swanned around the corridors with an air of learned arrogance and a sense of entitlement, looking down on and sneering at us from behind cold, disdainful, aspirational King's Park & Simshill 'working class but think they're middle class' eyes. I loved being in that remedial class. I looked forward to it every week and being a member of it was a badge of honour I wore with pride.

# 3.

# Psychic Jailbreak
# (The Boy Looked at Johnny)

One spring morning in 1977 I was sitting in class, ignoring the teacher droning on about some shit that meant nothing to me, looking out the window thinking about how I needed to get the fuck out of this uninspiring hole. I put my hand up and asked the teacher if I could go to the bathroom, just to get out of there. As I made my way down the concrete stairs to the ground floor I noticed a photocopied A4 poster pinned to the wall. It was advertising a night for the school debating society. I didn't even know that this society existed and I wasn't the kind of pupil who would be invited along to an event like this anyway. What drew me to the poster was the image of a young man kneeling on a stage, his brutally cropped hair cut as if by a broken bottle or a blunt knife. He had the desperate, frightened, angry, underfed look of a concentration camp prisoner. He was screaming into a microphone, wearing a torn crew-neck sweater, a white, short-collared, sixties-style shirt sticking up at the neck. His look was completed by a pair of old men's forties-style baggy demob suit trousers, striped football socks and Teddy Boy brothel-creeper shoes with a thick black crêpe sole. A beer bottle, a pint glass and a microphone stand were strewn across the stage; it resembled football terracing after it's been cleared of fans, littered with the debris of violence. The words at the top of the poster said, 'PUNK, WHAT IS IT AND

WHAT DOES IT MEAN?' I was transfixed by this image. I had never seen anything or anyone who looked like this guy in my life. I stood for ages just gazing at it. I tried to pull myself away a couple of times, but I kept returning to it, standing in silence and awe. I had to find out who this guy was.

Back in class on another day, a kid sitting at the desk beside me was looking at a music paper. I can't remember if it was *NME* or *Melody Maker* but what I do recall is an image of Queen Elizabeth's head. But this was no celebration of HRH, because the space where her eyes and mouth had been were torn out to make a blank space, and in their place were the words 'God Save The Queen' and 'SEX PISTOLS'. I was immediately drawn to this seditious image. I had been going to Celtic matches and I always enjoyed standing in 'the jungle', the terracing at Parkhead where all the craziest, drunkest, most violent, committed and fanatical Celtic fans stood. It was also the noisiest place, with the loudest singing, and it always had the most fantastic atmosphere. It was where the *energy* was. The Bhoys in the jungle sang Irish rebel songs.

Celtic were founded in 1888 by a Catholic priest called Brother Walfrid, in an act of charity to raise money for underprivileged children in the East End of Glasgow. Many of the Irish Catholic diaspora had settled in the West of Scotland, escaping famine and poverty and the oppression of British colonialism in their homeland. As economic refugees they were confronted with sectarian and racist bigotry on the 'mainland' and, like other victims of repressive regimes throughout history who find themselves resettling in a foreign country, they ended up surrounded by their fellow sufferers in religious ghettoes. It was out of this imperialist violence that Celtic evolved. The IRA bombing campaign on the 'mainland' was unceasing throughout the seventies. The Irish tricolour proudly flew up on the terracing roof, high above where we stood in the jungle. In between chants of praise for star players such as Kenny Dalglish or Harry Hood, Dixie Dean and Danny McGrain were IRA battle songs such as 'Sean South of Garryowen', 'The Boys of the Old Brigade', and the Irish Free State national anthem 'The Soldiers' Song', and there were also chants of 'If you HATE THE BRITISH ARMY clap your hands!' and 'If you HATE THE ROYAL FAMILY clap your hands!' To hear forty thousand people singing these martial songs lustily at thunderous volume in a mass rebellious hooligan choir was an unbelievable experience, an act of total sedition. This was happening way before I knew anything about the Sex Pistols or punk rock.

The image on the magazine, just like the debating society's Johnny Rotten image, transfixed and fascinated me. I loved the Sex Pistols even before I heard a single note of their music. I was primed and ready for the Pistols and punk. Guy Debord, leader of the Situationist International and author of *The Society of the Spectacle*, said: 'the world is image'. I agree. We are creatures who respond more deeply to images than to words. We are not too far removed from the cave paintings of yore. Image bypasses both verbal reasoning and cognitive rationality. They say a picture is worth one thousand words, which is a cliché, but in this case that was as true a maxim as there ever was. Rotten's dishevelled, emaciated intensity sucked me right into that photograph because no one else in the reality movie we had all been sold as 'British culture' appeared this strange looking and ablaze with such violent poetic intensity. This image burned a hole through the fakeness of the spectacle. My first outsider hero. No words needed. My imagination was lit.

A few years earlier, around 1974, I started looking in the window of Sound Track, a record store on Cathcart Road directly across from the bottom of Stanmore Road where I lived. New releases were advertised in the windows. I remember standing in awe before Bowie's *Diamond Dogs* album cover which had the unforgettable Guy Peellaert (of *Rock Dreams* fame) airbrush painting of Bowie as half-man, half-dog lying in front of a circus freakshow consisting of blue midget ladies. Mick Ronson's *Slaughter on 10th*

*Avenue* and Silverhead's *16 and Savaged* covers were others I remember from those days. Ronson had beautiful long blond feather-cut hair like a girl but it framed his tough, masculine face. I had a feather cut too at some point in the seventies. It was a unisex cut but I'm not sure that most teens saw it as such. The older, more sophisticated, sussed kids who were deeply into Bowie and Roxy may have understood the subversive and androgynous undercurrents of glam, but for someone like me, Arsenal's Charlie George, Man United's Denis Law and George Best, Rodney Marsh and Stan Bowles of QPR and very our own Kenny Dalglish would have been my style icons. Pop stars didn't do it for me until I saw Rotten.

Each day I would wear a Lord Anthony black Harrington jacket with red tartan lining, a navy-blue V-necked school sweater with a brown, light cotton, short-sleeved Simon shirt underneath, and high-waisted black Oxford or Birmingham bags, which were wool polyester trousers cut tight up at the waist and thighs, but spread out downwards in an 'A' shape becoming looser from the knee down (you can see some of the Northern Soul dancers at Wigan Casino wearing this style). There was also a craze for 'skinners', which were the same cut as Oxford bags, but the fabric was softer – indigo or brushed denim – in a lighter shade of blue sometimes splashed in a Jackson Pollock action-painting style by bleaching them in a bath or washing machine. These were sometimes worn high above the ankle to show off either high-topped Doc Martens 'Bovver boots', if the kid was 'tough', or a flash pair of platform shoes. I would always wear either Adidas Samba trainers or black leather brogues. My hair was done in a feather cut by the hairdresser on Cathcart Road. I may or may not have worn a 'star' jumper. This was a V-necked garment with a three-inch high ribbed waistband, and tight, ribbed cuffs that went halfway up your forearm in a very feminine style; the collar and waistband cuffs would be in the same colour, the chest and arms in another. Some sweaters were emblazoned by three stars and two rings on the upper left arm, inspired by American fifties college-boy fashion. Bay City Rollers and Gilbert O'Sullivan were both known for this style.

I had a pair of black Levi Sta-Prest in 1973 (not a flare, but a sharp, straight-leg cut like a Suedehead would wear, with a pair of brown 'monkey boots' with yellow laces from an Army & Navy store) that I bought from Dee's of Trongate and Krazy House, a big shop that stood on the corner of Glasgow Cross lodged between the Gallowgate and London Road. Between these two stores, an army of Glaswegian working-class droogs would make a pilgrimage each week to kit themselves out in the latest seventies street styles. I remember seeing boys walking around dressed head to toe in 'Glen check' suits, or a Crombie made in the same material, sometimes in only a white shirt, sleeves rolled up and Glen checked trousers held up by braces with a high, turned-up hem which showed off flash platforms with multi-coloured striped pop socks. The great glam band Slade made these fashionable.

Dee's and Krazy House were for the low-level initiates in Glasgow street style. The real top boys – the 'leader affs' (Glaswegian name for a gang leader) headed directly and exclusively to a tailor named Arthur Black. Kids would take in their own hand-drawn ideas of shirts, jackets and trousers and Arthur would measure them, make the pattern, cut the cloth and make precious bespoke items of clothing for these kids in whatever colours they chose. The fashions were flash and outrageous: double-breasted suits with big wide gangster lapels and patch pockets in fifties rock and roll star colours like powder blue, sometimes embroidered with black saddle-stitching, to be worn with a high-collared, button-down two-tone shirt. Very much based on the style of a Ben Sherman, these shirts were always monogrammed with the name of the kid in a rightward sloping classical font just above the heart, in some cases with coloured shoulder panels, and details like extra buttons or castle pockets and epaulettes.

You always knew an Arthur Black shirt whenever you saw one, cut perfectly to the shape of the proud wearer: sharp and deadly. A completely personalised custom outfit, a street uniform. The street was a stage to some of these kids, they walked the walk, and were not to be messed with. They demanded respect. As far as I was concerned, these shirts and suits designated style, class and status on the wearer. But you had to be 'gallus' to pull it off, and though I coveted one of these shirts, in no way did I feel that I possessed the necessary street flash hardness, nor did I have the readily available cash to buy one.

The first time I really took notice of the pop charts was when we moved to Mount Florida in 1972. From that moment I fell in love with songs like

MOTT THE HOOPLE
'All the Young Dudes'
'The Golden Age of Rock 'n' Roll'
'Roll Away the Stone'
'Honaloochie Boogie'

SPARKS
'Get in the Swing'
'Never Turn Your Back on Mother Earth'
'This Town Ain't Big Enough for the Both of Us'
'Amateur Hour'

SWEET
'Block Buster!'
'The Ballroom Blitz'
'Teenage Rampage'
'Fox on the Run'
'Hell Raiser'

SLADE
'Skweeze Me, Pleeze Me'
'Gudbuy T'Jane'

'Cum On Feel the Noize'
'Mama Weer All Crazee Now'

ALICE COOPER
'School's Out'
'No More Mr Nice Guy'
'Elected'
'Hello Hooray'

SUZI QUATRO
'Can the Can'
'48 Crash'
'Devil Gate Drive'

MUD
'Tiger Feet'

GARY GLITTER
'Rock and Roll (part two)'
'I Didn't Know I Loved You (Till I Saw You Rock and Roll)'
'Leader of the Gang'
'Do You Wanna Touch Me'
'Hello! Hello! I'm Back Again'

DAVID BOWIE
'Life on Mars'
'Space Oddity'
'The Jean Genie'
'Suffragette City'
'Starman'
'Drive-in Saturday'
'John, I'm Only Dancing'
'Sorrow'
'Rebel Rebel'

LULU (PRODUCED BY BOWIE AND RONSON)
'Man Who Sold the World'

WIZZARD
'See My Baby Jive'

HELLO
'New York Groove'

COZY POWELL
'Dance with the Devil'

BRYAN FERRY
'A Hard Rain's A-Gonna Fall'

T. REX
'Debora'
'Hot Love'
'Get It On'
'Jeepster'
'Ride a White Swan'
'20th Century Boy'
'Solid Gold Easy Action'
'Children of the Revolution'
'Metal Guru'
'Telegram Sam'
'Born to Boogie'

… oh my god, how I loved these songs.

The first single I ever bought with my own money was 'Hellraiser' by Sweet. It featured a heavy Zeppelin-influenced song on the B side called 'Burnin''. My brother Graham and I would flip between both sides obsessively, playing them at full volume on our parents' radiogram in the living room when Mum was out at the shops. We had gigantic Slade and Bowie posters on our bedroom wall manufactured by a company called Pace Posters. Dad would bring them back from his work. There was one magazine called *DISC 45* that I loved, a small mag which had the words to all the hit singles in the Top 20. Although I was hearing these records on the radio and seeing the artists perform the songs on *Top of the Pops*, 'Hellraiser' was the only record I owned.

I used to record songs off the chart countdown on a Sunday evening on Radio One, on a small cassette recorder that I received as a gift from Mum one Christmas. I borrowed some records from a slighter older boy who was in the 83rd BB. His name was Stephen Butchard or 'Butchie' as he was known in the street, and he was a fearless character. I would sometimes go up to Butchie's flat after a kickabout in the street, and he would play me records in his room. Amongst these records were *Meaty Beaty Big and Bouncy*, *Who's Next*, and *Live at Leeds* by the Who; he also had *Get Yer Ya-Ya's Out* by the Rolling Stones. I asked Butchie if I could borrow them. I can't remember the exact arrangement, maybe he moved away before I got the chance to return them or maybe he told me to keep them, but I ended up owning these albums.

*Live at Leeds* was the original 1970 pressing complete with the iconic 'Maximum R&B' poster showing Townsend wielding his Rickenbacker like a weapon with a super-sharp Mod 'Roman'-style haircut. Very punk. It also had promo photos, gig tickets and bills for destroyed instruments and other rock and roll paraphernalia inside to look and wonder at. Such fantastic packaging. It was a little glimpse into the occult and adult world of rock and roll. I later bought the *Story of the Who* double album in 1976, as well as *Stupidity* by Dr Feelgood, which I loved, and a couple of albums by Scottish rockers Nazareth. I *loved* their song 'This Flight Tonight' but had no idea it was written by Joni Mitchell. I was into songs I heard on the radio like 'Made in Heaven' by Be-Bop Deluxe and 'Only You' by Fox and 'Motor Bikin'' by Chris Spedding. I loved the Status Quo singles like 'Caroline', 'Down Down', 'Paper Plane', and I also had a copy of *Machine Head* by Deep Purple and a live 'Smoke on The Water' / 'Woman from Tokyo' / 'Strange Kind of Woman' seven-inch single. I owned *Changesonebowie* which had all the great Bowie singles on it. It's still one of my favourite albums, even today; an unbeatable run of hits. I also had all the Bowie and Bolan seven-inches, which were gifted to me by the Ahmed sisters, a Pakistani family we were friendly with who lived directly across the road from us.

Most of the boys at school carried albums under their arms like status symbols. Some had Peter Gabriel-era Genesis, Emerson Lake and Palmer, Yes, Jethro Tull and very occasionally Dylan. I knew nothing about these artists apart from how their record sleeves looked, because they were never played on Top 40 radio. I remember a kid letting me look at his albums one day in school at playtime. He had *Nursery Cryme / Foxtrot* and *The Lamb Lies Down on Broadway* by Genesis, featuring weird conceptual paintings of Alice in Wonderland stoner-type fantasies. These covers seemed forbidding to me, as if one had to be an initiate to understand them, to 'get them'. Maybe that was just my insecurity at not being hip to the prog scene.

One day in music class when I was about thirteen, the teacher asked us to bring in a record to play so we could all discuss it. I remember this kid pulled out *The Yes Album* and said 'I'm going to play a song called "The Clap".' I thought he was putting the teacher on, and it was gonna be a filthy, seedy song about vene-real disease and prostitutes, like 'Next' by Alex Harvey. But 'The Clap' was just a meandering, boring, acoustic guitar instrumental that said nothing to me, except I could tell the guitarist (Steve Howe) possessed great instrumental prowess. It wasn't exciting and noisy like Suzi Quatro or Mott the Hoople and it wasn't full of dread and evil like Alex Harvey singing 'Delilah' or 'Faith Healer'. I've hated Yes and progressive rock ever since, but I did own a couple of phantasmagorical Roger Dean posters: one was the Osibisa cover featuring a science fiction mosquito-winged elephant, the other showed a fly-like spacecraft landing on a distant planet; very trippy, prehistoric-psychedelic sci-fi airbrush art. I bought both of them from Virgin on Argyle Street next door to What Every Woman Wants.

\*

I hung around Sound Track after school each day just looking through the albums in the racks. The owner was a nice guy, I think he sensed that I didn't have a lot of money because I never bought anything much, but he let me hang out there nevertheless. I was beginning to explore around the edges of seventies hard rock, but I also really loved pop music. There were great singles by Bryan Ferry, the O'Jays, Hall and Oates, Stylistics, Billy Paul, Delfonics, Elton John, Rod Stewart, the Steve Miller Band, even the Eagles. Kiki Dee's 'I've Got the Music in Me' is godhead. The band that were mostly represented at our school was the Sensational Alex Harvey Band. Their explosive comic-style logo was seen on boys' (Wrangler) denim jackets, normally in the form of an embroidered patch, and scrawled into desks in pen and ink. Harvey was one of our own, a Glasgow boy who had made it after years of trying. His sensational band were accurately named. They took no prisoners and stormed the nation's pop charts and concert venues with a mixture of street-sharp hard rock, sea shanties, murder ballads and Weimar decadence. Alex was a literary man and he'd paid his dues. He started out in the fifties, winning a competition to be 'Scotland's Tommy Steele'. He was in Hamburg at the same time as the Beatles and performed in the cast of the hippie musical *Hair*. Then he teamed up with a bunch of young Droogs called Teargas and formed SAHB. I borrowed *Next* from Butchie and the album cover alone was a trip: Alex stood onstage in front of a microphone stand, yellow rag hanging off it, wearing a ripped black and white striped long-sleeved jersey, both sleeves rolled up to his elbows, his arms extended outwards, pointing, accusatory.

Some may have seen that as a typical messianic rockstar cruci-fixion pose but it was actually the stance of a Glasgow hard man offering out an opponent to 'come ahead'. In our city if someone stood like that and shouted, 'Come ahead, Your tea's oot!' it was both a threat and invitation to do battle. This image was not lost on the youth of Glasgow. I devoured this album. Side one, track one smashed me right between the eyes with the sleazy, priapic boogie-shuffle of 'Swampsnake' which slammed immediately into the amoral Dionysian frenzy of 'Gang Bang'. I was still a virgin so this orgasmic celebration to the glory of unleashed libidos filled my head with wild pornographic images. The onslaught continued, but he saved the best for last. My innocent teenage consciousness had been primed for the final seduction – my mind was about to be totally blown and warped forever as my soul was sucked deep into the black sound vortex of the hard rock voodoo dread epic 'Faith Healer', a sick pagan anthem built on malevolent throbbing sequencers and topped off with Zal's power chords and dramatic, soaring and swooping Bayreuth lightning-bolt lead lines. Alex played the shamanic pagan high priest of the title to the hilt, like Richard Wagner fronting a rock band. How the fuck did this guy, this band, come out of Glasgow? Celtic made me proud to be Glaswegian but *this*? He was just a guy from the same streets as me, from Tradeston.

I would see VAMBO or VAMBO ROOLS OK written everywhere in school and sometimes sprayed on walls in silver paint. I discovered that Vambo was a character from the imagination of Alex Harvey: a mythical superhero gang leader who would advise his fans 'Don't piss in your own water supply', and 'Protect your little sisters, there is no glory in rape.' Whatever bad shit or day-to-day hassles in the lives of the teenage SAHB army they were reassured that Vambo was always 'comin' to the rescue'. The guy created this alternative universe and took his army of teenage fans on an adventure of the imagination. His songs were peopled by amazing characters such as Sergeant Fury, Tomahawk Kid, the Faith Healer, Vambo Marble Eye, Midnight Moses, the Giant Stone Eater, Isobel Goudie and the Swampsnake. Songs like 'Action Strasse' placed you right in the middle of Hamburg's infamous Reeperbahn, in a dangerous, sleazy, rock and roll port town filled with sailors, prostitutes, dope dealers and strippers. SAHB seized Tom Jones's easy listening melodramatic sixties hit 'Delilah' and actualised all the feelings of vengeance and violence in the song that Jones had subsumed. It's a frightening, murderous record. You believe Alex when he sings the last line: 'Forgive me, Delilah, I just couldn't take any more'. Not sure I ever believed Tom, but I certainly believed Alex.

Dad came home one night and told me he'd been in a bar in Govan having a drink with Alex Harvey himself. Dad had friends that knew Alex's kid brother Les of Stone the Crows fame who was tragically killed by electrocution whilst his guitar was plugged into an amp that hadn't been earthed on stage. I was impressed, to say the least. Nothing, but nothing in my life had prepared me for the song 'Next': a diseased tango of sin, sleaze and venereal disease, the loveless tale of a frightened young virgin soldier told in unflinching, hard, graphic poetry courtesy of Belgian songwriter Jacques Brel. Harvey assumes the role of the narrator, half speaking the words with an ironic, mocking, Weimar cabaret-performer delivery, standing in a line with one hundred of his comrades who are all 'naked as sin'.

*I was just a child when my innocence was lost*
*in a mobile army whorehouse*

He sings of them having their arses slapped by a queer lieutenant: 'I swear on the wet head of my / First taste of gonorrhoea'. It's a nightmare song of dark eroticism and zero romance, an entry into the loveless world of adult sex which is both functional and bestial.

There's film footage of SAHB performing 'Next' on *The Old Grey Whistle Test*. Harvey dominates the screen and acts out the outrage and humiliation of the sexual initiate narrator of the song with facial movements ranging from fear and dread to self-pity and finally rage. It's an incredible performance. He's a completely malevolent presence. Guitarist Zal Cleminson was a perfect foil for the implicit threat of Harvey's street gang Vambo character. His psychotic, sick clown-face make-up and multicoloured, all-in-one superhero jumpsuits with a *Clockwork Orange*-style codpiece and platform boots completed his Droog image, so vital in relation to Alex's gang-leader persona.

The song that best defined the long hot summer of 1976 for me was 'The Boys are Back in Town' by Thin Lizzy. It was everywhere. A mix of tough street rock combined with a beautiful yearning pop melody worthy of the Ronettes and Springsteen-like minor chord runs, topped with Phil Lynott's street poet celebration of male camaraderie. It is a perfect record. Just perfect. I saw Lizzy on *TOTP* and was seduced by the vision of Lynott: a long, lean, tall, skinny, extremely handsome black Irishman, dressed in tight blue jeans, stack-heeled shoes and a loose-fitting glammed-out silver-streaked cowboy shirt unbuttoned halfway down his chest, revealing a silver necklace. He wore his hair in the afro style, tight like Jimi Hendrix. He was just so confident and outrageously flash. A good-looking guy, his big soulful eyes combined with the sly charming smile of a rock and roll stud obviously well versed in the dark art of seduction. Women loved him, and no wonder. His band consisted of master drummer Brian Downey and the twin guitar attack of Californian Scott Gorham and Glasgow's own Brian Robertson.

Later in the year I noticed an advert in the gigs section of the *Glasgow Evening Times*:

**SATURDAY 28th OCTOBER**
**APOLLO THEATRE**
**Thin Lizzy**
**+ support**
**Clover**

I immediately knew that I had to go. There was a new Thin Lizzy single that I really loved, high in the charts at the time, titled 'Don't Believe a Word'. It was pure rock and roll raunch and filthy boogie, a feral shuffle of sex and erotic danger, Lynott laying out his true intentions to any would-be conquests. I've never met a woman of my generation who hasn't dreamt of a night of sexual congress with Lynott, the lover, the Irish poet, the Afrocentric hard rocker. I had a burning desire to see Lizzy play. The only problem was that I didn't know where the Apollo was, nor had I ever been up town on my own on a Saturday night *ever*.

I concocted a plan. I was on nodding terms with a boy at school called Alan McGee. McGee was always to be seen carrying rock albums under his arm around our area. He got off the number 37 bus each day after school at a stop on Cathcart Road, King's Park, directly across from the private bowling club. We'd nod at each other the way teenage boys do, but had never spoken a word. I didn't know anyone who had actually ever been to a rock gig but I reckoned that this kid McGee might have done. I looked up all the McGees in the Glasgow telephone directory and found an address that corresponded with where I thought he lived. I called the number and his mother answered. She asked who was calling and I said Bobby Gillespie.

He came on the line and I said, 'Hi Alan, it's Bobby Gillespie, do you want to come with me and see Thin Lizzy play at the Apollo tonight?'

McGee said, 'Yes, what time do you want to meet?'

'Seven o'clock at the bus stop in Mount Florida?'

'OK, cool, see you there.'

And that was it. I was both excited and scared. I had no idea what to expect. Nothing could prepare me for it.

We met at the bus stop at 7 p.m. and took the 31 bus into town, where we got off at the terminus in Saint Enoch Square and walked all the way up to the top of Renfield Street and the Apollo Theatre. We waited in the queue of mostly teenage boys, a majority of whom were clad head to toe in double denim with the names of their favourite bands written on the back of their Wrangler jackets, and we managed to buy two tickets for the back of the stalls. Luckily for us the gig hadn't sold out.

The Apollo had been known as Green's Playhouse since the thirties. It held around four and a half thousand people and all the major rock bands had played there: the Rolling Stones, the Who, Roxy Music, David Bowie, SAHB, Led Zeppelin, Status Quo, Eagles, Elton, Rod Stewart. The Apollo audience was known in the music business for its extreme passion and loud fanatical appreciation of their musical heroes and god help any opening act the crowd were not impressed by. It was a legendary venue. Many acts recorded their 'live' albums here (double live albums were very fashionable in the seventies. Quo and Roxy both recorded theirs here) because the passionate response of the Glasgow fans drove the bands to play out of their skins. You had to be good in Glasgow or they would eat you alive. This goes all the way back to the music hall days. Hardworking people want to be properly entertained. If the cunt onstage ain't giving it his or her best then there will be a price to pay. There are stories of knives, hatchets, bottles and other missiles being thrown at shirking performers in Glasgow. Nick Cave told me that at the first ever Birthday Party show in Glasgow at the Night Moves venue in Sauchiehall Street he was singing, lost in the moment and suddenly he felt wet. He looked up to see if the roof was leaking only to see two guys with their cocks out pissing on him from the balcony above the stage. I told him, 'Nick, at least they liked you, imagine if they hadn't?'

Clover came on first – an American west coast soft country rock band, which may have featured Huey Lewis on harmonica and vocals. These guys were also the backing band for Elvis Costello's *My Aim is True* album on Stiff Records, a New Wave classic. We didn't pay much attention to Clover and headed out to the foyer where the Lizzy merchandising stall stood. I bought a Johnny the Fox tour programme, which I still have. Then we returned to the darkness of the back stalls and took our places, waiting for Lizzy. When the lights went down everyone got up from their seats and there was a huge roar like when a goal is scored at a football match. I held my breath. Suddenly Lizzy hit the stage to the sound of queasily psychotic screaming police sirens. There were revolving red flashing emergency lights placed atop each of the huge PA stacks and smoke-bomb explosions detonated with flashlight precision when the band hit the first chord of 'Jailbreak'. What an entrance! When the smoke cleared there stood Phil Lynott wearing a short-sleeved navy-blue Umbro Scotland football top with the diamond stripes on the sleeves, stalking the stage like a panther, wielding his black Fender Precision bass guitar like a rifle. His bass had a mirrored scratch-plate and each time he moved the reflection from the spotlights beamed out into the audience. I was hit throughout the night by mirror bass beams. I honestly felt that Phil had picked me out, that I was chosen. I never mentioned this to McGee. Or maybe I did. He probably thought I was mad.

I lost my rock and roll virginity to Phil Lynott and Thin Lizzy that night. I was filled with the Holy Spirit of Rock and Roll, never to be the same again. The classic Lizzy line-up of Lynott, Downey, Gorham and Robertson transmogrified my teenage soul with raw-powered street rock and flash glam electric sexuality. My love for Lizzy will never die. They were the first real musical love that I discovered by myself and they still inspire me to this day. Phil was the greatest, a true working-class hero. Every boy wanted to be him and every girl wanted to fuck him. He wore the sharpest threads and looked like he could handle himself in a street fight. He was a romantic poet and he was the Rocker. For Christmas 1976 I asked Mum for the *Johnny the Fox* album and Graham bought me the *Jailbreak* LP which had 'The Boys Are Back in Town' on it and the gorgeous, romantic 'Cowboy Song', the storyline of which I would live out for myself on an American tour with Primal Scream. That adventure lay way ahead of me. I wasn't thinking that far, yet. My romance with rock and roll was only just beginning.

# Part Two
# (1977–1981)

# 4.

# Apprentice Punk

There was a shop called Gloria's Record Bar in Battlefield. I'd sometimes go there and look in the window, too shy to ask the guy behind the counter for recommendations. I remember they always had *In the Court of the Crimson King* behind the glass. I didn't know what it was. I just thought it looked like a good record sleeve.

Through the early weeks of 1977 it felt like something new was happening. I remember seeing the Damned on *Supersonic*, a music show presented by the flamboyant Mike Mansfield. He'd announce each act from his control desk, high above the studio, with the words, 'Cue T. Rex, cue Tina Charles, cue David Essex, cue Be-Bop Deluxe', with his finger pointing archly to the studio technicians. It was on this programme that I saw the very first punk band on British TV, performing 'Neat Neat Neat'. It was thrilling. The music was so fast and hard. It was like nothing I'd ever seen or heard before. I didn't know the Stooges or anything like that at this point. I liked Deep Purple and Nazareth, so I knew a little bit about hard rock, but this was punk rock. It was different.

The first time I bought *NME* was Easter 1977 and the Clash were on the cover, Paul Simonon in the middle, Mick Jones and Strummer on either side of him. All three had the same brutally shorn hair like Johnny Rotten. It was shocking, both visually and culturally, because in early '77 *everyone* had long hair. Their first eponymous album had just been released. I went into Sound Track and looked at the sleeve. The image had a degraded quality to it, like a really fucked-up photocopy. It consisted of only three colours: the band photo printed in flat black framed on either side in a dark army-green; the slashed-up, battered-looking band logo leapt out at you in day-glo orange-red, with the three musicians posing in an alley like a gang who were just about to kick your head in. All three wore tight trousers and sixties-style 'bum-freezer' three-button Mod jackets; the exact opposite of the prevalent culture of flared or Oxford bag trousers and wide Al Capone jacket lapels then in vogue. When I flipped the record over it was even better: here was a scene of Black youth fighting white cops from the Notting Hill Carnival riot the previous August. I had recently watched a documentary about this on BBC2 with my dad, and had felt both inspired and excited by the footage of young Black people fighting back against the racism and oppression of the police. Then there were the song titles: 'I'm So Bored with the USA', 'White Riot', 'Hate and War', 'London's Burning', 'Police and Thieves'. All printed in a distorted, photocopied style in standard typewriter font. The whole package was visually violent and brutal in comparison to the Pink Floyd-Zeppelin-Hipgnosis-style concept art graphics dominant at the time.

It was exciting to even hold the record sleeve in my hands. I don't know why but it felt dangerous and illegal, as if I was holding a letter bomb; like I was about to commit an act of antisocial transgression. In fact it was a cultural mind-bomb. I nervously handed over my money to the guy behind the counter at Sound Track and took it straight home, slammed it on my parents' radiogram and cranked the volume up full blast. Its mix of amphetamine-powered high-energy rock and roll and seventies urban street poetry blew my still-forming teenage consciousness to bits. The scary things in life are always the best.

I'd already bought a few late sixties, early seventies rock singles from this guy, including 'Living in the Past' by Jethro Tull and 'Smoke on the Water' by Deep Purple. But I had no clue what most of the stuff in his shop was. I remember seeing Steely Dan's *Royal Scam*. That album cover was mad. I'd look through all the racks and check out records, not knowing the bands or artists but enjoying the sleeves. It fascinated me.

There was something about record covers that put a spell on me, even before I began buying records seriously as a fan. Album cover art was the first visual art I felt I had access to. I'd seen album covers like *Axe Victim*, with the skull-guitar, or *Sunburst Finish*, with a naked girl holding a guitar against the sun, by Be-Bop Deluxe, and I appreciated them, but I didn't find those so inviting. They fitted into the conventional seventies rock style of 'conceptual art': *knowing, intelligent* or *tasteful*. It wasn't street in any way. But then the first Ramones and Clash albums had photographs of the bands themselves, standing against walls or in alleys very much like the streets that I knew. The Sensational Alex Harvey Band albums were illustrated in a Marvel comics style and I loved them. They looked like a world you could fall into and get lost in.

Bowie and Bryan Ferry really stood out for me, style-wise. Ferry's wedge-cut with long fringe, and brown army shirt with sleeves rolled and black tie tucked into his shirt, around the time of 'Love is the Drug', stuck in my mind. *How cool*, I thought. And he had the three glamorous Roxy backing singers (the Roxettes) dressed in military shirts and tight fifties pencil skirts. Fabulous! I saw Bowie sing 'Golden Years' on *Soul Train* wearing a blue baggy suit and that made a deep impression on me as far as style was concerned.

I needed to hear more punk music. I heard that the Sex Pistols had released a song called 'Anarchy in the UK' which had been banned. That sounded really exciting to me, like these guys were a danger to the state. It was the days of the IRA, of the Red Army Faction (Baader–Meinhof Group) in Germany, the Brigate Rosse in Italy, the PLO (Palestinian Liberation Organisation); the days of bombings, kidnappings and plane hijackings, and of Carlos the

Jackal. I didn't really know what 'anarchy' was, but I knew that it was considered a danger to the established way of life in our country. I asked my dad what his definition of anarchy was and he replied, 'It's a great idea but very difficult to put into practice.' All the same it sounded thrilling to me and I wanted to know more. I managed to buy a copy of the single on import from Bloggs record shop in town on the French Barclay label. It said 'Banned in the UK' on the cover, which was itself a ripped-up Union flag. EMI had withdrawn the record after the media outrage over the Pistols' drunken and expletive-filled appearance on the Bill Grundy TV show and only a few thousand copies had hit the streets so the record was gold dust to converts like myself. The original UK EMI issue came in a plain black paper bag but the French version had a savagely distressed, photocopied, fucked-up quality to it which instantly spoke to my new-found and ever-evolving aesthetics. The seditious combination of the single artwork and the song lyric was thrilling to me. Of course, looking back with over forty years distance I can now see that Malcolm McLaren's clever marketing of the Sex Pistols using some of Guy Debord's Situationist theories was a genius move. Using capitalism to critique capitalism. Exploiting the rebellious energies of disaffected teens whilst further enriching a capitalist record company is one way of looking at it – 'turning rebellion into money' as Joe Strummer so beautifully and righteously sung. On the other hand, the fact that the Pistols under Malcolm's tutelage were widening the cultural and political frame of reference of the more curious members of that same teenage demographic at the same time is, to my mind at least, where McLaren's genius lay. His instinct for monetising cultural revolution was at worst opportunistic and cynical; at best, heroic.

The DJ John Peel had a weekly column in the music magazine *Sounds*. There was a picture of him naked in a bath, a younger woman dressed in a schoolgirl uniform standing to the side and looking at him adoringly. I thought to myself, if anyone's gonna play the Sex Pistols it has to be this guy. A few months earlier I had tuned in to the John Peel show on Radio One late one night, my cassette player lined up to record in case he played anything great, and Peel had introduced a song. He said, in his inimitable sardonic, sometimes ironic tones, 'This is a track from Eric Clapton's new album.' And I taped it. The song was called 'Hello Old Friend':

*Hello old friend,*
*it's really good to meet you and see you once again*

I remember thinking, he sounds like my fucking dad, that's *not* rock and roll. My dad's a bit more radical, mind.

So I didn't listen again until one night in 1977 with my brother, when Peel played 'God Save the Queen', and it felt like I had been possessed by the Holy Spirit, like I had been electrified. I had no words to describe how I felt because I had never before experienced such an overwhelming feeling. I had been converted. I had seen the light. My brother couldn't speak either. We looked at each other and we knew we had to buy this record.

The next day we put some money together and I went to the record shop. I didn't have a job. I was just a kid at school. I didn't have a paper round or anything. I was really nervous – like, fuck, I might get arrested here – as I walked into Sound Track and said to the owner behind the counter, 'Have you got "God Save the Queen" by the Sex Pistols?'

'Yeah, I do,' he said as he handed me the single, in a navy-blue sleeve with Jamie Reid's seditious image of HRH with her eyes and mouth ripped out, with 'Sex Pistols' and 'God Save the Queen' written in cut-up lettering, like the type you saw in ransom notes in the movies. I handed over the sixty pence. I'd done it, I'd bought it. It was an exhilarating experience, both liberating and transgressive. I left the shop in a hurry (maybe thinking I would be collared on the street by a Royalist cop) with the record in a brown paper bag with Sound Track written on it, sped over the zebra crossing on Cathcart Road, and ran all the way up the hill on Stanmore Road back to our house.

Graham (his street name was Gringo at that point; later he would be known as the Judge) was waiting for me. 'Did you get it?' he asked. I took the record out of the bag and he broke into a demented smile. I pulled out the black vinyl seven-inch record and put it on our parents' record player. We cranked the volume all the way up. Mum and Dad were both at work and we were just ORGASMING. I really believe that at that exact moment we both experienced psychic jailbreak. The way that we felt, thought, dressed, the way we looked at ourselves and the world, changed forever on that day. It would take a few years of immersion in punk culture to fully sharpen our dress, outlook and attitudes, but there was no going back after this. We had just been presented with an alternative route into the future. It was a Damascene moment. I have no other way to describe the feelings we had on that warm summer's day in Glasgow.

We flipped the record over and listened to the B side, 'Did You No Wrong', and for the rest of the day we played 'God Save the Queen' and 'Did You No Wrong' and 'God Save the Queen' and 'Did You No Wrong' on repeat.

But of course we couldn't speak to anybody about it, because no one else that we knew was into this stuff, certainly not my Quo- and Van Halen-loving friends who dressed in brushed denim flares and feather cuts. It was scary, intimidating and amazing at the same time.

The next few weeks, we bought 'In the City' by the Jam, 'Peaches / Go Buddy Go', 'Straighten Out / Something Better Change' by the Stranglers and 'Sheena Is a Punk Rocker' by Ramones. Then I bought this budget album for £2.49 on Phonogram (Sire), called New Wave. It featured more songs by Ramones and included US artists and songs like:

DEAD BOYS 'Sonic Reducer'
RICHARD HELL AND THE VOIDOIDS 'Love Comes in Spurts'
PATTI SMITH 'Piss Factory'
DAMNED 'New Rose'
RUNAWAYS 'Cherry Bomb', 'Hollywood'
FLAMIN' GROOVIES 'Shake Some Action'

And most importantly, New York Dolls ('Personality Crisis', 'Who Are the Mystery Girls?'). I thought, 'These guys sound *exactly* like the Sex Pistols – same guitar style and sound.' It took me a while to realise they were an older band from 1973 who had morphed into Johnny Thunders and the Heartbreakers.

*New Wave* was seen by older heads as a cynical punk cash-in album, but to someone like me it was great because it introduced all these foundational artists and broadened the scope of my taste. I played that album into the ground that summer. There weren't a lot of punk albums out at this point, it was mostly seven-inch singles. To get the more obscure records you had to go into town but I didn't know that yet. Later, I discovered the record shops in town. Luckily I had a job by then, so I used to go every day and buy something: Mink DeVille, Stranglers, the Jam, Tom Petty and the Heartbreakers, whatever was on *Top of the Pops*.

I bought *Teenage Depression* by Eddie and the Hot Rods after I saw the solarised psychedelic cover image of a quaffed-up teenager holding a pistol to his head in the window of Sound Track and knew I had to have it. It was a great time for singles. 'Gary Gilmore's Eyes' by the Adverts was being played on the radio. I loved the fact that they'd chosen a serial killer's last wish before he was fried to death in the electric chair as the subject matter for their hit song. How fucking cool was that? I saw these punk bands start to get on *Top of the Pops*, every week. I started buying the music papers and suddenly I could see photographs of these bands, and get a sense of their style. Almost overnight, I went from being a kid mostly just into football to being completely immersed in the world of rock and roll, with the same degree of passion and fanaticism.

I left school at sixteen with three O Levels, Art, English and History. A job opportunity came up through Dad's connections in the printing industry. John Horn's, where I started work in July 1977, was a factory in Pollock, bordered by Shawlands. It took me forty-five minutes to get there by train each morning. All the workers on the factory floor had to clock in at the gatehouse, so the bosses monitored your every move. I began my apprenticeship as a lithographic printer. I was quite young emotionally; I think most sixteen-year-olds are, but I certainly wasn't ready for the hardcore world of a working-class factory. I was sixteen but I probably looked about thirteen. I had shoulder-length hair. I looked like one of the Ramones.

They stuck me upstairs where the plate makers worked. I was to be taught the arcane process: how to make the lithographic metal plates from huge negatives of up to four different colours and burn the images onto plates as wide as my arm span, which the printers would than fasten to huge metal cylinders on their machines. The process involved using different types of chemicals. The factory floor stunk of this stuff, but I got used to it. I mostly just made tea for the 'journeymen', as the tradesmen were known. Each journeyman had his own personal room with a plating machine inside where he would work all day making plates. They'd print hundreds of thousands of Johnny Walker Red Label whisky or Smirnoff vodka labels, or boxes of Playtex Bra containers. The plan was that in September, I was going to college.

The platemakers were all guys in their thirties, forties and fifties. Suddenly I found myself thrown into the adult world, and it was initially intimidating. There was a noticeable hierarchy in the factory. The main guv'nor was a man named Stan, the factory manager. Stan dressed well in a grey suit and had a balding head with a combover, very much like Man United and England star

Bobby Charlton. I liked Stan, he was always fair with me and treated me with respect, maybe because of who my dad was. I think he had a tough job overseeing such a large number of workers, and he handled it with dignity and an unflustered, quiet intensity. The litho printers earned their high wages; it was a very stressful job. Everything was done in real time and they had to command these huge machines the size of bin lorries, sometimes printing eight colours at the same time. Nothing was computerised, and it was all done with total focus and application. The ink in one duct could go dry or too much water in another duct could alter the image and ruin the print run. This stuff was all down to the wire. These guys were working to order and the sheets had to be delivered on time. Total pressure.

I remember going for lunch one day and somebody had the radio on in the factory yard, out by the canteen, and suddenly 'Do Anything You Wanna Do' by Eddie and the Hot Rods came blasting out of the speaker, which was just heaven. I had already bought the record and had been playing it to death at home but to hear it at work was a call to arms.

*Gonna break out of the city*
*Leave the people here behind*

It was like, fuck, these guys are singing about my life, I don't want to be in this factory. I should have been in an art school. I found out there were guys next door to where I worked in the factory that were doing artwork, using Letraset. I used to go in there and chat to them. They would give me Letraset sheets and I'd cut up photographs and make little posters for imaginary bands and fanzine covers. I remember I made this band up in my head called Captain Scarlet and the Mysterons.

I spent the rest of the summer in the factory, but the upside of it was that I was getting £25 a week, really good wages for the time. I was a member of the NGA – the National Graphical

Association – which was a powerful union. Thatcher went after the NGA and SOGAT. She crushed the miners and then she crushed the printworkers, Wapping and everything, with the help of Rupert Murdoch. I lived at home at the time and after I gave Mum a contribution to the house each week I had all this money left to buy punk records. By the time I went to college in September I was buying *Sounds* every week, *NME* occasionally, whichever had a punk band on the cover.

I'd leave work at 4.15. If I was quick enough I'd get back home, turn the telly on and watch *The Marc Bolan Show* at 4.30. I still loved Bolan. I just had a thing in my heart for him.

The summer of 1977 was my punk revolution.

Buying those records really gave me a reason for living. I was like, fuck, this is just the way it is for everybody. You leave school and you've got to get a job. Or you go on the dole. That's what everybody does here. I kept looking around at the factory thinking, you're here till you're sixty-five. The printers were sweating, chain-smoking, drinking. They were getting hernias in their thirties, and heart attacks through stress and their lifestyle. Working hard, paying a mortgage. A guy said to me he was going to become a journeyman. That's what they call it when you're no longer an apprentice, if you get your City & Guilds Diploma. He said, 'When I become a journeyman I'm gonna get married, get a mortgage and a car and have kids,' and I remember thinking to myself, 'Really?' I thought, you want to be like your mum and dad, is that what you want? Because I was getting into punk, I was questioning the family, society, existential things. The received wisdom was that when someone got themselves onto the mortgage ladder and married with a wife and kids, then they were giving themselves a stake in society. But my reasoning was the exact opposite. They had neutralised themselves. They were now trapped financially and would have to be an obedient worker to keep up the house payments and the lifestyle that came with the good wages. It acted as a barrier to militant thinking and direct action and further enforced the class system.

One day at the factory all the labourers went on strike. The Father of the Chapel was a guy called Jimmy Grey and the rumour was that Jimmy Grey had a sawn-off shotgun. The printers were all scared of big Jimmy. Jimmy Grey liked me because he admired my dad. So I was kind of protected in the factory. If I got any shit I would just go to Jimmy Grey. Jimmy Grey was a hard man with big Coke-bottle glasses, and he worked a huge varnish machine right at the back of the factory. In the last year of my apprenticeship I was stationed on a new colour litho printing machine up beside Jimmy Grey's varnish machine. I got a contact high every day from the varnish. Jimmy had to pour gallons of that stuff into his machine. It was wild.

One day Jimmy Grey led all the SOGAT labourers out. The dispute was over an unfair dismissal of a fellow worker. When the rest of the factory stopped, the printers kept printing. However, the printers weren't allowed to load paper into the machine. Only the SOGAT members could do that. So the printers could only print until that load of paper ran out then the machines all ground to a halt. That was the agreed trade union rule: John Horn's was a 'closed shop', which meant to work there you had to be a member of a trade union and in an industrial dispute you couldn't take over another person's job if they had gone on strike. It was a beautiful thing. Closed shops protected the workers and built class solidarity. The worst thing in the world was to be a 'scab', a strike breaker, a class traitor. My journeyman was critical of the strikers. He said to me that he had a wife and kids and a mortgage to pay and didn't want to cause any trouble with the bosses. The usually heaving factory was now empty apart from management and printers, and it was ghostly, all the energy had disappeared. The factory slowed to a standstill without the SOGAT workers. An hour or so later the SOGAT labourers triumphantly walked back into the factory led by big Jimmy Grey;

after discussions with the owners their sacked comrade had been reinstated. I saw the power of the union that day. With a show of strength and worker solidarity they gained a victory. I was really impressed. I considered my NGA comrades to be more scared and a lot less militant than the SOGAT labourers. The NGA guys believed they had something to lose by striking, defaulting on their mortgage and car payments, family package holidays in Spain, etc., but the lower-waged SOGAT workers mostly lived in tenement housing and council estates and went to Blackpool for their holidays during the yearly Glasgow Fair fortnight so had no fear.

During my four years working in the factory I learned some important stuff about class. Of course I already had some solid grounding in this because of my upbringing; being around my dad instilled a sense of class consciousness in me. NGA were a powerful union and the power of collective bargaining by the trade unions in the sixties and seventies ensured that workers like myself had strong employment rights enshrined in law protecting us. There were no zero-hours contracts back then. Most factories and workplaces were closed shops and trade union membership was in the millions.

I started Print College in late September '77. I was the only punk guy in the class apart from this strange, skinny kid with long, straight, dirty-blond hair, and an angular, high-cheekboned face, like an emaciated Thurston Moore look. He wore tight black jeans and a white Seditionaries God Save the Queen shirt – black Queen head on white, capped sleeve. I was in awe of this shirt. He had an older brother who had gone down to London and visited Malcolm McLaren and Vivienne Westwood's shop SEX on the King's Road where he'd bought it. The rest of the guys were into football, hard rock and prog. But they were mostly nice guys.

I enjoyed the power of punk to make the straights feel threatened. I had already experienced this back home with my Status Quo-fan friends, who had one by one started to back off from

Glasgow's very own
Yuri Gagarin

Dad showing me revolutionary ways,
May Day, 1962

My beautiful mum, me and Graham,
Ardrossan, July 1967

Happy times in 35 Palermo Street, 1967

'Bobby does a Beatles' – Mum's caption, 1963

Aged 16, in my bedroom, walls covered in Lizzy, Clash and Celtic posters. Note tartan wallpaper

1970s fashions are timeless

'Boy about Town' – just about to speak to Paul Weller after a storming Jam gig at Strathclyde University, 1979

My first time on the road with Altered Images and Siouxsie and the Banshees, 1980 (Paul Kerr, brother of Jim, on the right)

My first ever live performance, drumming for Altered Images, Middlesbrough Rock Garden, 1980

Scowling with Alan McGee in my bedroom, Mount Florida, 1980

Playing bass with The Wake, Henry Wood Hall, Glasgow, 1982

First ever Primal Scream photo session, 1984

Moody bastard

Our first Primal Scream gig, The Venue, Glasgow, 12th October 1984

Mary Chain on *The Old Grey Whistle Test*, 1985

I loved throwing drums at the audience

Second album tour, leather and speed are all you need

Andrew Innes lays down the boogie

Throb heart and soul

me when I starting getting into it. They would knock on my door and ask my mum, 'Is Vic Vomit in?' and they would all start laughing hysterically when she went to fetch me. I could handle that, it was a bit of fun, but our games of football on the recreation ground had suddenly become more physical. One time this bigger kid kept hitting me with hard tackles. They got harder over the course of the game until he finally knocked me over and as I picked myself up from the grass he muttered threateningly, 'That was for Johnny Rotten.' Later in the match he did it again and said, '*That* was for Sid Vicious.' I made a decision not to hang out with these guys or anyone like them anymore. If they felt that something as innocuous as me liking a different style of rock and roll was a threat to them then I just couldn't relate to that in any way. There's this great line in 'Your Generation' by Generation X:

*Might make our friends enemies*
*But we gotta take that chance ...*
*The end justifies the means*

That was exactly my experience. I decided that I had to find other people who loved punk rock as much as I did. That was my only chance of making true connections.

# 5.
# New Religion

Suddenly my interest in punk gave new meaning to my life. It was something that was all mine. Nobody else I knew was into it in my area or my street, although Alan McGee's friend Colin Dobbins had a lot of picture sleeve punk singles like 'Swallow My Pride' by Ramones. I was jealous because I had the single too but no picture sleeve! I needed the cover art. These records were little works of art to be treasured. Records are fetish objects that we project our desires and longings onto. We give them meaning and power and they give us meaning and power back.

It was almost a sexual thing, looking at these talismans, these objects of desire and magic. Feelings similar to when you are extremely attracted to someone. The need to devour them. The terrible desire of wanting to be inside another human being. The urge to both transport and be transported to another place, somewhere out of this world with the love object. Sex and drugs and rock and roll all go together so well because they each provide some kind of escape or release from existence. Put them all together and you have a beautiful but potentially deadly cocktail.

Rock and roll totally consumed me. It became *my* religion. All I thought about was music and bands. I would read stories of the Pistols on tour in Sweden or the Clash in the UK, in particular Lester Bangs' epic three-part piece on the road with the Clash in October 1977, and it seemed like their lives consisted of one big adventure after another. They existed outside of normal society and lived by different rules. Rock and rollers were outlaws, cultural revolutionaries. I saw rock and roll as a place of freedom from the suffocating confines of straight society, where the participants could act out their fantasies, say the unsayable, think the unthinkable and ultimately be themselves. I slowly began to understand that rock and roll was a place of reinvention. These seditious images held a magical power over my teenage imagination. The aesthetics were so strong.

I really wanted to escape into the photograph on the cover of the Ramones 'Swallow My Pride'; to disappear into it and stand in an alley in New York City. This was a world that I wanted to be part of, this punk-rock world that they lived in, because I wanted to be out of the world I was in. I think punk did that for me. It was the beginning of a transformative process; through the portal of art, I was unknowingly beginning a journey that would eventually lead me towards a creative life. Ultimately this would be the thing that would save me.

At lunchtimes I would go to Greggs the bakers and buy two sausage rolls and a cup of tea and sit on the wooded benches dotted around George Square and eat. I never hung out with the other students very much, I liked to go off on my own and visit the record shops in the city centre.

There were six record stores within a five-minute walk of the college. 23rd Precinct was for proper serious rock-heads, next door to McCormack's Music Store where later I bought my first guitar. 23rd Precinct sold the new punk sounds, old prog, classic rock and other cool stuff, but it was for older music-heads, people way more experienced in rock culture than me. I mainly shopped at Bloggs and Listen, which were owned by the same people. Listen sold prog, country rock, singer-songwriter stuff, sixties and seventies rock, 'grown-up' music, the old wave. Bloggs sold punk. It had more of what you might call a New Wave punk aesthetic and I spent *a lot* of time in there. The windows were beautiful, always covered in the week's new releases with amazing picture sleeves of US and French imports. It was managed by a nice guy named Mickey Rooney (later the singer in garage band the Primevals) who was a Stooges and MC5 fanatic.

Further down Renfield Street there was an HMV which was mainly chart stuff and across from there stood Bruce's. Bruce's was a tiny store, selling mainly New Wave and punk records with some cool sixties stuff too, but I wasn't into that stuff yet. It was owned by an Edinburgh man named Bruce Findlay, who would later go on to manage Simple Minds. This was the Glasgow branch, but it was really an Edinburgh-based business. Bruce's had all the new release singles with lovely picture sleeves arranged in the window like a punk street art installation. The front door was always open, so if you stood on the street outside you could hear the cool sounds blasting out from within the shop.

Bruce's had their own fanzine called *CRIPES* which listed their extensive and hip mail-order catalogue records for sale. In summer 1978 I won a competition in *CRIPES* and the prize was a ticket to see the Rezillos play at Clouds in Edinburgh, a signed copy of their album and a meeting with the band. I went through to Edinburgh on my own on the train from Queen Street station on a hot August night and saw an amazing show. I loved that band. Afterwards the lead singer Fay Fife came out to meet me and presented me with the signed album and a kiss – WOW! Fay was the first rock and roll star I ever met. She was beautiful. I loved them, Scotland's own Rezillos, I had all their records and had seen them open for Ramones on the Rocket to Russia tour at the Apollo six months earlier, in December 1977.

Boots the chemist on Argyle Street also sold records. I remember buying Thin Lizzy's *Fighting* and *Nightlife* there. There were no noticeable rock and roll people in Boots, just women on their lunchbreak buying toiletries, make-up and stuff. I do remember, however, seeing *Raw Power* by Iggy and the Stooges glaring defiantly out of the record racks. The first two American records I bought were Ramones' 'Sheena is a Punk Rocker' and 'Spanish

Stroll' by Mink DeVille. I also loved 'Cherry Bomb' by the Runaways, 'Piss Factory' by Patti Smith, 'Love Comes in Spurts' and 'Blank Generation' by Richard Hell and the Voidoids, and 'Sonic Reducer' by Dead Boys.

There was a Virgin store on Argyll Street near Central Station beyond Hope Street where my dad's office was. This had a dark hippie head shop vibe to it. I had gone in there in late '76 or early '77 for a look around and it had an unfriendly, depressing, elitist atmosphere. This impression may have had a lot to do with me not having a clue what to buy and being too shy to ask the assistants any questions. My own paranoia.

The big deal for me with Rotten was he was working class and stylish, beyond anything I'd ever seen. His hair looked like he'd just been freed from a concentration camp, brutally shorn like a convict's. He looked like a deserter. The bright orange dayglo dyed hair sent out a message which corresponded with the screaming anger, rage and pain in his accusatory, strangulated, consumptive voice. In a world ruled by the reassuring, soft, country, album-oriented rock voices of Eagles and Fleetwood Mac, Johnny Rotten's voice was like a razorblade stuck through a cheek. His intense laser stare burned holes straight into my innocent teenage consciousness with the pure amphetamine hatred and contempt of a self-righteous paranoid speedfreak. Everything he said in interviews was deeply confrontational, and launched with a fusillade of hate. Venomous attacks. Like a starving rat or a mongrel dog trapped in a corner, there was something diseased and slightly rodent-like about him.

He wasn't conventionally handsome or a sex symbol like Rod Stewart or Mick Jagger but that was what was amazing about him. He was exactly like one of us working-class street kids. His looks were what would have been considered ugly by mainstream culture, but one of the important things that punk achieved was to make everything viewed by mainstream society and culture as ugly become beautiful, and everything viewed as beautiful became ugly. The culture was turned upside down.

And then there were the clothes! Oh my god. The glory of Malcolm McLaren and Vivienne Westwood's muslin Seditionaries Destroy shirts with the huge Nazi swastika and upside-down Christ crucified on the cross, with Karl Marx and Queen Elizabeth portraits screen-printed in bright pop-art colours. To wear this shirt in public was to invite violence for the wearer; Rotten was attacked in a pub on Highbury Barn by razor- and hammer-wielding Royalist thugs outraged by 'God Save the Queen'.

There was the black bondage look he previewed at Gibus Club in Paris. And I'll never forget the white tuxedo with the black and pink polka-dot kipper tie and bondage trousers with Teddy Boy brothel-creepers from the summer 1977 Swedish tour. He looked like a diseased Bryan Ferry lounge-lizard character ready to spit right in the faces of complacent rich hippy poseurs. Black leather trousers and jackboots, Mod bum-freezer jacket and Destroy shirt, the studded wristband, S&M belt and his digital watch. I thought he was the coolest-looking guy in the world.

I loved the fact he was into football too. I heard a radio interview with him that year on Radio One. John Tobler, the presenter, asked, 'What kind of music do you listen to, John?'

Rotten replied, 'Football chants and Irish rebel songs.'

I thought, that's me. I go the football, we sing football chants and Irish rebel songs at Celtic games . . . and he's in the best rock and roll band in the world. Johnny Rotten comes from a council estate, so do I. *This guy's like us.*

I'd read a centre-spread punk exposé article in the *Sun* or *Daily Mirror* one of the men at work left lying around. The title was TWENTY TIPS ON HOW TO BE A PUNK and it was stuff like: '*Get your hair cut short. Make it spiky. Wear black lipstick. Use a toilet chain as a necklace. Stick a safety pin through your cheek. Make a dress or T-shirt using a black plastic bin bag. If you go to a punk concert spit on the bands, they won't be angry because THEY LOVE THIS.*' Garbage like that. I wasn't going to be a 'plastic punk'. There were no shops in Glasgow selling real punk styles. There were no radical shops like the King's Road up in Scotland. I sent off to a mail-order company address I found in the back of *Sounds* and bought two T-shirts, one with the Clash and one with the Stranglers' logo on. The Stranglers shirt had the rat from the back of their brilliant *Rattus Norvegicus VI* album cover on it. I wore them both proudly in the streets and to gigs and college.

My college was a five-minute walk from the Apollo. One lunch-time I walked over there and bought a ticket to see Dr Feelgood with New Yorkers Mink DeVille on 1 October 1977. Sadly, their amazing, charismatic guitarist Wilko Johnson had just left the Feelgoods and been replaced by Gypie Mayo. He was a shit-hot player too, but it wasn't quite right and I knew it. I absolutely loved *Stupidity* (basically the best tracks from the two Feelgoods albums stuck together on one live album), but without Wilko it wasn't the same.

Willy DeVille was one sharply dressed motherfucker, all Lee Van Cleef gunfighter slit eyes and razor-sharp cheekbones. He wore his hair in a high rockabilly quiff and had a pencil-thin body enclosed in a tightly fitted buttoned-up shirt with a beautifully tailored waistcoat. He walked on pointed, black leather Cuban-heeled boots and wore his guitar slung low, sometimes hanging behind his back. He screamed style and cool. He lived up to the title of his brilliant song 'Gunslinger', the B side of 'Spanish Stroll'. He'd recently been on the cover of *Sounds* with his girlfriend Toots. She looked like one of the Ronettes: a Latina honey with black-kohl beatnik eyes, a beehive and a snakeskin bomber jacket that clung tightly to her body like a second skin. They were a perfect rock and roll couple. Mink had brought the Immortals over with him, a vocal trio consisting of three middle-aged Black dudes, real soul men dressed in Shaft-style, knee-length, brown leather trenchcoats. They looked lethal. It was quite a show.

I saw an advert in *Sounds* for the Clash's Out of Control tour in support of their incendiary new single 'Complete Control' which I was totally obsessed with, including the B side 'City of the Dead'. The advert was a black and white photo of a boy with short hair dressed in a ripped jumper and tight black trousers, sitting on a gas canister behind a barricade. All around him is waste ground very much like the condemned areas of Springburn and the Gorbals, and the boy is looking at a tenement house that is ablaze, his back to the camera. I later found out that it was from a book by photographer Clive Limpkin titled *The Battle of Bogside*. I thought it was a contemporary photograph of a punk rocker from 1977 but it's actually a Catholic schoolboy in Derry in 1969.

The image transfixed me. I ripped it out of the paper and stuck it on my wall alongside our huge fold-out poster of the Sex Pistols from *New Wave* magazine. The Clash were big into scenes of urban conflict and political violence. I was too. I had loved watching the riots at football games and seeing the cops on horseback retreat after being showered by hails of beer cans and wine bottles from high up in the terraces. It was thrilling to see these small acts of rebellion actually happening in person. It was always political, because in the case of Celtic and Rangers there was the ever-present disease of sectarian tension.

There was something rebellious in the air through the seventies in Britain leading up to punk, from the endless trade union strikes to the ongoing war with the IRA. There was a feeling of anger and resistance coming from below, whether it was working-class Catholics in Northern Ireland fighting for civil rights, Arthur Scargill's militant Yorkshire miners demanding better wages and working conditions, alienated Jamaican youths in Notting Hill or disaffected, disenfranchised teenage boot-boys who stood every Saturday afternoon on the nation's football terraces, the lower classes in society were at last standing up for themselves and talking back. The old ways of deference to authority, doffing the cap to the bosses, police, aristocracy and even royalty were being questioned, and punk was the musical voice of this disaffection and rebellion. A lot of people were pissed off at the state of their lives and made their voices heard in the only way that poor people can: direct action, civil disobedience and violence. There was widespread poverty all over the country in working-class communities, unemployment was rising as deindustrialisation was beginning to kick in, with massive lay-offs at the docks, car factories and steel plants, coal mines, and the future was looking dark. We were all fucking angry. Any kid growing up on the streets of Glasgow, Manchester, Liverpool, Birmingham, Newcastle, Belfast, Dublin, Cardiff and London or in towns and cities across the nation felt the same. Football violence was an inarticulate expression of the long-held anger and frustration of working-class youth.

On the terraces we thought the enemy were those on the other side of the stadium wearing different team colours. I remember my dad saying to me that the Celtic and Rangers sectarian conflict played nicely into the hands of the establishment, the old 'divide and rule' tactic the British had perfected over centuries of imperial conquest, learned from the Ancient Romans. The war in Northern Ireland was the perfect example. He told me it divided the working class of Glasgow. The Old Firm fans were all from similar backgrounds, lived in the same council schemes, but were wasting their energy fighting each other when they should be fighting the real enemy, the ruling class.

At the Clash gig I was two rows from the front. I was so excited to see my heroes in the flesh – I'd never actually seen a real-life punk rocker in person – but I was also a wee bit apprehensive because I'd read that punk shows often ended in violence. The night of the 28th October I boarded a train alone from Mount Florida station, got off at Central and made my way into the city centre. I walked up West Nile Street and at the top I saw a bunch of kids standing in a long line snaking around the block. I stood in the dark and watched them from across the street. Then I saw that there was more action happening over on Renfield Street. The Pavilion Theatre stood directly across the street from the Apollo, and the bright lights from the show signs of both theatres lit up the scene.

And what a scene it was.

Teenage punk girls with Soo Catwoman haircuts in school blazers stuck with razor blades, toilet chains hanging around shoulders like military braiding. Punk lyrics and song titles scrawled all over their blazers in chalk. Tight black leather mini-skirts, ripped fishnet tights, suspenders and high-heeled pointed shoes. Bug-eyed ratfaced underfed boys with dyed red spiked hair à la Rotten, in tight black leather trousers and homemade Destroy shirts. I saw beautiful girls with big kilt-sized safety pins stuck through their cheeks, right into their black lipstick-smeared mouths. All the girls wore sharp lined beatnik black-kohl eye make-up. A lot of kids had customised their school uniforms with punk slogans like DESTROY, BOREDOM, WHITE RIOT, HATE AND WAR written in black felt-tipped pen, and wore them with loosened striped school ties. Some girls wore only a black plastic binbag mini-dress with their fishnets, others wore paint-splattered boiler suits with punk badges and more slogans. It was as if Hieronymus Bosch's *Garden of Earthly Delights* was peopled with inmates who had escaped from a seventies lunatic asylum.

I was intimidated by the power and confidence that these punk rockers all seemed to possess. The audacity needed to go out onto the streets of Glasgow in 1977 dressed as outlandishly as these kids was awe-inspiring. It was totally confrontational. I can see why the straights felt challenged by the punks.

In Glasgow it was all about how hard you were. Violent confrontation was a test of masculinity; the 'crazier' someone was the more respect they got on the street. Most people dressed in conventional seventies styles. The trick was to keep your head down and hide in plain sight; don't stick out or you're asking for trouble.

The punks, on the other hand, stood out from the crowd in their outrageous and deranged cut-up and torn-down fashions. Their difference stood in proud defiance of the norm. These brave kids reinventing themselves and creating new apocalyptic identities freaked out the neds and straights, and it was glorious. I'd never witnessed anything like it. At the Lizzy gig everyone had dressed more or less like me, I blended right in. Here, I stuck out like a Celtic fan in the Rangers end.

I was initially too scared to go in. I stood on the street wondering what to do before walking away, back down St Vincent Street, my head full of the insane scene outside the venue. 'What the fuck was that?' I thought to myself. I was both confused and exhilarated. But then, almost immediately, I turned back and headed for the doorway of the Apollo, gave my ticket to the bouncer and walked into the stalls and took my seat amongst thousands of punks and waited for The Clash.

The first band on were the Lous, an all-female French punk band. The singer had short hair and a capped-sleeve T-shirt over muscular arms. She looked tough. They were good. I didn't know any of their songs but they held their own up there in front of a hard-to-please Glasgow audience.

Next up was Richard Hell. I had read that Hell was a poet and when he walked on stage at the Apollo he was carrying a book. I remember thinking to myself, 'Wow, he really is one.' I didn't know what a poet was. The only poetry I remember studying at school was in history class, when we looked at the war poets like Rupert Brooke and Wilfred Owen, doomed upper-class romantics. There was something strange about this guy. He was a junkie, though I didn't know that at the time. But he walked onto that stage with an air of self-possession and confidence. He wasn't there to entertain us. It was as if he had stuff he felt was important to say and he was gonna say it whatever the cost. I was held by his spell. His band the Voidoids were amazing, with the unforgettable Robert Quine on guitar, his style like no other.

His solos were the true sound of broken glass: electric fragments of shattered notes and angular distortions. Quine reinvented rock guitar playing. He was a one-off. His fractured solos perfectly complimented Hell's damaged-junkie symbolist-poet persona. Hell's lyrics and Quine's guitar wrapped around each other like two poisonous snakes. The combination was lethal. The sound of the Voidoids messed with your head. They sounded deranged. You had to think differently when you listened to them; they were true upsetters. I was obsessed by 'Love Comes in Spurts'. Richard Hell was a poet of the times:

*I belong to the blank generation.*

He looked great too: the original spiky-haired, ripped clothes, about to be torn down, derelict, punk look that Malcolm McLaren brought back from NYC.

I don't actually remember much detail about the Clash performance. All I can recall is that it had nothing to do with music because it wasn't musical. At the Thin Lizzy and Dr Feelgood gigs (and later Status Quo) I recognised which songs they were playing. I didn't know what the Clash were playing. They hit the stage in a blaze of light that burned for the whole show. There was no let-up, just a total high-energy assault. It was that energy I remember the most. When I think of that night all I can see in my mind is white light. It was beyond music and it was beyond words and it was beyond the normal accepted rules of performance and entertainment. It was energy, pure energy, and it sucked me into its vortex.

At college the next day I tried telling people what I had witnessed the night before, but I didn't know how to express it. I was babbling like an idiot, speaking in tongues. Seeing Thin Lizzy live was one thing; a sexualised, hard, street-rock thing. Seeing the Clash live was something else. It gave me another feeling entirely, similar to a religious epiphany. I'm not religious but something in me changed that night. Maybe the Clash ignited something that was lying dormant inside me already.

There was a song on the Sire/Phonogram *New Wave* album that I played endlessly over the summer of '77. It wasn't a rock and roll song like the other tracks, it was a spoken-word piece, a story narrated by a girl over a jazzy piano track, with a little bit of guitar thrown in. She came into the ring fighting with a sneer:

*Sixteen and time to pay off*
*I got a job working in a piss factory.*

This song was describing my life. This girl had lived and had written about the same experience as I was going through. Right at that moment. I wasn't alone in questioning the existential meaning of work. But blind acceptance of work was a fact of working-class life. As James Brown sang, 'If you don't work, you can't eat.'

We existed only to work in the factories, docks, coal mines, supermarkets, shops and farms owned by wealthy landowners, big business and the state. We existed only to make obscene profits for the capitalist bosses with the sweat of our labour and seconds minutes hours days of our precious lives spent away from our families and loved ones, and to know our place in the order of things. These teachings were burned into the skulls and souls of the peasantry and working classes over generations of exploitation and hundreds of years of degrading feudalism followed by the horrors of the Industrial Revolution. Now I had come of working age at the beginnings of post-industrialism.

I didn't realise it at the time, but this was beat poetry set to music. 'Piss Factory' was a song of resistance. A hymn to dissent and disobedience. A song of freedom and class consciousness. I completely identified with the story narrated by the character in the song – because *her* story was *my* story. I too worked in a piss factory for forty hours a week. That girl was Patti Smith, and I truly thank her for her song of experience, her poetry of resistance. 'Piss Factory' taught me that in order to change reality you have to confront reality. It also taught me that artists could write about 'ordinary', everyday experiences and in doing so make a deep soulful connection with their listeners, and also that the identification of shared experience between artist and listener was where the true power of art resided.

# 6.

# Cultural Revolution

On a summer's day in 1977 I was walking down Cathcart Road in Mount Florida and saw this skinny kid with a shock of ginger hair on the opposite side of the road. He wore a tight black T-shirt emblazoned with the slogan 'Chinese Rocks' written in a white font like the WANTED posters I'd seen in cowboy movies. I remember thinking, what a cool T-shirt. I knew who the Heartbreakers were – I loved that single, and 'Born to Lose'.

One night I stepped on a train at Glasgow Central, on the way back home from one of the Apollo gigs, and the ginger kid was sitting in a carriage all on his own. It was Alan McGee. I sat down beside him and got talking to him and asked if he'd also been to the show. He said, 'You should come to my house. I've got a load of punk singles and other records you may like too.'

Later that week I turned up at his parents' (semi-detached two-up two-down) house unannounced. His mother answered the door and shouted through to the living room behind her, 'Alan, Bobby Gillespie's here to see you.' I waited on the front porch for a few minutes then McGee appeared and took me upstairs to his room. He took out a single by the band Eater called 'Outside View' and put it on his record deck. On the sleeve the band were pictured behind a window full of broken glass. McGee asked me what I thought of it. I said, 'It's alright, but I don't love it.' (I do now, though, and their song 'Thinking of the USA' as well, both UK punk classics.) McGee told me he liked the song because he had an 'outside view' as well.

This was an important moment for me. Although the lyrics of 'God Save the Queen', 'Piss Factory' and 'In the City' had all resonated with me, I hadn't yet placed myself outside of society. I never thought of stuff this way; as far as I was concerned I was just a rock and roll fan. I had a feeling that I didn't really fit into the conventional ways around me but my consciousness was still forming, whereas McGee had seen this record as both a source of cultural critique and a way of creating a new identity distinct from straight society.

Alan was in the year above me at school. He had been buying records since the early seventies, and before punk had been heavily into David Bowie, T. Rex, Roxy Music and Cockney Rebel. We had a lot of the same singles but he and Colin Dobbins had a few more, all in the coveted picture sleeves. Alan worked as a clerk in an office for British Rail. His dad was a panel beater and had got him an apprenticeship at his garage. This ended badly when some of the older men stripped him naked, covered his balls in Swarfega and tied him upside down to a machine as part of an initiation ceremony. Alan's dad had given them his blessing. It was a common thing in working-class workplaces back then. When I was in the last year of my apprenticeship, a guy in the year above me who had just qualified as a journeyman threatened to strip me and cover me in ink so all the workers in the factory could come and witness me tied up and humiliated. I told him that if he ever came near me I'd smash his head in with a hammer. There was no one around on night shift. I would wait and I would get him. He never did it.

My gig-going had increased through 1977 – I'd seen Thin Lizzy (twice), Graham Parker and the Rumour, Status Quo, the Jam, the Damned, Dead Boys, the Clash (again) and the year had ended with that amazing Christmas show: Ramones supported by the Rezillos.

It was the Rocket to Russia tour and the Apollo was sold out. Ramones came out and totally destroyed us with their New York

City rock and roll Blitzkrieg, the four of them looking evil in their black leather biker jackets and ripped jeans. They were everything I ever dreamed they would be and more. They played with military precision and there was hardly any space between the songs, no tuning up or talking to the audience, just Joey drawling, 'This one's called "Rockaway Beach"!' and Dee Dee counting in every single song barking like a regimental sergeant with a clipped '1-2-3-4!' Ramones were perfect in both sound and vision. Ramones were a total assault on the senses. Ramones were godhead.

After the show I managed to steal a huge Rocket to Russia gig poster off the wall in the foyer of the Apollo. It had the band photo from the front of the album cover screen-printed in black and RAMONES written boldly in shocking pink. It was beautiful. My younger brother Graham had begged me to take him with him that night, but I was too embarrassed because he was only thirteen. He's never forgiven me to this day. I totally understand why.

The next year, 1978, brought more gigs. I saw Siouxsie and the Banshees, Elvis Costello, Eddie and the Hot Rods, the Stranglers (with the Skids as support), Thin Lizzy, Boomtown Rats, Aswad, Steel Pulse, the Clash (with the Specials and Suicide as support), Tom Robinson Band (with Stiff Little Fingers as support), Buzzcocks (with Subway Sect as support), Sham 69, the Jam, Dickies, Devo, Rezillos again. I was heartbroken that I couldn't see my beloved Poly Styrene and X-ray Spex play because their show was booked at Glasgow University and only students or their guests could attend. I was underage (I looked about fifteen) and didn't have a passport or ID card. I resented this. The night of the X-ray Spex concert I stayed at home stewing in a rage, knowing that Poly was playing half an hour away to a bunch of fucking disinterested straight students. What the fuck did that have to do with punk rock?

The Clash were booked to play Strathclyde Uni on the Give 'Em Enough Rope tour and I was sickened knowing I wouldn't be able to go. I loved the Clash more than anything. After the Pistols had broken up the Clash were carrying the punk flag. The story goes that Joe Strummer was up in Glasgow doing a radio interview at Radio Clyde and had wandered into Bruce's record shop on Renfield Street where he was accosted by some punks. A kid drove Strummer up to Strathclyde Uni on the back of a motorbike. Joe went up to the desk and asked to buy a ticket to see the Clash. They asked for his matriculation card, and when he replied that he didn't have one, they told him he couldn't buy a ticket. He cancelled the show right there on the spot. I thought this was heroic and proper behaviour from Strummer. That's how you look after the fans.

I attended some of these gigs with Alan McGee but mostly went on my own. Sometime in the spring of 1978 Alan introduced me to his friend Andrew Innes. Andrew lived up in Clarkston with his parents in a nice semi-detached house with a garden, five minutes up the road from Toledo Cinema in Muirend. Alan and I would take a bus from Battlefield that would take us practically to Andrew's front door.

Andrew and Alan were forming a band together. Alan on bass, Andrew on guitar. Andrew had a big amplifier and a Les Paul copy and he could play songs by the Clash, the Pistols, the Jam, Generation X, Ramones. You name it, Andrew could play it. To my mind, he played those songs as well as the guitarists in the actual bands. His older cousin had taken him to see the Jam play Zhivago's in St Enoch Square in May 1977 when he was fourteen, on the In the City tour. He could play the whole album brilliantly. He had a big Beatles songbook and a Beatles poster on the wall, and in amongst his punk albums lay the *White Album*. He could play *all* of the famous sixties songs by the Who. I thought this fifteen-year-old kid had amazing talent. I'd only ever heard guitarists on records or seen them on stage so it was a complete mystery to me how they achieved their sound and style of playing. A truly occult feat. But Andrew could do it aged fifteen. He had the chops and the confidence and could pick up the chords of a song just like that; he had an ear. It was mind-blowing.

Andrew had been in a punk band at school called the Drains and they had somehow obtained the telephone number for the Glitterbest office, Malcolm McLaren's management company, and called up asking him to manage them. Andrew was a pupil at Glasgow High School, which alongside Hutchesons' Grammar was one of the two elite private schools in Glasgow. Andrew got in on a bursary because he was a clever kid. He eventually graduated and went to university in London to study chemistry (the irony). His guitar heroes were Wilko Johnson, Steve Jones, Paul Weller, Pete Townsend, Mick Jones and the guys in Lynyrd Skynyrd. Andrew mostly dressed in straight-legged jeans and a T-shirt with a SPAM logo on it. One night on the way home after a few months of going up to Andrew's house regularly, McGee turned to me and said, 'You know Innes's dad owns the SPAM factory? That's why he always wears that T-shirt.' His house was quite big, bigger than ours at least, so I believed him. Gullible me.

McGee and I would go to Andrew's house every weekend and those two would get drunk on cans of lager and play our favourite punk songs with both Andrew's guitar and McGee's bass plugged into the big amp. I couldn't play an instrument so I started singing. We murdered great songs: all of *Bollocks* by the Pistols, 'White Riot', 'Janie Jones', 'I'm So Bored with the USA', 'Hate and War', 'Complete Control', 'Garageland', and the whole of the first Clash album. We played 'In the City', 'All Around the World', 'Away from the Numbers', '"A" Bomb in Wardour Street', 'David Watts', 'Tube Station', 'Mr Clean' by the Jam. 'What Do I Get', 'Love You More', 'Orgasm Addict', 'Fast Cars', 'I Don't Mind' by Buzzcocks, 'Ready Steady Go' and 'King Rocker' by Generation X, 'Rich Kids' and 'Ghosts of Princes in Towers' by

Rich Kids, 'Another Girl, Another Planet' by the Only Ones and 'Borstal Breakout' by Sham 69.

McGee says I would roll around on the floor screaming like Iggy Pop, but it was probably more like Jimmy Pursey. I'd say I was more of a Johnny Rotten disciple myself, having never seen footage of Iggy, the master, at this point (although soon I would see him play on the New Values tour in 1979 with real-life Sex Pistol Glen Matlock on bass). It was great fun. Andrew was a fellow punk and as obsessed with the culture as either McGee or myself. He also had *Spunk* and *Indecent Exposure* bootlegs by Sex Pistols. How fucking cool. *Spunk* was the Dave Goodman / Chris Spedding demo rumoured to have been released by Malcolm McLaren at the exact same time as *Never Mind the Bollocks* to say 'fuck you' to hippie capitalist Virgin Records' boss Richard Branson. *Spunk* was an amazing album. Andrew loaned me that and *Indecent Exposure* which was a recording of the Pistols playing at the 76 Club in Burton on Trent in 1976 with Glen Matlock on bass and they sound so fucking good. At the very end of the set you hear Rotten saying to the meagre audience, 'If you want more, you can *arrrsk*.' Holding these two records in my hands felt subversive and thrilling. I took them home and taped them. I also sent off to an advert in the back of *Sounds* or *NME* for a bootleg tape called *Anarchy in Sweden*, of the Pistols Swedish tour. The mixture of illegality and mystery added a frisson of danger to owning such underground documents. I felt part of a secret society of punk initiates.

In July 1978 McGee and I bought tickets to see the Clash at the Apollo on the 'Sort it Out' tour. 'White Man (in Hammersmith Palais)' / 'The Prisoner' had just been released and we were both dying to see them play again. The venue was to close later that summer and this was to be the last performance by a punk-rock band there. The rumour around town was that the infamously tough Apollo bouncers were going to take this last opportunity to lay some serious harm on the punk rockers.

I was still playing football for the Holyrood Youth Club team. It was mainly boys from the Prospect Hill Circus housing estate, two tower blocks built on a large expanse of waste ground between the districts of Rutherglen, Polmadie and Govanhill. These boys were the younger brothers of the feared local gang, 'The Circus'. Some of them were members of the 'Young Circus'. They could all play and were ready to fight anyone at any time. They had no fear, even when we went up to play matches in Castlemilk which was teeming with crazy gangs.

Paul Kerr, younger brother of Simple Minds' Jim Kerr, was our captain. He was hard as fuck and an extremely skilful footballer too, some player. I'd damaged my cartilage during a game so I went up to the show with a tight bandage wrapped around my knee, walking with a limp. Nothing was going to stop me from seeing the Clash.

First on were the Specials. This was a year before they dressed in sixties Mod two-tone suits and I don't recall their appearance or sound except that there were about seven people on stage, which in those days of four-man punk bands was quite unusual. Terry Hall sat on the edge of the stage singing and I'd never seen anyone do that before.

Then two weird guys appeared on stage, a singer and a keyboard player. There was no drummer, no guitarist *or* bassist. Apart from the Stranglers and Tom Robinson Band, Elvis Costello's Attractions and Tom Petty's Heartbreakers no UK punk or New Wave bands had keyboards, only guitars. Then the sound started up. What the fuck was this? It was a wall of noise. There were no 'songs' to speak of, and where were the drums coming from? The guy behind the keyboard wore huge X-Men-style sunglasses that crossed in the middle, making a huge white plastic X sign in the middle of his face. He had an afro as well, even though he was a white guy. He stood there frozen with his legs apart churning out unearthly sounds for the whole gig. The singer was insane. The Apollo crowd were baying for blood. Only the arrival of the

Clash up on that stage would be able to sate their junkie-like animal lust for punk-rock nirvana.

I didn't know what to make of Suicide. I loved their name. Ultimate punk statement right there. But neither McGee nor myself had ever heard their music before so the songs were all unrecognisable. We were not yet ready for this. The Apollo audience began ripping up the armrests and throwing these and other missiles at Alan Vega. He swears that an axe went whizzing past his head that night. He told me that story himself years later when we met. The punks went fucking mental. They didn't know how to deal with being confronted by these two out-there guys.

Of course when we listened to the records later on we understood what they were playing was totally based on rock and roll chord progressions (except it was a Farfisa organ and a cheap drum machine). At one point Alan Vega smashed himself in the mouth with his microphone and, bleeding, made an attempt at brokering peace with the hateful crowd of four thousand punks, saying, 'Hey man! You and me we're on the same side!' I'll never forget that moment, because although I too was waiting to see the main event of the night, Alan Vega and Martin Rev with their minimalist music had both confronted and challenged the audience's perception of what a rock and roll show could be, and by standing their ground they won my respect. Vega's impassioned but tender speech broke down the fourth wall between audience and performer. At that moment my heart went out to him. Although I could see he was even older than the Clash, I realised he was one of us. It was a movement. This reception lay waiting for them night after night on the Clash tour in every town in Great Britain. Later on I would discover that, consciously or not, Suicide were acting out Antonin Artaud's Theatre of Cruelty strategy in their no-compromise, freeform, sometimes violent performances. It took real bravery both physically and musically to improvise each night without a safety net. These guys were real artists.

The Clash had brought along their own tour DJ Barry 'Scratchy'

Myers to warm up the crowd each night before they came onstage. He played all the current punk hits plus older classics and all the kids were singing every word as if at a football match. Then he played 'Bodies' by the Sex Pistols and the mood changed. The Apollo crowd sang each and every word of this diseased tale of a punk girl from Birmingham carrying her abortion around in a plastic bag and when it reached the *FUCK THIS AND FUCK THAT FUCKING ALL THE FUCKING FUCKING BRATS* bit in the song it felt evil. There was a threat of violence in the air. Something that I was used to at football matches but not gigs.

Suddenly, without warning, the Clash hit the stage. Mick Jones ran on dressed in white under a red waistcoat and with shoulder-length hair. He ran up to his amplifier, plugged in and smashed straight into the pulverising opening riff of 'Complete Control'. There was a surge of kids running down the aisles from the back of the hall towards the front. They were immediately beaten back by the Apollo bouncers. I witnessed an eighteen-stone bouncer dragging a screaming girl of my age by her long blonde hair back up the aisle towards the darkness at the back of the stalls. Just a portent of things to come.

Me and McGee really wanted to get down to the front of the stage and be close to our heroes but two things stopped us: the ultra-violent bouncers and my injured knee. I tried to dance in a kind of one-legged 'pogo' movement and even managed to stand up on my seat to get a better view of the show. This time I recognised all the Clash songs and Joe Strummer looked amazing in his GET TO FUCK T-shirt. Paul Simonon wore tight white jeans, high-topped Doc boots and a black leather biker's jacket with no shirt underneath. He also had a black leather wristband with silver leather studs and a short blond spiked crop which showed off his movie-star high-cheekboned good looks. Such a great look. I can't remember what Topper was wearing, he was stuck behind the drums.

They looked and played like rock and roll stars. Me and McGee were in heaven. Joe Strummer kept stopping the gig to intervene in the battle between the teenage punks and the middle-aged bouncers. Their behaviour was appalling. Kids were being taken to the EXIT doors each side of the stage and battered by these bastards. Some were being dragged up to the back stalls and getting a 'doing'. You can see some of this in the film *Rude Boy*: Joe pleading with the bouncers to 'Control your temper', Mick screaming, 'They're dancing not fighting', but it was all in vain. The Apollo bouncers had planned to teach the punks a lesson they would never forget. I still believe to this day it was the way the punks looked that angered them. They couldn't handle anyone who looked different or unconventional. These guys were so fucking straight. They were frightened by the strangeness of the punk kids because it challenged their very limited perceptions of reality and propriety. Punk kids in Glasgow were not violent at that point. We were the outsiders who, by immersing ourselves in punk, were escaping the violence of the street neds and repressed West of Scotland working-class culture. I mostly remember the violence of the bouncers at that gig. They acted with impunity. These guys were sadistic bastards. Pricks.

I'd have liked to see them try and behave this way with my dad and his trade union friends. When the National Front attempted an intervention in Glasgow in the late seventies my dad and his mates went down to the school in Govanhill where the Front had planned a meeting. There was a huge anti-fascist presence massed outside the school. These were the days of the Anti-Nazi League and Glasgow had a proud tradition of anti-fascist action. In the thirties a gang of Oswald Mosley's Blackshirts arrived from London on a train to find hundreds of trade unionists waiting for them on the platform; their comrades from the NUR down in London had informed the Glaswegian cadres that a trainload of Fascists was heading north. The BUF never managed to set foot in Glasgow, they were too scared to disembark the train. Dad and friends also gave the National Front something they'd never forget from their visit to Glasgow and the Front never returned to our city ever again.

After the show finished and the crowd had dispersed McGee and I made our way up towards the back where we saw a boy my age being passed around a circle of about five bouncers in the now-empty Apollo. One of the men began laying into the kid as the others all stood there gloating and laughing and egging him on. It was a sick scene. We escaped through a door that opened onto the alley that ran down the side of the Apollo where we saw a crowd of punks standing outside the stage door. As we got closer we heard shouting and the sound of broken glass. Next thing we saw was Joe Strummer being carted by three plainclothes cops out into the middle of the road. The punks were all shouting at Strummer and the cops handcuffed him and threw him into a police car. Paul Simonon appeared out of the dark alley and made an attempt to help Joe, and was cuffed and thrown into the cop car too.

We stood there on the pavement, a voice behind us almost crying, 'Joe, Paul, oh no!' McGee and I both turned around and Mick Jones was standing right there in front of us almost in tears. What a moment, what a scene. Apparently some punks had felt the Clash hadn't done enough to stop the violence so were venting their anger on them. It looked to us like Joe and Mick had tried their best to diffuse an explosive situation. If they'd walked off stage halfway through the show the violence would not have been contained to just the kids down front. The whole theatre would have been a bloodbath. Some punks whisked Mick back to his hotel as Alan and I boarded the bus home. We couldn't stop talking about what we had just both witnessed. It was an incredible night.

There was something much more than just music happening at these shows. We were being changed. We were slowly learning to question not only straight society and the government but also ourselves. I went home and told my mum I'd seen the Clash get arrested. She was outraged and immediately made a phone call to the main police station in the town centre and demanded that they 'FREE THE CLASH, NOW!'

Throughout 1978 I listened to the John Peel Show each night on Radio One, Monday to Thursday. This was the only place you could hear the new singles and album releases that were being reviewed each week in the music papers. Bands like the Jam and the Stranglers were now regularly appearing in the Top 40 and could be heard on daytime radio but there was a new underground emerging on independent record labels.

I started buying *Zigzag* magazine, which (I didn't realise at the time) had been a cool publication covering a lot of the underground music of the sixties that I would later get into such as Love, the Byrds, Doors, Buffalo Springfield, Tim Hardin, and Tim Buckley. I bought *Zigzag* because it had an amazing photograph of Johnny Thunders on the front cover looking like a rock and roll pirate. Inside was a great interview with Thunders by Kris Needs, to promote his solo album *So Alone*. He spoke about Buddy Holly and how what he played was rock and roll, not punk. There was also an interview with the Subway Sect, one of the original London bands inspired by the Pistols who played the legendary Punk Special festival at the 100 Club. They had a single out on Braik Records, a label started by Clash Svengali Bernard Rhodes solely to release music by the Sect. The single 'Nobody's Scared' b/w 'Don't Split It' was an instant classic. I loved 'Nobody's Scared' so much that Primal Scream covered it at our very first gig on 12th October 1984 at the Venue, Sauchiehall Street, Glasgow. That night Jim Reid from the Jesus and Mary Chain would watch us soundcheck and then excitedly come up to me after we'd finished playing to say he loved our version and that we were 'The best band in the world'.

That was a long way off in the future yet.

John Peel's show often hosted unrecorded bands that didn't have recording contracts. You would hear professionally recorded live studio sessions by artists like Siouxsie and the Banshees, Joy Division, Psychedelic Furs, the Slits and Subway Sect. These Peel Sessions for the most part consisted of four songs and were very important to both the development of the artists and the cultural education of young music fans like myself. The artists could experiment and take chances with a Peel Session and they were also a great way of hearing these new exciting and challenging artists develop their sound and art in real time. Peel had been doing this since his pirate Radio London show *The Perfumed Garden* in the sixties. In fact previous to this the BBC had been recording the Beatles, Kinks, Yardbirds, the Who and the Rolling Stones in the early years of that decade. This is one of the great benefits a state broadcaster brings to the cultural life of the nation.

Peel's show turned me onto newer, more experimental sounds that some people would later label 'post-punk'. The weekly UK music press was also a vital source of news and influence. Towards the end of 1978 Siouxsie and the Banshees released their debut album *The Scream*. I'd fallen in love with the Banshees and became addicted to their summer hit 'Hong Kong Garden'. They had a sound unlike any other band and an image to die for. Siouxsie was like a female Rotten. Her dress sense was impeccable. She screamed style beyond. Everything she wore was perfect. *The Scream* was dark and oppressive. It was unforgiving. Like the sound of a cult. Siouxsie sang of suburban housewives disintegrating into nervous breakdowns, of her own 'jigsaw feelings' and the insidious fascism of militarism. She sang of being a carcass 'limblessly in love', and of a person so submerged in themselves they find it painful even to have to surface occasionally 'overground to normality'. These were songs of confusion and depression, of existential pain, and a realisation that life is difficult, not normal pop song material. *The Scream* was the first record through which I experienced these themes, where the band's music mirrored the lyrics perfectly. Kenny Morris's drumming was a mix of Glitter Band and Klaus Dinger motorik-style NEU! beats locked into a deep tribal groove with Steve Severin's primitive-modernist bass action. This rhythm section created a solid bed of powerful, reductive, paranoid horror movie soundtrack film noir atmosphere for guitarist John McKay to slice through with quicksilver notes of beautiful sonic violence. His riffs were the aural equivalent of the Anthony Perkins and Janet Leigh knife-murder shower scene in *Psycho* or the screeching sound of predatory birds in Alfred Hitchcock's *The Birds*.

Siouxsie's voice was like an echo from hell. She *was* the banshee. I loved her voice – it went deep into my soul and has stayed there ever since. It disturbed me with its ice-queen malevolence. Siouxsie has one of pop's great voices, once heard, never forgotten. There was a frozen coldness to the Banshees that was unlike any other artist, except maybe Nico, who used harmonium and drones and no real rhythms to speak of except ancient, medieval churnings deep from within her soul that only she could hear and feel. You can't dance to Nico (well, you can if you want, you just need real imagination) but you could certainly dance to the Banshees. They and Public Image Ltd were a new kind of rock.

In October 1978 Johnny Rotten returned with a new band and a single titled 'Public Image'. Rotten had changed his name back to his family name of Lydon, due to an ongoing court case with Malcolm McLaren over the rights to the Sex Pistols music: I believe ownership of the name 'Johnny Rotten' was up for discussion too. I heard it first on Peel. Nothing had prepared me for this monster of a record. How do you leave a successful chart-topping rock and roll band that changed culture and defined and inspired a whole generation?

The first rumbling of this new vision is the sound of Jah Wobble's heavy-duty dub reggae bass line which is then lifted upwards into forward motion on deeply echoed propulsive beats, as Jim Walker's Phil Spector-ish drums kick in hard; the ante is upped even further by the screaming, nerve-jangling arpeggiated

Byrds-on-biker-speed-laced-with-junk speedball genius guitar of Keith Levene. The Banshees' John McKay and PiL's Keith Levene reinvented rock guitar playing. After those two guys, people had to rethink how to play guitar. This was the future right here. The stage was set, and then on came Rotten, né Lydon, with a brand-new voice: higher in range and register and even more twisted and pained than his Pistols one, declaiming

*You never listened to a word that I said*
*You only seen me*
*For the clothes that I wear*

WHAT THE FUCK!!! No one expected *this*. This was a revelatory record. Johnny had come back, but even weirder and stronger.

The majority of people had been hoping he'd form another band like the Pistols. Disgruntled Pistols 'fans' would write into the music papers slagging him and PiL off. Fucking sheep. This was nothing like the Pistols. We'd never heard *anything* like this before. Who was Lydon declaiming in this accusatory, angry song? Malcolm McLaren? The Sex Pistols' audience? Society in general? I read it as: *Don't ever pigeonhole me, ever. I cannot be put in a box. What you the audience demand I will not give you. PiL are not here to entertain you. We are here to confront and lay bare our souls. If you don't like it, fuck you.*

It was art rock but malign and tortured. Lydon really was a guy in a lot of existential pain. I identified with him because he was working class but also because I saw him as a poet. I knew I could learn from him. He was my guiding star. Over the years to come myself, Jim Beattie and Andrew Innes would draw strength and inspiration from the stylistic changes made by artists like John Lydon and PiL. Their creative bravery and confrontational attitude gave us a blueprint for the band we wanted to be.

# 7.
# Altered Images, Altered States

Towards the end of the seventies is when I really started to develop some kind of personal style. I remember buying these cool black army trousers in 1978 and getting my mum to sew zips into the leg pockets so I could be like the Clash. I loved their military-chic look. A revolutionary rock style. They didn't have any clothes shops in Glasgow where you could buy stuff like that so you had to do an approximation of the look yourself. That was the idea anyway: DIY. I bought a black leather biker jacket from a woman's clothes shop on Renfield Street and sent off to a company called Dangerous Gear that I found in *NME* selling Clash T-shirts screen-printed with images of the Notting Hill riots, exactly like the one Joe Strummer and Paul Simonon wore back in '77. I made a stencil using a military typeface and wrote English Civil War and Safe European Home on the shirt. I also loved the pop-art, Constructivist-inspired T-shirts that bassist and songwriter Tony James had made for Generation X. My version was inspired by the cover of their 'Ready Steady Go' single. I found a tight yellow T-shirt, ripped the sleeves off and drew a black and red El Lissitzky-style Constructivist design on it. I loved that one. I had no idea who the Constructivists were, but I really dug these designs on punk and post-punk record sleeves that had been inspired by them. I would learn in due course.

Thanks to John Lydon and PiL we were all suddenly searching for old men's suit jackets from Paddy's Market. Paddy's Market was located in a lane that ran beside a row of dilapidated railway arches near the Gallowgate. It had piles of clothes stacked high on the ground outside the arches like something you'd see in photographs of a refugee convoy. They also sold bric-a-brac, mostly junk that even a jumble sale would think twice about displaying. Inside the arches there was a smell of damp and whenever you bought an item of clothing from Paddy's the smell remained no matter how many times you washed it.

I knew a boy called Rab H. who lived a five-minute walk away, just up past Alexandra Parade on the way to Provand's Lordship. Rab was able to get up early and down to Paddy's before everyone else and he always got the best stuff. He wore amazing original sixties pointed black leather winklepickers and chisel-toed shoes with sharp grey pleated pegs. His jackets were always cut short at the back. He liked a box jacket in the Italian bum-freezer style. He wore his black, greasy curly hair, like Gene Vincent's, in a quiff which really suited him. He also shared Gene's emaciated, underfed look and had a debilitating glue-sniffing habit. He lived for punk rock and was obsessed with psychopathic serial killers like Charles Manson or the warped personalities of the leading Nazis. He could be seen around town in a black leather box jacket and beret in homage to the Black Panthers. One night after a gig we walked through town together. He assured me that he didn't agree with the Nazis' racist philosophy, but that he admired their insane psychopathology. He was a gentle, sweet, mixed-up boy who lived with his grandmother.

Most Fridays I would get my pay packet from John Horn's, get on the train from Pollokshaws West and go into Glasgow Central to the record stores. Going home after record shopping on Saturday afternoons I would take the 31 bus home from St Enoch Square. I was regularly seeing these slightly younger guys who would always stare back at me, and I would look at them, because I liked the way they dressed and they must have liked the way I looked, too. Eventually we started speaking when we discovered we had similar tastes in new music. I got to know them a little bit from the bus stop and we'd chat on the way home. They told me they had a band. One day they asked me if I'd like to watch them rehearse.

They practised in a room at their school, Holyrood. I had always seen the same three guys together, Johnny, Tich and Tinny, but there was an older guy with them who they introduced to me as Caesar (real name Gerard McInulty). I liked the sound of the band immediately, they were obviously influenced by Siouxsie and the Banshees. I saw them rehearse a couple of times and then the bassist Johnny McElhone invited me up to his house. Johnny lived with his parents in a lovely bungalow in a village on the outskirts of Glasgow called Carmunnock. His dad was Frank McElhone, Labour MP for the Gorbals, one of the poorest and heaviest districts of Glasgow. The drummer, Tich Anderson, was really friendly. He lived up in the loft at his parents' house on Castlemilk Road. Tich had a great record collection. Caesar, the guitarist, lived in the street directly behind Tich, and Tinny McDaid, the other guitarist, lived in Allison Street, Govanhill.

We would hang out at Johnny's house and listen to the latest releases. I remember him always playing the twelve-inch single of 'You Can't Put Your Arms Around a Memory' by Johnny Thunders on pink vinyl. I was introduced to Johnny's older brother Gerry. Gerry was a handsome, charismatic guy who was attending Glasgow University. He dressed sharp in roomy sixties suits, De Niro *Mean Streets*-style Gabicci sweaters and PiL shoes from Robot on the King's Road. He cut an imposing figure. He had presence.

Gerry had an idea to try out a girl he knew to be the singer of the band, the little sister of his girlfriend, Kathleen Grogan. They auditioned her at the Holyrood practice room and everyone agreed she was good. She had an elfin-like presence, an ingénue quality, and she dressed in an interesting thrift-shop post-punk androgynous style all of her own. That girl was Clare Grogan and the band was called Altered Images. They got the name from the back of the Buzzcocks' record 'Promises / Lipstick', designed by the great Malcolm Garrett. He would put these messages on the back of the record sleeves he designed, slogans like 'assorted images' and 'altered images'. Every Buzzcocks single had a different one. I immediately got the reference and thought Altered Images was cool and modern-sounding. I watched them rehearse at Holyrood with Clare a few more times and then they started working on their songs in a church hall up in Carmunnock near Johnny's house. I would go watch them practise, normally on a midweek evening, and help drag the drums and amplifiers which were stored at Johnny and Gerry's house down the lane to the church hall.

This is where I learned how to set up and 'play' a drum kit. I would play Tich's drum riffs or 'Metal Postcard' by the Banshees: pretty simple tribal beats all done on the tom-toms and snare drum. When they had worked up enough songs they considered good enough to play in public they recorded a rough demo tape for £25 in a primary school in Govanhill, choosing the four best ones. Then they gave the tape to some of the local small venues in the centre of town. Their very first gig was at a pub called the Mars Bar, just off St Enoch Square. It was dark and hip. Local bands played there, such as The Cuban Heels and Simple Minds when they were known as Johnny and the Self Abusers. They then got a gig at a place called the Doune Castle. I designed the poster for this gig, and created a stencil in the same army typeface as I had used on my customised Clash T-shirt to spray-paint ALTERED IMAGES onto the band's guitar cases and amplifiers.

I started hanging about with these guys more and more, because McGee had got himself a girlfriend and Andrew was studying hard for university, and they had decided to start a serious band together.

The Altered Images kids were, like me, insatiable music fans. Gerry would always drive me back if I missed the last bus to Mount Florida. I remember the first time I heard 'What Goes On' by the Velvets was in his car. He had a cassette tape of it from the *Live '69* album and it was absolutely amazing. We would listen to that album all the time. I remember Gerry asking me on a drive, 'What goes on in your mind, Bobby? Are you up or are you down?'

The first time I heard *African Dub All-Mighty – Chapter 3* was in his car. He used to play those two albums, the Velvets *Live '69* and Joe Gibbs and the Professionals' *African Dub All-Mighty – Chapter 3* and I immediately loved them. *Best Dressed Chicken in Town* and the 'Born for a Purpose' twelve-inch single by Dr Alimantado were also big favourites up at the McElhone house. I loved the extended dub versions of Jamaican reggae songs. They blew my mind. This was real psychedelic music; you don't need to be bombed on LSD to have your consciousness warped by Errol T's mixes for Joe Gibbs, you just need an open mind. And our third eyes were wide open and receptive to these new sounds and innovations from the Jamaican dub masters.

Whenever the Clash and the Jam played now, I wouldn't buy a ticket; it had all become just too big for me, too normal. I wanted the thrill of seeing a band play in a smaller venue, and releasing their music on an independent record label. I was getting into the occult aspect of rock and roll, I guess. Some would say I was becoming a snob, but I say no way. I was just following the clues, looking for the new vital energy. Things were being done and said on records by artists such as the Slits, Au Pairs, Raincoats, Girls at Our Best!, the Pop Group and Modettes that were out of the commercial reach of major record labels, and I found this seductive. It was a new frontier of consciousness. First-wave punk bands had been mostly a male-dominated endeavour; the girls involved sometimes played bass but didn't lead the band or write the songs. But now female artists like Siouxsie Sioux, Poly

Styrene, Ari Up, Leslie Woods and Chrissie Hynde were telling us stories from a woman's perspective.

A new band I fell in love with were the Bunnymen. I saw them at Futurama in 1980 where I was roadie for Altered Images. Ian McCulloch kept saying after every song, 'A touch of class, a touch of class.' Every song. Fuck, that guy! Talk about great frontmen, he had it all: the looks, the hair, the voice. And they just basically played all of *Crocodiles*. The Bunnymen had a mystique. There was a detachment and an arrogant aloofness, but the music was so strong that it was all justified. They titled their second album *Heaven Up Here* because they believed they were the highest and the best, and who really could dispute that at that time?

There was this whole Zoo Records / Factory Records thing happening. You couldn't ignore it if your ears and eyes were open. I remember buying Joy Division's *Unknown Pleasures* for £2.99 in the secondhand section of Listen. Ten Commandments fanzine editor and future Bluebell, Robert Hodges kindly loaned me the money (which I paid back). I used to go to this place called the Art School on a Friday night on my own and they'd put on bands like the Poison Girls who were part of the Crass community who emerged from the anarchist commune scene. Their singer was called Vi Subversa, she was older than my mum. I didn't have her records, but I thought it was interesting. The Art School was a cool place to spend Friday nights.

I went there one night after I'd seen Joy Division open for Buzzcocks at the Apollo. I had broken into the venue by kicking in a side door in the alley. I took a seat in the empty balcony and watched Ian Curtis do his St Vitus dance of death on a huge empty stage to an even emptier hall. Another venue that opened around then was Glasgow Technical College beside Buchanan Street bus station. I saw the Cramps and the Fall play there on a double bill, which was unforgettable. Both bands were on fire. We saw Simple Minds promoting their second album, *Real to Real Cacophony*. It was pure art rock.

These smaller gigs were way more intimate and more inter-esting than the big gigs. It was where the new energy was. You could watch local acts like Positive Noise and the Berlin Blondes play too. The thing was, even if we didn't think the local bands were up to much, we had to admire the fact that they'd somehow got themselves together, written songs, formed a band and had the courage to present themselves up on a stage in public, risking derision, ridicule and humiliation from their peers. We all wanted to be the first into a new band or artist and catch them before they got really famous.

One night Gerry drove a few of us through to Edinburgh to see the Specials play at Tiffany's nightclub. This was just as their first single 'Gangsters' was released. We were all obsessed by it and we also loved their sixties Mod mohair tonic suits and button-down shirts. They looked sharp and hard as fuck. We arrived in Edinburgh early as we didn't have tickets and were taking no chances. We were dying to see the show and as we walked towards the venue we saw a gang of guys walking downthe street towards us. As they got closer we realised this was the Specials.

We approached Jerry Dammers and told him we had driven over from Glasgow to see the show. They were going to an Indian restaurant to have a meal; Jerry asked if we were hungry and invited us all along. Of course, we accepted his kind invitation. I had already eaten at home but had a Coca-Cola. As far as I can remember this was the first time I'd ever been in a restaurant. Jerry was so nice to us kids. He asked us questions about where we came from, what music we liked, stuff like that. When he was finished eating his curry he invited us to walk back to the venue with him. As we approached the door of Tiffany's the bouncer asked us all, 'Where's your tickets?' and Jerry said, 'It's alright, they're with me,' and we walked straight past the bouncer. We followed him into the dressing room where we found all the

Specials hanging before the show. I felt incredible. I just tried to keep my cool.

I'd seen a lot of shows over the last two and a half years of gig-going but here I was backstage as a guest of the visionary leader of the hottest band in the country, and said leader was not only a great songwriter and musician but also a decent human being who invited his fans for meals and asked them about *their* lives. This, I thought to myself, was *true punk rock*.

The gig was brilliant. The Specials were riding the crest of a wave. They would become figureheads of the 2 Tone label scene, a teenage craze out of which multi-racial bands like the Selector and the Beat would emerge and change the face of UK music. The Specials delivered on every single level. They had it down one hundred per cent perfect, both musically and visually, *and* they respected their fans.

We drove back to Glasgow that night buzzing with excitement. We couldn't stop talking about the gig and Jerry Dammers. I have carried the energy of that night with me forever and I hope that I have been as open and friendly with our fans as Jerry Dammers was to us Glasgow teenagers.

Caesar's songs were good. He had an instinct for how to construct a perfect post-punk pop song in the style of Pete Shelley. The other songs were written democratically. They would just jam them and then Clare would sing some words written down in her lyric book. I would go to the gigs and help them load and unload the gear because it was exciting to be involved. All the Altered Images drumbeats were like tribal drumbeats, not straight rock, and I could play them all.

The original line-up of Altered Images was really good. They really had something. They sent their demo tape down to Siouxsie and the Banshees' office in London and received a phone call: 'We've listened to your tape, we really like it, would you like to come and tour with the Banshees?' This was when 'Happy House' and 'Christine' were hits. The Banshees were a godhead band to all of us. We worshipped them. The songs, the image, the style; the lot. So you can imagine how we felt about this news. We felt like the chosen ones. I took a week off from my print-factory job to I could go on tour with the Banshees as Altered Images' roadie, to help set up and take down the band's gear each night. That tour changed my life.

We set off down the motorway out of Glasgow. I had a warm feeling as we crossed the border over into England. Gerry was driving and we listened to compilation tapes we had made of our current fave post-punk songs. We could feel the excitement and expectation building.

The first gig of the tour was at Sheffield Top Rank. When we entered the dark, empty venue through the stage door we heard the apocalyptic dread sound of funky polyrhythmic tribal drumming. We were met by the sight of Budgie, the Banshees' new drummer, laying down the martial drum law with feral confidence and a look of real pleasure on his face. Budgie was good and he knew it.

As we unloaded the gear from the Images van, Budgie stopped playing and we were invited to set up on stage so Altered Images could do their soundcheck. The venue looked massive from the stage, but when the audience came in later that evening it would feel just that little bit smaller. We set the band's equipment up directly in front of the Banshees kit. I remember looking at a big guitar tuner on top of Banshees guitarist John McGeoch's amplifier. It looked like something from outer space.

I made new friends that night. There was a guy dressed in an army officer's peaked cap with tight jeans and a capped-sleeve T-shirt, and another handsome guy, both roadies for Siouxsie. These guys were Jos Grain and Murray Mitchell, both of whom I call friends and who sometimes work for Primal Scream to this day.

The venue was packed by the time Altered Images came onstage. We knew that Siouxsie and the Banshees were in the dressing room directly across the hall. This was such an exciting feeling, to be *that* close to our heroes, but we were all playing it cool. A huge majority of the girls in the audience were Siouxsie clones, but with not even one per cent of Siouxsie's innate, immaculate sense of style or sartorial taste. Can't fault them for trying though. Siouxsie, Chrissie Hynde and Debbie Harry represented a new kind of woman. Not subservient in any way. A woman in control. A woman as artist. A woman in charge of her own destiny. Siouxsie was a formidable and indomitable character and her personality was a force of nature. She was a warrior queen. Her example inspired and empowered legions of young women to stand up for themselves and not take shit. These artists dressed up for themselves, not to impress men, as girls of their generation had been conditioned to through years of male oppression. There was no one more stylish than Siouxsie, apart from John Lydon. I loved them both.

I entered another world that night, crossed over to the other side. Although I wasn't a performer at this stage, being on the Banshees tour gave me a taste for it. We all watched Siouxsie and her boys from the side of the stage. To see a band as great as this in their prime work at such close range was an unforgettable experience. Siouxsie was at the height of her powers as a performer. She had something to prove; she'd lost half of her band the year before, when guitarist John McKay and drummer Kenny Morris had disappeared in Aberdeen on the eve of their Join Hands tour. Siouxsie and bassist Steve Severin had written and recorded a new album with Budgie from the Slits on drums and guest guitarists like Magazine's John McGeoch and Steve Jones from the Sex Pistols, and had come storming back with a new sound and two fantastic Top 20 hit singles, and here they were back out on tour with new songs debuting *Kaleidoscope*. She meant business, and her compelling shamanic performance held the entire audience spellbound. Steve Severin cut an imperious figure in his pleated trousers which were cut baggy at the waist and tapered down to become tight around the ankles. Steve wore loose-fitting black piratical blouses, and sported a dyed blond crop and Chinese ballet shoes. His bass playing drove and anchored the band at the same time. Banshees songs were powered by Severin's memorable, melodic, hook-laden basslines which featured high in the mix. I think Severin was a big influence on the style of Peter Hook from Joy Division and New Order, another of my bass heroes. Then there was McGeogh, a star signing on a free transfer. He was some player. It was a joy to stand beside his amp every night on that tour. He was one of the best I ever heard.

After the gig, the Banshees invited the Images back to the hotel. We told the man on the door that Siouxsie had invited us back. Her security guy Big Mick, who looked like an ex-wrestler, sorted it out. We excitedly entered the bar and sat in a circle around Siouxsie. I was on the chair right beside her whilst she chatted to the band, really engaged and interested in what they had to say. She was very fucking cool. I was shy at this point in my life so I thought it best to stay quiet and just listen. I did my best to keep my cool, but inside I was thinking that this was the greatest fucking thing to ever happen to me! I had posters and photographs of Siouxsie all over my bedroom walls, alongside Debbie Harry, Sex Pistols, Public Image Ltd, the Clash, the Jam. They had no ego or rockstar arrogance. That was how the old wave behaved, the rock aristocracy that Malcolm McLaren, Johnny Rotten and Joe Strummer had vowed to depose.

We all went down to Polydor Studios near Marble Arch which was owned by the Banshees' record company, who also released records by the Jam and the Cure. Steve Severin had wangled this studio time from Polydor, saying it was for him, but instead he gave the time to Altered Images to record a demo, free of charge. What an amazing gesture. The engineer on the session was a nice guy called Mike Stavrou who had engineered 'Hong Kong Garden' and produced *Join Hands*.

I walked around the streets near the Polydor building, just loving the fact that I was down in London with my mates who happened to be in a really cool little band and they were working with a Banshee. Life was good.

Through constant support from John Peel and glowing reviews and articles in the weekly music press Altered Images got themselves a record deal with CBS / Epic, and Steve Severin offered to help in the studio. This led to a great first single, 'Dead Pop Stars', which had lots of play on Peel and the coveted 'single of the week' spot in *NME*, and a second single, 'A Day's Wait', which I wasn't so keen on. Caesar wrote 'Dead Pop Stars', a cynical treatise on the pitfalls of pop stardom, a warning about the fate that awaits most rockers. Not a lot of people make it to the top and stay there, the rock and pop highway is littered with embittered deadbeats, burnouts and losers. Severin did a great job of producing 'Dead Pop Stars': it has a mix of PiL bass and drums, Caesar on slashing Banshees rhythm guitar, Tony McDaid's lead guitar riff; so good it could be straight off a Buzzcocks album. Clare's voice sounded as if Siouxsie Sioux had taken a huge hit of helium. It was great in a deranged, sixties garage-rock kind of way, very much like 'The Spider and the Fly' by the Monocles on *Pebbles Volume Three*.

After the second single, 'A Day's Wait', Caesar would leave the band. He was heavily into Joy Division, PiL, Wire, Paul Morley and *NME*. He took himself quite seriously and I guess he saw the way it was going with Altered Images. They started out as a kind of Banshees-influenced underground post-punk band, their songs a mix of dark pop melody and post-punk guitar, whereas Clare was a natural pop star. She took to the role effortlessly and without any self-consciousness. Like us, she read the music press every week and obsessed over the same new music and post-punk stars. People loved her instantly when they met her. She was polite, charming, stylish, a true romantic and very attractive, and that's why she made such a great pop star when the band started having hits. She was the kind of sixteen-year-old girl who brings *Lolita* to read on the bus to band practice. We were all romantics. That was the mutual attraction, the thing we all had in common. We didn't know that at the time though, we were just making it up as we went along, and it was a great adventure. None of us had ever really left Glasgow before, save for Celtic away matches. Clare was a brilliant frontwoman, stylish, flirty but untouchable at the same time. Everyone could see she *loved* being up there. Her joy was infectious; she was born to front a band. She was a pop star, no question.

Altered Images recorded the John Peel Session and played the Moonlight Club on the same visit. Severin was in attendance, so we were all really excited. A couple of weeks before Joy Division had played the Moonlight Club, just before *Closer* was released, it had been reviewed by Paul Morley in the *NME* and the feature was accompanied by photographs of Ian Curtis doing his frenetic dance, writhing and twisting his body into smoke-curled wind-like shapes, that is if the wind could ever be captured in a photograph. He had the look of someone tormented and tortured, in mortal agony.

The Moonlight Club in Hampstead was one of the last gigs with Ian Curtis. He'd experienced an epileptic fit after one of the shows. When you look at footage of Joy Division playing live you can see for yourself just how committed a performer Curtis was. The music surged through his body like electricity through a death-row prisoner in the chair, and he acted out his beautiful lyrics in all their terrible violence and apocalyptic imagery. To perform this dark, desperate, existential poetry each night must have taken its toll on Curtis. He plunged himself into the heart of darkness with each performance, and never held back. As a frontman I know that you've got to hold something back from time to time. You've got to pace yourself, especially over a long tour, or else you burn out fast. It must have used up all of his physical and psychic strength to do this night after night. Add this awful illness into the mix and it's heading for tragedy. But who was to know? It's impossible to pin down the forces that drove Ian Curtis.

We were all excited to be playing where Joy Division had played but the place was a shithole. It was just a structure attached to the side of the pub: the room was as wide as the stage and maybe three times as long. That night we were opening for Pete Petrol's new band Repetition. Pete was a bespectacled, nerdy-looking guy who had been the guitarist in Spizzenergi. Spizz were managed by Dave Woods who was the Banshees' booking agent.

Altered Images started getting gigs through the Banshees connection. We played the legendary Nashville Rooms (where the Pistols had played) over in Kensington. The headline act that summer night at the Nashville were called Margo Random and the Space Virgins. I have no idea what happened to Margo or her Virgins. Lost in a black hole in outer space somewhere, I suppose. Through the Banshees' office we met these fantastic people that worked for them in different capacities. There was Paul O'Reilly whose nickname was Suspect. He was a really good guy. Suspect always wore a black leather sixties box jacket and had a permanent grin on his face. There was Ginger Barwick, a solid and righteous human being who's still a great friend of mine to this day. Ginger made a life for himself in NYC. Suspect and Ginger were both members of the Banshees' road crew working in the band's office in Barbican. Ginger sold the swag and if there were ever any bootleggers outside the venue fleecing the fans and his beloved Banshees he'd be straight out there onto the street to kick the fuck out of them. Ginger had some temper on him. He never backed down from a fight and he never lost one either. He was hard as fuck. His dad had brought him up that way. He lived with his parents in a little house in Hammersmith where we would all stay when we were down in London. We also made friends with Billy 'Chainsaw' Houlston, a big, good-natured Brummie with a great sense of humour who ran the Banshees' fan club.

After the gig at the Moonlight Club, Severin invited everybody back for a party at the flat in West Hampstead he shared with Richard Jobson of the Skids. There were loads of pop stars and London scenesters there. I remember looking at his vast record collection. Severin had piles of albums on the floor, and at the front of one of the piles was *Electric Ladyland* with all the nude girls on it and I remember thinking, Man, that's a hippy record. I don't think that's allowed. That's how it was back in those days. I had the exact same feeling when I saw Andrew Innes's copy of the *White Album*. 'You're not allowed to like the Beatles!' It was a crime to admit you like anything before 1976 except the Velvet Underground, Iggy and the Stooges, New York Dolls and MC5.

The Banshees never asked Altered Images for any money to open for them, unlike other bands who we heard would ask support bands for 'buy on' money for the much-coveted opening slot on a tour. They helped the Images in every way they could, whether that was Severin conning Polydor into getting free studio time, making sure we had enough money to get a hotel for the night, or to buy petrol to make it to the next gig. *That* is punk rock.

The Spizzenergi gig was at Middlesbrough Rock Garden on Saturday 16 August 1980. The arrangement was to meet at nine o'clock Saturday morning in Carmunnock to load up the van with the band equipment and then head down the motorway to Middlesbrough. I got off the 31 bus at Johnny and Gerry McElhone's house and I saw there was a band meeting taking place. It looked serious. Tich Anderson, the drummer, had told them he wasn't coming. Tich was one of my best mates. I used to go to his house all the time and hang out listening to records. He had an amazing record collection: D.A.F., early Human League, Gang of Four, PiL, Heartbreakers, Raincoats, dub reggae, Joy Division, Wire, Cabaret Voltaire. He was just a brilliant guy. But on this day he didn't turn up. I think there were some inter-band politics I didn't know about.

Gerry said to me, 'Bob, you know the drumbeats – will you do the gig?'

I had to think about it on the spot with everyone looking at me. If I did the gig would I be betraying my friendship with Tich? This gig was a big opportunity for the band; Dave Woods had got it for them, and they couldn't be seen as unreliable and ungrateful. So I said, 'Yes, I'll do it, but only if Tich is allowed back in the band.' I thought, if Sid Vicious can do it with the Banshees at the 100 Club, so can I.

We drove down to Middlesbrough and played the Rock Garden. By the time we took to the stage it was rammed full of six hundred, deranged-looking, glue-sniffing third-generation Mohicanned-punks dressed like the Exploited with studded leather jackets and tartan bumflaps, cliché upon cliché upon cliché. They all looked completely brain-dead to me. There was also a big gang of angry-looking skinheads with their furious-looking girlfriends in tow throwing pint glasses full of beer at us. We never moved from the stage. We played our songs defiantly. In the end we got the audience's respect because we stood our ground and kept playing. That was my very first gig, my baptism of fire.

When you're young and believe in what you're doing nothing can stop you. Our gear was set up directly in front of Spizz's so there was hardly any gap between us and the malevolent front row. The feeling I had playing drums that night was one of complete exhilaration. It was a thrill like I'd never experienced before. It was one thing watching a band from the audience or at the side of the stage – which was an amazing buzz – but it was entirely different actually sitting onstage, dead centre, in the line of fire, in front of a living, breathing, judgemental and hostile audience; to find yourself in the maelstrom, in the high-energy vortex sonic force field that was the overdriven distorted sound of hundred-watt amplifiers and passionate young men hammering away on their Fender Twins.

What a feeling it was to be part of the magical energy summoned up by a rock and roll band, a band of friends. Magic being created in real time by like-minded spirits. Time seemed to slow down, like I was starring in a movie. This was a hit like no other; a deep hit to the soul.

I wanted more.

# 8.

# Factory Fodder (Shaved Heads and Kafka)

When Caesar quit the band in the summer of 1981, he formed the Wake, and I started to spend more time with him. He recruited a seventeen-year-old named Steven Allen as drummer, a young man who wore his hair in a wedge-cut with a fringe that hung just under his eyes. The bassist was Joe Donnelly. He was a nice guy, but not a rock and roller.

The Wake recorded a demo tape at a studio in a church basement situated at the bottom of Sauchiehall Street across from the Lorne Hotel. This was known as the Hellfire Club and was run by a soft-spoken, red-haired chap named Davie Henderson. One of the songs was titled 'Move with the Times' and I thought it was cool. It had a white-boy funk scratchy guitar riff very much like the kind of thing Josef K were doing on tracks like 'The Missionary' powered along by Stevie Allen's flying cymbal disco drumbeats. Caesar invited me to the recording session at Hellfire and I found myself really into what he was doing now.

Meanwhile Altered Images were fast becoming bona fide pop stars, featuring in colour spreads in *Smash Hits* and on the front cover of the *NME* at the same time. They released a single called 'Happy Birthday' which became a top ten hit and were on *Top of the Pops* every other week, Clare pixie-dancing in a ra-ra skirt with coloured ribbons in her hair and the boys playing gamely behind her. The cameras loved Clare and I was happy for them.

Tich called me up one night and invited me over to his house; he had just returned from an adventure in London and was buzzing, dying to tell me the gossip about which rock stars he had met in the London clubs.

When I got there, he was dressed in a really fucking cool Rock-Ola black leather waistcoat from Lloyd Johnson's shop on the King's Road. It was the type of thing that Martin Chambers of the Pretenders or Budgie would wear. Titch also had another Johnson's jacket based on the classic Levi's Lee trucker jacket in dark denim with white stitching. Very cool. No one had dark denim then, it was *all* blue, so this was very cool. He'd also started wearing tight black jeans and burgundy Chelsea boots and stacking his naturally curly hair high up into a Stray Cats-inspired quiff. He looked like a pop star.

He couldn't disguise his joy at having a real hit single and being on *Top of the Pops* and I was a wee bit sad that I was missing out on all the fun. Here I was working eight hours a day, five days a week, stuck on the treadmill of two weeks' night shift then two weeks' day shift, and my mates were living the rock and roll dream. Was I jealous? Yes.

I was happy for Tich, and all of them, but I also thought they'd presented themselves in an increasingly uncool way. Photoshoots with them all sat around a table with a huge birthday cake on it? This wasn't *Beggars Banquet*, was it? But good for him and the band, they deserved their success. That summer you couldn't escape Altered Images, they were everywhere. The music press called this 'new pop'.

I'd go see the Wake whenever they played a gig. Hardly anyone went to these shows. I often wondered how Caesar felt about this. He left Altered Images just before they started to really make it. I admired him for sticking to his guns and attempting to realise his vision.

Caesar, Stevie and I became good friends. Stevie was a little younger than me and totally obsessed with PiL, Pistols, the Clash, Joy Division. He had an older sister, Carolyn. She was into PiL too and especially Jeannette Lee, who lived at PiL's Gunter Grove headquarters and was a non-musical member of the limited company. Carolyn had the Jeannette Lee look down (from the front cover of *The Flowers of Romance*): shoulder-length black hair, black-kohl eyes, tartan miniskirt, black tights, flat shoes. She looked great. Carolyn, Stevie and myself would sit in Stevie's bedroom and listen to records on his Dansette. Stevie was an easy-going guy. He loved music the same way that I did and had a boyish enthusiasm. Carolyn conveyed a sense of someone who could be formidable given the chance. She had an erotic edge to her. She was into literature and spoke to me about books I hadn't read. She was smart, I thought. She had a steely, don't-fuck-with-me attitude hidden just beneath the veneer of friendliness.

We were inseparable, the four of us. We would go see plays each Friday evening at the Citizens Theatre which had a salubrious address in the Gorbals. The Citizens was home to the radical socialist 7:84 Company. They took their name from the fact that seven per cent of the population owned eighty-four per cent of the wealth, which was how it was in 1981, just two years into Margaret Thatcher's rule and the beginning of the free-market economy. The ratio is now much worse, of course, after forty years of neoliberalism. The admission at the Citizens was one British pound if you were a student or unemployed. We saw some amazing plays there: *The Rise and Fall of the City of Mahogany* by Bertolt Brecht, *Philosophy in the Boudoir* by the Marquis de Sade, *The Blacks / The Flowers / The Balcony* by Jean Genet. The Citizens' director Giles Havergal staged these plays beautifully and used Weimar-style harsh white lighting against an all-black background on a minimalist stage. He used Brechtian 'breaking the fourth wall' techniques, with the actors suddenly turning to address the stalls in the middle of the play, smashing through the barrier between 'performers' and 'spectators' to involve the audience in the play. Havergal was also influenced by the confrontational proto-punk techniques of Antonin Artaud's Theatre of Cruelty. This was radical and thoughtful stuff for us teenagers and made me look at things differently. The 7:84 Company took these experimental plays full of radical anti-establishment ideas by philosopher poets out on tour around Scotland to rural working-class communities. They believed that culture was for *everyone*, not just the middle and upper classes.

The Citizens was funded by the Labour-dominated Glasgow City Council, just as it should be. Art should exist for everybody, not only those with the wealth to afford it and the education that gives them a frame of reference; cultural knowledge being one of the many insidious ways the disease of class elitism maintains the old power structures and cripples critical thinking. It's for good reason that the children of working-class families receive a minimal education. The establishment understand the power and reach of cultural knowledge and information and so do everything in their power to crush any advancement in education for the lower orders. They want to keep us perpetually ignorant, in the dark. It's why the Tories slash school budgets and have abolished free further education. To have to pay tens of thousands of pounds and amass a lifetime of debt just to receive an education (which should be a birthright) is a way of dissuading poor kids from enriching their lives. It only benefits the already privileged and enforces the gulf between the classes. When I was a teenager, if you had good exam grades the state would pay for you to go to university, technical or engineering college, even art school. Wealth and corporation taxes were higher then and that's where the money came from to subsidise free further education. In this way society became a bit more equal. Until the Butler Education Act was passed in 1954 only the children of the upper middle classes and aristocratic families could afford to attend universities and art schools, so dancers, artists and poets were mostly from this stratum of society, because only they had access to 'high culture'. Everyone else was too busy working hard and scraping a living, with no time to realise their true potential. Before the war, the gates to the castle were firmly closed to someone like me.

The cultural and political advances and societal freedoms won as a result of the post-war consensus set fire to the sixties and seventies as working-class playwrights, authors, artists, filmmakers and pop stars took advantage of new educational freedoms. I am a child of social democracy, and although on an individual level I was failed by the education system many thrived within it and went on to live lives that would have been impossible for people pre-welfare state. By redistributing wealth, social democracy altered society for the better. That was all to change when Margaret Thatcher assumed power.

I cherish my memories of attending plays at this amazing place, where Giles and company gave me a cultural education that school had failed to provide.

In the winter of 1981 the Wake went through to Edinburgh to record a single, where 'Get Up and Use Me' by the Fire Engines had been recorded. 'Get Up and Use Me' was a godhead record for us; its spiky, angular guitar violence and low-fi drum-clutter powered by vocalist Davy Henderson's primal screams. It was a feral blast of dislocated consciousness, like Beefheart if he had grown up on an Edinburgh council estate rather than the Mojave Desert. It was post-punk perfection.

Recording a single at Wilf Smarties' Planet Studios was Caesar's idea and a good one. When we got to the address we found the studio was actually built inside a ground-floor flat in a smoke-black Edinburgh tenement (Edinburgh folk referred to their hometown as 'Auld Reekie' due to the constant smoke from coal chimneys in the old town and surrounding heavy industry from the industrial revolution). The band set up and played through the song that was to be the single's A side, 'On Our Honeymoon', a cynical take on the folly of romantic love and marriage. Once everyone agreed the sound balance was good in their headphones Wilf pressed RECORD and the boys played the song five or six times, and then Wilf invited them through to the small control room to have a listen. Everyone agreed it sounded great. The B side was next, titled 'Give Up', and Caesar asked me to play synthesiser on it. I had no idea he was going to ask me to do this, but I was excited, so I plugged in the Korg and Caesar and I messed around with the switches and patch settings on the synth until we arrived at a Giorgio Moroder-esque sequencer sound that we liked. Caesar counted the band in and I just fell in behind them. I'd had no run-through or practice. It was all improvised on the spot, in real time. Wilf spoke to us over the control room talk-back mic to tell us the take was great. We trooped through to hear it blasted on the big speakers. It sounded fantastic.

A few weeks later Caesar had test pressings of the single and I was able to play it on my little stereo in my bedroom and I was totally thrilled. Thrilled because the band were good, and thrilled because the single was good. Thrilled because I was actually playing on a real fucking seven-inch vinyl record.

Caesar asked me to design the cover artwork. I made a drawing of a Catholic priest holding up a baby during Holy Communion. It was a play on both the religious connotations of the band's name and the insidious power that the church held over people. Previously I had designed a single cover for the 'Ha Ha Hee Hee' EP for Alan McGee and Andrew Innes's band the Laughing Apple and arranged for an old printer guy in John Horn's to run off the covers on a small printing press which he kept in his garage at home.

An offer came from Altered Images for the Wake to open for their show at Tiffany's in December. This gig would be a triumphant homecoming. Caesar asked me if I would join the band to play guitar and synthesiser on a few songs. He taught me the riff to a

Byrds-style arpeggio guitar motif on a new song 'Favour', as well as the simple one-finger string machine riff to 'An Immaculate Conception', and I practised hard at home.

I borrowed a then in vogue red semi-acoustic guitar for the gig. I was nervous – it was one thing playing in Middlesbrough to a crowd of strangers, but here in Glasgow it seemed everyone was judging us; a feeling that would persist until Primal Scream's breakthrough in the early nineties. But adrenaline cut through any nerves and carried me through. It was a good show, we played well and played with attitude. A year before I had bought myself a Les Paul Classic copy from McCormack's music store in Bath Street, a cherry-burst reddish-brown colour – very Thin Lizzy. I also bought a Peavy Bandit amplifier. A proper rock and roll guitar. Caesar and Andrew Innes showed me some barre chords and I learned how to play 'Time's Up' and the two-note 'Boredom' solo by Buzzcocks.

Caesar managed to get hold of Rob Gretton's telephone number. Rob was New Order's manager and he'd been Joy Division's manager too. He was also a director of Factory Records. We went to Manchester to see him, and I recall asking if he supported Manchester United. Rob peered at me drily over his large glasses with the retort, 'Fuck off! *No one* from Manchester supports United – I'm CITY,' then he pushed his glasses back up into position from where they'd slipped. Classic Rob. He kindly let us sleep on his floor overnight and the next day we took the bus back home to Glasgow.

A week or so later Caesar received a phone call from Rob at his mum's house in Simshill asking if we wanted to support New Order and make an album on Factory Records. This was a gift from the gods.

The New Order gig was to take place on 26 February 1982 at Trinity Hall in Bristol. We went round to the bassist's house to pick him up and his mum answered the door and said she didn't know where he was. He had disappeared. My guess is he bottled it and didn't have the guts to tell Caesar so got his mother to lie on his behalf. He fucked up big time, what a fucking idiot. I despise people that behave this way. Spineless cunts. This gig was the band's big break. Caesar asked me if I would play bass. I didn't have one, but said yes.

We arrived in darkness and parked our van outside Trinity Hall, an old church – perfect for the gothic, depressed, doomy sounds of New Order and the Wake. We all helped to load the gear in and I saw Rob Gretton standing on the other side of the hall. I walked over and told Rob our bass player had vanished so I was playing instead of him tonight. 'The only problem is I don't have a bass guitar or amplifier,' I said. 'Have New Order got one spare that I can borrow, please?'

Rob looked at me and said in a droll, flat, unemotional tone, 'Ya better ask Hooky.' I looked around the backstage area for Peter Hook. I was shitting myself. Hooky was my H-E-R-O. I caught a glimpse of him bantering with some of the guys in the crew, plucked up my courage and sauntered over to him. I nervously told him who I was and repeated the same story I'd told Rob. There was an awkward silence.

Hooky stared at me and said, 'FUCK OFF!' And then, 'Of course you can. They're up there on the stage – use the Yamaha and tell Eddie I said it's alright.'

I wish I could describe how I felt at that moment. A mixture of fear and elation carried me up onto that Trinity Hall stage as I picked up the huge Yamaha bass, plugged straight in to Hooky's hi-watt bass stack and was nearly blown off the stage by the sheer sonic power of his thunderous Thor-like Viking bass sound.

In the dressing room after soundcheck Caesar ran through the songs with me. I knew the basslines because I'd heard the demos and seen the band practise enough that they were easy to pick up.

The gig sped past in a nervous blur. I struggled to contain the power of Hooky's amplifier set-up. My hands were shaking so fucking hard with nerves that it's a wonder I managed to hold any of the notes down at all. But I absolutely *loved* the buzz from playing. The experience of being onstage was one of life lived on the edge of my nerves, an altered state of consciousness. The Yamaha bass I was using was the one Hooky played in Joy Division's 'Love Will Tear Us Apart' video. How fucking cool was that?

Afterwards Rob Gretton came into our dressing room and asked if we wanted to play some more dates with New Order. After some drinks we all went out into the darkness of Trinity Hall to watch New Order and they were magnificent. They started the set with a new song we'd never heard before called 'Temptation' and played most of the recently released *Movement* album. There was a dark power and majesty to their music and their group image was cloaked in mystery. It was an incredible night. Caesar and Stevie both complimented me on my performance, and asked me to join the band.

Every time the Wake played with New Order I would make a bootleg tape for my own enjoyment using a portable cassette recorder, and there were always new songs we'd never heard before in the set. Over time, with every gig, these songs would develop, change and improve. New Order's music was a great example of the 'work in progress' technique. They were never afraid to fuck up and would play the songs in a different way each night. I learned a lot from my time touring with New Order that I would put into use in the future with Primal Scream.

When we returned to Glasgow I bought myself a black Fender Mustang bass guitar and an Electro-Harmonix Clone Theory effects pedal. I loved the way bands like PiL, Joy Division and the Cure (on *Seventeen Seconds*) had the bass guitar featured prominently high up in the sound mix, like a lead instrument. I also loved the basslines in the reggae records I listened to. The bass was as much of a hook in these records as the actual song. Traditionally in pop and rock the hook was the lead vocal or guitar, the bass a hidden undertow that kept rhythm with the drums. It only featured strongly in Black music genres such as funk, disco and reggae.

The Wake began practising at the Hellfire Club for the Factory album sessions. Caesar already had some of the songs all worked out with lyrics and chord progressions but other songs were written collectively. I always saw him as the leader. He had formed the band and it was shaped in his vision. Carolyn Allen joined us on keyboards. To my knowledge she had never touched an instrument before, and that was very much in keeping with the spirit of the times too. Punk-rock bands were all a mix of amateurs and accomplished players. She played childlike three-note riffs using two fingers because the keyboard only had one setting: synthetic orchestral strings, an icy and distant sound. This was a very early eighties post-punk musical style used by artists such as Fad Gadget, Depeche Mode and New Order on these cheap-sounding, simple, almost toylike instruments.

Rob Gretton called Caesar to inform him the album was to be recorded at Strawberry Studios in Stockport. Joy Division had recorded their classic *Unknown Pleasures* album at Strawberry only three years before. The producer was to be Chris Nagle who worked with Martin Hannett. Hannett was, of course, Factory's very own Phil Spector. We were going straight into the fire. We all felt that Rob must really believe in us and were beyond excited as we made the trip south.

We pulled up outside Strawberry and loaded the gear into an industrial lift. The lift took us down one floor below street level and as the concertinaed metal doors were pulled open we stepped out into the legendary Strawberry Studios. Later in the session Chris Nagle told me that Martin Hannett had him mic up the lift doors and that was the clanking, mysterious industrial sound like sheet metal that you hear on *Unknown Pleasures*.

We were all shocked when Chris Nagle explained to us how we were going to record the album. The strategy was this: Steven

Allen would record his drum parts beginning with a track of bass drum, then a track of snare drum, then a track of high hat. The tom-toms and cymbals were to be recorded separately. Nagle made Stevie record every single song on the album this way, which was very difficult because Stevie was used to playing off of my bass or taking his cues from Caesar's vocals or guitar riffs or Carolyn's keys. Once Stevie had completed all the drum tracks it was my turn. I played through every song from memory with my bass isolated and only Stevie's drums for guidance. Then Carolyn laid down her string machine parts; she had never been in a studio before so it must have been nerve-shredding but Nagle was a really nice guy and his relaxed, gentle manner both pushed and encouraged us to play as well as we could. Out of all of us, Caesar was the most confident. He had experience of studio recording and many gigs under his belt with the Images. He was also an accomplished guitarist and believed in the words he had written. I believe the Nagle recording technique had been learned through his work with Martin Hannett. Hannett recorded bands this way so he would have complete control over every single instrument with no chance of any unwanted sounds 'bleeding' from one track onto another. Hannett would then manipulate the instrumental tracks by putting them through various state-of-the-art digital sound effects outboard gear he had purchased, and psychedelicise the isolated tracks so he could sculpt the sound to achieve the desires of his futurist sonic vision. Martin Hannett was a postpunk Godard, an auteur of sound.

Sometime during the sessions Rob Gretton came down to have a listen and see how we were getting on. Tony Wilson paid a visit too. We were all a bit shy in his presence and none of us said very much. Tony was wearing a khaki shirt then very much in vogue around Factory, reminiscent of A Certain Ratio's style, and had his hair cut in a thirties aristocratic *Brideshead Revisited* way, with a slight floppy fringe. He had a well-educated Oxbridge air about him in comparison to Rob who was definitely

Mancunian working class. Having Rob and Tony visit the studio was encouraging and inspiring for us. We didn't want to let them down. The fact they arranged for us to record this album meant that they believed in our band, and that gave us a self-confidence vital to a young artist. Patronage from people who have achieved great things in their life can sometimes just give you that extra encouragement. Nagle recorded and mixed the album in a week and we drove back to Glasgow feeling joyous and blessed.

# Part Three
# (1982–1985)

# 9.

# Working-Class Glaswegian Industrial Blues

I was buying and reading books by authors like J. G. Ballard, Franz Kafka and William Burroughs. I loved *The Atrocity Exhibition* and related to the ever-present feelings of dread and paranoia in *The Trial* and the dime-store detective narco-pulp of *Junkie*. I also read Orwell's *Homage to Catalonia* because I had an interest in the Spanish Civil War; in fact my dad had recently helped have a statue of Dolores Ibárruri, a.k.a. 'La Pasionaria', heroine of the Spanish Civil War, erected down by the bandstand on the River Clyde. The statue was put up in honour of the men and women of Glasgow who had volunteered to go to Spain and defend the recently formed democratic Republic against General Franco's Fascist army. Caesar was into *The Outsider* by Colin Wilson, which led him to Albert Camus and other existentialist writers. That book was his literary roadmap. I borrowed it from him but felt that Wilson was a dry, boring writer. I didn't find it inspiring in any way.

The Wake's album, *Harmony*, was released on Factory in 1982 as FAC 60. The cover art was designed by the band and James Kay and features an illustration of a wreath drawn in the style of the industrial imagery so prevalent in Eastern European Communist regimes. It had an authoritarian feel to it, somewhere between Fascism and Communism. This illustration was drawn in black line against an all-grey background. It resembles a tombstone.

Everyone in the band was a socialist and it was a sleeve very much in keeping with the Factory Records aesthetic. We all loved Peter Saville's cover art for Joy Division, ACR and the Durutti Column and this was our tilt at that. Caesar also had a fascination with the rituals of Catholicism and the sleeve for Joy Division's *Closer* gave him creative licence to be open about that. His mother went to Mass every Sunday.

I hated all religions. I saw them as a way to control the masses and enforce class and power structures all over the world. The oldest con besides romantic love. That was the way I felt as a young man. I still have many reservations and criticisms regarding organised religion but I have also grown to understand that for many people faith in god and the church is the bedrock of their lives and I respect that. I am related to someone who is a practising Christian, a truly good and moral human being who follows the teachings of Christ and lives her life accordingly, a person who does nothing but good in the world. She has an inner strength that is something to behold and she is very inspiring. Mystery and spirituality are beautiful things. My father has always spoken highly about Christ's Sermon on the Mount and the Gospel of Matthew. He sees it as a socialist text. Pierre Paolo Passolini even made a wonderful film about it. The tenets of Christianity and socialism are very similar.

The album received middling reviews but a writer for *Sounds*, Dave McCullough, came to Glasgow to interview us. They did a full-page feature and McCullough was supportive. The piece featured a nice photograph by Paul Slattery of the band standing inside a municipal building beneath a domed roof. I was dressed in a four-button black leather sixties box jacket with a creamy yellow psychedelic paisley scarf which had belonged to my deceased grandad. My hair was shaved high at the sides and round the back and combed to the side, parting on the left with a short fringe that hung just right on my eyebrow. None of us said much in the piece. McCullough was *Sounds*' 'post-punk' writer and a lot less pretentious than Caesar's beloved hero Paul Morley of *NME*.

After the album release we played a show at Henry Wood Hall, a church near Sauchiehall Street up town. We promoted the concert ourselves. A friend of mine, Jim Beattie, opened for us that night. Beattie played bass and sang over pre-recorded tracks that came from a miked-up cassette recorder. Beattie had recorded his backing music onto this machine. It featured an inbuilt drum machine with four settings: rock, samba, waltz and disco. It had a then-popular two-track recording facility from which you could record sound onto a C-90, C-60 or C-30 cassette tape. Beattie overdubbed his ideas onto these tapes and had recorded enough tracks to play a small live set. I had been making music with Beattie since the summer of 1981. He was in the same school year as my brother Graham and lived with his parents in a Mount Florida tenement at 39 Brownlie Street, just one minute down the hill from where I lived on Stanmore Road. We practically lived on the same street, me at the top and Beattie at the bottom.

Beattie's mum had the keys to a hall where the Boy Scouts and Girl Guides would meet. Beattie and I would go there on a Saturday night when it was empty. He would take his really cheap Japanese Les Paul Classic copy and a small guitar amp and I would take the metal lids from the dustbins by the shed which stood between his (shared) back garden and the scout hall. Once inside, Beattie would plug his guitar and amp in and I would place two dustbin lids on the parquet floor and he would play a one-chord Banshees or PiL-like screaming guitar riff and I would join in with primitive tribal beats on my dustbin lids making a clanking metal industrial sound and we would both SCRRREEEEAM! SCRRREEEEAM! SCRRREEEEAM! endlessly – no lyrics, no words, just SCRRREEEEAM! SCRRREEEEAM! SCRRREEEEAM!. We made an amazing sound. Neither of us could really play but we didn't care; that wasn't the point, the point was to make an exorcism happen. Those sessions were cathartic without us realising at the time. We always pissed ourselves laughing afterwards and never took it seriously; it was just something to do on a Saturday night that kept us off the streets. Beattie made tapes of these screaming sessions onto a cheap portable cassette recorder. Sometimes we both hammered with our fists on the big ventilator or central heating shaft that ran alongside the scout hall wall. The ventilator shaft made a fantastic sound, a polyrhythmic cacophony. The empty hall had a high roof, concrete walls and parquet flooring; this made for a cavernous, echo-laden sound. The drums sounded like war music, martial and violent. Working-class Glaswegian industrial blues.

Sometime earlier I had borrowed an album from Caesar by the Fall called *Live at the Witch Trials*, and on that record there was a spoken-word piece, 'Crap Rap', that I loved where Mark E. Smith says

*We are the Fall*
*the white crap that talks back ...*

He ends the piece with

*I believe in the R & R dream*
*I believe in the primal scream*

I suggested to Beattie that we use Primal Scream as a name to describe the music we were making in the scout hall. Beattie really liked the name because it was punk *and* post-punk, therefore perfect. So, we had a name for our noise experiment stretching all the way back to the summer of 1981. Over the years people have asked me if there was a John Lennon influence but we had zero idea about the Lennon and Arthur Janov therapy links back then. We were young punks and had a year-zero mentality. We never listened to the Beatles until Paul Weller ripped off 'Taxman' for

'Start!' and Beattie bought *Revolver* as a result. Even then we only dug 'She Said She Said', 'Tomorrow Never Knows' and 'Taxman'. We thought the rest of the album was rubbish. So Beattie and I both saw that the name had multi-layered meanings and could be representative of anything we ever did in musical terms. Beattie performed under the name Primal Scream solo at Henry Wood Hall, singing and playing bass over pre-recorded sound-collages he'd made on his two-track cassette player. The first proper, full-band Primal Scream show was way off in the future.

I had a friend named Elliot Davies who sold bootleg tapes at Glasgow tech college on Saturday mornings. He would pay me ten pounds to help out and he always had loads of great stuff: Velvet Underground live gigs and rare studio sessions at a time when no one was into them; the infamous Doors Miami show from 1968 where Morrison tells the teenage audience that they are 'all a bunch of fucking slaves' whilst the instrumentalists vamp on 'Back Door Man' for about fifteen minutes. This was totally inspirational stuff to me. I had started listening to the Doors obsessively after hearing 'The End' in Francis Ford Coppola's *Apocalypse Now* a couple of years earlier. My brother Graham and I would drive around Glasgow late at night in Mum's little Renault listening to a C-90 cassette tape which had the singles compilation album *13* on one side and their self-titled debut album on the other. I absolutely loved Jim Morrison's confrontational diatribe. Like Bertolt Brecht – whose 'Alabama Song' featured in the Doors' repertoire – he was into breaking the 'fourth wall' between performer and audience. Morrison's whole schtick was that people were coming to rock gigs and convincing themselves they were committing a 'revolutionary' act by just being there. Any true rebellious energy manifested in the sixties counter-culture had been bought up by corporate record labels, packaged by Madison Avenue advertising companies and sold on to rock-hungry kids as 'revolution'. Morrison was hanging out with San Francisco beat poet Michael McClure and had been attending performances in LA by the Living Theatre, a radical troupe of hippie actors who wanted 'PARADISE NOW'. Morrison was deeply into all aspects of the anti-war counter-culture and knew that the potential of rock to make any changes in mass culture had been neutered, soaked up, repackaged and sold back to the masses as mere entertainment. The masses were not ready to commit themselves to revolutionary change yet and Jim knew it.

So, he let them have it. That show virtually ended the Doors' career. Their financially lucrative US arena tour was cancelled by worried promotors and Morrison was arrested and tried in court in Miami on a charge of public lewdness. Some kids at the show had told the local Miami TV news channel that Jim had exposed himself during the show. There were photographers present that night but no photographs exist. The cops hated Morrison because he would antagonise them in every city. He got busted onstage in New Haven, Connecticut for telling the audience a story about how a cop had burst into a toilet backstage where Jim was making out with a girl. Jim makes fun of 'the little man, in his little blue uniform, with his little stick' who had put a stop to his backstage fun. The cops are pictured circling the stage, prowling like hyenas stalking a deer, waiting for the moment to pounce and eventually they arrest him onstage in front of the audience, a clear image of old world uptight conservative Christian racist AmeriKKKan establishment power versus hippie counter-culture anti-war free love youth.

*Five to one, baby*
*One in five*
*No one here gets out alive*

Jim Morrison truly lived the things he was singing about. In the future I would personally find that was a very dangerous game to play.

Elliot took an interest in what I was doing with the Wake. I'd been friends with him since before I'd become a band member and he saw that we were getting somewhere with the Factory records connection and wanted in on the action. Through our contact with New Order's manager Rob Gretton, Nick Lowe, an old schoolfriend of Andrew Innes', managed to secure the right to promote New Order at Glasgow Tiffany's. The Wake were going to open for them at Edinburgh Assembly Rooms on 12th April, St Andrew's University Stirling on the 13th, followed by Glasgow Tiffany's on the 14th. 'Blue Monday' was riding high in the charts and a sensation everywhere. It felt like a victory for underground music: not only was 'Blue Monday' an experimental electronic dance track but it had no recognisable song structure; compare it to any other chart hit of the time and you'll see what I mean. The fact that it was released on the Situationist-inspired Factory Records excited me, because naïvely I loved the way they applied ideas of anarcho-syndicalism to the music business. The record deal was a profit share. When enough records had been sold and the company had been reimbursed for the album recording costs then any royalties would be split equally between the label and the artist. If for any reason the label were ever to close then Tony Wilson would return the recordings to the artists, so the workers owned the copyright to their work, not the company.

It sounds mad today but that's how it was back then. Punk had opened up new ways of doing 'business' and the corrupt practices of the established record industry were being questioned by labels like Factory. The band's no-compromise attitude even extended to their chaotic *Top of the Pops* performance when manager Rob Gretton had insisted they perform it totally live in the *TOTP* studio. I don't know if this is true or not but someone once told me that Bernard Sumner performed 'Blue Monday' whilst tripping on acid. That was fucking legendary as far as Jim Beattie and I were concerned.

The tour was doubly exciting because New Order's second album, the Orwell-quoting *Power, Corruption and Lies*, was just about to be released on 2 May so expectations were high. The Wake played well each night of the tour and after we'd removed our equipment from the stage and packed up the guitars we'd go out into the audience and wait for New Order to come on. This was New Order at their very best. They still possessed the dark power that drove Joy Division and a cloak of mystery shrouded them. They never spoke to the audience. Peter Hook spent much of the gig faced up against his amp stacks with Bass Nero & Salford painted on them, his back to the audience, arrogant and contemptuous. It was definitely not 'entertainment'. From seeing bands such as Suicide, the Pop Group and the Fall I had developed a love for confrontational performance, the 'fuck you' attitude that these bands possessed. Audiences are sometimes like cattle, grazing idly in the field waiting to be herded to another field, shepherded all their lives, unthinking, unknowing. Artists have to be brave; as the old saying goes: *pioneers take the arrows*. It's lonely out there on the perimeter, on the edge of consciousness, the dark, unknown regions of soul dread and psychic derangement where the straights are too scared to go; the great herd gather around each other, take safety in numbers and all move together in the same direction safe in the knowledge that the farmer will feed them regularly. They know their place in the great (or not so great) scheme of things, while the lone wolves go hungry, always searching for the meagre, unwanted scraps that society has forgotten and seen no use in; but the lone wolves use this cultural 'garbage' as soul food and through a kind of feral alchemy create powerful art. To use Kipling's well-worn but true maxim, *he who travels fastest travels alone*.

New Order were on a high for these shows. The success of 'Blue Monday' and the excitement of their imminent album release meant that their music had a light and lift to it that hadn't been there before. I feel blessed to have seen them on this tour.

They made a very powerful impression on me; not just musically, but in the way Gretton dealt with people. They were so gracious and helpful to the Wake. I managed to thank Hooky about this years later, in the late nineties, and he said, 'You treat people the way you'd like to be treated yourself', and they did, very well. Amazing people. I love them all.

Something strange happened earlier that year. The Wake had opened a show for New Order at the Great Hall, Cardiff University on 29 January. I remember sitting backstage waiting for New Order to soundcheck and Bernard Sumner was walking around wearing a sixties cotton anorak very much in the style that Will Sergeant of the Bunnymen wore. He looked cool. His head was shaved in the Hitler Youth style with a side parting and small fringe. I wore mine the same way except my fringe was a bit longer. Bernard had a startled, spooked look, like Oskar in the movie version of Günter Grass's *The Tin Drum* directed by Volker Schlöndorff which I'd recently seen at the Glasgow Film Theatre. He was so fucking charismatic; onstage he seemed both dissociated and possessed at the same time. His guitar playing was total godhead, his choppy punk-funk rhythms as good as Lou Reed's or Sterling Morrison's on *Live '69*. His three-note lead lines and the sound of his voice in songs like 'Age of Consent' caused deep emotional breakage in me; it's like his soul is crying. I loved his tone and his timing. There was a dissociative emotionality to it. He was a great frontman. Still is.

Anyway, 'Barney', as Rob always called him, was walking around in this blue anorak with a tiny pornographic book sticking out of his pocket. He was a few distant galaxies away, his eyes fixed on other planets and visions that we could not see. New Order were big into acid at this time and maybe Barney was tripping in Cardiff that day. What I thought was really cool about Bernard apart from his very obvious charisma was the little porno book. It was the exact opposite of the Wake's muffled Catholic guilt and austere virginal sexlessness. Caesar dreamed of having a conversation with New Order about fifties French existentialist novels, but when I overheard Barney and Hooky and the roadies all they spoke about was 'birds' they'd met on the road. They were a rock and roll band; there was nothing 'anti-rock' about them; that was all just projection from pretentious *NME* writers showing off their literary influences. People had this image of New Order as miserable young existentialists dressed in forties raincoats with Joseph Conrad or Albert Camus novels falling out of their pockets. Barney had a cheap porno book and he didn't give a fuck. I loved him for that.

By the time the Wake came onstage the Great Hall was rammed with people. No one knew who we were because we never got any radio play apart from a couple of spins on Peel and only *Sounds* had featured us. The set was going well, then, halfway through the gig, I began to lose interest. Bored by the band and bored by the songs, all of which were around eight minutes long now, with no rock dynamic to speak of; the songs started and ended on the exact same level, forever unchanging in their gloomy, fugue-like, flat, depressive manner.

So, I unstrapped my Shergold six-string bass and placed it in front of my bass amp and walked across the stage, right past Caesar who was singing and Steven who was lost in his drumming and Carolyn who had her head down looking at her keyboard, all of them still playing, and off the stage into the dressing room. There I sat down on my own and waited for them to finish the set. I could hear them still, loud over the PA. There was a small smattering of applause from the New Order-hungry student audience and then silence. The dressing room door opened and they came rushing in. One by one they all started shouting at me, a cacophony of fools justified in their self-righteousness and anger. I just sat there and said nothing. I'd never seen any of them lose their tempers before, their pose was always one of passive indifference and studied 'cool', although it wasn't 'cool', it was just boring. For a while I sat there and said nothing, I just let them all continue shouting at me and when they asked why I had walked off I eventually said, 'The songs are all too long, they're boring.' That went down well. I had embarrassed them in front of two thousand people, but more importantly they were scared about what Rob, New Order and Factory would think. The truth was they didn't give a fuck – they had their own shit to deal with and were too busy preparing to go onstage and play themselves to be bothered by my little act of rebellion.

The atmosphere in the dressing room was extremely awkward and uncomfortable now, a forced silence gripped the space and it was emotionally claustrophobic. It was a small, cramped room with nowhere to escape. I had begun dissociating onstage during the show. It was how I made myself disappear in any situations of emotional pain, violence or confrontation. I have done this since childhood. Once these take over my consciousness my disengagement is complete and then I am simply not present in any situation. My body is there but my mind and spirit are not. It's a reaction to trauma, a way of protecting myself. Whenever my parents fought I wanted to be anywhere else in the world except my house. It filled me with fear and anxiety and I wanted to escape, but as a child I couldn't, so the trauma triggered my mind and body in this way. I used to sometimes experience it onstage singing with the band. I'd be really up for the show backstage dying to get out there and play but when I walked on and saw the audience I wouldn't want to be there, and no matter how hard I tried to get into the show I just couldn't. It was as if my whole body and mind were frozen. It feels like I am on a ketamine-like drug. I am present but not present; I am in the world, but not in the world; I am within reach, but unreachable. Something triggers this reaction in me. Usually a fear of deep humiliation or emotional violence and physical confrontation. I'm a strange character. The emotional distance required to keep myself 'safe' and cut off from the world whilst still walking through it is something I have built up over the years. I am good at it. My nerves are very close to the surface of my skin, which makes me perfect lead singer material.

I walked out on my own into the anonymous darkness of Cardiff's University's Great Hall, and waited for my heroes, New Order. They didn't disappoint.

That summer of 1983 we were asked if we wanted to record a single for Factory Benelux. Benelux had released some cool singles like Josef K's 'The Missionary' and Paul Haig's version of the Sly Stone classic, 'Runnin' Away'. Rob Gretton set up a studio session at Revolution Studios in leafy Cheadle Hulme, Manchester, and he suggested that New Order front-of-house guy Oz be the producer. We all thought this was a good idea as New Order sounded mighty and powerful live and Oz always balanced the sound mix perfectly.

There were two new songs we had worked up: 'Something Outside' and 'Host' (another Catholic reference from Caesar), from jamming out ideas during band rehearsal at the Hellfire Club. I played the low E string on my guitar using heavy dub reggae-inspired basslines in both songs with Steven playing rim shots in a reggae style too. Oz recorded us exactly as Chris Nagle had. It was a very eighties way of doing things, banishing all the things that made rock and roll great, like the tension between instruments fighting each other to be heard over the racket and the 'bleed' from screaming amplifiers. There were no amplifiers used in this recording session either. Oz had me plug my bass straight into the mixing desk to record. This is known as DI – direct input. It works for disco and electronic music where you want a clean, airless effect, but rock and roll needs freedom. Spillage and chaos make rock records sound better, giving the listener an aural impression of anarchy and the churning sound of sedition. It was a cold and unemotional way to make music, very forensic. The record was released in October 1983 as a twelve-inch single wrapped in a sleeve which featured the painting *Beat the Whites with the Red Wedge* by Russian artist El Lissitzky who alongside Kazimir Malévich was a member of the Russian avant-garde Suprematist group of artists from the twenties. The Suprematists supported the aims of the Bolshevik Revolution and believed that with their art they could be 'agents of change'. I had seen *Beat the Whites with the Red Wedge* in a book of Russian Constructivist art and showed it to the band, suggesting it might make a good sleeve for the single.

I enjoyed getting involved with record sleeve design and it's something I would develop and work at over the years, right up to this day. I have had a hand in the concept and design of every Primal Scream record sleeve. I love the design process. It's an amazing experience to see the tiny little germ or seed of an idea take life and become something tangible that you can hold in your hands. Records are fetish objects that possess occult power, but you have to work at that connection, it doesn't come for free. You have to invest them with psychic energy and make spiritual connections using your own will and imagination.

One grey Glasgow autumn day when nothing was happening I heard a knock at the door. I was met with the sight of Caesar and Steven Allen. They had never come round to visit me there before so I was already thinking something weird was going on. They both looked nervous and then Caesar blurted out, 'We don't want to play music with you, we don't want you in the band anymore,' and Steven Allen parroted him word for word. I was in shock, I hadn't seen this coming at all. Then they both walked away. I closed the door and went into the living room and sat down, really upset. I didn't just lose a band that day, I lost three friendships, and I was heartbroken. A few days later, once I'd got myself together, I called Caesar and asked him if they would give me another chance. I met up with them and made my case to stay in the band, but it was a humiliating and undignified experience because they had already made their minds up before I got there. I felt they wanted to hurt me and see me plead for forgiveness; it was cruel stuff, sadistic even. There was a dead silence, a whimper of nothingness. That was it. I was sacked. So be it. End of story. Goodbye. Finito. Kaput. I felt humiliated, in real emotional pain. I walked out of the flat and across Battlefield Road, turning the corner past ex-Celtic player Jim Brogan's garage, the one with the cycle speedway track behind it, then walked up past the Church of Scotland hall where the 3rd Boys' Brigade met and over to the home stretch, past McGee's ma's house where Cathcart Road becomes Castlemilk Road and crossed over to Fourth Avenue and my dad's house. Once inside I picked up the telephone and called Beattie's house.

'I've just been kicked out of the Wake, do you want to form a band?'

Beattie said, 'Yes, what you doing tomorrow night, d'ya wanna come over to my house and write some songs?'

I said, 'Yes.'

He said, 'Seven o'clock?'

I said, 'Cool, see you at seven.'

The following night we started Primal Scream for real.

I'm proud of the records we made whilst I was a member of the Wake. If Factory had cloned a perfect 'Factory band' that would have been us. We were 'Factory Youth'. We had the thirties shaved Wehrmacht style haircuts, we dressed in old men's secondhand clothes, and comported ourselves with a deadly serious, depressed, cold, stony, humourless demeanour and took ourselves way too seriously. You can do that when you're twenty or twenty-one but someday you have to wise up.

A huge part of my frustration and boredom with the Wake's music stemmed from the fact that I'd been listening to a lot of psychedelic-era sixties music with Beattie. We were both so untouched and underwhelmed by what passed for contemporary 'rock' that we began unearthing the holy sounds of Syd Barrett's Floyd, Dylan, Velvet Underground, Arthur Lee's Love, the Doors, the Byrds, Rolling Stones, and the Kinks and that lead us both to dig down further, deep into the netherworld of 'garage punk' artists like Thirteenth Floor Elevators, the Seeds, Electric Prunes, Chocolate Watchband and the Pebbles album series of obscure teen-punk garage singles. These songs were mainly two-minute-thirty explosions of high-energy rock and nearly always tales of teenage sexual frustration and societal anger. Drug psychosis, paranoia and psychic derangement were also themes in the 'heavier', more literate bands. We recognised that some of these sixties artists shared a similar spirit of rebellion with the seventies punk bands we loved. We already loved Iggy Pop, indeed I had seen Iggy play the Apollo Theatre in 1979 on the New Values tour when his classic single 'I'm Bored' was out. We would play 'The Passenger' single on repeat at Beattie's house and Stooges were godhead to us. I used to take acid and listen to the first two Stooges albums lying on the carpet with my head between the speakers. You haven't lived until you've heard 'We Will Fall' and 'Dirt' in this way, I'm telling you: beautiful primitive urban blues. To paraphrase the great Memphis pianist, producer and shaman Jim Dickinson: the Stooges were 'primitive modernists'. The Stooges played the blues but they were not slavishly copying the original Black American artists in the same way that British Blues Explosion bands like Peter Green's Fleetwood Mac or John Mayall & the Bluesbreakers did. Instead, Iggy, the Asheton brothers and bassist Dave Alexander created a post-adolescent urban white blues sound that encapsulated all the fears, hopes, sexual frustrations and yearnings and existential boredom of teenage outsiders everywhere. They were so far ahead of their time and way too much for the straights. They were even too much for the so-called 'hip' counter-culture; the 'turned on' people of the time who preferred the Californian soft-rock singer-songwriter 'adult' sounds of CSNY, Joni Mitchell, Neil Young and Carole King. The

Stooges were the true sound of young America, but as usual no one was listening. The masses are stupid; feed them horseshit and tell them it's caviar and they will believe you if it's packaged in the right way.

# 10.

# Scream of the Sky-Blue Vox Phantom

The songs we had been playing in the Wake had zero rock dynamic. They began and finished on the same energy plane. Fine. That was then. We were all young and still learning, finding our way slowly into the infinite possibilities of the world of music and songwriting. Shane McGowan once said to me about songwriting, 'It's not a competition.' He was right, and it's not a race either. I've always seen it as an experiment in real time. Each time you write a new song you get excited and think it's the greatest song ever written. Then you record it. Then a couple of years later you hear it somewhere by chance and think to yourself, 'I could have written that line better' or 'That guitar riff isn't that good' or 'The arrangement is all wrong' and on and on and on ad infinitum. It is always a 'work in progress'. It's all about the journey (as clichéd as that sounds), and about improving your songwriting technique or musicianship, your singing, your record production. The process never ends and is forever fascinating as a result. It's why we keep making new work – because the old work is never truly satisfying. You always feel that you can improve and express yourself using clearer, better, more poetic language. I'm on a creative journey and I hope it will never end.

Beattie and I loved the way writers like Jagger and Richards, Jim Morrison, Lou Reed, Ray Davies and Iggy Pop could say what they needed to say in a song in two or three verses at the most. We dug Dylan too but his spiteful and malevolent put-down amphetamine phantasmagorias lasting seven or eight verses of Symbolist and Beat imagery were way out of our reach. We knew that Bobby was a natural-born poet and way out of sight; after all I'd listened to him at home since as far back as I could remember. I had been writing poetry since 1980 using my mum's typewriter and cutting out the finished poems and sticking them in a blue notebook. I was into words but never told anyone and kept it to myself, even when I had been a member of the Wake. I was biding my time. I had been inspired after reading that Paul Weller of the Jam had started a publishing company: Riot Stories. Weller announced this in the music press and asked for kids to send in their poetry, short stories or novels and if he dug 'em enough he would publish them. Then as now the literary world was way out of reach for working-class people, especially the teenagers who made up the Jam's mass audience. I saw Weller's intervention as a truly punk-rock gesture. I love that man. I never ever intended to send my poems to Riot Stories but just knowing that it existed made me feel good, that someone *cared* about people like me.

Beattie and I set about attempting to write songs using the techniques and structures of the classic sixties tracks we had fallen in love with. It wasn't easy. Back in summer 1981 when Beattie and I had been primal screaming in the scout hall we also recorded straight onto his two-track tape machine. Beattie would play his bass guitar through an echo unit. He pushed the sound until it became extremely distorted and each note resembled the broken, orange-coloured stone fragment muscle-panels that make up the body of the Thing from the Fantastic Four. Sometimes I can visualise sound, almost synaesthetically, and Beattie's bass sounded like the Thing looked, bursting with supernatural cosmic power. I kept time by putting a microphone inside PiL's Metal Box, the actual film can replica, and that went through the echo unit as well. We recorded a primitive version of 'Good Times' by Chic and 'Fever' by the Cramps (Mum owned the original Peggy Lee version on a ten-inch 78 rpm single which was cut loud as fuck). Some record that is; sexy like only they could do in the fifties.

Beattie bought an acoustic twelve-string guitar because we really liked the idea of folk-rock bands like Love and the Byrds, and he was hooked on Roger McGuinn's jingle-jangle magic Rickenbacker guitar sound. I also became addicted to the Byrds and Love. I found a sixties original-issue Vox Phantom guitar for sale for £150 and arranged a time and date to take the train out to Motherwell to pick it up. The seller's house resembled the ones in *Brookside*: it was in a working-class suburb and had a little garden outside. I knocked on the door expecting to see an old burnt-out hippie but a really normal un-rock-and-roll man in his forties answered and invited me in. He took me into his living room and there it was: a beautiful sky-blue Vox Phantom as played by my hero Sterling Morrison, guitarist extraordinaire of the Velvet Underground. I picked it up, strummed a few chords and instantly it felt familiar. In fact this guitar *was* to become my 'familiar', a magical object capable of summoning up psychic power and divining lightning. I handed over the money and put the guitar back in its case, walked out of the little house and all the way back to the train station. When I got home, I started writing the first Primal Scream songs.

Beattie and I would hang out in his mum's front room where the record player was. The albums were laid out on two different shelves under the record deck. His big brother's albums (Camel, ELP, Tull, Yes, Genesis, Peter Gabriel, Tangerine Dream) on one side and Jim's (Sex Pistols, Clash, PiL, Joy Division, Banshees, Jam, Psychedelic Furs, Velvet Underground, Iggy, Doors, Bunny Wailer, Lee Perry and Dr Alimantado) on the other. We would sit and listen to music and jam song ideas on the Phantom and twelve-string. I had written a song called 'Gentle Tuesday' and sang it to Jim playing my chord sequence. He joined in and immediately began playing beautiful, highly melodic arpeggiated guitar chimes that curled around the lyric like stoned cigarette smoke whilst supporting the song with a gentle, propulsive, oceanic rhythm.

We wrote another song called 'Leaves' in the same way, then 'All Fall Down' and 'It Happens' and 'We Go Down Slowly Rising'; over the summer of 1984 the music just poured out of us. We wanted to record these new creations of ours to see if they sounded as good coming out of speakers as they did in our heads and so I got in touch with Elliot Davies. Elliot had a TEAC (Tokyo Electro-Acoustic Company) four-track recording machine through which sound could be transferred onto a common C-90 cassette tape. These TEAC machines were fashionable for a while because they enabled people to demo their song ideas cheaply at home instead of shelling out loads of cash to enter a professional recording studio. Elliot knew and liked Beattie. He thought Beattie was eccentric and unhinged, but in a nice way. On a sunny day we recorded two early versions of 'Gentle Tuesday' and 'Leaves', with me on rhythm guitar and vocals and Beattie on twelve-string acoustic and bass. Beattie programmed the drums on a Roland 606 drum machine. Once we'd bashed out the tracks we mixed them to our satisfaction. Beattie was very good at balancing sounds, he loved recording and manipulating sound.

As we listened back to our new demo Elliot said to me, 'The songs are both very good but, Bob, you're no singer.'

I said, 'What do you mean, Elliot?'

'You're not a proper singer like Al Green or Marti Pellow, you're more like Bernard from New Order.'

I replied, 'If I sound like Bernard then that's good enough for me.'

Elliot had a great, wide-ranging record collection, because he'd worked at the Listen shop: lots of Stax, Motown, Philly soul, disco, UK indie punk, post-punk and psychedelic sixties, but his thing wasn't really rock and roll. He loved Marvin Gaye, Al Green and Dexy's Midnight Runners, especially their *Too-Rye-Ay* era. He was always kind and generous towards me and he was a lot like me in so much as he was a loner. He was a skinny, bespectacled Glaswegian Jewish kid who loved music with a passion. He also discovered the comedian Jerry Sadowitz doing card tricks in the street one day and asked him if he had a manager. When Jerry said no, Elliot offered his services. At this point Elliot, just like myself, was claiming unemployment benefit and having the rent for his two-bedroom flat on Pollokshaws Road paid by the Social. He saw the dark, devastatingly hilarious comic genius of Sadowitz way before the rest of the world and he deserves credit for that. That summer of 1984 he was managing Sadowitz and Wet Wet Wet from the opulence of his social security Pollokshaws Road flat. Not a bad start in showbusiness.

One evening I went round to visit Elliot and the writer Andrea Miller was there. Andrea was *NME*'s Glasgow stringer. I had read her emotionally detached, slightly imperious live reviews in the paper, a bit snobby, I thought. In real life she was very friendly although in a guarded manner. Never get close with a music journalist, ever. Andrea had brought a friend along, an eighteen-year-old girl named Karen Parker. As the night progressed and they raced through two bottles of wine I discovered that Karen worked in Barclays Bank and was also a photographic student taking night classes. That is where she had met Andrea. Karen was heavily into the Birthday Party and the newly formed Nick Cave and the Bad Seeds.

Karen reminded me of a young Leslie Caron: dark brown hair cut short in an androgynous bob, her cat-like eyes burning with energy and intelligence. Her voluptuous figure and bee-stung lips drew me in like nectar. We went along with Elliot and Andrea to a couple of music-related events and I could feel that there was a strong mutual attraction developing between us. I asked Karen out on a date – my choice of meeting-place was the Necropolis cemetery in the centre of Glasgow. Ever the romantic. To my great delight she agreed and we arranged to meet there on a Saturday afternoon. There was a playful erotic frisson between us as we walked amongst the dead and the ostentatious tombs and statues commemorating the extremely wealthy Glaswegian tobacco barons and industrialists of the nineteenth century. Glasgow wasn't known across the world as 'the Merchant City' for nothing, you know. Our walk and talk amongst the gothic monuments of Imperial grandeur seemed to go quite well and pretty soon afterwards we became a couple; when I wasn't writing songs with Jim I'd spend most of my time hanging out with Karen. I'd go into town to meet her on her lunch break from her job at the bank where she worked as a teller, and we'd go to Pizza Hut for lunch. Karen was as much into music as I was, and when I went to her house I discovered she had a great record collection. Alongside her Birthday Party, Cramps and Iggy albums Karen had records by artists such as John Lee Hooker, Hank Williams, Lightnin' Hopkins, Nina Simone and Howlin' Wolf. I was very impressed. I liked the way she dressed too – black and white tartan skirt just above the knee combined with a sixties brown suede box jacket, black woollen tights and flat shoes – never heels, at that point, though they came a couple of years later when she really got into Vivienne Westwood's designs. Sometimes she wore flower-print dresses, always sleeveless, again, a very fifties, early sixties style. We were all taking ourselves out of the present – removal as rebellion – a kind of dissociative rebellion into style, secondhand dreams of a future now. In a sense the prevalent indie-girl style of the mid-eighties was very non-sexual and kind of androgynous, which makes sense as a lot of the girls and boys who came to see the early Scream shows were teenagers – schoolkids not yet settled in their sexuality and self-awareness. The indie-girl style was a conscious reaction against the sexualisation and commodification of the portrayal of women in society, an act of rebellion against expectations of how women should present themselves exclusively for the male gaze and pleasure. It was a rebellion against straight society. It was also the only way that most people who were fans of indie music could afford to dress: charity-shop chic, jumble-sale aesthetics. Mostly we were looking for clothes from the sixties, which was another androgynous time.

Out in the straight world the eighties was a time of big-shoul-dered suits for men and tight waists, shoulder-pads and plunging necklines for women; the concept of 'power dressing' was all the rage. In tailoring, 'maleness' was exaggerated to boost the already inflated, cocaine-driven egos of the new lords of the world, the 'City Boys' of financial capital which had replaced heavy industry as the main driver of the UK and US economies. Women were encouraged to 'power dress' too – getting ready to do battle in the boardroom as a prequel to the pleasures of the bedroom was the selling point of a certain strain of eighties designer fashion: money + desire + success + sex = 'style'. Greed was good; rich was sexy and poor was not. The winners take it all and the losers take the fall, every time. Capitalism is all about winners; a Porsche car and an Armani suit were the sure signs of success in the age of greed.

But as we know, money doesn't buy you style; style is some-thing you are born with. Dressing like a boy is a good place to hide for girls, just as boys were feminising themselves and dressing and acting androgynously. There was a blurring of boundaries, a rejection of the old differences. I was aware of these stylistic acts of agency and the potency of putting it into practice on the street and stage. I remember one evening going over to Karen's house and when she answered the door she looked really different. She'd hennaed her hair to a reddish colour and it had transformed her somehow. Her lips looked even fuller and redder than before and it made her complexion more translucent, more ghostly. Her new hair colour gave her more confidence, which in turn is very sexy. I think she got the idea after seeing a photograph of Anita

Lane, Nick Cave's girlfriend, muse and sometime songwriting partner.

Karen would accompany me to Paddy's Market to look for secondhand clothes. She was an avid reader of *I-D*, *BLITZ* and *The Face* and also *Elle* magazine. There was a model who featured in *Elle* a lot named Jeny Howorth who we both admired. She had her hair cut short like a boy's and wore tight black polo necks and black tights with miniskirts; hardly any make-face up except a touch of black liner and blood-red lipstick; a very clean, sharp and timeless image. Karen was influenced as much by Jeny's style as the rock boys and girls she worshipped.

Later on when I made some money playing with the Jesus and Mary Chain I was able to buy Karen some nice designer pieces by Vivienne Westwood (a 'Versailles'-style eighteenth-century bustier and a black velvet ruffled flap skirt which looked DYNAMITE together) and a fantastic deep-red corduroy dress with a really unusual, eye-catching feature around the chest (Björk wore one when she was in the Sugarcubes) from the Glaswegian designer and my great friend Pam Hogg, which we bought from her stall in Hyper Hyper on Kensington High Street. We had a lot of fun going through to Edinburgh on the train from Queen Street Station looking for record shops and just being young and in love. Karen was such a beautiful, kind, gentle soul and I had the comfort of knowing that she really cared for and loved me. This in turn gave me confidence. She was a cool girlfriend. Sometimes her openness and welcoming personality was perceived as naivety by some. She had a childlike sense of wonder about the world and life and she really did live for music. Her love of her favourite artists like Rowland S. Howard, Iggy or Suicide was unconditional. Karen, like myself, was a romantic. And romantics feel things more than most people. It's easy to hurt romantics because they already feel too much. Karen could sometimes be a touch oversensitive and at times lacking in confidence. But together we made a strong couple and we empowered each other. Life was good.

One time I came home from a Jesus and Mary Chain tour in Europe or America to find that Karen had a present for me: a riverboat gamblers' tie, just like the ones bad guys wear in cowboy movies. It was tied in a bow at the top and had two ribbons coming out at angles either side beneath the bow. The fabric was an off-white colour with flecks of blood on it. I asked her where it came from and she replied, 'Me and Louise Wright went to see Johnny Thunders play at Night Moves and we got down the front row. We were practically sat on the stage directly at the feet of him. We were both tripping on acid. Johnny's tie fell off whilst he was singing and I grabbed it as it fell on the stage; he was asking for it back over the microphone but I put it in my pocket and kept it as a gift for you as I know you were sad to miss his show. So here, it's yours now.' I was totally blown away by this show of devotion and love.

I have kept Johnny's bow tie with me all through the years, through every flat and house move I've ever done, from town to city, and it's become a kind of talisman for me. I even wore it when I married my wife Katy in 2006, along with a Gram Parsons and Nudie Cohn-inspired suit that was made for me by Alexander McQueen. You can't put your arms around a memory, but I can always hold Johnny Thunders' tie in my hand and feel the mojo magic of rock and roll. It is a true fetish object invested with occult power, stained with JT's blood. When I put it on I remember the innocent glory days of young love.

Over the years of our relationship Karen also bought me great books on songwriting, with sheet music and lyrics by masters such as Bob Dylan and Neil Young. These books were a huge influence on my development as a young songwriter. I learned about song structure and new guitar chords from these books at the same time as being inspired by the power and poetry of the words. Thoughtful presents indeed.

*

Earlier that year Beattie and I had gone to the Candy Club, which took place in the function suite of the Lorne Hotel on Sauchiehall Street, across the road from the Hellfire Club. The Kitchenware band Hurrah! were playing that night. We went out for something to do on a cold miserable Sunday night because I knew the Club was being promoted by Nick Lowe; not, of course, the amazing genius who wrote '(What's So Funny 'Bout) Peace Love and Understanding' and 'Cruel to be Kind'; this Nick Lowe had been at Glasgow High secondary school and was Innes's best friend. Nick was a lovely guy, very gentle but sharp and intelligent too. He's a successful BBC Radio producer these days.

After the show finished Beattie and I went over to say bye to Nick and he asked us what we were both up to. We replied that we were going to start a rock and roll band but we only had two members and at some point we were going to have to find other people, but weren't sure how to find anyone who was into the music that we loved.

By 1984 punk rock was seen as an embarrassment in the UK music papers, and the self-appointed 'hip' people in Glasgow were all Bowie Young Americans casualties dressed in awful clothes and dry, limp quiffs playing white-boy 'funk' that was as funky as Margaret and Dennis Thatcher attempting to dance the Funky Chicken: naff central. Glasgow was full of Postcard rejects or aspirational neds who thought they were Young Soul Rebels. The one thing they all had in common was that none of them had any class whatsoever, either in the way they dressed or the soulless music that they made. It was always all about fame, not being an artist, none of them had anything to say. Nick told us that a couple of guys had given him their demo tape at the Candy Club only the week before. He told me that *he* wasn't into the music, but he really impressed upon Beattie and me that *we* were both gonna dig it (plus there was a Syd Barrett album taped on the other side of the cassette; Nick knew how into Syd we were so he took that as a sign that we would have a connection with these mystery guys).

# 11.

# The Sash My Granny Wore at the Acid Factory

I got out of bed and opened the package that the postman had dropped through my door, excited to see what it contained. I didn't receive much in the way of letters or messages from afar in those pre-Scream days, and was delighted to see that it contained a C-90 cassette tape and a short note from Nick Lowe.

Dear Bobby,
So good to see you and big Jim the other night at the Candy Club. Here is that tape I was telling you about. Maybe you could ask these two guys to join your band?
All the best,
Nick

On the cardboard cover of the tape were written these words in black ballpoint pen in an almost childlike scrawl: '*Jesus and Mary Chain* – Never Understand, Upside Down, Inside Me, In A Hole'. Then it said, 'Contact Douglas Hart' and an East Kilbride telephone number. I placed the tape into my red Japanese Mitsubishi cassette player and a distorted drum machine came bursting out of the speakers followed by blasts of white noise synthesiser. Then the singer came in.

*Sun comes up, another day begins*
*And I don't even worry about the state I'm in*

Fucking hell! This sounds like Suicide with Billy Idol on vocals. As the song progressed I realised that these two guys could actually write a proper pop rock and roll song with hooks. The next song was titled 'Upside Down' and it too possessed the same Suicide–Billy Idol killer combo sound. The other two songs were very Joy Division to my mind but I dug them all the same.

I was so excited by my discovery that I immediately called Beattie to tell him about this tape I had just received. We both agreed we should get in touch with these guys and ask if they wanted to form a band with us. I called the number on the tape cover and an older woman answered, obviously the guy's mother. I asked if Douglas was in and she replied that he was at college but if I gave her my number she would get him to ring me back when he got home later that afternoon. Douglas Hart says that on that first phone call his mum asked me, 'Are you famous?' and I replied, 'Not yet, but I will be.' I honestly have no recollection of that, but hey, I'll take it.

At around 7 p.m. I called Douglas again. I explained who I was and that I had a copy of their demo and loved it. I also asked if he and his partner wanted to make a new band with myself and Beattie. Douglas told me that there were actually four of them and that they had a new name too: the Jesus and Mary Chain. We spoke excitedly for at least two hours about bands, records and films we both loved and discovered to our mutual delight that we shared a lot of the same obsessions and influences. He told me that the 'white noise synth' was a guitar. Fuck, what a guitar sound, I thought to myself: a totally overdriven fuzz-tone dementia psychosis transformed into soundwaves of brain-crashing heavenly bliss. These guys had songs to die for. He asked if we wanted to co-promote a gig with them in Glasgow as they had sent their tape with these four songs out to every radio station, newspaper, student union and pub venue in Scotland and to all the gig venues in London but had had no replies or interest. He told me that I was the first person to like their music and show any positive interest in them. I informed him that Beattie and I had only just started writing songs plus we had no band and that's why I was calling him.

After the call I felt totally energised and inspired. Beattie and I had thought we were the only two people in Scotland who still believed in the power of punk. We were both psychedelic obsessives and had been greedily finding any information on the ultra-damaged poster-boy of underground rock: the dark, doomed, romantic, poetic boy from Cambridge who was crucified on a lysergic cross, Syd Barrett. Back in the eighties, before the information deluge of retro rock mags such as *Mojo* and *Uncut*, no one knew anything about misterioso figures such as Arthur Lee, Syd Barrett, Brian Wilson, Alex Chilton; these guys were shrouded in myth and underground legend. Their unavailability and disappearance from the contemporary music scene only added to their mystery and otherworldly attractiveness to people like myself and Jim Beattie. Not a lot of people were really interested in these artists. They were all seen as sixties drug casualties and burnouts, embarrassments from another era.

I arranged to meet the Mary Chain boys on a Tuesday, a beautiful June afternoon, outside Boots the Chemist on Argyle Street. I got there slightly earlier than planned to find the three boys waiting for me. We introduced ourselves to each other and went to find a café. They all wore ripped blue jeans like Ramones. I was wearing ripped jeans too, clearly a good sign. They all had hair stacked high, not like goths, more like an exaggerated Bunnymen thing. Jim and William both had brown curly hair that was wispy and light in texture. Douglas's was jet black with tight curls. He was noticeably younger than the other two. They were very polite and friendly. I asked about the other member. Where was he?

'Murray, the drummer, oh, he's at school.'

We found a café and sat down and they asked me if we would play a joint show with them. I told them our predicament but said that when we had a drummer and a couple more songs we would definitely play with them.

Luckily, though, the band had already started to expand. Robert Young, or 'Dungo', as he was known around the Mount area, had grown up on the same street as Beattie. He played bass in a band called Black Easter led by a kid from King's Park named Blair Cowan. I'd known Robert from the early seventies when we used to play football together. He was a short, chubby kid who always seemed to be wearing a purple and white Hibernian away strip. Robert is the only person in my life that I've ever seen wear a Hibs top in Glasgow apart from psychotic Hibs fans travelling through from Edinburgh for matches.

Dungo was a soft little boy who was bullied a lot. I remember one Christmas in the late seventies when I was making my way back home from a day's shift at John Horn's. As I climbed the steep slope on Brownlie Street I saw him at the bottom of the stairs to his tenement. We called over the street to each other.

'What did you get for Christmas?' I asked him.

'A telecaster guitar,' he said.

'Wow! That's amazing,' I said, 'can you play it?'

'Yes,' he said. 'Do you want to come up to my house and see it?'

We climbed up to the second floor of the tenement, my first and only time in his home. His dad had a weird energy surrounding him and whenever us kids would see him on the street we'd all look the other way. He gave off an unfriendly vibe. I followed Dungo down the dark hallway and into his bedroom where he excitedly took the cream-coloured Fender telecaster copy out of its cardboard box and picked it up and started playing the tense, clipped opening riff to the Clash song, 'English Civil War'. I couldn't believe what I was hearing: this fourteen-year-old kid who was being bullied on the street was playing a Clash song nearly as good as Mick Jones himself. What the fuck is this?

He sounded amazing. Robert was a street friend of my brother Graham and they were both in the same year at school. Graham had hipped him to punk rock by playing him some of my records back at our house, and Dungo had asked me if I would make him compilation tapes of my best punk rock albums and singles. I made him some tapes and I enjoyed turning the young kid on. He was a humble boy then though clearly quietly delighted that I'd admired his new guitar and more importantly that I recognised his ability to play it. I left his house that night thinking how cool it was that this little kid had worked out how to play punk guitar. Years later I would think back to that night and realise that Robert just *had it* from the start. Pure fucking talent, raw and passionate and straight from his heart and soul, just as the tattoo on his arm said.

So in summer 1984 I poached Robert from Black Easter, and Robert added his unique melodic bass playing to our psychedelic stew. He respected the fact I'd been a member of the Wake and he recognised that Beattie and I were much more serious in our ambitions than the guys in Black Easter. The original Primal Scream sound flew high on Beattie's newly discovered guitar style; the product of time spent mainlining Roger McGuinn's twelve-string jingle-jangle chiming arpeggio magic on repeated listening to the *Mr Tambourine Man* album. Robert had been similarly fixing on Love's first album as well. His bass style was a folk-rock–post-punk mash-up with a killer mixture comprising Byrd Chris Hillman's McCartneyesque folk–funk stylings with more than a dash of Love bassist Ken Forssi's ultra-hoodlum attack setting mixed with Peter Hook's driving romantic melodicism. My words and vocals sat dead centre between these twin instrumental magicians and the 606 drum machine was programmed with 'flying cymbals' disco beats. We were aiming for a mix of ecstatic sixties joyous transcendental psychedelic pop and modern eighties electronic dance beats.

\*

At that first meeting with the Mary Chain they told me how no one would give them a gig anywhere. I mentioned that I had a friend in London who had just recently started up his own small independent record label, Creation Records, who also ran a club called the Living Room above a pub in Fitzrovia near the Post Office Tower. I said I would call him on their behalf and insist he give them a gig. I rang McGee that night, ranting and raving about this new band I'd met called the Jesus and Mary Chain and how he *had* to give them a gig. I added their songs were brilliant and that of the tracks that I'd heard, they already had *two* classic singles ready to be unleashed on the world, and that he, McGee, should be releasing the record. Alan said, 'Cool, Bob, if you're into it, it must be alright, give those guys my address and tell them to send me their demo tape, if I like it, I'll put them on at the club.' I did so, and McGee thought the tape was OK, nothing brilliant, but he gave them a gig anyway on my recommendation.

One Sunday afternoon McGee called me and he was babbling at a thousand miles per hour like he'd just swallowed three grams of the Essex Hells Angels' finest bathtub amphetamine. 'Gillespie,' he said, 'the Mary Chain were *total genius* last night.'

I said, 'Wow, tell me what happened.'

McGee gurgled out that Jim and William got so pished on beer before the gig that during the first song William played the chords to 'In A Hole' but Jim was singing 'Upside Down' and Douglas was playing the notes to 'Inside Me'; they only got a verse or so into the song before the whole thing collapsed and the brothers had a fist-fight onstage but the punches never landed because they were both so pished. Then they all ran off and that was the end of the gig. Alan kept screaming down the phone to me, 'They're GENIUS! GENIUS! GENIUS!' It was no surprise to me at all.

Throughout the summer of 1984 Alan got the JAMC gigs through his contacts on the London indie circuit, mostly in the back rooms of pubs or in small Soho clubs where there was a scene that catered to neo-psych and psychobilly tastes. McGee knew them all.

I was their champion. I really believed in them. They were real outsiders, just like Beattie and me. Eventually, this support paid off; people were starting to notice the Mary Chain, so McGee decided to cut a single.

In the summer of 1984 the Reids, Douglas and I and a few others decided to take an acid trip together. We went up to East Kilbride where they used to trip at this place they called the Acid Factory. It was an abandoned post-industrial wasteland. The Mary Chain would go into this abandoned factory, listen to music and take photographs. It looked post-apocalyptic, like something from *The Omega Man* starring Charlton Heston, really cool.

Jim, William, Douglas, myself and Beattie met at the factory one Saturday afternoon in mid-July, the 12th, as it happened. We took another couple of mates with us, one called Paul Harte and another mate of his from Castlemilk called Big Paul (he eventually formed the band the Submarines, who opened for us at Splash One a year later). Paul Harte was a close friend of mine and we used to listen to Cabaret Voltaire's *Sensoria / Crackdown* album and bit of Psychic TV and watch those *Doublevision / Ralph Records* VHS compilation videos together up in his flat. He was into post-punk industrial stuff, Pistols and PiL. On this occasion the two Pauls didn't take any acid, only Beattie, myself and the three Chain boys.

I remember telling McGee about our psychedelic date over the phone a few days beforehand. I said, 'The Scream and the Mary Chain, we're gonna take acid together this Saturday.'

McGee said, 'It's a meeting of minds. It's gonna be legendary.'

The trip began well and there was some deep soul bonding going on between us and the Mary Chain. They had a cassette player with them which played compilation tapes they had made especially for the trip. I remember 'I Wanna Be Your Dog' playing as Jim Reid smashed a metal pipe he'd found into a concrete wall, making a beautiful percussive sound. I wished I could have recorded that moment on audio tape, I still have it in my visual memory, like Neubauten meets Yoruba, the sound of primitive violence meets industrial ritual. 'Caveman' by the Cramps was playing as I sat on my haunches on the burning ground as the sun beat down on us. I picked up stumps of two tree branches and beat them in time to the Cramps primitive-modernist rock and roll classic. I seemed to regress backwards through time, and I felt myself undergoing a transformation through millions of years of anthropological 'civilisational development', returning to my true primitive state until I became the caveman in the song. Each beat of my tree-branch drumsticks reverberated in bluish-purple sound and images became noise. I could hear the colours as well as see them; this was some powerful motherfucking acid. My outwards and inwards vision was synched in perfect time with the rhythm, I felt godlike.

But the god delusion wore off and soon I had visions of millions of locusts everywhere. Everywhere I looked the greeny-brown texture of the grass had turned into locusts. We were outside East Kilbride in the Scottish countryside, the Acid Factory was surrounded by farmer's fields and a wood. There was green grass everywhere and somehow in my warped, paranoid and fast-melting acid-zapped mind, I told myself that if I stood on a tree stump or a stone I was safe from the locusts. I wouldn't move from the tree stump because everywhere the grass looked like locusts to me and I was so gone on the acid that I couldn't speak. I was imprisoned in my own self-made private hell.

By this time Jim and William had gone off together some-where. I later found out that William had been having a bad trip as well and was freaking out because he had hallucinated spiders crawling into his brain via his eyes. He had that long curly fringe hanging over his eyes and imagined it was spiders intent on eating his brains. Real horror movie stuff. The two Pauls, not on acid, were saying, 'Let's go, let's get out of these woods.'

I was saying, 'I ain't fucking moving, I ain't fucking moving.' None of them could see what I was seeing. Later on I would write the lyrics for the song 'Burning Wheel', which describes the self-induced paranoid psychosis I wrought on myself through my years of chemical experimentation. This was the beginning of all that.

After the trip I discovered that during my freak-out I had taken all my clothes off and clambered on Douglas Hart. He didn't know how to push me off. He was so terrified, tripping out, he just lay there. He later told me that the longer I lay on top of him out there in the woods, the more he felt like he was being slowly reduced to a piece of cardboard, getting thinner and thinner and thinner and thinner with me on top of him like a naked corpse. He was nervously mumbling, 'Bobby! Bobby! Bobby! Please get off me.' Douglas also told me that while we were in the woods tripping he heard the sound of gunshots hitting the trees and saw a local ned firing an air-rifle in our direction. Doug walked over to where the rifle-toting ned was standing to tell him that I was on acid and having a freak-out and to please not aim in our direction. Mr Trigger-Happy thankfully acquiesced to Doug's plea.

I have a near-complete blackout about these two episodes, something that would reoccur again and again in my future drug and drinking career. I also have a blackout regarding running out into the middle of the country road naked to attack moving cars, though I'm told it happened. When I eventually got home that night and looked in the mirror I could see that my face and hair were smeared and matted, covered in filth and dirt from the hard, dry ground in the countryside. I had been rolling about in fucking dirt in the forest, all day, naked. My friends later told me that they'd had to dress me.

Once the acid had begun to wear off and some of my rational senses had returned, we left the woods and started to walk back towards the town centre of East Kilbride so that Jim, myself and the two Pauls could get the bus back to Glasgow and the sanity of civilisation. As we walked up the neverending steep hills around East Kilbride under an unforgiving hot sun I was sweating buckets. But the nightmare wasn't over yet. Walking up towards the town I saw some buildings. They were five storeys high at most, these flats, and I was walking up this fucking endless hill, puffing and panting and sweating, on the hottest day of the year so far. I could just see the buildings expanding and contracting in time with my breathing. I breathed in, they contracted inwards; I breathed out, they expanded outwards ... and I kept thinking that the roofs on this council estate were all gonna explode at any moment and blow right off. When the roofs blow off the houses then the top of my skull would too, and my brains were gonna come flying out just like the inhabitants of the flats and all their furniture and belongings. My heart was beating fast and hard, pounding with existential fear, echoing BOOM! BOOM! BOOM! in my brain as I walked up the hill to my personal Golgotha. I felt dirty and guilty and told myself I deserved to feel like this, that I only had myself to blame for my psychedelic sins because only a fool would mess with this demonic stuff. It was the devil's own poison. Only seasoned trippers could navigate the treacherous, psychotropic oceans onto which each mysterious journey into the uncharted territories of deep mind and soul exploration that was an acid trip could take you. I was ashamed to admit that I was just an amateur, a weekend sailor who had crashed on the rocks and was now cognisant enough that within a few minutes' time I would witness the true price of my folly. I heard the sound of a martial drumbeat echoing around my frazzled skull. What the fuck is that, I thought, then I stopped walking and turned around.

Through the heat haze of the late afternoon and my skewed, goggle-eyed acid vision I saw the sight of an Orange pipe and drum band marching slowly up the road towards where us acid-stragglers were stood on the pavement. I swear that the pipe band and Lodge members morphed into an enormous creature resembling a huge orange slug, leaving a trail of greasy orange slime behind them. They had set off from East Kilbride earlier that morning and marched into Glasgow playing their triumphalist Protestant battle songs, all instrumental on flute with drum and accordion accompaniment. I knew all the words to these songs. I had grown up with them. The Orange Order had gathered yearly in Palermo Street every 12th July to commemorate King Billy's victory over the armies of the Catholic King James at the Battle of the Boyne in 1690. You couldn't escape that date. It was spray-painted on walls all over Glasgow, denim jackets and school desks; some headcases had it tattooed on their arms as well, in a rough, homemade 'prison style'. As an innocent child I had watched the band leader throw his mace in the air, topped with a heavy, imperious, gleaming silver head-stock. The length of the mace was covered in red, white and blue ribbons. I'd made my own version out of an old mop handle painted silver and festooned it in garlands. All the boys on my street did it, and we would have competitions to see who could throw their stick the highest and catch it before it hit the ground. I was good at this game. We copied the way the band leader moved the mace from side to side, over his back and round his neck before throwing it high in the air again to the cheers of the marchers and camp followers.

The pipe bands and their leaders looked glamorous and exciting to a seven-year-old with no idea of the sectarian bigotry that the Orange march represented. To us, the band looked just like the soldiers we saw in Medieval or Napoleonic-era action adventure movies minus the armour and horses. By six o'clock the Orange band and their followers had endured a day of seriously heavy drinking. Once the speeches had been made by the high-ranking Lodge leaders in Glasgow Green, camp followers and band members would get seriously tanked up for the long journey home to whatever part of Glasgow or Lanarkshire they came from.

As the big orange slug crawled past us at funereal speed my eyes fixed on the fat, sweaty faces of the pipe band musicians: up close they all had bright red faces from being exposed to the sun all day without wearing suncream. Their burnt faces were exaggerated on the acid, their Hiroshima-like faces melted in the summer heat. I had no cause to fear the Orange men and women because I was no threat to them, merely watching their final ascent back to their home town. They didn't even notice me, Beattie and the two Pauls. They'd had a long day and so had we. I remember thinking whilst watching them march that I had got what I deserved. My psychic crucifixion was complete.

We took a bus home to Glasgow in a changed mood, the two Pauls giving me strange looks. They told me scattered stories about my behaviour and I said nothing. I couldn't defend myself – I was still only just hanging onto reality. Jim was still tripping too, so he was quiet, staring out the window and at his feet. He normally always had something sick and sarcastic to say but he kept schtum.

When I finally opened my front door there was nobody home, thank god, so I climbed the small flight of stairs in our semi-detached house in Croftfoot, entered the bathroom, quickly stripped my dirt-covered clothes off, looked at myself in the mirror and saw that the contours of my face and eyes were outlined in purple and blue trails of colour that would jolt every few seconds as though someone had fitted electrodes to my body: *jolt! jolt! jolt!* My central nervous system was fighting back after being unnaturally overloaded by the poison I had discharged into my body six or so hours before. Drug sweat poured out of every pore in my body and my hair was thick with clumps of dirt, greased and matted. No matter how much soap or shampoo I used, I just couldn't wash the dirt out of my hair and skin or the sin out of my soul.

I really did feel a sense of deep guilt and shame about the embarrassment of the two Pauls' revelations. I hoped that once the acid had subsided and had finally been sweated, pissed and shat out from my body that I would somehow retain my sanity and return to my normal state of mental and spiritual balance; even though that 'balance' was sometimes tipped by melancholic tendencies, it was easier to deal with than this lysergic horrorshow. I called Karen and asked if I could stay over at her house. I boarded the 31 bus into St Enoch Square in town then took a bus from Argyll Street all the way over to Mount Vernon, a suburb in the East End, way out beyond Bridgeton, Parkhead and Shettleston. She opened the door to her parents' house and took me up into her bedroom. Sweet sanctity at last.

We took quite a bit of acid over that summer. We would give our money to a guy nicknamed Joogs who had also been present that day at the Acid Factory. Joogs would go find the acid dealer Sammy, who we renamed 'the Tripmaker': The Tripmaker was maybe in his late thirties. He had shoulder-length stringy orange hair and was a wiry, slightly nervous, suspicious little man. He was a hangover from the hippie days of the early seventies and the skin on his face looked like it was permanently peeling, not from sunburn but some unseen cosmic force chipping away at his mortality, like his very being was being stripped away slowly, in real time. He was a real-life acid casualty. Aside from all that, I think he was a nice enough guy, no hassle and not a heavy in any way.

Joogs was a guy I'd been seeing around town at gigs and record shops and Paddy's Market for a few years. We would nod to each other in mutual punk recognition but nothing more. One day or night somewhere we got talking and discovered that we both loved a lot of the same music. The Cramps were a mutual favourite. He was also, like us, bored of ninety-nine per cent of the contemporary music scene and had started to explore the forgotten garage punk, psychedelic rock sounds of the sixties. He invited me to his flat in Govanhill to check out his sounds.

Joogs lived with his family in a tenement flat in Allison Street, just across the street from the old guy barbers where Beattie and I would go to get our haircuts. This barber was wild. When you walked into his 'salon', a storefront at street level, you found yourself in a dark den with a few sinks and mirrors, four leather barber's chairs, no lightbulbs, the only light coming in through the traffic-stained window from the street. He had slats of wood that he would place across the chair arms whenever a mum or dad would bring a little kid in for a trim so the kid would be lifted high enough in the chair. The barber (I never knew his name) didn't seem to have many customers. Whenever Beattie and I went in he was always stood on his own sharpening an open razor on a black leather belt, proper Sweeney Todd gear. He'd ask what we wanted and we'd both say 'Hitler Youth'. He didn't need to see any photographs. He shaved us high at the back and sides and I always kept my fringe long. He was lethal with that razor, so we had to be careful not to let him go too mad. One pound eighty a cut. When Beattie and I left the 'salon' people would laugh at us in the street, children would point at us and giggle and neds would shout insults at us. This way we knew the cut was good because 'if it upsets the straights it must be great'.

Visiting Joogs at his flat in Alison Street was an experience. My family were very working class and I'd grown up in a nine-teenth-century tenement, but this place was like taking a time machine back to the thirties. There were no carpets in the hall, just bare floorboards worn down over years of proletarian living. The house had a dank, depressing air hanging over it, as if every-one and everything in it was suspended in a state of permanent inertia. Once inside Joogs' bedroom he asked me if I wanted a cup of coffee and I said sure.

Joogs was first and foremost a Cramps fan. He also had twelve-inch singles by Sisters of Mercy and the Birthday Party. He was obsessed by Rowland S. Howard, the Birthday Party's legendary guitarist. He didn't have a lot of sixties stuff yet but was working on it. He did, however, own an album credited to the Seeds on the French EVA label which was a comp of Sky Saxon's early sixties doo-wop singles under the name Little Richie Marsh. This was a bootleg with the classic post-Seeds proto-punk single 'Bad Part of Town' and 'Did He Die'. When we listened to these tracks we realised Johnny Rotten must have been a huge fan of Sky Saxon. Beattie, Joogs and I scoured the monthly record fairs held at the McLellan Galleries on Sauchiehall Street and scored original vinyl by the Electric Prunes, Love's debut on Elektra, Eddie Floyd, Isaac Hayes, Stax singles, Syd-era Floyd singles, Thirteenth Floor Elevators, the Byrds, the Misunderstood . . . and so our search continued.

I found an address for a record shop in Devon in a psych fanzine and sent off for classic garage psych compilation albums such as *Acid Dreams*, *What A Way To Die*, *Perfumed Garden*, *Back from the Grave* and sent off directly to Rhino Records in LA to buy their fantastic *Chocolate Watchband* comp. Line Records in Germany had just reissued the complete Seeds catalogue which was great. We could buy these on import at Virgin in Renfield Street. I went through to Edinburgh with Karen on day trips and shopped at Bruce's where they had a great garage psych section, much deeper than anywhere in Glasgow.

The summer of 1984 we were tripping all the time. We wanted to be like our psychedelic heroes: Jim Morrison, Lux Interior, Roky Erickson, Syd Barrett, Arthur Lee. We just felt, well, if we're gonna play psychedelic music, we need to take psychedelic drugs otherwise you can't be psychedelic. You need to take the trip and experience it. I honestly thought it was going to help me write songs. Obviously you can't write anything when you're on fucking acid. You're too bombed. But I guess the perception, the way you look at the city of Glasgow changes. I remember one night we all did a trip and walked from the Griffin pub all the way home to Mount Florida and then Croftfoot. I remember being down by the Clyde just looking at the suspension bridge and across to the Communist Club, where we used to rehearse, and the Trade Union Club. The Trade Union Club was where my mother worked in the late sixties and early seventies. I remember just thinking it all looked like a beautiful impressionistic oil painting, like a Turner, so beautiful at night. So magical.

One night Karen and I came back to my house after scoring acid at the Griffin. We were in bed and during sex she turned into a badger-like creature, her true feral sexuality revealed to me. One of the things that I loved about drugs was how they break down the day-to-day defences that people erect to protect themselves; all inhibitions are scattered on the winds of lust.

# 12.
# Jesus Walks

I managed to get the Mary Chain their first gig in Glasgow that summer through this guy I knew called Tam Coyle. He'd put on little gigs here and there, nothing big or fancy, but he was really into music. A speccy, nerdy, harmless guy, a gentle working-class boy. Tam always had a big smile when he saw me, he was sincere. 'Alright there, Bobby, how's it goin'?' He occasionally promoted gigs at Night Moves, the rock and roll club one floor above a Chinese restaurant in Sauchiehall Street. I saw a lot of good bands play Night Moves: 23 Skidoo, the Fire Engines, Aztec Camera, REM on their second album tour, Theatre of Hate, A Certain Ratio. It was a place that could hold four, five hundred people so bands at a certain level on the indie circuit could play there. I approached Tam and told him about my friendship with this band from East Kilbride. So he gave them a gig opening for local bands called Rhythm System and Project GK. The Mary Chain's first gig was in Glasgow, 19 June 1984. The band turned up with only their guitars and asked the headline band if they could borrow their gear, drum kit and amps. At this stage they had an eighteen-year-old kid named Murray Dalgliesh playing the drums.

The venue was half full and then the Mary Chain came bounding onto the stage, obviously absolutely battered out of their brains. They were banging into each other. They were bouncing off the amps. It was just noise, carnage, like a junkyard having a nervous breakdown. I mean, it was the sound of a Metallic

189

K.O.; not that they sounded like the Stooges but the *sound* of that album title.

It was so sexual, as well. The sight of these young, skinny guys dressed in rags banging into each other, all of them charged up with high-voltage electrical energy and nervous adrenaline. It was very homoerotic. Other Scottish bands Aztec Camera, Orange Juice, Josef K and the Fire Engines did not possess this malevolent sexuality. The Mary Chain gave off an unhinged aura of violent threat and sexual confusion. They were so shy, nervous, edgy, suspicious and paranoid in real life that when they were on stage it transformed into this four-headed monster of fuzz-tone psychosis and inner space ultra-violence of mind-melting proportions. They were channelling something so deep and powerful that I don't really believe they were aware of how powerful it was; they couldn't control the malevolent spirit energies they summoned. They played about three songs, if that, and it was a cacophonous, violent, fuck-you noise. It was completely unmusical, but at the same time it made complete sense to me and Beattie, because we understood the language. It was innate to us both because we were way into noise. We came from noise, chaos and carnage and their music possessed that same visceral anger. Like all the best music it existed just beyond the reach of language. No words were necessary; their uncontrollable black energy and blank, emotionless faces spoke volumes.

Beattie and I were both thrilled at this display of dissident dissonance and balls-to-the-wall, passive-aggressive confrontation. We stood in the front row up beside the stage. No one liked them except us two. Then they were thrown off stage. The Night Moves bouncers came up on stage and pulled them off to the side and the gig came to an end. The headline band had complained because the Chain were falling into the amps and throwing mic stands around. Later I found out they were so nervous about playing they got drunk so quickly they could hardly stand up. As they were thrown off by the bouncers and hauled through the exit door down the stairs to what we imagined was going to be a beating, Beattie and I looked at each other and said, 'Let's go and help them.' Not that we could help, we weren't tough guys by any stretch, but that's what you did back then.

So we ran after them. I remember standing in the street with Douglas, this wide-shouldered, good-natured, intelligent, curious-minded, handsome eighteen-year-old boy. The girls all liked him. Beattie and I were like, this is fucking religious. We had witnessed the unleashing of this undiscovered black planet of energy in the universe. We both felt like we'd been plugged into the National fucking Grid. Actually, it was better than the National Grid. These guys were supping straight from the source of universal psychedelic punk energy. It was as if we'd been transported to a place we'd always hoped existed but hadn't known whether we'd ever experience it in real life. Tonight we had.

We both poured out the love to the Chain boys, telling them that the gig was a mind-blower and game-changer. These guys would spearhead the next revolution. It was obvious to anyone with a brain and a good set of ears. There was no competition out there, rock and roll was dead in 1984. We all believed in our own romantic way that we could redeem rock and roll, that if kids were exposed to the true primitive power of rock and roll instead of the safe, clean, asexual mind-garbage that they were force-fed by mainstream media and music papers they would respond and be inspired. We needed change, a revolution. There was a shift in consciousness coming and I was going to be part of it. I fell asleep happy.

In September Alan McGee finally recorded a single with the Mary Chain, who were getting little bits of coverage in the weeklies but nothing significant. He called me raving about the genius of the newly recorded single. He told me he was coming all the way up to Glasgow on the overnight bus to see me. He said, 'I'm gonna get the Stagecoach tonight and I want to play it to you – there's two versions and I can't make up my mind which is best. I want you to decide.' So he got the overnight. It cost £10 one way and they gave you a caramel and a small carton of orange juice when you boarded. You could sit anywhere. The overnight Stagecoach going the other way, from Glasgow to London, always had the feeling to me of a bunch of unconnected strangers whose only thing in common was that they were all heading to London to escape their bleak, impoverished pasts and hopefully disappear into a better, more fortunate future. Some luck. It would disembark on a bit of waste ground surrounded by a corrugated iron fence at 7 a.m. on the side of St Pancras Station, on the exact spot where the British Library now stands. It always looked to me like a bomb crater. Welcome to London.

McGee arrived at my house at 8 a.m. which was well early for me at that time being on the dole. He was buzzing, even after the eight-hour trip. He pulled the cassette from his coat pocket and I put it on. I really dug the sound it made, all distorted treble and attack. Alan proceeded to play me two versions of 'Upside Down': the Joe Foster version without feedback, which sounds like Ramones, and then the William Reid and Alan McGee version which is the one everybody knows and loves. I just went, 'That's the one. It's fucking genius.'

'I knew you'd think that,' he said. 'OK, that's what I'm releasing.'

For the B side they'd recorded a cover of the unreleased Syd Barrett / Pink Floyd song 'Vegetable Man'. This song was a favourite of mine and Jim's. We had it on a bootleg vinyl album bought from the record fair at McLellan Galleries. We loved anything from the psych-punk underground that was rare and unreleased. We loved the mystery, myths and stories that surrounded such psychedelic rock misteriosos as Arthur Lee, Sky Saxon, Roky Erickson and Syd. The Mary Chain version of 'Vegetable Man' was as unhinged as the Syd / Floyd version.

These guys were special. This single was killer. Now the rest of the world had to realise it too.

Beattie and I were still trying to put a band together. All through the summer I'd walk from Croftfoot to Mount Florida carrying my Vox Phantom guitar to work on songs we had written together. Once we had worked up a song to the point of having a completed lyric with accompanying guitar chords, top-line vocal melody and Beattie's chiming twelve-string riffs, we would jam it with Robert Young so he could write his bassline. The three of us would sit in the small, cramped, bedroom Beattie shared with his big brother David, gathered around the Tensai two-track tape machine going over the song again and again until Robert was inspired to find a bassline that we all felt was right for the nascent song. This was the real, true essence of the early Primal Scream sound. Three boys from the same street in Mount Florida synching their minds, hearts and souls deep in musical harmony. We were invoking the psychedelic gods. At least to our minds we were. I have always loved the way that music can truly bring people together, because when it's right it is without ego, it's all for one and one for all, and that only happens with certain souls; not everyone can achieve that state of rock and roll grace. It's why only a certain combination of people make classic albums or become a classic band and if they lose a crucial member the sound of the band changes irrevocably forever.

Rock and roll at its highest point is serious magic. An alchemical transformation is possible, but only if people with the right attitudes, minds and spirits are involved in the ritual. Beattie, Robert and myself never really needed to talk much about the songs – or anything else, really – because we had a deep knowledge that can only be learned through the shared experience of living life together on the same streets as kids. Robert was one of the most gifted, talented, natural-born musicians I have ever had the pleasure of working with. Music just poured out of the guy and his melodic inventions were endless. All we had to do was touch his beautiful but damaged soul by writing a song that inspired him, and the ideas just flowed from his heart, mind and body, out through his fingertips onto the strings. He never seemed to have to try too hard to play something great; the best ones don't, they just 'have it', and Robert had it in buckets. Beattie had a raw, untutored natural talent too. His soul-piercing, inventively melodic, uplifting yet plaintive twelve-string guitar excursions chimed with a sun-kissed psychedelic sound summoning up visions of tripping – tripping on sunshine. His golden riffs suggested imaginary flights of escape from the greyness of our surroundings; folk-rock hallucinatory sounds from the Glasgow tenements. We psyched out up there too, you know. Beattie and Robert both played wonderful music that complemented the lyrics beautifully.

I found that whenever I wrote about myself in a true and honest way then the songs were always better, even if I wrote in a codified way using metaphor or in the third person. I could write about my own existential doubts, pains and fears whilst disguising myself as a girl as in 'Gentle Tuesday'. I also discovered that if I wrote lyrics just to fill up some space because I had nothing to say that day then the song wouldn't travel very far. If it was meaningless to me then how could it mean anything to anyone else?

There's a melancholic sadness to a lot of the early Primals music, songs like 'Gentle Tuesday', 'Bewitched and Bewildered', 'May the Sun Shine Bright for You', 'We Go Down Slowly Rising', 'All Fall Down', 'Love You' and 'Aftermath' all have a lovesick, melancholic yearning to them. They are written and sung by a young, depressed boy who views life from a pained, detached, cynical position. The desperation of life and love weighs heavy on the mind. The world is filled with beauty and danger. Existential blues, Glasgow style. The music was deliberately gentle. I sang the most beautiful melodies I could summon from my soul.

Writing melody came easy to me because Beattie and Robert's guitar magic created a chiming lysergic heavenly dream world. We aimed to scramble people's senses with beauty and declaim our poetry in whispers. A soft revolution, a gentle seduction.

I had invited the Govanhill punk rocker Joogs to hang out with us at Beattie's house to listen to the songs we had written. After a while someone suggested he hit a tambourine so he would have something to do instead of just sitting on the edge of the bed listening to us three play and sing. We often tried to be inclusive like this (with mixed results). What Joogs didn't possess in natural rhythmic timing he made up for with garage punk attitude and a certain amount of sartorial style. Still, it showed us what we were missing – we knew that in order to play gigs we had to ditch the Tensai cassette drum machine and find a human being who could keep time.

I don't know how or where we found him, but we did. Tam McGurk lived in a district called Pollok, quite a hard area, on a deprived council estate. He was deep into Echo and the Bunnymen, Simple Minds and the Smiths and not much else. He didn't dress like us, or think like us. We really wanted to play this date with the Mary Chain so we just thought he'd do for the time being. McGurk had a bit of an attitude, he was up for a drink, a fight and a fuck, in other words a typical twenty-year-old kid from a Glasgow scheme full of spunk.

The year before, in late '83 or early '84, we'd been writing songs and we auditioned a couple of people to be the singer. I wanted to be the guitarist, but I didn't have the confidence, so Beattie and I put an advert out on Radio Clyde on the *Billy Sloan Show* which was very popular in the West of Scotland. Our advert said, 'Primal Scream are looking for a psychedelic punk rock singer', with Beattie's telephone number on it. Beattie's mum, Bettie, worked on the switchboard at Clyde and had passed the message directly to Billy Sloan.

We had one guy come up to Beattie's house to audition. We ran through a few songs with him by Iggy, Velvets, Byrds, and we knew pretty much immediately what the decision was going to be. Once the kid left, I looked at Beattie and said that *I* had to be the singer in the band. It was weird to be writing lyrics for someone else to sing. Beattie agreed and that was it. Jim Reid told me that he had been listening to the *Billy Sloan Show* the night the 'Scream looking for a singer' ad went out and was seriously thinking of calling us up for an audition, but was eventually talked out of the idea after discussing it with his brother William – who was writing and demoing early JAMC songs on the Portastudio in their shared East Kilbride council flat bedroom – who convinced Jim to stick with him. Can you imagine if that had actually happened?

The Screamers and the Mary Chain were destined to meet someday. Ironically, the correspondence between the two bands was soon to take quite a different turn.

Sometime in late September McGee called me up out of the blue and said, 'The Mary Chain have sacked their drummer and they want you, are you in?'

I replied, 'Well, it's a nice idea, McGee.' (I always spoke to him this way, using his surname.) 'The thing is, I'm not a fucking drummer.'

'Yeah, I know you're not,' he said. 'But I know you can do it. I told Jim you drummed with Altered Images and they love Altered Images. They really want you to be the drummer.'

How could I refuse? 'Alright, McGee,' I said. 'In that case, why don't we have a rehearsal at the Hellfire Club, and if they like what I do then cool, if they don't, then that's cool too, but in my opinion they need to hear me play first.'

I booked some time down at the Hellfire Club and arranged to meet Jim, William and Douglas one weekday afternoon. They had all brought their guitars with them on the bus. I knew seven JAMC songs from the two demo tapes I had heard. We played through a couple of loose versions, feeling each other out, which is what musicians do whenever they encounter a new player. The fact that we were already good friends defused any potential tension from the situation. This type of thing can be extremely uncomfortable: auditioning a total stranger can be one of the most painfully embarrassing experiences. I don't recall that we'd actually been playing long when Jim or William just stopped and said, 'It sounds great, will you join our band?' I of course said yes and that was it. I was now the drummer in the Jesus and Mary Chain.

Years later, Douglas told me that afterwards the three of them took the bus back to East Kilbride and they were all really excited after the rehearsal, all of them looking at each other saying, 'That was amazing, we've now got a band, this is proper now, we're finally a band.' Doug said they were so happy to have me be part of it but of course being the Reids they never gave much away emotionally unless they were fighting each other. Jim and William were both pretty quiet and never really said too much. Douglas was the conduit for their communications with the outside world at this point. From what I could see, the fights between Jim and William were mainly verbal insults and sarcasm, and occasionally inanimate objects would be destroyed. The fights I had with my own brother were different. Graham would come home drunk from work and suddenly attack me for no reason. One time he picked me up and threw me down on the floor and attempted to jump on my face. I turned my head to the side just before he made contact and he went flying into the sideboard, then I got up and ran out of the room to get a knife. It had been lucky for me he had been wearing nylon socks and he slid off the ski-slope of my long, shiny, newly washed hair. Brotherly love, Glasgow style.

# 13.

# Crusaders

McGee had arranged for the Mary Chain to tour Germany; a package tour with Alan's own band Biff Bang Pow! and a gang of garage Mod punk rockers from Aberdeen called Jasmine Minks. I can't explain how excited I felt. I'd been signing on the dole for four straight years and was now feeling depressed and frustrated about having no direction. Writing Scream songs with Beattie and trying to put a band together had energised me but we hadn't even played a gig yet. We were still in our formative stage and the money I had saved up from working at John Horn's was beginning to run out.

I'd only ever been out of the United Kingdom once in my life, for a school trip to Belgium when I was twelve to see the war memorials in Flanders, the row upon row of white crosses. I've never understood the message they were sending with these trips. Were we supposed to feel 'Never again!', 'No more war!' or were we there to honour the blood sacrifice made by past generations? I felt the point of the trip was the glorification of war, just as they do each Armistice Day when the Queen and heads of state lay wreaths at the cenotaph in Whitehall. I was brought up a pacifist, not to fight in a capitalist's war. I have more in common with an Iraqi citizen than I do with the Chairman of Blackwater or BP Shell, they're the real enemy.

So we were going to go on tour in Germany, only I had a problem: I didn't have a passport. I arranged a date with the passport office. Douglas and I went up together to the office which was just at the bottom of Sauchiehall Street, and on the way I went to the photobooth in Central Station. I'd grown my hair into a long bowl-cut somewhere between Michael Clark of the Byrds and Sky Saxon of the Seeds, but had it shaved high and left the fringe long. It felt fresh and clean in the way that good haircuts often do. After we'd received our passports, Douglas and I went looking for a café and sat down for ice cream. Douglas was so excited. He said to me, 'Bobby, it's gonna be like the Beatles in Hamburg. We'll be there, all of us dressed head to toe in black leather and when we come back to Britain we're gonna be rock and roll stars.'

I just laughed at him across the café table and said, 'Hope so ...'

Primal Scream finally had enough songs for a short set and a full band line-up so I contacted the Mary Chain and we set up a gig at the Venue in Sauchiehall Street for 12 October 1984. I put half of the money in for the costs to hire the venue and PA system and the JAMC boys put up the other half. We co-promoted the gig. The line-up was Primal Scream, the Jesus and Mary Chain, Alan McGee's band Biff Bang Pow! and a band from East Kilbride called Ochre Five. Grant Morrison, the famous DC comic book writer whose credits include *Batman*, *Fantastic Four* and *2000 AD*, was in Ochre Five.

They turned up for the show wearing public schoolboy uniforms and capes. I thought they were trying to look like Malcolm McDowell and his revolutionary chums in Lindsay Anderson's film *If....* Weirdly enough, I had designed the flyer and poster advertising the show using the hand grenade image from the poster for that very film. *If....* was a favourite of the Chain and the Scream. On that first phone call to Douglas we had both enthused about it. Malcolm McDowell is stood in front of a huge hand grenade, dressed half in his public schoolboy uniform and half in a flying jacket like the one Julian Cope of the Teardrop Explodes wore in the 'Reward' video. He's holding a machine gun and at the bottom of the image are the words, 'Which side are you on?' I thought this was a confrontational question and image and it suited us: Beattie and I were on a mission and so were the JAMC. I overlaid that image with all of the band names using Letraset. I added 'with psychedelic punk rock disco, admission two pounds'.

Alan asked if I would put Biff Bang Pow!'s drummer up for the night, a guy named David Swift. Swift arrived late on the evening of the 11th. He was an *NME* writer from New Zealand and a regular at McGee's Living Room club. We chatted for a bit and went to bed, a big day ahead. On the morning of the 12th, my dad woke me up to tell me the news that the IRA had blown up the Grand Brighton Hotel in an attempt to assassinate Margaret Thatcher and the Tory Cabinet. I hated Thatcher like I would've hated Hitler had I been alive during the war years. I had watched powerless from the sidelines as Thatcher and her government waged systematic war on the British working class through mass factory closures and changing employment laws to weight them even more in favour of big business bosses – giving them even more power and a bigger share of the profits than they had already whilst further impoverishing workers. She was a right-wing revolutionary who had vowed to crush the Trade Union Movement and the working class with it. The summer of '84 she had politicised the police force and used them as her own private army in her battle against the National Union of Mineworkers. The NUM, led by Arthur Scargill, had heroically resisted Thatcher's war against them, to the point of being starved into submission by a coalition of scabs, police, the full force of the state machinery, print and broadcast media and anti-union laws designed to destroy any dissent.

I also knew, from all-night political discussion with my dad, who was very involved with the miners' strike, that this assault was the first of many that the British state would launch on working-class people to take away their hard-won employment rights and wage bargaining powers, and that Thatcher was totally committed to ripping up the post-war 'social contract' consensus, thereby destroying the social democratic system that I had been born into and replacing it with a neoliberal, privatised, competitive capitalist society. Thatcher envisioned a 'dog-eat-dog' economy. She did not believe the state should assist the poor. Her take was that if you were poor, then you deserved your lot – it was because you hadn't worked hard enough. She had no concept of circumstance, of the evidence that people born into poverty have poorer life chances than people born into inherited wealth. Or maybe she did, and the bigotry of her own petit bourgeois English lower-middle-class upbringing just could not be hidden. She despised working-class people. Michael Heseltine, one of her own government ministers, described her as typical of so many of her kind. Her family had just about scraped into the lower-middle class, pulling the ladder behind up them as they ascended and despising those that had been 'left behind'. Thatcher described the striking miners as 'the Enemy within'; she used warlike analogies in her speeches, and she had even cynically engineered a war against Argentina over the British-owned Falkland Islands (Las Malvinas) to guarantee her a second election victory in 1983, causing the needless deaths of young British and Argentinian men who were sacrificed to further her career of evil.

The way I saw it, Thatcher was using the full force of the British state: powerful vested interests like the CBI bosses, business elites, the newspapers owned by right-wing billionaires and the state-owned BBC TV and radio. To this she added a highly politicised police force who were ordered from on high to act violently against the miners on the picket lines. MI5 agents and Special Branch officers were used to gather information and spy on Trade Unionists. Indeed, our telephone at home was bugged during this time and Dad's Union offices in Charing Cross were broken into a couple of times by Special Branch.

Dad helped raise money to buy vital food supplies for the miners. He sent huge lorry-loads of fresh food down south to the food kitchens in Lancashire and Yorkshire each week, in an act of brotherly solidarity and comradeship. Different unions would have buckets going round the factories raising money to help strikers in other industries and parts of the country; that was impossible now because the government had frozen the NUM bank account. So Dad and the Scottish Miners leader, the great Mick McGahey, a communist from Fife, hatched a plan to send food instead. I was so proud of him. Sometimes we'd get these weird phone calls at odd times and when I would answer there was never anyone on the other end of the line, just silence, then a couple of clicking noises. We would say stuff like, 'We know you're listening, you stupid Tory bastards, go fuck yourself, you servile cunts.' We thought it was both funny and pathetic. The government had said the strike was illegal because NUM leader Arthur Scargill had called it without balloting his members, then they brought in emergency laws that froze the Union bank accounts and gave the government the power to sequester any money that had been saved in order to fight a strike of this magnitude. The miners couldn't sign on as unemployed or claim housing benefits; Thatcher's strategy was to starve them and their families into submission. Her main plan was to close down all the pits so that the NUM could never shut down the country the way they had done during the powercut days of 1974 that had brought down Heath's Tory government. She was out to avenge that humiliation and crush the power of the unions forever.

I have always seen laws passed by Parliament and enforced by agents of the state as direct acts of violence against the poorest people in society. Look at David Cameron and George Osborne's 2010 'austerity' budget; they completely slashed public spending whilst giving tax breaks to big business and lowering income tax on the wealthiest. It's nothing short of a class war waged on the working class. Poverty kills and they know it. They enjoy causing other, less fortunate people to suffer. Why do this when our country is wealthy enough to clothe, feed, employ and house everyone to a very good standard of living? Well, *because they can*, and because it's been like that for hundreds of years. That golden time of wealth redistribution known as 'social democracy' was only a tiny blip in history between the early fifties and 1979. The societal advances and freedoms won during the sixties by workers, Black people, gay people and the women's movement, all those civil and social rights, had been just too much for the ancient regimes all around the western world and the neoliberal revolution being waged by Reagan and Thatcher was the beginning of a long-term strategy to claw back all those hard-won freedoms and hand power back to the corporate and political establishment.

I had watched her crush the miners and wished I could have done something to help them stop her. She was a malign and malevolent presence, not just in British life but in the world. She inspired many similarly warped and deceitful disciples; sleazy, smarmy, Oxbridge-educated spiv politricksters such as Tony Blair, Boris Johnson, Nigel Farage and George Osborne – all are Thatcher's children and I hate them all equally. But I hate her more. She was their Elvis.

That night at the Venue was to be my first gig playing for both the Mary Chain and the Scream. The Brighton bombing made it seem like an even more momentous day and I was quietly excited. I had never once rehearsed with the Mary Chain. That initial thing in the rehearsal room had been at my insistence so the boys could hear my primitive drum skills for themselves and make their minds up. We never rehearsed any songs, ever. Every single gig was freefall. Every gig. Even when we made *Psychocandy* it was freefall. Just the way I like it.

I had planned an outfit to wear for the first Scream gig. I wore a red crew-neck jumper and played a red semi-acoustic guitar which I borrowed from Paul Harte. I decided not to play the blue Vox Phantom – it was a colour-scheme thing. My whole look that night was my tribute to Subway Sect, who I saw support Buzzcocks in 1978 on the second Buzzcocks album *Love Bites* tour. The whole band were wearing red sweaters and Vic Godard played a red guitar. I remember it stuck in my head. That image was Bernie Rhodes's (manager of the Clash and Subway Sect) idea. Bernie had told Vic that if the group all wore red the audience would remember them. The Sect's image had been all school-uniform grey during 1976 and '77, which I had also loved. I liked the way schoolkids could identify with that look. I remember berating McGee and Innes for not watching the Subway Sect at a gig; they were stood in the foyer probably eyeing up all the punk girls or something. I went out after the set and found them and gave them both shit. McGee has said that I was a confrontational, annoying little bastard back then. Not much has changed since I guess.

The Scream that night comprised myself on electric six-string and lead vocal, Robert Young on bass, Tam McGurk on drums, Beattie on miked-up acoustic twelve-string and our pal Joogs hitting that tambourine. We had pored over the Arthur Lee albums and dug the way there were seven members of Love on the cover of *Da Capo*. They looked like a weird psychedelic street gang, and although he couldn't keep time that well Joogs's inclusion onstage was a great visual element – plus he was full of enthusiasm and encouragement for our band's fledgling musical experiments, and he was in possession of a snide, sarcastic sense of humour that gelled perfectly with ours.

I remember at the soundcheck Jim Reid was standing out front in the dark, empty club watching us and he came up to me excitedly after we'd finished and said, 'Bobby, you're the greatest band in the world.' That made me feel instantly good because I knew he had great taste in music.

When it was time for us to go on we all lined up across the front of the stage. Robert and Beattie were right up there at the front beside me. Three of us up front like a gang, with me flanked by these two tough guys playing guitars. They were up for a fight. Both of them up for a fight but playing this kind of gentle folk-rock music. Robert never strayed too far from his Glaswegian punk roots. He saw life as struggle and confrontation. So did I, and so did Beattie. We all shared that. The world was a hostile and unforgiving place and people like us had to fight for everything we had, no one was going to give us anything for free and you never knew what kind of shit life was going to throw at you. It was a game of 'no-chance', so you'd better be ready for it when it came. The truth is we were young guys in our early twenties with romantic dreams of rock and roll glory. Our economic and educational backgrounds gave us a drive and determination and political outlook that was markedly different from the Home Counties suburban indie boys we encountered on the London gig circuit. I don't remember much about the first show. We played a short Scream set, probably six or seven songs, all around two minutes long, no guitar solos, and one of the songs we played that night was 'Nobody's Scared' by Subway Sect. Then there was a short ten-minute break, after which I was back onstage again playing drums with the Mary Chain. Both gigs were creatively satisfying and it felt good to be in two cool bands.

Just before we went on the Creation tour of Germany we played a Mary Chain gig at the Three Johns pub in Islington. Alan McGee had invited *NME* and *Sounds* journalists along to promote the soon-to-be-released 'Upside Down' single. We played a really disciplined set with no fuck-ups or stoppages, just the songs as they should be, clean and powerful and no messing. I was really proud of how well we had played, we all were. After the show, in the hallway that doubled for a dressing room, the four boys in the band were all smiling at each other, satisfied with our performance. In the early days of JAMC we had these lovely moments of group solidarity and mutual satisfaction and enjoyment. We were a great little rock and roll band and we knew it. As the band's fame and notoriety grew these moments would become suffocated in the violence and chaos surrounding the group, so these are some of the most precious memories I have of my time with them. At the Three Johns I could feel that there was a momentum and an energy building around the Mary Chain.

I remember the gig took place in a room above the pub, maybe one hundred people, if that. It was very dark, with a couple of single naked bulbs at each side of the 'stage' space, on the same level as the audience. There was a small vocal PA. McGee had borrowed a snare drum and floor tom for me and they were miked up and put through the PA with Jim's vocal, William and Douglas's guitar amps blasted straight into the crowd.

JAMC live were an unfriendly white noise wall of sound that brought to mind images of broken glass and barbed wire; a psychic storm, a fractured dissonance, with world-weary words of dark romanticism and existential failure. William Reid wrote about the bitter truths of post-adolescent no-future blues and teen-punk futility, romantic love as a doomed and diseased thing. Even sex was full of dread, doubt and fear. Their songs spoke of an isolation and hopelessness which I totally related to. They had a warped poetry and a take-it-or-leave-it, fuck-you attitude; songs *for* the dispossessed *by* the dispossessed. There was also a sadness in the songs which I tuned into, even the aggressive ones like 'Inside Me' and 'In A Hole'. It was outsider music.

The JAMC stage presence was an uneasy mix of confrontational passive-aggressiveness and explosive spasms of violence and anger. Each of us possessed an inner rage at the inequities of the world and the existential pain we all felt as sensitive, curious and questioning young men. We never spoke about politics, it was mostly music and films, but there was a real anger there, you could feel it in the words, music and performance. I never spoke about it with the Reids at the time but later on, I found out they grew up in the exact same conditions as me in a tenement in Parkhead.

# 14.

# Leather Boys on Amphetamine

We took the train down to London on a Sunday afternoon. The journey took eleven hours instead of the usual five. We just commandeered a room in the first-class carriage and the guard didn't mind when he came to check our tickets. We were going on our first tour together. A rock and roll dream coming true.

When we reached London we got on the Tube at Euston and took the Victoria line to Tottenham. McGee had a spare room and he let us sleep there. I have a lovely memory of the four Mary Chain boys in sleeping bags on the floor all snuggled up against each other to keep warm against the cold, autumn London night. Great camaraderie.

Once we disembarked at Calais we drove through the night to a little town somewhere outside Cologne in Germany where we met Thomas Zimmerman who was the tour promoter and a fan of British indie music. Thomas was a gentle guy, an idealistic music fan. I would meet other people who shared Thomas's evangelism over the next few years. The support and encouragement of guys like him and Jeff Barrett – who we would soon meet – were really important factors in our development as performers because they promoted gigs by unknown bands and took a chance and made a commitment of belief in rock and roll; a romantic gesture for sure rather than a commercial endeavour.

On the tour the bill was supposed to rotate each night with a different headliner, but JAMC were seen as the minor act and therefore mostly bottom of the bill. We didn't care. We knew we were good and we were just grateful to be there. It was an adventure. In the eighties the Federal Government in West Germany subsidised the arts and gave a lot of money to local towns and villages. So someone could apply to the Federal Government and say they were promoting gigs in a small town and they'd give you a grant so you could put a gig on. American and British bands like the Gun Club and Green on Red went and did the circuit of small-town gigs in underground clubs and village halls. We were on that same circuit.

One of my best Mary Chain memories happened in Vienna. We had a night off before the gig. The local promoter took us to a gig in a high-ceilinged, gloomy place, maybe built in the eighteenth century. It had a real Nazi vibe to it. My World War Two–obsessed imagination ran riot in Germany and Austria. I imagined brownshirts and Hitler Youth and SS and all sorts of totalitarian horrors taking place only fifty years before. I can't recall which band was playing, someone local I'll guess. There were a few hundred people standing around between bands drinking, talking and smoking – except us four Mary Chain boys. In those days we used to just sit on the floor, never chairs. From floor level you can't be seen but you can see everything. I looked at Jim, William and Douglas and I felt so content. I thought to myself, *I belong with these guys*, and I smiled to myself internally. It was one of the best moments of my life. I hadn't felt the need to say anything to anyone, because so much of our communication was unspoken; just a look, a nod of the head, the best relationships are like that. I recognised this was a truly spiritual moment, that I had finally made deep connections with other people, and that there was some calling, some purpose for me and all of us to be here. I felt we were all the same, together for a reason, and that I belonged in a way that I'd never felt before and maybe haven't since. I was part of the gang, and I just loved them. They were young men, but I loved them. I was in love with them all.

We spent the whole tour in a minibus with a broken window. I didn't care. This was heaven.

Our first trip to Berlin was amazing. We had to drive through the 'corridor' to get there – the only road allowed for travel between West Germany and Berlin, in Communist East Germany, nearer to Poland than the then-capital Bonn. We were stopped by these East German soldiers who were as young as we were. They looked in the van and asked to see our passports but they were dead nice. I thought about how hard it must've been for them, conscripted into the army whilst we were free to be in this rock band, and I felt a bit sorry for them.

We played at a club called the Loft, run by a woman named Monica. She was in her forties then. She's still there, in her eighties now, promoting shows. Truly rock and roll. From the look of her, Monica had obviously been having a good time throughout the sixties and seventies. She was a proper music-head. She loved us. People loved the Mary Chain. This is before we had even made a record. I remember Douglas getting off with one of her mates, a sexy chick in her early thirties, and we were like, whoa, how cool, go on Doug!

At that gig I drank half a bottle of vodka and then in the middle of our set I jumped over the drum kit. The tour kit had been set up on top of a drum riser and I got so carried away that I ended up doing a fucking swan dive over the top of the kit during the set and landed at Jim's feet, right in front of the monitors. He just laughed and carried on. It was a moment of pure joy and madness. Rock and roll does stuff like that to you.

Once the tour was over, we all piled into the bus and our roadie Dave Evans started out on the long journey home. Dave was a good driver. Maybe the Berlin speed helped . . . The drawback with Dave was that he only had one cassette tape, the *Crazy*

*World of Arthur Brown* album, which he played non-stop at full volume from Berlin all the way to Calais. First time it was on, I thought OK, I've never heard this album before, I'll give it a chance, and then about the tenth time it was like, fuck, it's too much. It was as if Evans was brainwashing us with the *Crazy World* album. He pummelled our brains with that tape. Something must've worked on some level because three years later the Mary Chain gave Dave a job as rhythm guitarist on the Darklands tour – from roadie to band member, just like that. Anyway, at this point we didn't have any power and just kept our mouths shut and suffered in silence, but not for long.

We landed in Dover and when we touched dry land I said to the boys that I was going to go and get the *NME* because they would have reviewed the Islington gig and 'Upside Down'. The rest of them were too scared to see the reviews for themselves.

I got off the bus, bought both the *NME* and *Sounds* and came back. 'There you go, guys, have a look at this.' Neil Taylor in *NME* said, 'This band are the new Sex Pistols.' 'Upside Down' by the Jesus and Mary Chain was single of the week everywhere, in all the music papers. The Three Johns gig got amazing reviews and it *was* just as Douglas had predicted: 'We'll go away to Germany like the Beatles in Hamburg and come back as rock and roll stars dressed in black leather.' We went away as nobodies and when we came back, suddenly there was all this excitement about the band in the music press and major record labels were sniffing around McGee looking to sign us up to recording deals.

When we returned from Germany we played one more show at the end of 1984, at the Ambulance Station on the Old Kent Road, an anarchist squat that put gigs on occasionally. McGee had fixed this up as a 'showcase'. I remember climbing through a big hole that had been knocked through the wall in a room upstairs that led to where our 'dressing room' was. We scored some nice amphetamine sulphate from one of the squatters and had more than a few slugs of vodka before hitting the stage at street level below. The place was rammed full of people, all of whom wanted to see the 'new Sex Pistols' in the flesh for themselves. McGee later told me that Johnny Marr and Morrissey from the Smiths were there. This pleased me no end. I admired them both for their music, their tastes and attitude. The Smiths had single-handedly kick-started a grey, depressing, moribund indie scene into life. It was *pre*-Smiths and *post*-Smiths. It was a bit of a dislocated gig because people kept invading the 'stage' and knocking over our drums, amps and Jim's mic stand. At one point I hoisted my floor tom above my head and launched it straight into the audience. I was very drunk and lucky that I had a wall directly behind me which helped prop me up for much of the show.

There were some great photos taken that night. We are all pissing ourselves laughing, huge grins on our faces. William is on his knees with his back to the audience, facing his Fender Twin amp, his guitar wringing out the screeching psychotic feedback sounds that only he could make. Jim is wearing a homemade punk shirt with the words 'CANDY CUNT CUNT CUNT' stencilled in black spray-paint on a secondhand shirt that had been dyed grey and ripped across the bottom. I wore a blue and white checked plaid American shirt which I'd picked up from Flip in 1980, black wraparound shades, straight-leg dark blue jeans and George Cox Diano Creeper shoes which I bought from Robot on the King's Road. I had a shaved head with long fringe. The look was always very important to me.

The chaos and secrecy surrounding the Ambulance Station gig just added to the band's growing mystique. 'Upside Down' would eventually reach number one in the independent charts after months of support from DJs John Peel, Janice Long and JAMC 'outrage' pieces that filled the weekly music papers. This chart was taken from sales in shops around the UK that were linked into 'the Cartel', a co-operative alternative distribution service set up by labels such as Factory, Rough Trade, Mute, 4

AD and other smaller independent record labels in conjunction with independent record shops all over the UK. This meant that alternative music could exist on its own terms, outside the reach of the major record labels who also owned the old established UK-wide record distribution services. The idea was rooted in the Marxist maxim about how workers would only be free once they owned the means of production. At least this was the way I always thought about it.

Rough Trade boss Geoff Travis came up from London to sweet-talk the Mary Chain into signing to his new WEA-funded label, Blanco y Negro. The meeting was arranged to be at McGee's mother's house in King's Park. I remember the meeting was a bit odd. Us four Mary Chain boys must have come across as inner-city urchins to the more culturally sophisticated and upper-middle-class Travis. We all just sat there on McGee's mother's couch, saying nothing. McGee did all the talking. I recall asking Geoff some questions about Vic Godard and Subway Sect. Rough Trade had released a few solo singles by Vic and Travis was still involved in his career, so I was curious to find out how things were going. Geoff possessed the kind of confidence that people from his background always seem to have. When you first encounter it, it's completely alien and intimidating; not to say that there was anything wrong on Geoff's part, it's just that guys from our background lacked the experience and confidence to hold a conversation with someone like him. He was at least ten years older than us for a start, and he'd been involved in the music business for a decade or so, running shops and labels, so he had the power of music-biz experience and knowledge behind him – plus, of course, WEA's money. JAMC wanted to release their records on a major label, get a big money advance to get off the dole, have hits and be rock and roll stars, and Travis was a way into that world.

Geoff was just being himself; he was as much a product of his upbringing as we were of ours. I don't know if the others observed things the way I did, but the class differences were something I couldn't help but notice. Travis's pedigree with outsider underground artists on his Rough Trade label gave him a sheen of credibility.

So JAMC signed to Blanco y Negro, and Geoff sent us into the studio in December 1984 to record the follow-up to 'Upside Down'. Stephen Street, who made his name working with the Smiths, was to be the producer. The recording would take place at Island Studios in London. 'Never Understand' was chosen as the A side, and we recorded 'Ambition' by Subway Sect for the B side and an improvised 'noise' song titled 'Suck' at the same session. Street recorded us separately, just as Chris Nagle had recorded the Wake. This style didn't suit the Mary Chain at all. We were a punk rock band and the sound was all about four guys playing the song together, really laying into it with passion and power. In the words of MC5 manager and White Panther John Sinclair, 'Separation is doom'. The problem with Stephen Street's 'Never Understand' was it just wasn't very good. It sounded too clean, too 'produced'. There was no sex, danger or violence. He just didn't get the band at all. After hearing it, we decided to record it again and produce it ourselves. Alan booked a day at Alaska Studios and Noel Thompson engineered it. Alaska was owned by Pat Collier, who had been the bassist in the Vibrators. Away from the pressures of corporate producers we laid 'Never Understand' down with ease. I remember it was a great session. Just us four boys, McGee and Noel, no record company involvement. When we were listening to the final mix playback we all knew we'd captured the song perfectly. On 'Never Understand' I made a suggestion to Jim. The lyrics on the last verse went:

*Looking so hard but you just can't see me*
*I tell you the truth but you don't believe me*

And I said, 'Why don't you sing "You're pushing too hard" as a tribute to Sky Saxon of the Seeds?'

Jim said, 'Do you think I should?'

'Yeah, go on,' I said. 'It'll be great.'

So he sang 'You're pushing too hard and you just can't see me.' And when he came out from the vocal booth to hear what he'd just sang he looked at me and smiled and said, 'Yeah, it's cool, let's keep it in.' It was a way of saying, 'Hey, we're carrying the flame now.' It was a nice moment. A homage to the rock and roll ancestors.

To promote our first major-label single release Warners had fixed it for us to appear on *The Old Grey Whistle Test* at 9 a.m. on a cold February morning. It was McGee's idea for the Mary Chain to get there that early so they would be sober for their first big TV appearance, but of course that didn't happen. In those days we used to stay in McGee's back room. McGee had us in there folding the 'Upside Down' sleeves that I'd had printed up in Glasgow. We were so bored we'd write rude messages in them, like 'Get it right up you, you fucking slag.' Abusive messages: 'Your dad sucks off policemen whilst you sodomise your mother', etc. etc. ad nauseum, puerile porno abuse, just trying to outrage each other and amuse ourselves to alleviate the boredom of folding the fucking sleeves. We were like, 'I bet Duran Duran don't have to do this.'

McGee woke us up at eight in the morning. None of us had got up that early for *years*. Jim, William and myself had all been on the dole for ages and we were never up at 8 a.m. I used to get up at 11 a.m. and stay up all night till five in the morning listening to music, reading and shit. Suddenly McGee had got us up at eight in the morning and we were all huddled up, freezing in this little minibus going to the BBC. Jim and William suddenly got these cans of beer out of a plastic carrier bag and started necking super lager at 8.30 a.m. and I was saying to them, 'What are you doing? We're going live on TV in a minute!'

They're going, 'We're nervous, we're fucking nervous, we cannae dae this sober.'

So by the time we got to the BBC studios Jim and William were both smashed. I was sober, there was no way I was blowing this. Our performance was brilliant. We conveyed the correct attitude and played ferocious versions of 'Inside Me' and 'In A Hole'. This was the first taste of the Mary Chain for hundreds of thousands of people and momentum was building.

The month of the *Old Grey Whistle Test* broadcast we played a one-off gig at the Dome in Brighton. The place was bursting with people eager to see us. We took to the stage full of confidence. 'Upside Down' was number one in the independent charts, 'Never Understand' was just about to be released. We'd recorded two Peel Sessions and he was raving about us. We were in the music papers every week.

The Brighton gig was a sell-out and we could feel the noise and anticipation from the audience out front. We started with a powerful version of 'In A Hole', a statement of intent. The band were tight and I was soaring on the drums, grooving out to William's screaming barbed-wire fuzz-tone guitar symphonies. I was in punk heaven, totally locked into the groove, keeping that beat and intensity of focus. I imagined that each time my left arm rose high in the air and my drumstick came down with a hard crack on the snare drum that I was whipping the entire audience in their faces. I hated them. I didn't believe that we were there to entertain them but to punish them. They were an angry, ignorant mob; post-punk scum who came to see a freak show, all of them dressed in the styleless uniformity of shite biker jackets, bleached, splattered jeans and Doc Martens that even the Exploited would've thought too gauche to wear: a trenchfoot tribe of moronic cultural impotence. They had all missed out on punk the first time and now in true Pavlovian fashion felt the urge to spit on us and attack us with bottles. *They* were the freak show.

Two songs in I felt a missile whizz past my head. *Just carry on*, I thought, *fuck them*. Then another missile, then another went flying past my head and smashed against the wall behind me. I could feel the missiles were coming down on us from above so I momentarily looked up, without missing a beat, and saw a big guy who had climbed on top of the PA column to my left. He had a bag of bottles and fuck knows what else and was raining them down on us. I stopped drumming mid-song and went over to where Jim was. He was still singing near the front of the stage, totally lost in the moment and looked confused as to why I had stopped drumming and was out front with him. William and Douglas were still playing, deep in concentration. I screamed into Jim's ear that we should get off the stage, that there were too many missiles, and I pointed up towards the guy on top of the PA. Jim looked puzzled and then SMASH!! we both got hit in the face with a bottle. Fortunately it didn't break and we were both just shocked.

Then, I saw Karen, who was there with us, get hit full in the face with a wine bottle. That was it for me. I proceeded to pick up any bottle that had landed on the stage and started throwing them back at the audience. I'd done a bit of bottle-throwing at football in my teens and knew how to aim for the head. I despised these cunts out there. We were a great high-energy rock and roll band who wanted to play our music and these imbeciles had only come along to throw bottles at us and try and kick our heads in if they got the chance. Violence at the football was one thing, but we started playing in a rock and roll band to get away from that madness. After fifteen minutes or so, the lights went up and the crowd went fucking mental, people screaming, more smashing of bottles, and our equipment got smashed up in the melee.

The promoter came into the dressing room pleading with us to go back on, worried the hall would be destroyed and he would have to pay for the damages. We told him to fuck off. I was screaming in his face. By this time the lump on Karen's forehead had swollen to the size of a cricket ball and she needed to go to A&E. Joe Foster and I took her to Brighton Hospital in a taxi where the doctor looked at it and told her she was lucky that her face hadn't been lacerated by the bottle. There were people who had attended the concert in the waiting room who started screaming abuse at us because they had been bottled too. Joe and I went over to them and told them all to fuck off, that they deserved it for being part of that audience of fools.

That night set the template for Mary Chain gigs for the rest of 1985. We were a freakshow, fair game for any psycho in town. The 'New Sex Pistols' tag, although very flattering, was to prove a millstone around our necks. People were stupid. There was a lot of anger in British society in the eighties. There were uprisings by urban youths in riots against the police in Toxteth, Brixton, Bristol and Manchester and the violence at football grounds up and down the country exceeded even the seventies as the firms became more organised. But as far as I know only the Jesus and Mary Chain gigs attracted violence on a similar scale in the world of rock and roll. We were a conduit of hate. To be honest I loved that. Although it became dull when every gig ended after ten minutes in a hail of broken bottles smashing onto the stage, I enjoyed being the focus of all that hatred. I carried a lot of anger inside me and I enjoyed annoying people, being a member of such a confrontational band, who, if the truth be told, also enjoyed offending the audience in any way that they could. Jim Reid can be heard on film denouncing a sold-out audience at the Electric Ballroom in Camden, summer 1985: 'Where were you all six months ago? We fucking despise you.' No other successful band spoke to their ever-growing audience in such a way. We were good and we knew it. We had the arrogance of youth and we wanted to rub the audience's faces in the broken glass from the bottles they threw at us. At least I did.

# 15.

# Psychocandy

In early 1985 we filmed the 'Never Understand' video with Tim Broad in a warehouse in Wapping. Tim was a lovely, gentle man. He directed all the Mary Chain videos whilst I was in the group. He died tragically of AIDS in the nineties. Tim had been around the Derek Jarman scene. Those videos have lots of crotch shots, you'll notice, of me; slow-motion crotch shots with the leathers on in 'Just Like Honey', very homoerotic. I loved Tim's videos. But the video for 'Never Understand' was amazing. Every member of the Mary Chain looked great on camera, the stillness translated into cool defiance and a remote kind of confrontation, no histrionics. We were visually alienated whilst the music was a high-energy onslaught of psychotic feedback and murderous screams mixed with a gorgeous lovelorn pop melody that Brian Wilson would die for. A deadly combination of the psycho and the candy. Sweet violence, love and hate in equal measures: the true sound of confusion. As if all the existential bewilderment and psychic pain that had tortured us all for years was being unleashed in a rock and roll exorcism.

The sessions for the *Psychocandy* album took place at Southern Studios in Wood Green. Southern was owned and run by a guy called John Loder in his early forties. He engineered the album and he knew what he was doing in that little studio. It sounded good. Southern was situated in a terraced house. The 'live' room consisted of two smaller rooms that had been knocked together to make a larger one. There was just about enough space to set up a four- or five-piece rock band and record them playing live. The 'control room' where the mixing desk sat was outside in a little corrugated iron shed where the patio had been. It was all very low-fi but cool.

John Loder also ran a distribution company. Southern distributed records on the Crass label run by the anarchist group of the same name. They also handled a lot of the new US underground punk-rock labels like Dischord; in fact I recently found out that Ian MacKaye from Fugazi was also present during the *Psychocandy* sessions, assisting John, patching leads, making tea. Adrian Sherwood did a lot of work there for ON-U Sound, Mark Stewart, Bim Sherman, Tackhead and New Age Steppers.

After the Stephen Street debacle and the success of 'Never Understand', Travis and WEA trusted the Mary Chain to produce the album themselves. This was all Jim and William with help from John Loder. William especially knew exactly what he wanted from the studio in order to realise his vision for the songs he'd written. Jim wrote songs too but William was three years older and had a natural, deep understanding of the potential effects that the deadly combination of a good song and the right production could have on a listener's consciousness.

I recall the one time I was ever a guest in the Reids' parents' house in Calder Avenue, East Kilbride in late 1984. I was up in their shared bedroom and William was spinning 'Susie Q' by Dale Hawkins on a 45 RPM vinyl single on the little record player, maybe it was a Dansette. He spoke about how 'dirty and sexy' it was. He was critically analysing what made a great rock and roll record. He noticed that the speed of the song corresponded with the grind of the groove, creating a breathing space in the sound and a predatory and menacing confidence which made it sexy in a way that, had it been faster, it wouldn't be. He asked me why Ramones were not superstars as they should have been, after all they had so many amazing songs that we all loved. I answered that the masses were not hip and that cool stuff never sold in huge amounts. He countered that with, 'What about the Stones then?' His take was that although Ramones were genius their music was not sexy and you had to make sexy music to make it big. I got a lesson that day in a deeper understanding of the art form. Thanks, William.

We were recording the album, and William wanted me to play 'Just Like Honey'. He said, 'Play like the Ronettes' "Be My Baby" drum beat – can you do that?'

I went, 'Yeah.'

He goes, 'Then pick it up in this bit.'

I went, 'OK.' And I just did it. I just knew what to do. It was easy because it was all done on pure feeling and instinct and I loved their songs. I felt so great being a part of recording *Psychocandy* because I knew the songs they had written were great. Jim had a brilliant rock and roll voice: the right mix of, alienation, pain, anger, disgust and lovelorn yearning. He was a natural frontman too: his schizoid onstage character consisted of a surly, passive-aggressive, saturnine teenage boy poet one minute and a murderous, psychotic, self-destructive, nihilistic vandal the next. Offstage Jim was as quiet as a rural churchyard: a tough but fragile personality crippled by a painful shyness. He protected himself by shutting down all communication with the outside world. In some ways his onstage persona was really just a more extreme version of his true inner self, which was naturally depressed, confused and dissociated. I was similar to Jim and I think we both knew and understood this. There were a few different reasons why I fitted in with the Reids and a shared emotional temperament was one of them.

Everything on the album as far as the backing tracks were concerned was recorded really fast and once these were done they started doing the overdubs. William would record layers of guitar on the songs. He knew instinctively what sound he wanted to achieve. The Mary Chain fuzz-tone sound came from a cheap Japanese fuzz pedal made by a company called Shin-ei. The boys bought them for twenty-five or thirty quid a pop at a music store directly across the road from the world-famous Barrowland Ballroom venue in Glasgow. No one else wanted them. It was the mid-eighties and everyone's records had huge gated snare drums like Phil Collins and record productions were sterilised, machine-precise, airtight and super-clean with no messy sound spillage whatsoever. The guy in the shop couldn't give them away. Only the Chain ever bought them I think, because they were highly unfashionable. People wanted chorus pedals to sound like the Police at worst or the Cure at best. The sound from these pedals was virtually uncontrollable. Imagine the sound of a gigantic hornet's nest being cracked open and thousands of giant angry hornets flying out to protect the nest and sting the assailants to death in a mondo-style Japanese science fiction horror movie. Or think of the movie *Them* with giant ants and replace them with giant hornets instead. Shin-ei fuzz pedals made a truly dark, psychotic, apocalyptic sound and somehow William Reid was able to control this sonic monster and bend it to his will, sculpting sound-collages of shrieking violent feedback, designing carefully chosen edits of feedback loops and punching them back into the mix of the songs on *Psychocandy*. This was done with the skill and vision of a fine artist. William created an illusion in the mix where, at certain parts of the song, the feedback would get louder and more fucked up and crazy in a seemingly random fashion. It was a genius touch. It was truly artful what he was doing, totally considered.

No one had ever done this before as far as I know. Jim and William had recorded their early demos in their bedroom at home on a Tascam Portastudio, a four-track recording machine, recorded directly onto an everyday C-30, C-60, C-90 cassette tape. Their dad had been laid off from his job. He worked in Rolls Royce or one of the big car factories in East Kilbride and was made redundant, so he bought the boys the Tascam with his redundancy money and that's where the first demos were recorded, the ones that I'd first heard on that cassette. They had learned primitive overdubbing techniques by trial and error. They had experimented with this stuff at home, maximising its rock and roll potential in such a beautiful way. William is such an instinctive artist. His musical intelligence, songwriting vision, genius guitar-playing and intensity of focus at this point in time was just so *on*.

I came down from Glasgow to join the band to record the album. The sessions took place in a friendly and easy atmosphere. We had already recorded 'Never Understand'. Over the next five or six days we laid down 'You Trip Me Up', 'Just Like Honey', 'Sowing Seeds', 'Taste the Floor', 'Taste of Cindy', 'Inside Me', 'The Living End', 'My Little Underground' and also some more slow, druggy experimental tracks that became B sides like 'Head' and 'Cracked'. I knew most of the songs already, but one afternoon William said, 'I want to show you a new song that we're going to record today.' He ran through the chords of 'The Hardest Walk' and I immediately knew what I was going to play on the drums. I remarked to him that it reminded me of the chorus of a song by a Glasgow band called Friends Again titled 'Honey at the Core' and William said, 'How did you know?' I just smiled at him and then went over to my drums and began working on the song with the rest of the boys.

At the end of the week Karen came down. William and Jim had asked her to sing backing vocals on 'Just Like Honey' because a few months previously she'd been at the *John Peel Sessions* with me and they'd asked her to sing on it right there on the spot. She hadn't sung on any record or anywhere in her life, but she said yes after a little bit of Mary Chain persuasion. They liked her voice and thought Karen possessed the naïve charm of Moe Tucker of the Velvet Underground. The Peel Session sounded great with Jim and Karen singing together so they wanted her to repeat it on the album version of 'Just Like Honey' which would later be released as a single.

Just before the release of 'You Trip Me Up' we set off on a short tour of Europe. Blanco y Negro boss Geoff Travis flew over with a test pressing of the single so William and Jim could OK it. After the soundcheck we went to a music journalist's house to hear the test pressing. I remember it was a bright sunny evening and the guy had a lovely flat; music journalists were very grown-up over there, they took rock seriously as an art form, and respect the people who make it as artists.

The guy put the record on his deck and 'You Trip Me Up' came blasting out of his hi-fi speakers. It was a mind-melting psychedelic pop-punk feedback and fuzz masterpiece, like the orphaned lovechild of Phil Spector and Einstuzende Neubauten. Jim and William were saying, 'It sounds like a hit, it's gonna be a hit.' I said to myself, *In a perfect world, yes, but not in* this *world*. Part of the reason I loved them both was their romantic belief in the transcendental power of rock and roll to save souls and make good a hostile and imperfect world, even if only for three minutes and twenty seconds (the average length of a pop single back then). I shared the same belief. I knew that 'You Trip Me Up' had no chance of daytime radio play alongside Sade, Wham! and Tears for Fears because it was the most extreme record they ever released. It was a statement of intent, a perfect declaration of everything they were and everything they believed in, a beautiful punk gesture destined to fail in a straight world but successful like the Velvet Underground and Stooges before them in inspiring thousands of young punk rockers and garage bands to form and give voice and comfort to outsiders everywhere. It was classic teen-punk rock and roll made by four freaks from dysfunctional Scottish working-class backgrounds, the real thing, pure alienation. You can't fake that shit. It's all in the feeling, and the Mary Chain were all about feelings. I was so fucking proud to be part of a record this extreme and beautiful.

When *Psychocandy* was released the Chain put the lyrics

*Love like the mighty ocean*
*when it's frozen*
*that is your heart*

beside my photo on the inner sleeve. I loved that, it was my favourite line in the song, and I always wondered if Jim or William picked up on my slightly melancholic vibe and attributed that quote to fit my character. Whatever the reason, I think it's cool.

After listening to the test pressing we were taken out for a meal with McGee. None of us had ever been in a restaurant in our lives before we entered the music business and we had zero table manners. We were used to basic West of Scotland food like fish and chips and had no idea what to order when the menu was passed around, especially in a foreign country where we had to have the promoter translate the menu for us. We would all sit there mute as dummies waiting until someone ordered something and then the rest of us would immediately order the exact same thing, trying not to embarrass ourselves. On our German tour in 1984 with Biff Bang Pow! I had ordered a coffee and when the waiter brought the order I said to him, 'I ordered a coffee, not a fucking eyebath!' He had brought me an espresso and I'd never seen one in my life.

Anyway, something funny happened at this meal. I have no recollection of this but Douglas Hart and Alan McGee have both told me this story on separate occasions and they both maintain that it happened. All us Mary Chain boys ordered exactly the same thing on the menu and the waiter brought the first two plates out and gave me and Douglas our food first. Then Geoff Travis reached over the table and grabbed our plates and gave them straight to Jim and William who got stuck in. This is a very typical scene in the music business: the people deemed to be 'important' or 'the talent' are always picked out for special treatment by record company starfuckers and management and hangers-on, looking after the golden goose. I've had the 'special treatment' myself. But it's weird that I don't remember the scene at all. Maybe it never happened, maybe it's a revenge dream story from two of my best mates who sussed something out about the shapeshifting creatures of the music biz early on. The thing about the music business is this: if they're fucking someone else today you can be sure they will fuck you tomorrow. Best to keep most as acquaintances and hold on to a few trusted friends. Life is like that anyway.

That first trip to Scandinavia was memorable. In Copenhagen the Chain played a sold-out show to a crowd of mainly goth kids. It was the same all over the European continent. I remember us doing a soundcheck at the Helsinki show. We were running late. The promoter asked if he could open the venue doors whilst we soundchecked because there were a couple of thousand kids waiting in the cold outside. As we were playing our song the dark, vast empty room suddenly filled up with hundreds of goths; a plague of goths. It reminded me of the scene in Werner Herzog's *Nosferatu* when the ghostly barges sail down the canal and thousands of rats come off onto the quayside and bring plague to the city. I never realised how widespread the goth movement was until I toured Europe. They were *everywhere*. It was like a pestilence. I was never a goth but somehow the Chain attracted them. William especially liked goth girls. Not the music though, which he thought was a great idea but never realised. He had a point. I went astray that night. The road throws up all sorts of temptations and traps. You live and learn.

There was a fantastic atmosphere in the hall when we took the stage. I was really looking forward to this one. We started off with 'In A Hole' and we meant business. It rocked like fuck: all of us playing razor-sharp no-frills no-meat-on-the-bone psycho-boogie hard rock as it should be played. We were flying high. I was totally sober as were Jim and Douglas. We were *on it*.

Then, in the middle of the show, William, the only one of us who'd been drinking, walked over to Jim's mic stand and started berating the audience. Doug and I looked at each other; he hadn't done anything like this before. Most of his rant was unintelligible and the Glasgow accent would have been impenetrable to the Danish crowd, but the one bit that stuck out clearly was, 'You're a bunch of bacon-eating bastards.' Jim was incensed, totally shocked at his brother's crazed and drunken intervention. Doug and I started laughing but we tried to hide our mirth. We both knew it was wrong but it was so fucking outrageous at the same time. William seemed possessed as if by an evil spirit, almost demonic. He wasn't himself at all. Where the fuck was this poison coming from? McGee was standing side stage and he motioned to Jim, Douglas and myself to leave the stage. We all swiftly climbed up the ten steps to the dressing room which overlooked the hall and closed the door and looked at each other in a blank, shocked silence. William was still onstage on his own, continuing to harangue the Danish audience. When William eventually finished ranting he came into the dressing room and Jim laid into him (in the way that only brothers can), saying that he'd ruined a great show and for what? William exploded. He picked up a wine bottle and threw it against the huge wall-to-wall dressing room mirror, demolishing it. He picked up vodka bottles, chairs, any other object he could get his hands on and proceeded to destroy the room and all of its contents. Jim and Douglas both left speedily whilst McGee and myself stayed and egged him on, both of us loving the anarchic and violent chaos of the scene. That was the first time I'd witnessed William's deep-rooted anger. I was carrying some myself, so I related to him. When there was nothing left to trash, McGee put his arm around the now mute and placid William and took him back to the hotel. I went down into the hall to see what was happening and found Douglas chatting to some fans, a bunch of lovely Danish girls who invited us to their flat for a party. We took up their invitation and hung out there all night. They were nice gentle people, all music fans, and we had fun there. Much more preferable than the doom-laden Mary Chain hotel scene.

It was often like that between the Reid brothers. On my last tour, February 1986, we played at Coventry University. Peel favourites We've Got a Fuzzbox and We're Gonna Use It, an all-girl punk band – a riot of Day-Glo colours, fishnet tights and highly spiked and teased bottle-blonde goth hair and Doc Martens – were our opening act. We took to the stage after Fuzzbox's set and went about delivering the Mary Chain gospel to the many black-clad disciples waiting for sonic deliverance. We nailed it, man, we were hot that night. We now had our act down and played with total professionalism (well, by our standards, anyway).

Three quarters through our set, in the space between songs, I saw William quietly call over to his brother. Jim was facing the audience and had his back to William, and I could see that he couldn't hear the message. We rocked on and finished the set, then we left the stage and walked into the dressing room, very pleased with our performance, or so I thought. Once inside, with the door closed behind us, William said to Jim, 'I called to you onstage between songs and you ignored me.'

Jim looked incredulous. 'What? What are you talking about?'

William's voice rose in anger. 'What am I fucking talking about? You humiliated me in front of two thousand people!'

'I what? I never heard you,' Jim said. 'Honestly. . . are you fucking crazy?'

Everyone in the room was silent, frozen with tension. It felt awful. William picked up a bottle and smashed it into the floor.

Jim sarcastically spat out, '*Very* Sid Vicious. . . well done, William.'

William exploded and was lost in a blizzard of rage. With one single arm movement he swept the band rider of cans of lager and bottles of wine and vodka off the table in front of the dressing room mirror and destroyed everything in sight. This time, McGee and I didn't think it was funny at all. We left the room with Jim and Douglas and left William in there, screaming and shouting on his own. A sad end to a great show. The only thing I can say in William's defence here is that touring does that to people. It's a highly intense environment and the scrutiny of two thousand pairs of eyes can feel like a forensic intrusion into your soul, if you leave yourself open to it. I was the drummer boy at the back; and not the visionary songwriter and leader that William was. I had zero pressure, no worries. I just had to play and I loved it. It's harder for frontmen, because they are thinking all the time, *How can I make this better?* They can never really relax. The self-examination doesn't stop with writing the songs, the art has to be complete, that means record covers, staging, presentation, dress, interviews, the lot. There is no let-up. Being in a band can expose the many deep insecurities and neuroses of the artist in ways that anonymity serves to hide. Many artists have almost nothing to shield them between their nerves and the world – sensitive cats for sure. You have to be able to build defences and be tough, no two ways about it. Many have tried and many have fallen. The road is long if you want it to be, but you need a strong spirit and a thirst for discovery. You have to be curious and searching, and the very best always are. They never stand still. The road is not for everyone.

My time with the Jesus and Mary Chain taught me a lot. Jim and William were obsessive about the way they presented themselves to the world in every aspect from the sleeve graphics to their non-interaction with the audience, everything was thought through. They watched old *Ready Steady Go* clips and saw how the classic artists had presented themselves. I remember them going on about Them performing 'Baby Please Don't Go' on *RSG* where Van Morrison scratches his nose during his performance and they were shocked that he'd blown it (in their eyes) by doing so. Their attention to detail was inspiring to me. In the Chain we had a perfect image and line-up. We all looked good, like a gang: black leather, ripped black shirts and good hair, whereas in the early Primals the image was still all over the place and I knew it. I connected with the Reids because we were all dissociated to different degrees. Douglas was more down to earth. In the Chain we were almost all of one singular mind. It was unspoken, but we knew. We were all students of punk rock and glam, sixties and seventies pop, and had digested McLaren and Rotten's punk tenets. We were all outsiders, a word that is used too liberally these days. The Reids shared a bedroom in their parents' house in East Kilbride and as far as I knew William had no friends and Jim only had two – Douglas and a guy called Cass.

All of us were obsessed by rock and roll. It was a religion to us. In the Mary Chain everyone was a fanatic, equally obsessive about music and image whereas, at this point, it always felt a bit dislocated in the Scream. The thing about bands that fans don't realise is that, in the main, the members are on *not* all on the same trip, there is no shared quest. People join bands for various reasons – mostly to get laid and famous and all that normo-straight jazz shit. Only the holy bands such as the Velvets, Stooges, MC5, Thirteenth Floor Elevators, ever possessed this unity of visionary purity (the Clash came close; even the Sex Pistols were not all on the same aesthetic level). This monomaniacal level of visionary purity is difficult to maintain for too long a time because the intensity of focus required for the communistic commitment of actualising the quest for musical myth, magic, beauty and mystery inevitably leads to physical and spiritual burnout. The chemtrails of heroic, quixotic, drug-mangled art-rockers' career-crashes scar the art-poet dream-skies with warnings and inspiration. To my mind, in a band, there has to be a congress of intellect, a way of looking at the world and oneself in accord with the art-quest. Most are just not up to it, and although they can hide beneath the camouflaging battle dress of rock band uniforms, they are deaf and blind to the source philosophy that drives the music. The Muse does not call to everyone. During my time in the Mary Chain I felt part of a heroic quest. I knew what we were doing was of some cultural importance. There was a deep, unspoken connection that all of us shared. It felt fated that we had been brought together for this sole purpose. The Scream hadn't yet reached that point. I knew and understood this to be fact. Would it ever get there, I wondered to myself?

JAMC felt like a real band. Like a force field everyone was tuned into. In Primal Scream at this point there were some part-timers in the band, and we had guys coming and going on guitar. I only really thought me, Beattie and Robert were taking it seriously. In the Mary Chain everybody was a fanatic, equally obsessive about music and image.

When the JAMC walked into a room or onstage I felt amazing in the knowledge that we looked like we meant it for real. It wasn't a pose, it was a way of life. None of us wanted a 'real' job, we wanted to live a creative life, to spend our days writing songs and making music and looking good whilst doing it. We all knew that the straight life of job, marriage, kids was not for us. We saw the straight life as a trap. Punk rock had opened up our consciousness to the fact that there was another way of life, that kids like us could lead creative lives, that we too could be artists and rock and roll stars. Rock and roll is a great democratic art form: any kid can make a band, you don't have to be an accomplished player, enthusiasm can carry the day, and the mere fact that a kid can discover that how they express themselves can be a revolutionary act. The shared belief in the power of punk was a powerful tie.

# 16.

# A Splash One Happening

I wanted to write songs, but I was still trying to work out what to say. I didn't want to reveal myself, so a lot of it was codified. The lyrics were good, by which I mean they alluded to something which is good. However, they were not direct. Later on I became more direct because I was influenced by the honesty of soul and country writers like Hank Williams and Dan Penn and I had a lot more courage in terms of what I was prepared to reveal about my life. Initially, though, I was just writing lyrics to go with the melodies, because we were writing songs with a really strong melody and lots of chord changes. I wrote unusual songs because I only knew a few chords. Everything was dictated by melody, it wasn't about the guitar riffs. In Primal Scream Beattie wrote guitar riffs to go with the songs, but the songs were written from melody. The songs had some kind of sadness in them, disappointment married to a sense of wonder, a bittersweet duality, a mix of resignation, romance and melancholy.

I was doing stuff in Europe and England with the Mary Chain, so I was hardly in Glasgow. We self-promoted another Primal Scream gig in a place called Lucifer's in Jamaica Street which became the Sub Club, a famous acid house venue in Glasgow. I made the poster for that. It was from a Herschell Gordon Lewis movie: a girl with her face covered in blood, but looking really trippy. The support band came from Cumbernauld and were called the Original Mixed-up Kid, taken from the Mott the Hoople song of the same name. I just brought them in because they put some money towards the PA and venue hire and they would bring a crowd of their mates in as well, so we'd break even. The idea was not to lose any money. My friend, the artist Jim Lambie, told me he was at that gig and it fucking blew his mind. That was the Scream's second gig. I think it was reviewed in the *NME* by Andrea Miller, which is amazing for a second gig.

After that, Jeff Barrett put Primal Scream on in Plymouth at a little club called Ziggy's, and McGee had us come down to play some gigs in London at the Clarendon Ballroom. McGee released our single 'It Happens' / 'All Fall Down' and they gave us a full page in the *NME* alongside a great photograph taken of us by Lawrence Watson. We're standing in a church doorway and I'm dressed head to toe in black leather with long hair. My head's back. I look really feminine, like I'm wearing make-up.

In the summer of 1985 I started this club in collaboration with a few friends called Splash One. I came up with the name, inspired by the Thirteenth Floor Elevators song of that title:

*I've seen your face before*
*I've known it all my life*
*and though it's you,*
*your image cuts me like a knife*
*and I am home, home to stay*

It was about sending out a message to other like-minded people that this club was going to be somewhere for all the psych-heads and underground rock freaks to gather. I met these guys through Paul Harte who had a flat in the West End in Byres Road, and who joined us playing rhythm guitar around this time. There was a guy called Grant MacDougall who lived in the flat opposite Paul's – a really good guy. He worked at Christie's, the auctioneers. He was into the Pop Group, Throbbing Gristle, and 23 Skidoo. Grant had the brilliant collage poster from the first Pop Group album up on his wall and an original Nazi swastika flag hanging too. He was absolutely *not* a fascist; it was post-punk bohemian decoration. Grant was into Factory Records and flirting with fascist imagery was something that was seen as transgressive for the time, though that's hard to explain now. There was a promoter in London called Final Solution who put gigs on by Joy Division and Killing Joke, but no one in the music scene was outraged. It was the culture of the time, and one that feels very distant now. Bands like Throbbing Gristle toyed with fascist and authoritarian imagery and Joy Division changed their name to New Order. Both names with Nazi connotations. A Certain Ratio took their name from a Brian Eno lyric by way of a Heinrich Himmler quote: 'A certain ratio of Gentiles are Jews.' This stuff was in the air back then, and it was sure to have an effect on teenagers. A lot of it was shock value, a statement. In the seventies I used to go to football matches with a guy we called Big Hartie, who was a total fucking headcase. He was into public acts of transgression. I witnessed him do some outrageous stunts. Once when we were playing five-a-side for Holyrood Youth Club in the gymnasium in Holyrood School he climbed up on the wall bars and shouted, 'Hey boys, look!' Everybody stopped playing and looked up, and he dropped his shorts and shat from the top of the wall bars, straight onto the parquet wooden floor. Transgressive art. We didn't know whether to laugh or be horrified. We were caught between the two emotions. It was like he'd smashed through the cinema screen of reality. It was a statement – a statement against teenage boredom. It was amazing.

Between Grant, his friend Derek Loudon, myself, Karen, Louise Wright and some other people, we clubbed in our money and hired this club called Daddy Warbucks. It was situated on West George Street, a minute's walk from Queen Street Railway Station and just around the corner from George Square where the Glasgow City Chambers are. There was a small flight of stairs that led from the street up into the club. Once you were past the bouncer on the door you were greeted by the sight of a hotel concierge-type desk with a till where we would all take turns taking the entrance money from the punters. There was a cloakroom on the right and the entrance to the dancefloor straight in front of you. It was always very dark inside. The walls were painted matt black and there were flashes of silver here and there, nothing too flashy but just enough to remind you that you were in a nightclub. The lighting was minimal. There may have been disco lights and a mirror ball but we never used them, preferring to keep the club dark but for the few stage lights that allowed the bands to see their instruments. The admission fee was £2, which for five hours of high-energy rock and roll sounds you couldn't hear played anywhere in Glasgow, plus a live set from an up-and-coming new contemporary garage-rock band, was pretty good value. I remember manning the door when Sonic Youth played the club for their very first show in Scotland and a bottle-blonde punkette girl complained to me that we had raised the price to £3. I said to her that the band had come all the way from America and had touring costs to meet (we paid Sonic Youth £500, but I never told her that) and she was lucky that we had brought them up to Glasgow.

The crowd that came to Splash grew with each month as we successfully managed to promote a number of the new happening bands on the UK music scene, mostly from the Creation label, which I of course had links to. Bands such as Jasmine Minks, the Pastels, the Weather Prophets, Felt, Meat Whiplash, the Bodines and the Shop Assistants all released exciting singles in 1985 or '86 and were getting music press features and plays on John Peel's BBC radio show, and there was definitely a cultural spin-off from the whirlwind that the Jesus and Mary Chain had whipped up that also attracted new faces to come to the club.

We ran Splash One on a non-profit basis. Everyone involved did it for the love of music and to bring exciting new bands to Glasgow and it felt like we were building a 'scene' in the city after so many years of nothingness. For a long time, there hadn't been a rock and roll scene. Sure there had been Postcard back in 1980 but that wasn't rock and roll, that was something else.

Rock and roll was a despised form in the eighties, ridiculed by *NME* writers who mocked anyone or any band who they decided was 'rockist'. In some sense they were correct that 'rock' had to change and be more culturally aware of societal changes and incorporate feminism and be done with its sexist, male chauvinist superiority gimmickry which only reinforced established power structures. They were also correct that the 'feminisation' of rock was an exciting new development which gave us challenging bands and artists such as the Au Pairs, the Slits, Siouxsie Sioux and Chrissie Hynde writing songs and telling us stories from *their* point of view. There were no men controlling these girls. No way. Men were *scared* of these women.

However, somewhere along the way everything seemed to get lost in a swirl of cocktail music and an aspirational non-confrontational style championed in the *NME* as 'new pop', where chart success and non-threatening lyrics and safe, nice, 'boy and girl next door' personalities were the order of the day. Some brilliant records like ABC's 'All of My Heart' came out of this time – we used to play a version of that classic song at early Scream soundchecks in 1985 and '86 and Martin Fry is a cool guy. But in the main things got awful in UK music somewhere around 1981 in my opinion. The idea of music as rebellion was mocked in the music press. The Clash were seen as has-beens, also-rans, even as they were releasing fabulous singles such as 'Magnificent Seven' in which they combined Strummer's anti-work beat poetry with a Grandmaster Flash / Sugarhill Gang NYC rap rhythm:

*Ring! Ring! It's 7 a.m.!*
*Move y'self to go again*
*Cold water in the face*
*Brings you back to this awful place*

I thought about that line every morning when I got up at 7 a.m. to get ready to go to work at John Horn's printing factory, as I splashed my face with cold water in our council flat bathroom. I loved songs that described the true reality of my life. The power of that connection hit deep into my consciousness. Strummer *knew*.

'New pop' was about aspiration to a fantasy life. Wham!, Haircut 100, Kid Creole all made good pop singles, just as the New Romantics had too. But those records said nothing to me about my life. I could tell by looking at certain bands that they were mostly just Bowie casualties. All form and no content. It was all about BEING FAMOUS. They had nothing to say.

Nothing cut as deep as songs like 'A Town Called Malice' or 'When You're Young' by the Jam. Paul Weller, like Strummer, was still carrying the punk flame. A true working-class poet. Weller's lyrics were as sharp and hard as his Mod / punk image. No messing. He meant it. Another song I loved around that time was 'Grey Day' by Madness. That song described my life perfectly in 1981:

> *In the morning I awake,*
> *My arms my legs my body aches,*
> *The sky outside is wet and grey*
> *So begins another weary day*

I loved pop music when it both chimed with and described my life. That sensation of being able to completely relate to a lyric was very powerful. To be moved by poetry and music was something I continually craved. That's why emotionally numb pop music that was only ever touching the surface of things never really turned me on. I wanted to go *deep*.

Daddy Warbucks was the kind of place that was open through the week for neds to go and pick up girls, get wasted and have fights. We hired it on a Sunday night which was always quiet.

We played cassette tapes because everybody was such an anal fucking record collector, no one wanted to take their records, their precious singles, and get them scratched. So through the week everybody would make a cassette tape. Every time we had a gig we'd make a different compilation. It was good. Playing the Velvets, Stooges, Shangri-Las, Ronettes, Pistols, Electric Prunes, Seeds, that kind of thing.

There was no other club like it in Glasgow. Night Moves was about touring goth bands, and then there was a place called Henry Afrika's that put on Bowie-casualty jazz-funk bands. I think the Apollo had closed down by then. There was also Tiffany's, where bands of a certain size like Hüsker Dü or the Bunnymen played, but the smaller clubs were for neds, and there was nowhere for people like us to go. I remember we went to the art school one night tripping and I got thrown out because they had these bits of rope suspended from the ceiling with little pennant flags hanging from the ropes. I was tripping out my skull, jumping up and pulling on the flags, trying to fucking destroy the place, and the bouncers threw me out in the street. I was just shouting at everybody. I used to get quite aggressive on drugs. There was a car outside and I climbed on the roof. That was all there was to do: take acid and jump up and down on a car roof. There was nowhere to go basically until we started Splash One and then it became popular and loads of bands met and formed there.

Because of our club all these kids were forming bands in places like Bellshill. Suddenly you'd meet somebody like Norman Blake, who was in a band called the Boy Hairdressers with the artist Jim Lambie. The Boy Hairdressers split up and Norman formed Teenage Fanclub. The other band that started there was the one Kurt Cobain loved, the Vaselines. Frances and Eugene met each other at Splash One. They became boyfriend and girlfriend and then Stephen Pastel put their records out on his 53rd & 3rd label. Kurt Cobain heard them and fell in love with them. He covered two of their songs on the Nirvana *MTV Unplugged* album. I met Eugene through his big brother Charlie, from a club called Maestros in the early eighties, the New Romantic period. Charlie was a really stylish guy, he always had a great look on.

I remember making Eugene tapes of Velvets bootlegs and stuff, and he started growing his hair like John Cale. It was a cool scene and people would take acid and come to the club tripping out of their skulls to groove to the psychedelic punk-rock soundtrack.

I met Stephen Pastel through McGee and Creation. I had to meet him to get the artwork for the Pastels single 'Something Going On', which I was putting together for McGee – something I used to do on those early Creation Records sleeves. You'd print it out on A3 and then cut it in half and fold it and then put it in a plastic bag. I had them printed by a guy that I used to work with in the John Horn printing factory. I immediately liked Stephen. He was a freaky kid, total outsider in his own way, but I remember I was shocked when I asked him if he dug the Pistols and he said to me, 'No, I don't like the Sex Pistols.'

I was like, 'What?' I said, 'Why don't you like the Pistols?'

'They're like heavy metal.' Stephen was more into Dan Treacy, TV Personalities and Swell Maps. We agreed on the Shangri-Las, Velvets and Subway Sect though. In the Scream we craved rock and roll stardom with major hit albums, singles and fantasies of drugged-out *Performance* (the classic sixties Donald Cammell and Nicolas Roeg movie)-style decadent reveries, but Stephen had no truck with any of that stuff. He had no desire for dissolution and fame. His whole aesthetic persona was shaped by the ideas that emerged from the independent music scene of the eighties, especially the Rough Trade and Whaam! labels. Whereas I wanted the musicians in our band to aspire to be great players, as good as the musicians that we heard on our favourite records from the sixties like Love, the Doors and the Byrds, Stephen was more attracted to the wilfully amateurish sounds of bands like the Raincoats – artists more grounded in the realities of the mundane and everyday, like a kitchen-sink sound version of British cinéma vérité; in love with the idea of making music with friends just for the joy of it with no great career plan involved. Very pure, very idealistic. I admired him then for his convictions and still do today. He's still making fine music and is very involved in the Glaswegian musical community. He also owns a fantastic record shop called Monorail in Glasgow.

For the front cover of our very first single 'All Fall Down' I took an image from a sixties Françoise Hardy album that I'd seen lying on the floor of Joe Foster's Dalston bedsit; it had stuck in my mind as a great image I could use. I cut it so it was just half her face, her hair blowing in the wind, so you didn't know it was her. I just liked the image, the shape her hair made. It was abstract and mysterious. On the back of the single was a photograph of the band that Karen took.

Primal Scream had come down to London, to Alaska Studios, under a railway arch directly across the road from Waterloo Station, to record a single, 'Crystal Crescent'. Many years later, in 2009, we would rehearse there with legendary Motor City high-energy heroes Wayne Kramer, Michael Davis and Dennis Thompson of the MC5 for a show we would play together at Massive Attack's Meltdown. Joe Foster co-produced it with us, as he had with 'All Fall Down', one of the earliest songs we wrote and not a very good choice for a single. We tacked some trumpets on in an effort to sound like the Teardrop Explodes and Dexys but the truth was, it was a flat and uninspiring recording and I was embarrassed by it. I pleaded with McGee not to release it because I thought it was shit but he had spent something like £160 recording it so he insisted it had to be released.

'Crystal Crescent' was released in a proper twelve-inch and seven-inch sleeve. I designed the cover art and put a still of the filmmaker and actress Maya Deren in *Meshes of the Afternoon* – an underground experimental classic – on the front cover, which had only the band name Primal Scream, no song title, in homage to Peter Saville and Factory records. Maya was friends with Kenneth Anger and into free love and the occult. She looks so beautiful. I had her printed in silver on a blue background. It's a great cover. For the back I used a picture of our then tambourine player looking like a psychedelic lone-ranger bandito taken by Dick Green. I just liked the fact that his face was covered with a neckerchief.

For the B side of 'Crystal Crescent' we recorded a song that I'd written on my sixties sky-blue Vox Phantom, called 'Velocity Girl'. It only had one verse and one chorus, because I felt that I'd said everything I needed to say in that time frame. I imagined it to be a ballad like 'Caroline Says II' by Lou Reed, but when the band got hold of it, it became really fast. I don't even think we practised it before recording it. We just went into Park Lane Studios in Pollokshaws Road, Glasgow and smashed straight through it. And that became the version everyone loves, produced by the band and engineer, Bobby Paterson. At the same session we also recorded a wigged-out Link Wray-style garage instrumental written by Beattie titled 'Spirea X' which samples Malcolm McDowell in *A Clockwork Orange* saying, 'It's funny how the colours of the real world only seem really real when you viddy them on the screen.'

The inspiration for sampling film dialogue came from two records we loved: 'No Sell Out' by Malcolm X, an electro-rap twelve-inch on Tommy Boy Records, and 'E=MC$^2$' by Big Audio Dynamite in which Mick Jones and Don Letts had sampled dialogue from films by the director Nicolas Roeg. It's difficult to convey how big an effect *A Clockwork Orange* had on my generation. I was too young to see it when it was originally released in 1971 and it was quickly withdrawn and banned from UK cinemas by the film's director Stanley Kubrick. There had been violent gang-related incidents purportedly inspired by the film with kids dressing up in white overalls and bowler hats unleashing a wave of 'ultra-violence' on Britain's streets, so Kubrick pulled the film. Weirdly, the film was only banned here in Britain. By de-platforming himself Kubrick assured that the film became a hot cult classic amongst cinephiles of a certain delinquent disposition, and it could only be viewed by purchase of a bootleg VHS video cassette. VHS home video machines only came into mass usage around 1983, so it was very difficult to see the film and this just added to its transgressive mystique.

I managed to find myself a copy at a record fair at the McClellan Galleries in 1983 and was thrilled to finally sit down and feast my eyes on Kubrick's masterpiece. I'd read the Anthony Burgess novel a few years earlier and already knew the trajectory of the narrative about young Alex and his gang of droogs speaking their occult Nadsat language, drinking vellocet at the Korova Milkbar to sharpen them up for a bit of 'the old ultra-violence'. In these days of high-definition TVs and Blu-ray players we take it for granted that picture quality is sharp and clear but back in the eighties things were not so. My bootleg VHS copy of *A Clockwork Orange* leapt out of my TV screen with a hallucinatory shudder. It must have been a fourth or fifth generation 'bounce down' – recopied so many times that the moving images jarred and the colours bled into one another like photocopy art using a colour printer, the picture quality degrading and disintegrating each time it is recopied. When that happens a new image is born and the picture becomes something else. All this added to the dark, violent, transgressive and forbidden mystique of *A Clockwork Orange* and the film was a big influence on myself, Jim, Robert Young and the Mary Chain too.

Years later, in 1992, Douglas Hart hipped me to the fact that the Scala cinema in Kings Cross was going to screen a one-off performance of *A Clockwork Orange*. I excitedly travelled up to London from Brighton with my then-girlfriend Emily and met Douglas outside the cinema. I remember it was a cold, grey afternoon. We thought the screening would be rammed with 'Clocky' fans but when we went inside there was only us three plus maybe four other people scattered around the stalls. Seeing it on the big Scala screen for the first time in glorious technicolour was quite something. It really is a film unlike any other. Sadly, Warner Brothers got wind that the film had been screened without permission and they sued the Scala, which led to the cinema closing down; a real blow to cult cineastes in the London area. The all-nighter Friday night into Saturday morning Scala screenings of 'underground', 'cult' movies were legendary. I attended a screening of sixties psychedelic exploitation movie *The Trip* directed by Roger Corman there one night whilst tripping on acid myself. Taking the Underground from Kings Cross at midnight to get the train back to Brighton was a lysergic subterranean mindfuck. The other late-night revellers and passengers resembled creatures in Hieronymus Bosch's *Garden of Earthly Delights*. It was 'real horrorshow', to quote Alex in *A Clockwork Orange*.

The 'Crystal Crescent' / 'Velocity Girl' single came out in 1986, and it coincided with some writers at the *NME* deciding there were a bunch of new underground British bands who had something in common; they gave this 'scene' a label, designating it as a new movement: *C86*. *NME* used to release cassettes of what they thought was the best new music of that year. It was like a taster, a sampler. The first track on *C86* was 'Velocity Girl' and people went mental for it. People were buying the single to get the B side and it reached number four in John Peel's Festive 50:

1. There Is a Light That Never Goes Out – THE SMITHS
2. Kiss – AGE OF CHANCE
3. Mr Pharmacist – THE FALL
4. Velocity Girl – PRIMAL SCREAM
5. Panic – THE SMITHS
6. I Know it's Over – THE SMITHS
7. The Queen is Dead – THE SMITHS
8. Safety Net – THE SHOP ASSISTANTS

9. Some Candy Talking – JESUS AND MARY CHAIN
10. US Eighties – THE FALL

That was a very big deal in those days.

Once we'd played a few gigs you'd get kids at university who read the *NME* and listened to John Peel call Creation up and say, I want to promote Primal Scream, and you'd go and play for like £150. Basically, petrol money and van hire. We did loads of these gigs everywhere, from Plymouth to Middlesbrough, little gigs promoted by fans. This is how we met Jeff Barrett, later of Heavenly Recordings. Jeff put the Mary Chain on at Ziggy's in Plymouth in the spring of 1985 and then the Scream that summer and we became lifelong friends and co-conspirators. We played places like the Duchess of York in Leeds and that's where I met Tim Tooher.

Tim and his mate Mike Stout were both dropouts from Leeds University and they were big Mary Chain, Scream and Birthday Party fans. Obsessive music-fan guys and girls like them would promote us and other bands such as the Loft, Jasmine Minks, Felt, the Weather Prophets, the June Brides, the Bodines, the Pastels, all over the country. Little pockets of cultural resistance; kids who wanted to hear high-energy garage rock with a romantic, literate bent, kids who were sick of the corporate pop lie that persisted on radio and TV and ruled imperiously over the broader culture. For example, I found the smug hubris on show at the Live Aid concert at Wembley Stadium sickening. In 1984, breaking a United Nations cultural boycott in condemnation of apartheid, Freddie Mercury and his band Queen had played a series of shows at the Sun City luxury resort in South Africa at the same time that P. W. Botha's Boer death squads roamed the country undertaking state-sanctioned, extrajudicial killings, assassinating anti-apartheid dissidents and activists. Nelson Mandela was still imprisoned, and while the Black majority population were herded into poverty-stricken 'townships' and 'bantustans'

243

(Black-only areas) much-loved and revered UK recording artists such as Queen, Rod Stewart and Elton John had all taken the apartheid gold. The dark irony of playing Sun City then Live Aid was seemingly lost on everyone concerned.

The self-congratulatory hubris of the rock elite who had 'survived' the excesses of the sixties and seventies and the awful music they were all now making was something so nakedly disgusting that it gave us something to kick against. Most of the former counter-cultural heroes of the baby-boomer generation were on display on the Live Aid stages in London and Philadelphia; a globally transmitted horrorshow of talent gone to waste, the dissolute proof of their over-privileged, decadent wastrel lives written all over their once-beautiful, but now twisted, bloated, drug- and alcohol-ravaged faces. They played the hits that had helped spring the hippie revolution into mass consciousness in the sixties without energy or sincerity. Looking distracted and befuddled behind a wall of coked-out, numbed indifference, they displayed nothing except an arrogant contempt for both their audience and their own rich songwriting legacies.

The lie was that the sixties pop revolution changed anything, except in a deleterious way, the narco-zapped brain chemistry of many of the formerly shamanic performers was plain to see up on those stages. There was a lesson to be learned somewhere. I remember William Reid telling me it had made him feel sick, and I knew exactly what he meant. The punk revolution hadn't changed anything at all. The same superstars still lorded it over the pop culture as they had done in 1977, just as they still do today.

It's easy to be judgemental and high on self-righteous purity when you are only young and starting out in your career. You haven't made many mistakes yet, have hardly played any shows or made any notable artistic statements; the young artist thinks they know it all and, in their certitude, damn anyone or everything that cleared the path to make space before them.

In a way this year-zero generational attitude is needed to

clear the decks and start again, revive culture and make it both relatable and accessible to young people. Youth needs to have its voice and only youth can speak for itself. The disappointment we felt at the artistic collapse of some of those who had come before us and inspired us was something we vowed never to surrender to ourselves. This time it would be different. . .

One notable thing about the new bands was a shared political consciousness. There was a mainly unspoken left-wing anti-establishment ethos (maybe with the exception of Lawrence from Felt who was 'apolitical'). This leftist attitude was prevalent throughout the UK independent music scene in bands such as the Smiths (GLC benefit), New Order, and the Style Council who were all active in some way in class politics. Margaret Thatcher had polarised the entire country and the rockers were not immune to it. Even if sometimes the musicianship was lacking in places there was an overall feeling of youthful sincerity to the records that bands were releasing. You could tell that they *meant it*. There was an urgency in records such as 'Every Conversation' by the June Brides or 'Up the Hill & Down the Slope' by the Loft that encouraged the feeling that the band and singer were all playing as if their lives depended on it, that the song *had* to be written.

Again, I am reminded of the sincerity of youth, when one is constantly living in the moment and everything seems to be a life or death scenario. One's perception of time hasn't been grounded by experience yet – time is of the essence and there never seems to be enough of it, and everything seems *so important* and has to be done *now*. The feeling that the newly written song HAS TO BE RECORDED NOW BEFORE I DIE. . . The rush and thrill of these seven-inch 45 RPM mini-manifestos on vinyl was addictive to my young ears and some of the great records released around this period (mostly on single because no one except Felt had recorded full albums of their repertoires as yet) such as 'Ballad of the Band' and 'Primitive Painters' by Felt, 'Think!' by Jasmine Minks and 'Baby Honey' by the Pastels provided an alternative soundtrack to the corporate sugar-pill schmaltz that ruled the airwaves. With the combination of support from certain music paper journos like Neil Taylor at *NME* and John Robb at *Sounds*, and Radio One plays from the likes of John Peel and Janice Long, the word was getting out about this sonic resistance and kids all over the country were calling up the Creation offices in London (in reality a single room at 83 Clerkenwell Road) offering us and the other bands gigs that the kids themselves would promote. It was a word-of-mouth scene and fanzines were springing up all over the place. I first met future *NME*, *GQ* and *Loaded* editor James Brown when he collared me as I came offstage after a Scream show in Leeds University refectory. This sixteen-year-old kid was a ball of pent-up enthusiastic energy who asked if he could interview me for his fanzine *Attack on Bzag!* – I of course said yes. A guy named Jerry Thackray who under the nom de plume 'the Legend' had released the very first single on Creation, wrote a 'zine called *The Legend!* in which he enthused about band such as ourselves, the Pastels, and the Shop Assistants. Jerry always supported and wrote approvingly about Primal Scream, even when he wrote for *Sounds* and *NME*, when no one else from the muzak press would. Alan McGee himself had a fanzine called *Communication Blur* which I designed the front cover for one time.

This flurry of youthful enthusiasm and activity had been brewing at a low level, very much under the radar, for a while I think. Post-punk had fizzled out by early 1981 and aside from bands such as the Sisters of Mercy, the Birthday Party and the Smiths there wasn't much excitement in indie-rock. It took the explosive emergence of the Jesus and Mary Chain to really shake things up again and a whole generation who had missed out on punk the first time around now had a band to get excited about. All the Creation artists like ourselves, the Loft, the Jasmine's, Slaughter Joe (Creation staff producer, and cultural provocateur Joe Foster) were carried along in their slipstream. It was a good time to be young and playing in a rock and roll band. It felt that cultural change was possible again for the first time since 1977 and we were at the vanguard.

Sometime in 1986, Paul Harte, the Scream's guitarist, quit the band. I don't think he thought there was much future in it. So this guy called Stuart May, who was a regular at Splash One and always hassling me for info on garage psych records, joined the band at my insistence. Stuart looked good, with an asymmetric haircut, long fringe, shaved at the sides. He always wore a polo neck sweater, tight jeans and pointed Chelsea boots and he was into sixties music. He was quite a handsome boy, and his nickname in the band was 'the Brat'. He became a kind of whipping boy for the more aggressive members of the band. I remember Robert Young saying to me, 'This band needs a scapegoat.'

Stuart came up to my house one sunny afternoon and I played him 'Some Velvet Morning' by Lee Hazlewood and Nancy Sinatra. He'd never heard it before and his eyes and mouth both widened. His facial expression showed that he was awed by the time-altering sensation of the song's thrusting galloping cowboy beat suddenly turning into a psychedelic waltz and then back to the high plains gallop. It's a cut-up masterpiece of Greek mythology and cowboy psychedelia, as if William S. Burroughs was sitting in the producer's chair. After it finished I asked him, 'What did you think?'

He replied, 'It sounds like bad mushies.'

I thought that was a genius observation.

McGee sent the Scream on a tour with the Weather Prophets in May 1986. We had some double-bill gigs with them in Belgium and Holland. We were friends with Pete Astor and all the guys in his band. After a show one night I walked up the stairs in this hotel – we were staying on the first floor, on this long corridor with fifteen rooms – and the Brat and Tam McGurk, the drummer, were both standing at the very end of the corridor. I was at one end, they were at the other. The Brat had the firehose in his hand and as I walked towards him he had a big smile on his face. I said to them both, 'What the fuck are you guys doing?' The Brat turned on the hose and a tsunami of water went flying from one end of the corridor all the way down to the other and he just looked at me, smiled and said, 'Stones material.' He just soaked the fucking corridor. We were all crying with laughter.

There was always great camaraderie with the Scream. A few of the guys in the band could fight, so there was never any trouble at gigs. The front row was me, the tambourine player, Beattie, then Robert Young and Paul Harte or the Brat and we lined up across the front of the stage so we'd intimidate the audience with guitars held high. We took that from seeing Dexys Midnight Runners performing 'Geno' on *Top of the Pops* looking like an army. It was an aggressive stance and Beattie, especially, loved this. He read this quote about Arthur Lee's Love where another unnamed LA musician said, 'Those guys are called Love, but really they're Hate.' He loved the fact you could be playing gentle music, but at any point you'd let some cunt have it.

We started to get noticed in the music papers. I remember a gig in New Cross on a Friday night and it was rammed. We went onstage and it was a fucking disaster. It was like being on acid but I was completely clean. Our two guitarists and bass player had all tuned their guitars separately by ear; there was a very loud disco being played over the PA system in the room next door and we only realised they were out of tune once we were onstage. I remember trying to sing the songs and I couldn't. The poor audience were looking at us in shock and we were looking at each other, equally appalled. We walked offstage after three songs and that was the end of the gig and we were the headliners. It was like I'd been turned inside out. The most embarrassing thing ever to go from the Mary Chain to this. I wanted to die.

We had some fun times on the road early on, though. One time in 1986 we were all standing on a grass verge by the hard shoulder just off the motorway somewhere in England on the way to a gig having a piss, all seven of us in a line, and somebody said, 'For fuck's sake, would you look at the size of that thing!' Everybody turned round to look at what was causing the commotion. Robert had a huge cock; he was hung like a horse!

Robert was saying, 'What's the problem, guys?'

And I said, 'The size of your cock, ya bastard, it's like a fucking python!'

He just laughed and said to me, 'It's not that I'm that big, it's just that you guys are all too wee.'

From then on he was known in the band as Throb, not Dungo anymore, because of his throbbing bass lines and also because he liked putting it about. He was flying the flag for the band.

We set out from Glasgow one Friday afternoon for gigs in Leeds, Sheffield and Manchester; then back up the motorway to Splash One on Sunday. We had rented a white van from the hire company in Pollokshaws Road. Josh Dean, a Creation-obsessed kid from Brighton who promoted us at the Basement Club in his home town, had volunteered to drive us. Normally Douglas Hart's brother Alan drove us on tour but he wasn't available. The hire company only had a big white transit van with no seats in it so we 'borrowed' a couch and two chairs from Paul Harte's flatmate whilst he was at work. We were sure he would understand. We loaded the couch and chairs plus amps drumkit and guitars into the van and all piled in, looking forward to a weekend of gigs. Leeds and Sheffield went well, then we set off for Manchester. Manchester was always good to Primal Scream.

Picture this scene. We were on the motorway, Josh driving, with a compilation cassette I had made blasting cool sounds. Throb and McGurk were riding shotgun up front. The rest of us were sitting in the back of the van on the 'borrowed' couch, drum cases, and in my case a hundred-watt Fender twin reverb amplifier. We were bombing down the motorway and McGurk said to Josh, 'Hey! The turn off to Manchester is right here, you're gonna miss it, quick!' In a panic Josh steered the van violently to the left and it shot over onto two wheels then violently to the right and up on the opposite wheels. Then he pulled the steering wheel left again and the van spun all the way round in a 360-degree turn. All of this seemed to happen in a slow-motion, cut-up dream state, as if we were trapped in a giant washing machine travelling at eighty miles per hour I was pinned down against the van roof, buried under a pile of amplifiers, guitars, drums and a big living room couch. I could feel the van screeching down the motorway with only the thin metal roof between the skin of my back and the three-lane blacktop.

This horror scene probably only lasted for a few seconds, but seemed like half an hour. Time dissolves and melts into air in my experience of accidents, very much like a jagged, psychedelic, psychotropic time lapse. The van finally skidded to a halt. There was first a silence then a low moan of pain from an unknown voice, a pathetic death-rattle timbre. I guessed it was Joogs. I knew I was alright, but what about the others? The van doors burst open and Josh and Throb pulled out all the drums, amplifiers, guitars and the couch. We staggered out onto the hard shoulder and I saw that the van was totally wrecked. The boys all sat on the grass verge. Joogs, who had a gash on his knee through a cut in his leather jeans, was still moaning; another boy was concussed, but these seemed to be the only casualties. Josh was crying and came up to me saying he was sorry again and again until I had to say to him, 'Enough!' I showed no emotion. Now wasn't the time for crying. I checked how everyone was feeling and if they were hurting. We were all good apart from Joogs who needed to go to hospital. We didn't need him to play the gig but the amps and drumkit were totally trashed and we still needed to get to the soundcheck at the Boardwalk. Joogs was in pain so he was lying on his back covered with a jacket and busloads of tourists would slow down to take a look at the crash scene, our van still sitting smashed up in the central lane, and then drive on without asking us if we needed any help. I thought they were macabre, so a few V signs were sent their way. Cunts! Josh walked to find a phone and tell the police and the AA there had been a crash. Nathan McGough who was promoting the show sent out a couple of cars to drive us into Manchester and get Joogs to hospital. He also arranged for us to borrow the necessary equipment we needed. In the end, we made the soundcheck and played a great show. I've heard that some of the Stone Roses were there that night. As I said, Manchester has always been good to us. Nathan found us places to stay, couches to kip on and the Brat repaid that kindness by running off and spending the night with Nathan's girlfriend, Ailie. That was the road.

I first met Nathan when I was in the Wake. He was managing Factory band the Royal Family and the Poor. We just got on straight away. He is actually from Liverpool; his dad is Roger McGough, the poet. Some people think Nathan looks like Paul McCartney. He was a very handsome young man, women loved him. He later managed Happy Mondays at the height of the Madchester era. It's still great to run into Nathan to this day. He's a proper character.

We were now without a van to take us to our sold-out hometown gig at Splash One. I told the boys in the band to meet at the bus station in Manchester on Sunday afternoon where we would take the Stagecoach back home. We couldn't afford train fares and this method was cheaper. We got on the bus with what was left of our equipment, determined to make the Glasgow show a great one despite the crash. A crisis is always a good test of character. It allows you to see who believes in the cause and who doesn't. I remember the feeling of determination I had to make it a good show, Beattie and Throb too. Nothing was gonna stop us from playing those gigs, nothing.

# 17.

# Electric Ballroom Blitz (Brained And De-Chained)

On tour with the Jesus and Mary Chain I would share a room with Douglas. Doug was very easy to connect with, open, agreeable and intelligent; a curious young man, always enthusiastic about stuff he was into whether that be films, records, books or football. He was a beautiful soul. The girls all loved Douglas and so did I. Once or twice I doubled up with William and that was good because I got to know him a bit more that way. We would have discussions about stuff long into the night. In public William was quiet and reticent, but one on one with someone he trusted he would open up. In music paper interviews William wouldn't say much, preferring to let his songs speak for themselves, but he had strong opinions on a lot of subjects and was a very interesting thinker; his and Jim's vision for the band was so pure and well thought-out. They didn't arrive there by chance. The Mary Chain had a vision of what a rock and roll band *should* be and what it *shouldn't* be. I learned so much from being around those guys.

Beattie and I also had a vision for the Scream, but we were still in the embryonic stage of forming it, creating it in the moment. We knew we didn't have the perfect band yet but we had to get out and make records and play gigs so we were learning how to do it in real time. The Mary Chain already had the luxury of a backlog of brilliant songs, and Will was three years older than me and had been writing songs longer. The Chain as a band was perfect as it was: four punks with clear minds and a defiantly powerful, well thought-out group aesthetic. There were no neds in the Mary Chain. There were a couple in the Scream. I loved the purity of the Mary Chain; it was kind of religious. Actually, it *was* religious. Pure rock and roll.

As we got bigger we were given single rooms with double beds, but even then, some of the hotel rooms on tour would be creepy, low-rent affairs and I could feel the ghosts coming through the walls. I remember one time in Berlin we stayed in a modern concrete skyscraper block. It was an alienating place and I thought my room was haunted, so I asked Douglas if I could room with him and we shared his big double bed. We did that a lot. I remember sharing his room at the Iroquois Hotel the first time we visited NYC in 1985: cockroach central with the hairdressers on the ground floor where James Dean got his hair cut. Cool.

Every time the Mary Chain played a London show it would end in a riot. On 15 March 1985 we had a gig at North London Polytechnic on the Holloway Road. That was insane. It was the first time in my young life that I'd ever flown on an aeroplane; McGee flew me down for the show from Glasgow. When I landed I couldn't hear a thing because my hearing had been severely disabled by the intense air pressure in the cabin during descent. I arrived at the venue and the first person I saw was the Jasmine Minks guitarist, Adam Sanderson. Adam had a Glen check Crombie on, which was a real ned thing from the seventies. He walked over to me and he opened up his coat and said to me conspiratorially, 'Hey Bobby, look,' and he had a fucking claw hammer in the pocket. He's from Aberdeen.

I said, 'What the fuck's that for, Adam?'

'Just in case.' Then he went on, 'Word on the street is they're coming to get the Mary Chain tonight. There's a bunch of boys coming to do the Mary Chain in.'

I was like, 'Oh, right, fuck . . .'

The band that went on first were called Meat Whiplash, friends of the Mary Chain from East Kilbride. A garage band with one classic Creation single to their name; total *Pebbles* or *Back from the Grave* scenario. They really couldn't play, but that wasn't the point. During their set somebody threw a bottle on stage and McD, their singer, who was a brilliant guy, threw it straight back into the audience, fair enough if you ask me. That spark lit the flame and some more missiles arrived onstage, bottles and stuff. Then the Jasmine Minks were on. I don't know if the hammer came out. I don't know. I was in the dressing room with the Mary Chain boys. Then somebody came backstage and said there were hundreds of people in the street that couldn't get in. So myself and Douglas went out through the crowd and into the foyer of the venue and we kicked the fire doors wide open. Hundreds of leather-jacketed, spiked-hair gothic punks stampeded towards us through the open doors and got in for free, which swelled the already huge and hostile crowd inside. It was a sold-out gig of about five hundred people but suddenly there were seven or eight hundred people there. By the time we came on, deliberately late, the atmosphere was ugly and we hadn't been playing too long before the missiles started raining down on us and then Jim was dragged into the audience. People had to jump in to get him back because these guys were trying to beat him up. And the missiles were coming the whole time.

Eventually we had to leave the stage after twenty minutes, if that, because the constant hail of missiles and bottles was just too much and someone was gonna get seriously injured. I had bottles flying past my head. The gig got stopped so many times. After we finally walked off the crowd began tearing down the PA stacks and trying to get up onstage. I heard the noise and commotion and ran out of the dressing room to the side of the stage to witness the insanity. Geoff Travis risked being glassed when he ran onstage to get my drums and I picked up any bottle that hadn't been broken on the stage and began throwing them back at the audience. I was in stitches. McGee came to get me and locked us all in the dressing room because he thought if the audience did manage to storm the stage then we were all done for. I remember guys crawling through our dressing room windows *before* the show to get in, so maybe he had a point. It was a shame though because we were playing really well. We were a great band. We did those gigs in Scandinavia and America, and there were no riots, only in England.

Every night we would make up a song. We never rehearsed the songs, we would just start them and finish them. It was free-form madness and I loved it, whatever dirge drone sounds Will, Doug and I would conjure Jim would sing fractured beat poet utterances around the phrase JESUS FUCK. We also did a cover of 'Mushroom' by Can; a kind of airless, parched, doomed, gothic un-funky plague-rock version. I made up a different drum beat, because I couldn't obviously play polyrhythmically like the great Jaki Leibzeit. So, instead I came up with this incessant tambourine and floor tom pulse that the boys could hang their barbed-wire guitar violence on. I have described our version as a 'creepy crawl death-rattle low moan blues'. I think that sums it up.

An Australian film crew filmed that gig with an interview at the end of the riot. There's a bit of me in the interview. I'm sitting on the stage after the hall has been cleared of people and the lights have gone up. I'm speaking in an almost posh voice for some reason: 'We just want people to come and listen to our music. We don't want violence.' Like some young fucking aristocrat. The same guy who forty-five minutes ago was throwing bottles at the audience. It was my first time being interviewed on TV and I loved it. I spoke slowly and clearly so I could be understood by anyone who viewed it. I was self-aware enough to know that had I spoken in my usual burr Glaswegian brogue it may well have come across as unintelligible and I dearly wanted to be understood. The truth was, I was slightly nervous and slowed my diction down to try and come across in a cool manner and not seem stupid. Coming from nowhere to instant fame like we did and having zero 'media training' made for some crazed TV appearances. There was the one on German TV where, as Jim Reid is both proclaiming his own genius and lambasting the legacy of Joy Division to the interviewer's complete astonishment, Karen and I are getting off with each other on the interview couch oblivious to the cameras in a Warholesque show of insatiable young love and exhibitionist abandonment. Amphetamine sulphate and love do mix. . . sometimes.

It seemed that every time we played in England there was a riot. The next one was at the Electric Ballroom and that was even more extreme. There were now people coming to kill the Mary Chain. Jim Reid had gone to see Nick Cave and the Bad Seeds at Hammersmith Palais, and some thug had come up to him and said, 'Are you the singer in the Mary Chain?' and six guys beat him up. Gave him a doing. Kicked fuck out of him. He told me as he was lying on the floor they said, 'Just tell your fucking drummer he's next.'

On 21 September we 'played' the Electric Ballroom in Camden Town. After the NLP riot McGee had got these ex-paratrooper guys, or so they claimed, to be our security. These were really horrible, weird sexist guys; where McGee found them I don't know, maybe he had a subscription to *Soldier of Fortune* magazine. There was an atmosphere of expectation and excitement backstage as we waited to go on, thick with hopeful intensity and dangerous energy. We could feel it backstage in the drab, nicotine-stained dressing room. Oh, the 'glamour' of rock, eh? When we finally took to the stage a wine bottle whizzed past my head before I'd even picked up my drumsticks. *Here we go again*, I thought to myself. We played brilliantly that night, we were so tight after the Scandinavian tour, but the crowd hadn't come to hear a great rock and roll band play their songs, the mob had come to crucify us and vent their rage. We were merely a blank screen onto which they could project all their hatred, anger and frustrations and the fusillade of bottles and pints got too much after a while. It's impossible to focus on the music when you're watching out for flying missiles and around the twenty-minute mark we walked off stage. This act was met with a vast howl from the angry mob who were now baying for our blood like the macabre ghouls who would congregate at Tyburn, or Marble Arch as it is now known, in centuries past to watch criminals hanging. Someone came backstage and said they were tearing down the huge PA stacks and trying to storm the stage, so once again we were locked up in the dressing room for our own 'safety'. One of the paratroopers got bottled on his bald head whilst attempting to retrieve a guitar amplifier. He stormed into the dressing room trapped in his impotent rage, cursing us; he really wanted to hit us but professionally that would have been a disaster for him. We just ignored him, staring blankly and without any empathy or emotion and when he left the room we all burst out laughing saying stuff like, 'The stupid cunt deserved it.' He was a nasty man.

If you're wondering how I felt in those days about going onstage with the Mary Chain, and if I was scared, the answer is no. Some nights, before I had even picked up my drumsticks, there would be bottles, pint glasses and full cans of beer whizzing past my head. I was young and thought I was invincible. I didn't think they could touch me, because of the music, the power of the music. I felt that we had a force field between the four of us, a magical force field generated by the power of the Mary Chain sound. I just felt like it was us against the audience and we were always gonna win.

There was a lot of anger at gigs in the eighties. I don't know why, if it had something to do with the Thatcher era. We'd had a long period of Thatcherism by the mid-eighties and I guess rock gigs and football matches were places to vent anger. Gigs could get violent. I remember being attacked at a Johnny Thunders gig in about 1987. I was walking back from the bar with four pints for my brother Graham, Throb and Andrew and some guy came up from behind and punched me in the back of the head and ran off into the crowd. It got tiresome because every time we played a gig the violence was more extreme and people in the theatres were getting hurt.

I travelled to New York for the first time with the Mary Chain in April 1985. Punk city of my dreams. It was incredible. My first stop was to go to find the Gem Spa on St Mark's Place to pay homage to the New York Dolls because that's the picture on the back of their first album. Then I headed to Midnight Records in Chelsea, because I'd discovered that they sold psychedelic records: *Back from the Grave* and *Psychedelic Unknowns*, *Acid Dreams*, all the stuff you couldn't find in the UK then. You always had to send off for mail order to the States for these vital records. As I was looking through the racks I was aware of the guy standing right beside me focused on the next rack. I took a double look and there was Robert Quine, guitarist from the Voidoids. Fuck! I asked him, 'Are you Robert Quine?'

He went, 'Yeah.'

I said, 'Can I have your autograph please for my friend? Could you write *To Jim*?' I thought it was a shame Beattie was missing out. He loved Robert Quine's guitar playing so much, we all did. He played like no one before or since.

The whole time we were in New York was so exciting, I felt like I was in a movie. It was a great life experience for me, as well as those gigs in Europe, the Scandinavian tour. I loved being a rock star. It was a trip being in the most exciting band on the planet at that point. Even bands that we loved such as Echo and the Bunnymen were recording tracks that sounded like us. I had been given a pre-release tape of the next Bunnymen single 'Bring on the Dancing Horses' by Mick Houghton, their PR. The B side was titled 'Over Your Shoulder' and it sounded like the Mary Chain. It was the Bunnymen doing the Mary Chain! Fucking hell, these guys are gods! Years later in the sleeve notes on a Bunnymen box set Ian McCulloch comments, 'That was just us showing the Mary Chain how it should be done.' Classic Mac.

That American tour was great, two weeks visiting some of the major cities of the United States. Rock and roll nirvana. I love America. Forget about the politics, I grew up on American comics, movies, TV shows and rock and pop records. I was so happy during that tour and the band played great every night: no ultra-violent riots, just great music and the band camaraderie was tight.

Onstage, I would have only William's guitar sound coming through my monitor and he played different every single night. He'd start off with a recognisable riff so we knew which song it was and then proceed to free-form around the established chord sequence that held the song together. He was an incendiary musician. Some nights it felt like he was action painting in sound. He was a truly sonic artist, all instinct and emotion, and he possessed a deep musical intelligence. William Reid was both visceral and artful at the same time; his guitar sound would energise me as if I'd mainlined a shot of high-grade amphetamine sulphate, it was pure white light, white heat, wired soul genius. His gonzoid riffage and energy sprawl would propel me forward rhythmically, jolt-feeding me with constant energy zaps. Douglas and I would maintain eye contact throughout the gig, sometimes laughing at each other, both of us full of ecstatic rock and roll joy, meanwhile Jim would be going full spastic psychotic out front, rolling on the floor, smashing the mic stand to pieces, moaning and cursing and occasionally fully losing consciousness and speaking in tongues, falling betwixt the lyric poetry of the songs and the clang and clamour of the band's feral sounds. Often he would fall on the floor and curl up in a foetal position, overwhelmed by the sonic maelstrom. He was the eye of the hurricane and he knew it. A dangerous place to be.

Jim was a shy boy who somehow transformed himself into a shamanic performer each night, totally possessed by the music. Between the four of us we formed a high-voltage electrical circuit. A psychic force field. A wall of sound both impenetrable and mighty. Fuck you fuck you fuck you. What other band screams *we fucking despise you* to their new-found and still-growing audience? That psychic connection between a configuration of certain human beings is the alchemical formula for creating great rock and roll. Why does it work with some people more than others? Same songs, different people and the spell won't work. Some people are just magical is all, and when it's right you don't question it. It feels right and it's unspoken. That's the occult power of rock and roll, and with the Mary Chain in the early days, it was right.

We started the tour at a rumoured to be Mob-owned venue called the World situated at 254 East 2nd Street in the East Village. We played Boston, Washington, Toronto, Chicago, San Francisco, San Diego and ended it in LA at the Roxy. We were asked to be on Rodney Bingenheimer's KROQ radio show which was popular with LA Anglophiles. Rodney had long been a supporter of the most exciting new British pop and rock bands going all the way back to Bowie, Slade, the Sweet, Pistols and the Clash with his Rodney's English Disco club on Sunset where underground freaks like Kim Fowley, New York Dolls and Iggy Pop caroused with superstars like Led Zeppelin and Quaalude-damaged teen queen glam-rock groupies such as Lori Maddox and Sable Starr. Rodney was the first person on the west coast to play New Wave and punk bands like Blondie, Ramones and Sex Pistols on US radio. His love of great rock and roll was legendary.

On the show one of us mentioned that we were fans of the sixties garage-rock band the Seeds. Rodney told us he was friends with Sky Saxon and that he would arrange a meeting with him if we wanted. So we went for lunch with Rodney at Denny's diner where he ate breakfast, lunch and dinner every single day. Sky Saxon turned up with a retinue of what seemed at first to be homeless, unwashed, middle-aged men wearing raggedy clothes, damaged acid casualties from the sixties counter-culture. This was a desperate and motley bunch. Rodney introduced us to Sky and he seemed friendly enough. I guess he was curious to meet this young British band who were name-checking him. Sky hadn't had a hit since 1966 with his classic 'Pushing Too Hard', the very phrase Jim Reid had sung on 'Never Understand'. It was obvious to all of us that Sky was very much down on his luck and that was sad to see. In our eyes he was a rock and roll hero. We all worshipped the Seeds; they were part of the reason we formed our bands after all. We invited Sky to our show at the Roxy Club later that night. He said he'd come along to see us and we loved the idea of that.

The Roxy Club was opened by David Geffen in 1975 with Neil Young playing the opening night. A bunch of Hollywood post-hippie cocaine cowboy cognoscenti turned up to hear Neil play his Laurel Canyon singer-songwriter soft-rock hits like 'Old Man' and 'Heart of Gold'. Instead they got a whole set of unknown songs that documented the dark side of hippie culture. In the tradition of Raymond Chandler and other 'LA noir' authors who wrote about the hard, sick underbelly of the City of Angels, Neil had written about the amorality, seediness and violence that often accompanied the counter-culture drug world. It wasn't what they wanted to hear.

The Roxy was a licensed venue so we were playing a seven o'clock show for underage kids. The singer-songwriter Beck told me he queued up to see that show as a sixteen-year-old and loved it. That makes me happy because I think Beck is a brilliant artist.

The first gig was great. There was a couple of hours break between shows. I was bored and since we were in the cocaine capital of rock and roll I shouted to Alan, 'Hey, McGee, no snow, no show!' which is what Ian McCulloch allegedly said before each

Bunnymen show. Alan pulled one of the guys aside and asked him if he could get coke and the guy sent this incredible-looking girl out to get it. She came back half an hour later with the goods. Jim, Douglas and myself found another room to chop it out and I swear we snorted everything that was in the bag. By the time we hit the stage for the second show the three of us were bouncing off the walls, wired to fuck. Jim forgot some words; Doug's bass playing was erratic and I found myself lying on the floor on my back once or twice instead of keeping time. The only member who played it straight and great was William. That's the show the radio station recorded and it was pressed up into a vinyl album to be sent to radio stations around the country. Unfortunately not a very good advertisement for the band. If only they'd taped the early show!

After the gig I somehow calmed down; my nerves were less jangled and I felt great on the coke. They say the first time is the best and for me it was true. Here I was sat on the lip of the Roxy stage surrounded by beautiful blonde Californian girls listening rapt to my every word; it was like a Beach Boys–Led Zeppelin fantasy come true. Sky Saxon made his way across the stage and whispered in my ear, 'Hey, Bobby, do you have any drugs?'

I replied, 'Sorry, Sky, we did them all.' He shuffled away disappointed. Thurston Moore and Kim Gordon of Sonic Youth were also there. A few days before we'd seen them play a fantastic co-headline show with Swans in an abandoned factory somewhere out near the desert. Swans' sound was both crushing and claustrophobic and Sonic Youth were in their *Bad Moon Rising / EVOL* period and sounded both mysterious and evil. Kim and Thurston came backstage and chatted. Sonic Youth felt an affinity with the Jesus and Mary Chain. We had met Thurston in NYC in the spring but this was my first time meeting Kim and she was great, Douglas and I both got on with her immediately. Later on we all arranged to meet with Rodney at

Cantor's Jewish Deli which is where Phil Spector would send out for supplies whilst he was cutting his Wall of Sound classics. Phil and the Wrecking Crew lived on Cantor's nosh. Thurston came with us and Kim drove Douglas, giving him a tour of the Hollywood Hills. I was still flying high on the cocaine and the ragged glory of the Roxy shows. Hanging out with Sky Saxon and Sonic Youth in LA was fun. Douglas and I had also met our guitar heroine Poison Ivy Rorschach of the Cramps in a record store earlier that week and I remember I bought a Rhino Girl Group compilation that day and I was so nervous I couldn't even speak. Doug did all the talking whilst I gazed on in mute wonder and awe. Ivy was so fucking sexy. The queen of rock and roll. I loved LA. I didn't want to go home to Glasgow. I never wanted the tour to end.

A couple of months later the Jesus and Mary Chain asked Primal Scream to open for them on two summer gigs. We were excited about this prospect. The first was at the legendary Nottingham Rock City on 25 June 1985. I had just turned twenty-four and life was good. I was playing in two cool rock and roll bands. Before our set we were chatting to one of the Hells Angels who did security at the venue, and he offered us all some speed, which of course was gratefully received. The Angel pulled out a huge Bowie knife and plunged it into a plentiful bag of pure white powder and stuck the speed-laden tip of his knife up each of our noses and we snorted the medicine. Man, that shit was good. After the Scream finished our set we were hanging out downstairs again, drinking in the small corridor that links all the Rock City dressing rooms. One of McGee's muscled, bald paratroopers called us over to where he was guarding a door and we walked down to see what was going on. He said, 'Look here, guys.' Lying on the floor in an empty room was a comatose girl aged about twenty, out stone cold; she must've fainted in the crush upstairs waiting for the Mary Chain. The paratrooper looked at us all then at the comatose girl and said, 'We could have a gangbang with that. Anybody in?' We just looked at each other in disgust and walked away from the creep. I went to the venue security and told them to monitor the girl.

I was staying in a hotel in Nottingham with the Mary Chain because McGee wanted me to stay with them, and the Scream were staying somewhere else. I went out to get a newspaper or a can of Coke or a pie or something the next morning and the bald paratrooper was running about looking at the buildings surrounding our hotel as though there was snipers out there ready to take a shot at me. 'Stay there! Stay there! Where you going?'

I said I was going to get a newspaper.

'Fucking stay there! Stay there! Stay inside!' He was looking at the buildings across the road, at the buildings above. Ridiculous. *He* was the danger.

I decided I should travel up to Manchester with the Scream boys. It was a beautiful summer's day and we were playing the Hacienda, a dream come true. Throb's got *Heart and Soul* from the Joy Division song tattooed on his arm. Me, Beattie and Throb are massive Factory disciples, so for us, the Scream, playing the Hacienda was genius. We travelled the short distance from Nottingham to Manchester and when we arrived at FAC 51 Karen was already there. She'd come down on the train from Glasgow. Just before soundcheck Karen said to me, 'Eh, Bobby. . . the Mary Chain have asked me to play drums tonight.'

I said, 'What? Are you taking the piss?'

'No,' Karen said. 'William just asked me to play with them.'

'What did you say?'

'Well at first I said no, I've never played drums in my life, then William said is there anything we could give you that would persuade you, what do you want and we'll get it for you. . .'

'Right,' I said.

'And I said if you get me a gram of speed I'll do it.'

'So you said you're gonna do it?'

And Karen said, 'Yeah.'

She'd never played drums in her life before, ever. I was like, fucking hell. There had been no discussion with me. I don't even know if McGee was present at that gig, but no one in the JAMC organisation mentioned it to me. And I just thought, well, if that's what they want what can I do? Fuck it. Just focus on the fact that the Scream are playing the Hacienda.

So we were playing, and looking out to the audience and on the left there was a door. That door led to the dressing rooms downstairs and who was stood in the doorway watching us but Mark E. Smith. I loved that guy, really respected him, and he was watching *us*. So we finished the gig and Throb went off first and tried to walk past Mark E. Smith but he wouldn't move, so Throb said, 'Excuse me, can you move please?' And Mark E. Smith just stood there ignoring him. So Throb said again, 'Could you move please?' and MES just stood there ignoring Throb and blocking his way so Throb just fucking knocked him out the way with his shoulder.

After the Scream had played the Mary Chain came on and I had to stand side stage and watch my girlfriend play with my band. Karen, who couldn't play drums, had never picked up a drumstick in her life. It was a Moe Tucker move by the Mary Chain, but the difference was Moe could play. This was something more and I sensed it. Sold out for a gram of Pink Champagne (Manchester speed). It was weird. The Scream boys were all asking me why I wasn't playing. What could I say? The Reid brothers wouldn't speak about confrontational stuff like this, and I couldn't speak up either. I accepted it because it was their band. We were all dysfunctional truth be told. But it left a bad taste. That was the start of me getting moved out of the band.

*Psychocandy* was finally released in November 1985, the music press loved the album and it quickly went silver. We all received silver discs which the record companies gave you in those days for sixty thousand sales. It went gold not long after which was a hundred thousand album and cassette sales. I lost the silver somewhere along the way, maybe when we moved to Brighton in 1988: I have the *Psychocandy* gold disc hanging proudly in my toilet. The band were all over the music papers. People loved the album and it went straight in at number thirty-one and stayed in the charts for ten weeks. They loved the single 'Just Like Honey' too, which reached number forty-five. Bands like JAMC were not getting any daytime radio airplay so the fanbase were all buying on first day of release but we weren't reaching the masses. You need radio play to do that and the charts were full of straight garbage, puppet performers and plastic people. It wasn't until the nineties that Radio 1 and commercial radio would willingly play guitar band music and by that point it was mostly neutered and safe. There was no sex and danger or revolutionary consciousness in Britpop.

Nineteen eighty-five had been a momentous year for me, and I wondered what surprises the new year would bring. Early one evening that winter, around tea time, I was sitting at home and the phone rang. It was Jim Reid. This was unusual because my point of contact for the Mary Chain had initially been Douglas Hart in the early days but now it was mostly McGee.

'Ah,' I said. 'Nice to hear from you, Jim, you alright?'

Jim got straight to the point. Quickly and nervously he said, 'We want you to be the drummer in the Mary Chain full time. We don't want you to be in Primal Scream anymore. You can't be in both bands, you have to make a choice.'

Well, I'd never seen this coming. My memory of this phone call is still very hazy, I think I immediately froze in a state of shock, all the strength draining out of my body. I couldn't speak; I went silent for what seemed like ages but was probably just a few seconds, and then answered: 'OK, I'll just be in the Scream then.' And that was that. Nothing more to say. It was a very short conversation. I felt fucking awful. That was it. Over. I loved being in that band. They were my soul brothers. I had given them everything I could. I'd never let them down. I always looked good, played well and turned up on time for every job we had. Plus, we were great friends. I felt part of the gang. I knew I brought something important to the band. Maybe my worth was more than I knew.

I reasoned with myself that my drumming abilities were strictly limited to the few beats I could play: two drums and a cymbal pounding out the tribal heartbeats of primitive rock and roll. In the current context of the group it worked, it was perfect. My two drums created a lot of space in the Chain's music that a regular rock drummer would have taken up with crashing cymbals, tom-toms, riffs and stuff, trad rock clatter shit. Boring. Predictable. But I knew that if they wanted to develop past the primal garage-rock sound we had then they would probably need to get somebody in that could play a bit more than me. I could dig that. I was into Buffalo Springfield, Love and the Doors, all bands with syncopated drummers who could play rock, soul, shuffles, waltzes. I'm very primitive. I thought I was the perfect drummer for the Mary Chain at that point, but knew they wanted to develop their sound further and become more musically sophisticated so this was probably the right thing to do.

No matter what I told myself it still hurt. But I also knew that I had the ability to write my own songs, tell my own stories, although I had no illusions about how good they were yet. I had a long way to go, but I believed that one day I would become a better songwriter. My respect for Jim and William was such that I would never have dreamed of offering them a song that I had written with Beattie as a potential Mary Chain recording. No way! My contribution to the Chain was strictly image, rhythm and band cheerleader. I was happy with that position. I loved being part of their band. I couldn't be the truly creative person I wanted to be in the Mary Chain: they already had two great songwriters. I knew I had to be my own man, master of my own destiny, because I couldn't be at the mercy of these guys forever.

\*

I had noticed as the Mary Chain were getting bigger and receiving more media attention, sold-out concerts and chart success, that the Reid brothers were becoming more isolated; being famous seemed to make them even more introverted and hermetic. There were fewer laughs now than in the early days on the Creation tour of Germany '84 and the gigs in NYC, Europe and the UK that spring and summer of 1985. The American tour that November had been a laugh because the camaraderie in the band was solid. We were a gang riding around the USA in our little tour van, instruments and amps in the back, just us four, McGee, and our pals Dave Evans and Luke Hayes as our roadies. Perfect. But that Psychocandy tour in February of 1986 wasn't as much fun. For one thing, I knew this would be my last tour with the band. We were playing great sets, now nearer forty minutes than the crazed fifteen-minute riot days, but it seemed to me that they were going through that thing every young guy who dreams of being a rock star does, when they start getting it they suddenly don't know how to handle it.

Jim and William are both shy guys, but they wanted to be the biggest band in the world and change pop culture. However, the pact you sign with the devil includes fame and fortune alongside artistic success. Some people can handle it, can even love it, because they enjoy it for what it is. Douglas and I both had a ball as Mary Chainers. To others it's anathema, a poisoned chalice. The Reids did take themselves very seriously, maybe too seriously at times. Everybody does at that age. Even more so if they are the authors of a multi-generational all-time classic rock and roll album such as *Psychocandy*. They thought they were going to change the world. And why not? That album changed a lot of people's lives. Over the years many people have told me how much *Psychocandy* meant to them as teenagers, both lonely middle-class suburban kids and alienated tower-block council-estate kids. In a band that's really what it's all about, connecting with other lost and lonely souls. It's why we formed bands in the first place. Boredom and anger. Alienation and pain. Looking for kicks. Fuck you.

Looking back on it now, I think the Mary Chain set me up. They were clever. In offering me the choice between being their full-time drummer or the leader and songwriter of Primal Scream, they already knew which path I would choose. It was a way of getting rid of me without openly sacking me. They gave me a soft parachute. We never fell out. I love both William and Jim Reid to this day and Douglas Hart was the best man at my wedding in 2006. If the boys play in London, I'm there every time. I love hearing them play live. They kill it. And they did replace me with a drum machine, which is cool. I liked that a lot. The next album they released, the classic existential blues record *Darklands*, is my favourite Mary Chain album, and it's all drum machine. I was irreplaceable. And that was fine.

My final Mary Chain performance was at the Liverpool Empire in February 1986. They already had a new guy lined up to take my place and he was scheduled to play on the last couple of gigs on the tour. His name was John Foster Moore. I remember feeling a bit weird about it, but, I thought to myself, 'Well, that's just the way it goes.'

The morning after the Empire gig, a cold February morning, I boarded the tour bus for the short journey from the hotel to Liverpool Lime Street, where I said my goodbyes to the guys, walked through the ticket barrier and got on the train back to Glasgow. I was filled with a cold, strange, sad feeling. Once on board I put on my headphones and played Big Star's *Third/ Sister Lovers* album from my Sony Walkman cassette recorder all the way home. Alex Chilton's darkly beautiful, plaintive songs of hopeless, fractured relationships and drug-numbed nihilism seemed appropriate under the circumstances. I was on my own again now.

# Part Four
# (1986–1991)

# 18.

# Sonic Flowers and Strawberry Switchblades

We played a few gigs in 1986 but nothing big because we were still an underground band. Janice Long was a big supporter of the Scream, she loved us at the very beginning and is still on board to this day. John Peel, however, was never a big fan. I don't think there were enough girls in the Scream for him. He seemed to drool over bands with girls in them, especially if they couldn't really play their instruments. The more amateur the better so far as he was concerned. But, hey, you can't expect everyone to dig what you do.

The Mary Chain sacked McGee after they parted with me, so he was on his own again too, and more than a bit hurt, dejected and lost. He was gonna quit the music biz until his hero Tony Wilson of Factory encouraged him to keep going. Then, Rob Dickins offered McGee his own label, feeling that they could have some fun working together. Dickins always liked me and McGee. In the seventies he signed the Sex Pistols to Warner's Publishing. Rob's old man worked in Tin Pan Alley on Denmark Street and started the British charts so they would have a newspaper and could sell the advertising space. That's why and how the *NME* was started, to sell advertising space. Clever guys. Rob Dickins liked characters. He signed the Bunnymen to WEA and worked directly with Bunnymen manager and KLF mojo man Bill Drummond. Rob is a bit of a character himself. He's married to

Cherry Gillespie, one of Pan's People. He was the most powerful man in the UK music business in the eighties and nineties.

McGee's new label was called Elevation, named after a Television track on *Marquee Moon*. That's how he signed us and the Weather Prophets to Warners. Rob Dickins was very supportive of the Scream and he dug that we were obsessed by bands like the Byrds, the Doors, Love and Tim Buckley.

I don't know how much we got as a recording advance from Warners, maybe seventy-five grand to sign, plus thirty grand publishing. Beattie and I split the publishing advance because we were the songwriters. From that £75,000 advance we would have to pay the recording costs and find a living wage for each of us. When McGee asked me who should produce the album, I suggested Jimmy Page or Prince. I was one hundred per cent serious. Aside from his virtuoso guitar-playing and compositional talents Jimmy was also a master producer of rock and roll. I also thought he would understand our folk-rock sensibilities from his Yardbirds days. Obviously I was buying all the Prince records as they came out. I love Prince. That run of singles in the eighties is unbeatable. They're as good as the Beatles or the Stones, Bowie, Phil Spector, Tamla-Motown, Stax, anyone. They're incredible. McGee just laughed at me and said well that's never gonna happen. In the end, we got Stephen Street.

I don't know how this happened. I wanted our records to sound like the Doors and Love. I knew nothing about the production side of things, the art and craft of the recording process, but from listening to Zeppelin and Prince I knew *they* did. I didn't know *how* you made records. Although I'd had studio experience with the Wake it was still a mystery to me. We'd only made two indie singles with the help of Joe Foster who had great taste in music. He was there to help us fight our corner against the prevailing eighties production values that most engineers aspired to back then. We didn't really know what a producer did because we had no experience of working with one; all we had to go on was what was written on record labels or album covers. Stephen Street had engineered *The Queen is Dead* with Johnny Marr producing, and we liked the sound of that album. I loved Johnny Marr and the album felt like a good contemporary take on the sixties. We wanted to make an album with a sixties *feel* and a contemporary sensibility. We didn't want to sound 'retro'.

I'd already had experience of working with Stephen Street, of course, with the Mary Chain, and it hadn't gone brilliantly. He was nice guy, but kind of straight and ordinary, not rock and roll at all. He came to see us play in Edinburgh at the Onion Cellar sometime in late summer 1986. I remember telling him I didn't think our drummer was good enough. After the gig Street said to me, I think he'll be fine. We went to Rockfield Studios in Monmouthshire, Wales, that winter and it was a total disaster. Our drummer Tam McGurk just couldn't keep time. He would slow down and then speed up within a bar, not even over sixty bars or thirty bars, *within a bar*. It was impossible for Beattie and Throb to play to. When McGurk wasn't needed in the studio he was away at the pub in the local village getting pissed, trying to pull birds. He was in it for the birds and the booze, which is fine, as long as the job is done well beforehand. He wasn't on a creative quest, like we were. Under the microscope of the studio all the truth comes out.

Stephen Street was still early in his career as a producer. It's easy to say in hindsight that he should have replaced McGurk immediately and brought in another drummer, but he persevered with him, probably because he liked us all as a band and felt it wasn't in his remit to sack the drummer. But I wish he'd been brave enough to have that conversation with me during the recording sessions when it became apparent how bad McGurk was. And as leader of the band I wish I'd been brave enough to sack McGurk on the spot.

We were in Rockfield for weeks and weeks just slogging it out with nothing much to show for our labour, only three or four tracks. I discovered that I couldn't sing a couple of the songs and this was puzzling, frustrating and embarrassing. I'd written them and sung them live and on BBC radio sessions. So what was the problem?

Throb had this Scott Walker album from the Scott Walker TV show with a gatefold sleeve which folded out to reveal Scott dressed in slim-fitting brown corduroy trousers and a black cardigan. He has a very Parisian sixties Left-Bank intellectual bohemian look with his hair cut short in the Roman style, very Mod, with a key on a chain around his neck and slip-on loafers to complete his look. I had that image in front of me on my music stand to inspire me. I had Scott in front of me, my vocal hero, and every time Stephen would press the 'record' button and the red light came on to warn everyone that it was recording I'd go to sing but found that no matter how hard I tried I just couldn't hit the note. To my horror this happened again and again and again. I felt like I was standing in front of a twenty-foot brick wall and somebody was saying to me, *jump over the wall, jump over the wall*, and I could only jump about four inches high or something. I couldn't hit the first note and I felt humiliated.

This was our big chance to record an album for a major record label. We'd signed off the dole and we were finally earning a living as professional musicians. We were in Rockfield Studios, where the Bunnymen recorded their classic debut *Crocodiles*. Iggy Pop had recorded *Soldier* here. I was determined to make a classic debut album, and I couldn't even sing; couldn't even get the first words out.

The reports coming back to the Creation office from Stephen Street were that we were getting nothing done, and we heard that McGee was coming to pay us a visit. I was totally focused on getting something going, recording-wise, but Throb had other things on his mind. He'd met this sexy married woman, quite posh, cut-glass accent, in her late twenties, and she was driving up from the Plymouth area to visit him. She'd had an affair with a friend of ours who had brought her along to a gig where she took a shine to Throb. The feeling was mutual. She was actually really nice but our friend's name for her was the Rich Bitch. She arrived with a big wicker food hamper with champagne and wine, dressed in white jodhpurs and knee-length boots. She looked like she'd stepped straight out of the cover of a Jilly Cooper novel. After the recording session finished she and Throb disappeared to his chalet and he told me the next day that they had a very debauched time. He was happy and I loved to see that wonderful big smile on his face full of light, mischief and humour.

Shortly after, McGee came down and listened to what we'd recorded and we decided to send both the drummer and rhythm guitarist home. It was useless. McGurk's drums were all over the place and May was just thrashing away aimlessly. Live it was OK because it was just a noise. May added a wash of sound and some extra visual and guitar power to the mix, but in the studio he just couldn't cut it.

Now it was just me, Beattie, Throb and Stephen left in the studio. We laid some tracks down with a drum machine and McGee suggested that we bring Andrew Innes in. Within a couple of hours Andrew came through to the control room and said, 'I can't play guitar to these songs. The drums are so out of time it's impossible.' Stephen had been cutting up the two-inch master tapes to try and edit Tam's drums together, but even that didn't work. Andrew also realised that most of the songs had been recorded too high for my vocal range. 'They're all in the wrong key,' he said.

'What's a key?' we replied. We were self-taught punk musicians and didn't have any knowledge of musical theory. Under the cold scrutiny of the studio recording inexperience is exposed. Andrew changed a couple of song keys around on his guitar and asked me to try and sing them again. It worked.

Still, in the end McGee said that we were going to have to cancel the album sessions. All we had to show after five weeks in Rockfield were two or three tracks, including 'Gentle Tuesday'. Beattie and I flew back to Glasgow almost defeated. I felt deep shame, guilt and embarrassment. We didn't really speak on that flight back home because there was nothing to say. We had failed and we knew it. We weren't angry at each other. But we thought we'd blown it. We'd secured the backing of a major label to make our debut album. WEA had enough faith in us to send us to a well-known commercial recording studio and we didn't even have an album to play anyone. We both thought we'd be dropped by the label, I think, though we didn't say that to each other. We didn't speak a lot those days. Nobody spoke about their feelings. Nobody.

A week or two later, I received a phone call from McGee with some good news. He'd just been to see Rob Dickins who loved our song 'Imperial' and his plan was to send us into Abbey Road with Clive Langer to produce it as a single. Clive Langer digging the track was insane because he had produced *Too-Rye-Ay* by Dexys, *Reward* and *Passionate Friend* for the Teardrops and the classic Madness hits. After a fortnight in the void of despair it was on again! We arranged to rehearse 'Imperial' with Clive before recording it: 'pre-production', as Clive described it.

The band was now me, Beattie and Throb. We asked Andrew Innes if he wanted to join full time, and we kept the useless tambourine player, for some reason. Everybody was on equal wages, even the fucking tambourine player. We were totally socialist about it, except me and Beattie got an extra fifteen grand each because we wrote the songs.

Beattie, Throb, myself and Innes met Clive Langer at a rehearsal studio in Camden and he brought along a session drummer; he was a bit of a crash bang walloper, not my preferred style of drumming. I like a lighter, more soulful touch. He was a bit too heavy for us and a bit too straight, but I thought we should give Clive the benefit of the doubt. We played the song a few times to Clive in the rehearsal room. He 'routined' us, as they say, which just means to put you through your paces and listen to the arrangement. He came up with this idea to put a key change halfway through the guitar solo, which was inspired. He's very musical, Clive.

When we arrived at Abbey Road Clive took us into Studio 2, where the Beatles had recorded all their pop and psychedelic masterpieces. Clive set up the perfect conditions for us to record 'Imperial', and we had a great time on that session. It was our first ever truly professional recording session with a name producer. An affable, cautious Scot named Colin Fairley, who'd worked with Elvis Costello, engineered the track. He was very, very good. We all felt huge relief because just six weeks before we were thinking we had fucked it up for good, but thankfully Rob Dickins believed in us.

The track sounded great coming back through the big speakers, Beattie's twelve-string chimed like McGuinn's and Throb and Innes were hanging tight in the rhythm pocket with the session drummer dude. Clive said the key was good for me and I sang well under his guidance. We all thought the drums were a bit heavy, but at the same time we liked the way the Bunnymen and the Teardrops had heavy drums, so we felt relaxed about it. We wanted a hit record, because we didn't want to go back on the dole. We wanted to be rock and roll stars and have a great time and make some money and get out of where we were, stuck in Glasgow, out into the world as a touring rock and roll band.

Making that record was a great experience. Whilst we were in Studio 2 we discovered that Robert Fripp was in the studio next door recording a version of Iggy's 'The Passenger' with his wife Toyah Wilcox. We could hear it through the door in the corridor. Clive suggested we ask Fripp to come and play guitar on 'Imperial'. We all thought it was a good idea because of his sterling guitar work on 'Heroes' by Bowie. Clive went next door and returned with Robert Fripp himself carrying his guitar in a case. He introduced himself to us all and seemed like a gentleman. He went down the staircase that joins the high control room to the studio floor. Imagine a huge, gymnasium-sized room, big enough to play basketball in. He set up his guitar and pedals, and played through Andrew's Vox AC 30 amp; Colin Fairley ran the track down to him through the headphones and he just started playing improvised Frippertronics. We recorded maybe three tracks of his stuff until Clive thought we had enough. Then Fripp packed up his axe and pedals and went back to his wife next door. When we were mixing the track we couldn't find a space to use any of his wild Frippertronic shredding, sadly, but it was certainly all good stuff. When he plays forward it sounds like it's backwards, a really intense, metallic, psych-mathematical style. Maybe one day if we find the master tapes we can have it remixed.

We were in Abbey Road for two days and towards the end of each night Clive would have a wee drink and get quite emotional. One night down in the studio floor we were talking and he looked down at Beattie's winklepicker Chelsea boots and asked me, 'Bobby, do you know who the last people to wear boots like that in this studio were?'

I knew the answer already but replied, 'Who?'

With tears welling up in his eyes, Clive blubbered, 'Them, *them*, they could do anything,' of course meaning the Beatles. He was as much of a romantic as we were. That's why we connected so well.

On the night he was mixing the track Clive turned to us all and said, 'I'm gonna get Cedric in. It's time to get Cedric in.' Cedric was reputedly Ronnie Wood's coke dealer. So we were all like, 'Yes, Clive, great idea! Amazing!'

An hour or so later Cedric turned up looking like Jason King from *Department S* with the big moustache, wearing a high-end

Afghan coat. He looked like he had stepped out of a time machine from 1974, like a white English version of Ron O'Neal in *Super Fly*. So there was Cedric chopping out lines of coke in the anteroom outside Studio 2. Beattie licked his finger and went to dab the coke and Cedric stopped Beattie's hand in mid-air.

'Hey man, you don't dab coke, not like speed.'

The rest of us were embarrassed. Like, 'Beattie, what the fuck are you doing?' He'd never done coke before, only speed. Of course we loved the Stones connection. We were walking around the corridors buzzing until we found a staircase and climbed up onto the roof at Abbey Road, high as fuck, feeling like rock and roll stars. It was an amazing feeling, surrounded by huge pictures of the Beatles everywhere, lining the corridors. I had my photo taken alongside a picture of Lennon that night. It was a real bonding experience. Me and Throb were in heaven.

Rob Dickins was very pleased with the way 'Imperial' turned out so he gave us another thirty grand to go and make an album. Sadly, that wasn't enough to hire Clive Langer to produce the whole thing, so instead McGee suggested Mayo Thompson. Mayo had been in a band called the Red Krayola (formerly the Red Crayola), labelmates with the Thirteenth Floor Elevators on the legendary Texan International Artists label.

We met up with Mayo and mostly just asked him questions about Roky Erickson. Of course he was a lot older than us, and he gave off the air of an upper-middle-class academic guy. He had co-produced some singles with Geoff Travis for Rough Trade by the Fall, Stiff Little Fingers and the Raincoats; all good stuff that I'd bought back when they were released but very primitive-sounding and really just audio verité recordings of the bands laying their songs down live, not 'production' in the way I envisaged our record needing, with layered guitars, vocal harmonies and string arrangements. But after messing up at Rockfield we didn't really have much choice and the Elevators connection won us over. He seemed interested. We absolutely loved *Hurricane Fighter Plane* and *Transparent Radiation* by the Red Krayola and thought that maybe if he'd had a hand in those recordings then he might help us achieve the sound we had in our heads for our album. We were naïve.

It was decided we would do the sessions at the Greenhouse Studios just behind Old Street Station. It was a new studio facility opened by Pat Collier, who had been bassist in UK punk band the Vibrators. Pat had moved from his former place, Alaska, in Waterloo, over to Old Street. This was way before Old Street became trendy, back in 1986.

Each day I would get a Tube from Kings Cross or Euston depending on which guest house I was staying in. We were kicked out and banned from so many for partying. Old Street back then was a post-apocalyptic Thatcher's Britain terminal drag scene. There was no silicon roundabout hustle and bustle or coffee shops filled with busy young tech and banking professionals, just homeless people drifting with the debris, old newspapers and plastic bags blowing through the deserted subterranean Old Street Station walkways, the void beneath the roundabout.

The band was now a four-piece: me, Beattie, Throb and Innes. We still had no drummer but we were friends with the Weather Prophets, so we asked Dave Morgan to play drums on the album because we'd been on tour with him and we thought he was good.

Our producer Mayo Thompson was asleep most of the time through the recording of the album. He was interviewed a couple of years ago in *The Wire* magazine and they asked him about bands he produced, and when asked about *Sonic Flower Groove* he said, 'I slept all the way through that one.' I thought, *You cheeky cunt*. I'd forgotten about it, but he actually did. He just sat in his chair by the mixing console with his eyes closed, and occasionally he would wake up and push his glasses back up into position on his nose and make an encouraging comment. He was never negative, and always patient with us, which was good because we were all hard on ourselves and were never sure when we'd done a good take. We always thought we could do better. But it felt as if he was just going through the motions. Mayo wasn't really a record producer in the true sense. He was no Phil Spector, but then again I'm no Ronnie Ronette.

When I was younger I couldn't understand how people could do something like that. I thought they worked with you because they liked you and your band. I was naïve. Now I'm older, I get why he did it. He had to earn a living. Fair enough. He did an alright job, but it was really Pat Collier who engineered and co-produced the record with us. It was a group effort. To be fair to Mayo I think he saw his job as one of helping us birth the record without too much trauma. He didn't have any ideas for arrangement, because we had all those already, so it was really just a straight recording of the songs exactly as we would perform them live but with a few guitar overdubs. We knew how we *didn't* want it to sound.

I remember Mayo crying once or twice, and I think it must've been the way we sang and played with sincerity that moved him. He wasn't a bad guy, in fact we all liked him, and he did the best he could I suppose with the material we had. When I listen to it now I wish we'd added two- or three-part vocal harmonies to lift all the choruses; the songs are crying out for that classic folk-rock effect. It wasn't really a 'produced' record like *Piper at the Gates of Dawn* or *Forever Changes*, with strings and horn arrangements, but then again we weren't Syd's Floyd, Love or the Springfield. We set our bar too high and we were bound to fail. We were unreasonable in our aims and confined by our songwriting and musical abilities as they were then. We were still learning how to write, play and arrange songs. Still, I think we captured the spirit and sound of the original band on the album. It is full of a youthful, ecstatic joyousness, a melancholic yearning and a naïve sincerity. It has the energy of youth with a twist of bittersweet sadness. There's a metaphorical yearning for sunshine and light whilst acknowledging the existential truths of failure, loss and pain.

I was still learning how to write lyrics, working out a lot of stuff internally and still struggling to express myself. In Glasgow, feelings had to be submerged and no weakness shown. Writing these songs was a way of breaking that fearful, blank wall, that bluff, macho front. By writing from the heart I was learning to express myself. I knew that in some cases I was struggling to say what I wanted but I also delighted and surprised myself with some of the lines I wrote. I knew if I was to do this properly it would be a lifetime's work, and that I was only just starting out as a songwriter. It was all just an experiment, I thought to myself, and sometimes you're going to fail. But you can't be afraid of creative failure. It's the only way to find out what works and what doesn't. I saw the band as a work in progress. I knew I had it in me to improve my craft and so did Beattie, Robert and Innes. We would never give up the struggle.

On our second album, *Primal Scream*, there are songs addressed to imaginary girls such as Ivy or Wendy. These names were picked randomly out of syllabic necessity rather than as actualisations of real sentient beings, although, saying that, whilst writing 'Ivy Ivy Ivy' I did have in my mind the vision of a girl similar to Poison Ivy Rorschach of the Cramps, who was, and remains, the ultimate example of unattainable female beauty. In her erotic coolness and shamanic intensity, Poison Ivy possesses all the mystery and power of a Pagan love goddess – a true heroine and eternal inspiration. These were written to be played in a high-energy rock and roll setting. They're kind of trashy, an exercise in writing classic rock songs. Maybe not fully realised yet, but an experiment of sorts. When Beattie left the band, after *Sonic Flower Groove*, he took his signature twelve-string Rickenbacker sound along with him and we had to start again from zero. For some reason the 'year zero' challenge seemed to suit our backs-against-the-wall survivalist mentality.

*I wanna scream I wanna shout*
*When I see your religious mouth*

That's the opening of 'She Power', our lunge at a hybridisation of T. Rex and the Ronettes. And in 'Lone Star Girl', which bleeds Throb's Johnny Thunders-inspired New York Dolls gutter-thug guitar violence with my Beach Boys-style pavement surfer sun-kissed melodic cadence, I sang

*Protest songs won't stop the bombs*
*Nor soft rebellion neither*

What were we thinking? We were from Glasgow! Not New York or California! I guess we were attempting a marriage of urban sleaze and plaintive yearning – sex and danger, romance and longing – a great idea but extremely hard to pull off. The Mary Chain had done it successfully on their *Darklands* album from a couple years before. Songs like 'April Skies' and 'Happy When it Rains' nailed this aesthetic beautifully. God how we LOVED those songs of theirs. We were just feeling around in the dark for a new direction, away from the folk-rock days of early Scream, and heading out onto the hard rock highway looking for thrills, spills, chills, sex and danger. All of that would come to us, only later, in a new and different form, as yet unheard. At this point we were still apprenticing, out on the road, paying our dues, giving our all each night to rabid audiences of curious outsider kids in small down and dirty clubs up and down the country, searching for truth and enlightenment in the rock and roll wilderness, waiting for our Guru to find us, which he would. But more of that later.

To this day I still love some of the songs on *Sonic Flower Groove*. 'Silent Spring' was a good song I wrote in 1984 about impending ecological disaster. I read an article in a left-wing magazine about the ongoing effects of Agent Orange dropped by US fighter planes on Cambodia and Vietnam in the seventies, destroying farmers' food crops, and how it had created horrific birth deformities in the children there. I stole the title from Rachel Carson's sixties novel about pesticides but enlarged the subject matter to an imagined future of planetcide.

'Imperial' was inspired by the miners' strike, and my first attempt to write about the history of the Left, how the Left is forever factional and fighting internecine wars and not standing together, whereas the Right always shows a real class consciousness and therefore wins every single time

*Thee and thine*
*Who build a shrine*
*To that which takes away*
*Without return*
*Witches ye burn*
*Clandestine mass*
*A looking glass*
*Exterminating angel might well find*
*Just a matter of time*
*It goes around and around and around again*
*To converse*
*Into reverse*
*As always, while in opposite is found*
*A solid ground*
*A broken tree*
*A bended knee*
*Forever or until revolving knowing*
*Change winds are blowing*
*It goes around and around and around again*

'Gentle Tuesday' and 'We Go Down Slowly Rising' are beautiful songs. I also love 'May the Sun Shine Bright For You'. When

Kim Fowley asked Jim Morrison how you write a great song, Jim responded by asking Kim if he was in love with anyone. Kim replied 'No'. Jim said, 'You will never be able to write a great song until you are in love.' Well, I was in love when I wrote 'May the Sun Shine Bright For You' and it has all the hope, yearning and naivety of infinite possibility that only young lovers feel:

*Every day with the dawn*
*Horror-beauty unknown beyond*
*Here with you I know I belong*
*May the sun shine bright for you*
*Autumn, winter and spring*
*And the summer, a feeling within*
*Evergreen honey-blade sweetly brings*
*May the sun shine bright for you*
*Girl, you take me inside*
*Honey-blade carnival of delights*
*On our love rollercoaster we glide*
*May the sun shine bright for you*

An ode to my love Karen in 6/8 time. A naïve psychedelic love song. My days back then were mostly spent hanging out with Karen, either in her room or going for drives all over Glasgow late at night listening to music on compilation cassettes we had made. Sometimes we'd drive out to Glasgow Airport, sit in the café with some tea (the price of admission) and watch the planes take off. Neither of us could afford a plane ticket to anywhere, but the sight of the planes on the runway hitting speed and shooting up into the air became some kind of metaphor for me. I saw myself and the band as a jet-plane that was gearing up ready for take-off, up into the cosmic skies above us and out into the world of possibilities, a journey to a new creative life. We had to escape the current state of our depressed, grounded signing on the dole existence in Glasgow. I hoped that one day I would be on those very same planes, flying off to gigs or recording studios in the major cities of the world. I was desperate for travel and life experience outside of our beautiful city. I knew that I had to leave to learn about myself and meet interesting people who would introduce me to new ways of viewing things. I *had to* widen my frame of reference. I had left school at the age of fifteen and had no further qualifications to fall back on out in the straight world. It was rock and roll or nothing for me.

My times with Karen were golden. Love is a strange thing, as everybody knows. It hits you from out of nowhere, like a lightning bolt from a cosmic sky, suddenly dominating your every waking moment, thought and action; a soul-shaking shock that rocks both your spiritual (un)consciousness and central nervous system. These fleeting pleasures can disappear again as swiftly and as unexpectedly as they first came, or rot slowly over time like the biblical 'bottle in the smoke'. This ineffable phantom – the unseen force of erotic love, the sweet vampire-taste of godlike ecstasies and pleasure-burned synapses – is a drug we all crave. The experience of young lovers is of such a deep intensity. With age comes the knowledge that the sweet blindness of youthful romanticism can eventually become hammered out of you. Bitterness and cynicism may now reign where naivety and youthful hopefulness once did. Love and sex are strange bedfellows. I'm still not sure that they mix for too long. I guess there are many different kinds of love. Love is what you make it. My philosophy is to love while you can, because we don't have too long in this life; like love itself it is here and then it's gone, too quickly. 'Enjoy every sandwich', as the great American singer-songwriter Warren Zevon said.

After everything I've been through I still like to see myself as an incurable romantic. Sometimes I think I'm a 'romantic cynic', then other times a 'cynical romantic', but really I suspect you cannot be both romantic and cynical at the same time. Maybe what I'm pushing at is the idea of experience well-earned, and pretending to myself that I have attained some kind of realistic, mature vision of 'love'. Only a fool would really think that is the case; as I said, when it comes, it hits you like a thunderbolt out of nowhere. I'm still open to the shock and awe of love. I'm still a believer.

There's a song we recorded for Janice Long called 'Bewitched and Bewildered'. It's one of our best ever, and why we didn't record it for *Sonic Flower Groove* I'll never know. I also recently discovered an unreleased track from the Greenhouse sessions called 'Tomorrow Ends Today'. It sounds like it could have featured on the first Stone Roses album. On the surface it's an ecstatic and joyous psych and folk-rock pop song but it has an underlying bittersweet, sexual twist in the lyric too:

*I've a thousand things to do*
*Every one of them to you*
*I surely will*

We had some fun during the *Sonic Flower Groove* sessions. Rose McDowell, the black vinyl catsuit-clad polka-dot singer from Strawberry Switchblade, hung out with us a few times and we shared some nocturnal adventures together. Rose was a bona fide pop star with top-ten hit singles and *Smash Hits* front covers, and could be seen performing on *Top of the Pops* regularly. She had a taste for S&M & psychedelic sex. Her fetish was young, leather-clad rock and roll boys. Her flat in Muswell Hill was legendary. Pet monkeys roamed the place as another acid-dosed victim surrendered to her will. She was friends with Genesis P. Orridge and Psychic TV and sang backing vocals on their classic single 'Godstar' which was dedicated to Brian Jones. Rose was brilliant to hang out with.

Good times they were indeed, and funny times too. One day Beattie was having difficulty obtaining the desired guitar sound he heard in his head onto tape so he called Pat Collier and said, 'Can you make my guitar sound more satanic?'

Pat replied drily, 'Well Jim, *you* have to play it more satanic if that's what you want.'

We all cracked up. Beattie was starting to get into heavier guitar sounds and longer guitar solos. With the early version of the Scream, the songs were a minute and a half long, two minutes at the most, with no solos. On *Sonic Flower Groove* the songs all started to get a bit longer because there were longer guitar intros, solos and outros. The musicianship on the album was first class. Beattie played beautifully, his Rickenbacker twelve-string chimed heavenly golden like the Bells of Rhymney and Throb, Innes and Dave Morgan formed a tight and propulsive rhythm section. It went against the shambling, wilful, amateur indie orthodoxy of the day and alienated a lot of our original fans.

When we released the album that autumn nobody was that excited; not our press officer Mick Houghton who also worked with JAMC, Cope and Bunnymen, nor McGee, or the fans. It didn't get great reviews. It reached number sixty-two on the UK album charts, not high enough for WEA to renew our contract. We did a three-week tour of Britain that culminated in us headlining the Town & Country Club with These Immortal Souls supporting us led by the legendary guitarist Rowland S. Howard. We did a short European tour that winter which was fun but when we returned home I knew things had to change.

# 19.
# Brighton Rock

When we'd played in Brighton in 1987 we took acid and at night it looked beautiful, the Regency houses beside the ocean all clean and fresh with all the pretty lights sparkling along the seafront like diamonds in the blue velvet sky.

At the end of that year I moved to Brighton with my brother Graham, Karen and Throb. Whenever we played gigs in Brighton the people were so friendly, and it felt as far away from Glasgow as could be imaginable, both geographically and aesthetically. The proximity to the sea was also attractive. Our friend James Williamson who later founded the Creation Books imprint had helped persuade us. He was into eighties underground transgressive culture and nineteenth-century decadent literature, books like *Maldoror* by Comte de Lautréamont, *Against Nature* by Joris Karl Huysmans, Arthur Rimbaud and the whole 'poet maudit' scene. Williamson was a devotee of Kenneth Anger's occult movies and bands like Sonic Youth and Swans early on and was a huge fan of the counter-culture from the fifties through to the eighties. He was a fan of music and he loved Primal Scream. He owned the Meat Whiplash record shop in Plymouth with the huge Bobby Gillespie sign above it.

I first played in Plymouth in 1984 with the JAMC and returned with the Scream a year later. This strange guy would come to the gigs and just stand there at the bar, have a drink and not say much, but Jeff Barrett introduced me to him and told me he loved both bands. After a gig someone said to me that I should go and see his record shop. So they took me down to the shopping precinct in Plymouth. His shop had a burning, porno-red neon sign in the window with the words MEAT WHIPLASH, after the Fire Engines song. I thought that was pretty fucking cool for starters. Above the window in the space where the shop name normally sits was written BOBBY GILLESPIE in black block type-face against a lipstick-pink background with two black six-pointed stars either side of my name. I was like, what the fuck?!

I was a bit embarrassed, but at the same time I thought it was great. I went in and behind the counter were Jeff Barrett, James Williamson and a kid named Simon Ashton. They had a huge Some Bizzare poster up on the wall of Foetus crucified on a cross. They only stocked cool underground records from the eighties like Bad Seeds, Sonic Youth, Swans, psych-garage records from the sixties and bands like the Cramps, Stooges and MC5. No chart shit. They were all mad guys obsessed by rock and roll exactly like we were. If they fancied a drink they'd just shut up the shop, go to the pub and get wasted. Their opening hours were elastic. I think James had an inheritance.

I was sick of Glasgow, but Beattie didn't want to move. In the end for his own reasons he left the band. That was quite a painful situation for a few months, because he wouldn't say outright that he was leaving. I think he would have rather the band split up than carry on without him, which is understandable but Throb, Innes and myself were determined to continue whatever the outcome. Eventually Beattie officially left, but not without some drama. He made it quite difficult for himself and us because at that point he didn't have the emotional intelligence to make such a big move and neither did we. It's not an easy decision to make and I'm not judging him for his behaviour. We are still friends to this day. Beattie is an amazing guy and stellar musician. A true punk in heart and soul.

Our rent was eighty pounds a week for our new flat. I paid my half through housing benefit and Karen was working at Barclays

Bank. Throb was single and so was my brother, so they were going to the indie clubs with James Williamson and having a great time running riot with the student girls. We were drifting a bit creatively speaking because we'd just lost Beattie.

Innes lived on the Isle of Dogs in a council flat with his girlfriend from university, Christine Wanless. Like Innes, Christine had a science degree. She would make clothes for Innes: paisley Nehru shirts, velvet trousers, satin shirts, really cool shit. I commissioned her to make me one silver and one gold lamé shirt which I later wore in the 'Movin' On Up' and 'Higher Than the Sun' videos. Christine was a really good seamstress. At the gigs I'd wear those shirts with black leather trousers and the polka-dot shirt I wore on *Sonic Flower Groove*. I always had brilliant shirts made. We were really into clothes and how the band should look.

How a band dressed was equally as important as the music. Sound and vision had to be in complete accordance. Sex Pistols, Clash, Ramones, Jim Morrison, Love, the Byrds, Stones, Stooges, MC5, Velvets: all sartorially and musically *correct*. Remember how I was drawn to the photograph of Johnny Rotten on the school landing – his amphetamine stare, shredded hair and ripped clothing created an aggressive, visual intensity that I had never seen in anyone before except maybe men and boys lost in the delirium of violence at football matches, certainly not in a 'rock star'. The power of a strong image can seduce people, can lure them into your world, a dark, seductive spell of visual metaphor and imagist poetics come to life.

And what is style except a kind of street theatre? We are creating characters from out of our imaginations whilst living out a dream as a way of navigating our immediate surroundings, be they societal, familial, or the suffocating influence of our immediate peer group. Style is survival. It's a way of asserting one's individualism in the face of straight conformity. Clothes as battledress. Style as a weapon. It takes bravery to dress a certain way, in a certain area, at a certain time, to stand out from the crowd. We all know that everyone dresses like everyone else because there is safety in numbers: *safe with the herd from the wolves out there.*

Can clothes and a sense of style transcend the culturally repressive boundaries that class imposes on us? Of course they can. Back in the late seventies, early eighties one of the poorest kids that I knew had the best style of anyone in Glasgow; my mate, Rab H. His own personal revolution was not political, except that his sense of style gave him both admiration from his post-punk peer group on the streets and clubs of the city, and a feeling of self-respect that he would never ever get from straight society, not that he wanted it of course, being an unemployable drop-out who didn't want a job or to grow up and take part in society's games. But style alone won't save your soul. You gotta be sharp in other ways too. The way that the correct combination of clothes, shoes, hats, make-up, haircut, hair colour, can transform one's character immeasurably, instilling a new-found confidence and dynamism, is something that can't be discounted.

A true stylish person cuts through reality like a blade, and not everyone has the sharpened sense and taste to wield that deadly weapon. When we emerged in 1985 the UK music scene was short on style and extremely drab. It was all oversized jackets, shapeless T-shirts and Doc Martens. UGH! There were no dandies on parade. The nearest to that sartorial obsessiveness was the care that some of the goth bands took with their image. That look was never for me, but I did admire the fact they had obviously spent a lot of time thinking about how they should present themselves, and it took a lot of bravery on the part of some of these kids to get all dressed up and made up and leave their mum's council flat, bedsit, or middle-class suburbia to get the bus into town to go to the local indie or goth club. Whenever I went out during those times I wore either a sixties two- or four-button black leather box jacket, black leather pants or blue jeans ripped in the ass and both knees à la Ramones, along with some sixties nylon sweaters I'd pinched from my dad's wardrobe (they didn't fit him anymore) in fab colours like turquoise with a black and white stripe detail on the turtle neck.

I had also picked up a beautiful sixties dark green mohair two-button suit in Camden Market in 1983 on one of my visits to see McGee which I wore a lot. Sometimes I'd wear just the jacket with straight black jeans and a Shelley's Chelsea Boot. I had a beautiful black satin shirt made to measure for me from a tailor in Brighton's North Road, and I also commissioned a pair of navy-blue velvet trousers from there too. I loved having clothes which were self-designed and made for me by tailors. It made me feel apart and above everyone else, out there in both the music biz and straight worlds. I seemed to live in a dream world of my own making, starring in a movie that I was constantly directing. This is the power of clothes and style. It was as if I was creating a new version of myself. I don't think that was a deliberate strategy as such, more a natural outcome of the journey I was now undertaking with the band and my submersion in songwriting and rock and roll folklore.

McGee got us a few one-off gigs that summer. One was in Lisbon, where Nikki Sudden got stabbed trying to buy smack for him and Throb. The thieves were trying to cut the rings off his fingers with their knives. The other was supporting the Butthole Surfers at Brixton Academy. Teenager Frankie Stebbings from the Wolfhounds played drums and McGee was on bass. We mostly played covers like ''Til the End of the Day' by the Kinks or Jody Reynolds' 'Fire of Love' which we did in a sleazy Gun Club swampy style. There were a couple of new songs but nothing from the Beattie era at all.

At some point we started writing new songs. I'd write the beginning of a song in my flat and take it round to Throb's and jam on my guitar with him. It was so easy for him, he was a natural. His style was so funky, bluesy and sexy, always just behind the beat the way I like it, and very emotive. He was an expressive player. I persuaded him to move onto guitar because I wanted us to have the power of the MC5. He was a real Johnny Thunders disciple. I said, 'You can play like fucking Johnny Thunders. You can play all of *Tonight's the Night* and *Zuma* almost as good as Neil Young and I hear you playing along with the Dolls and Heartbreakers albums all the time. You're the new guitar player. You and Innes.'

I believed we could be the rock and roll band that we wanted to be. We could only be a folk-rock band before, with Beattie. We felt held back – we wanted to rock out, but previously all of our old songs had been written from a melodic perspective and for rock and roll you need rhythm and blues. Melody doesn't really come into it. The idea was that we could kick out the jams like MC5 with Throb and Innes on twin guitars like Sonic Smith and Wayne Kramer as our models. We just had to write songs that suited the new line-up and high-energy ethos. Behind the onstage fuck-you confidence and black leather rocker image Throb was actually quite a shy, self-deprecating guy when it came to certain things like his musical talent, but after a little bit of persuading he agreed.

I was used to the working relationship I had with Beattie, and I'd never written songs with anyone else before, but I knew from Revolving Paint Dream (the band that he and his girlfriend Christine were in) that Innes already had some good commercial songwriting chops in a sixties style and that if we transferred Throb's gift for melodicism on the bass guitar into actual rock-pop song structures then something new and different might come of it. I knew we had to keep working together to keep the band going, to develop our style.

We played a gig at a seaside festival in Italy. We rehearsed into the night before on speed and I remember reading most of *Carburetor Dung* by Lester Bangs on the plane the next day still speeding off my tits. Throb decided to bring the speed to help us through the gig and was stopped at customs on the way in by the Italian security services. We all watched as he was led away into a room by the police, thinking he was going to prison, and we were all gonna get busted too. He looked like a biker, a big, handsome rocker with long hair and leather trousers and pointed Chelsea boots; he probably hadn't slept for days, it was no wonder they picked him out for inspection. We were all tense. After about twenty minutes Throb came walking through the electronic doors that separate the customs and baggage section from the main airport concourse with a big smile on his face. I asked him, 'What happened there? Have you still got the speed?'

'Yeah!'

'How come you never got busted?'

And Throb said, 'The cops asked me to take all my clothes off and I took everything off except my socks, where I was hiding the speed. Then they set the sniffer dogs on me but I haven't had a bath in ages and my feet are so fucking smelly that the dogs just left me alone and they decided to let me go.'

We all cheered at this great news and of course we were speeding out of our brains at the show later that night.

We did that gig with Frank Stebbing on drums. We played another gig, headlining some indie festival at Dingwalls called Panic Station, and I wore a red tartan plaid shirt customised with a photocopied picture of Arthur Rimbaud gaffer-taped over my heart. I'd grown my hair really long, down to my chest and Throb had as well. We did '99th Floor' by Moving Sidewalks and a brand-new song I'd written with Throb and Innes titled 'You're Just Dead Skin to Me' but in a Neil Young *Zuma* style with a stinging guitar riff written by Throb. We had a song that was a complete rip-off of 'Till the End of the Day' by the Kinks, same riff but I wrote new lyrics, and also 'Swallow My Pride' by Ramones. We were trying to start again and we weren't playing any of the old songs from *Sonic Flower Groove*.

\*

Innes would come down for the weekend and stay with me at my flat on the seafront on Regency Square by the dilapidated, ghostly West Pier. We had these jam sessions which would eventually result in the second album, *Primal Scream*. 'I'm Losing More Than I'll Ever Have' is on there and that was the first blues song we ever wrote together. I wrote the lyrics from true life experience. It was something that had happened to me, a song of experience. Making that leap of telling the truth in a song and not hiding behind symbolism or metaphor was a big deal for me at the time. I was learning to put real-life experiences into songs. I found the ones that hurt the most were the best. For a lot of people 'I'm Losing More Than I'll Ever Have' is their favourite Primal Scream song – it was Andrew Weatherall's, as he would later tell me. I think he related to the song in a very personal way. Revealing painful truths is the way to making great art. That style of confessional writing also has personal value in the way it can be cathartic and spiritually cleansing. There's something purifying about coming clean, unloading the poisonous shame of guilt and betrayal that's eating up your soul. That is the beauty of the blues.

My lyric-writing style was influenced by listening to the brutal honesty and plain-speaking poetic directness of Hank Williams and blues artists like Howlin' Wolf and Robert Johnson. I admired the way these artists laid out all their pain, suffering and low-down sinful ways for all the world to see and hear. True primitive modernists. Songs of sin and redemption, good and evil, they seemed to inhabit a dangerous Manichean universe alive with sexual immorality and dark magical realism, true blues. As a young man in a rock and roll band temptation was everywhere.

In the original iteration of Primal Scream I would write songs and Beattie would come up with twelve-string guitar riffs. But he wasn't there anymore so, I thought the three of us should jam the songs and see what came of it; make it democratic, because that was the new vision. This was a new band. We wrote a bunch of new songs and then put an advert in one of the music papers looking for a drummer. We auditioned Toby Tomanov and we all liked his vibe: he was into the Heartbreakers so that was good enough for us. He'd also featured in that brilliant James Young book *Songs They Never Play on the Radio*. We thought, well he's played with Nico, he likes Jerry Nolan and he was in the Nosebleeds with Vini Reilly and Morrissey. Ed Banger and the Nosebleeds had this punk single, 'Ain't Bin to No Music School', and a lot of Mancunian musicians passed through it, like Billy Duffy, Vini Reilly from Durutti Column and Morrissey. He was in the band when Morrissey was the singer and Vini the guitarist. Ed Banger was a bit of a headcase.

Toby had a posh girlfriend, Liz, who played saxophone, and they lived in Dalston. She was part of a music collective who used to hang out in a West Indian community centre in a building directly across the road from where Café Oto is now. Me and Throb would come up from Brighton once a week and rehearse there. We told Toby we were looking for a bassist and he introduced us to Henry Olsen who had also played with Nico. His real name was Henry Laycock, and Toby's was Phillip Tomanov.

Henry was originally from Stratford upon Avon; a real lovely middle-class gentleman, into jazz. He was a bit insecure. He wore suits and loved all these jazz guys like Ron Carter, Mingus, Monk, Miles, Coltrane etc. Apart from playing in touring bands backing Nico and John Cale he had absolutely nothing to do with rock and roll culture. I don't think he was really a bassist. I think he was playing keyboards when he was in the Nico band and he played guitar with John Cale. We just liked the fact that he'd played with those two.

Toby was a bit of a lad, but he was a rock and roller. He loved Mott the Hoople, Thin Lizzy, Dolls, Stones, MC5 and seventies rock. He was from the hard, working-class area of Wythenshawe in Manchester and had been a participant in the original Manchester punk scene. He'd been drummer in the Blue Orchids with Martin Bramah and Yvonne Pawlett, original members of the Fall, and he knew Mark E. Smith. He'd shared a flat with Nico and John Cooper Clarke. He had serious UK post-punk credentials and he was also an ex-junkie.

At this point our mate from Plymouth Jeff Barrett was the press officer for Creation, so at 83 Clerkenwell Road you had McGee, Dick Green and Barrett in two little offices and then Nicki Kefalas and Dave Harper who were pluggers for the radio. McGee went up one day to see Nicki about something and Tony Wilson just happened to be there. Tony asked McGee how he was doing and he replied, 'I feel like giving up, Tony, I've lost the Mary Chain and I had this record label Elevation with Warners, I've lost that. Primal Scream, they don't exist at the moment.'

Tony gave him a pep talk and told him not to give up, to keep doing it and stay independent. So McGee kept on pushing with the label and then he signed House of Love who none of us were ever fans of. Soon, they were on the front pages of all the music papers with a number one single in the indie charts and John Peel loved them. McGee flogged them to Phonogram for hundreds of thousands of pounds. He was back in the game and it was great for his confidence.

We recorded some tracks in a studio near Fulham Broadway: 'You're Just Dead Skin to Me' and 'You're Just Too Dark to Care', two of the ballads. The guy who owned the studio and engineered the session was called Graham Shaw. We recorded the heavier rock tracks at Bark Studios in Walthamstow owned by a guy called Brian O'Shaughnessy. Brian had built a recording studio where most other people would have a kitchen extension or a garage. It was an appendage to a suburban terraced house in Blackhorse Road. The studio consisted of a small control room and a little live room. We recorded most of the second album in there, all the rock tracks at least. I don't think we were there very long because we didn't have a big budget from Creation.

We had a song 'Ivy Ivy Ivy' which we thought was good, like a mix of the Shangri-Las and the New York Dolls, all high-energy rock and roll attack. I remember rehearsing it and during a break Toby and Throb disappeared and when they came back it was apparent that he'd shot Throb up with some smack. Throb had asked Toby to get him some and Toby had dutifully obliged. I think Toby was still using even thought he was telling us he'd stopped, not that we cared. Jacked up on the smack Throb played amazing that night and when the rest of us stopped playing Throb just kept going, lost in the music, zoning out somewhere else in a junked-out reverie, totally oblivious to what the rest of us were doing. He kept soloing long after we'd finished the song, playing endless Johnny Thunders-style riffs, really beautiful music just pouring out of him as though the smack had unlocked any emotional blockages he held deep within himself. He played so freely. On the train home to Brighton afterwards he told me how much he had loved the effects of the smack on his playing that night.

I think initially Throb was very self-conscious about not being a guitarist. He was self-conscious about a lot of things because of his upbringing and his father being so hard on him, even his looks. He was such a handsome guy, he could pull women like *that*, they loved him. But he also had these hidden insecurities and I think the heroin made him feel liberated. I think he was anxious about taking Beattie's place in the band because he was a really good guitarist. I kept telling him he was a great guitarist as well. I loved hearing Throb play guitar. It was a joy every time. The smack definitely gave him some kind of courage and rid him of his inhibitions, that's one of the great attractions of heroin.

Ever since he had moved from bass to lead guitar, a pattern had emerged where Throb's critique of his own (and the band's) musical performance could be self-laceratingly cold and overly extreme in its harshness. He always felt that he/we could be *better*, but for now he was luxuriating in the warm opiated glow of the smack; his seductive lover-boy big brown eyes had been transformed into black smouldering coals, burning with new pleasure and relaxed contentment; his charmed smile hung slyly from his lips like imitation jewellery on the neck of a young bride just about to take her wedding vows. It represented a commitment to another way of life; the swap of youthful idealism for adult artifice and sacrifice, a dark romance pregnant with necromantic erotic possibilities. Some of us are born suckers for anyone or anything that rushes the blood or stills the mind. We crave the magic elixir of the creature that will quieten the wolves in our heads and soothe the pain in our souls. I'd get used to seeing that same look on the faces of many of my friends over the next few years and they, most probably, on mine. I had the impression that in his mind at least, he had at last found the key to the door of unselfconscious soul-liberating freedom and he was ready to open it and step over the threshold through to the other side to see what life was like over there in the sweet bye and bye where the wild buffalo roamed and psychedelic outlaws rode the frontiers of consciousness.

There was a rehearsal room in the basement at 83 Clerkenwell Road, underneath the Creation offices. We would get in there at night because we didn't have much money and you'd get a cheaper rate. McGee's office was near the front door and the toilet was right at the back of the corridor. One night as I was coming back down after a piss I passed McGee in the corridor and he stopped me and said, 'Nobody wants this kind of music anymore, Bob', and he pointed down to the sound of the band playing downstairs.

I said, 'What do you mean?'

'It's so old-fashioned, nobody wants to hear this kind of music anymore.'

'Well,' I said to him, 'we do and we're gonna keep playing it because we fucking love it,' and I just walked on, thinking why the fuck did he have to say that? I went downstairs and told the band what McGee had said: even that guy doesn't believe in us anymore. This was the spring of 1988.

Our second, self-titled album was produced by Sister Anne, which was actually just us collectively having a laugh with an MC5 reference. Half the album, five songs, are high-energy rock and roll screamers featuring Throb and Innes's twin Les Paul attack and the other five songs are dark, lonely, lovelorn ballads. In retrospect I think we should have made one side high energy and the other side exclusively ballads. I don't know why nobody at the record company suggested that but nobody seemed to give a fuck. There was no A&R. I think we sequenced it in that mixed-up style because we admired the Beatles' *White Album*: the way that it started with 'Back in the USSR' and went straight into 'Dear Prudence'. The Stones mixed their albums in this way as well. McGee just left us to get on with it. By that point he'd signed My Bloody Valentine and he was far too busy to worry about the sequencing of our album.

Things were starting to get very lively on the road. The music was always great and I carried around a big box of tapes which had either been compiled by myself or our young friend Tim Tooher. I'd met Tim in Leeds around 1987 when he and his fellow university drop-out friend Mike Stout promoted a gig for us in a high street discotheque where the tiny stage was situated annoyingly, directly above the bar. We just about squeezed all of our equipment and six-piece band onto the stage. There weren't many people there but the love and enthusiasm Tim and Mike showed for our band more than made up for that disappointment. It felt great to know that what we were doing actually mattered to someone. And these kids were pretty hip.

The records that Tim DJ'd with before and after the gig were all fantastic; the kid had *great* taste in rockin' sounds and that's *always* the way to my heart. Later on, after the show, he took me back to his student bedsit and I saw his vast record collection all laid out on the floor around his bed. He owned a lot of stuff that I had, but he had also begun to dig deeper into American roots music and it seemed he owned every album that Johnny Cash,

Lee Hazlewood and John Lee Hooker had ever made in mint condition and all on the original 1960s labels too. His taste was wide and varied. Along with the requisite Dolls, Stooges, Stones, MC5 high-energy gods that we worshipped, he had loads of funk, blues, soul, country and psych records. Tim's lovingly made compilation tapes which he would post down to my Brighton flat were both an inspiration and an education in music. Being young and voluntarily unemployed had some good sides to it; in Tim's case he seemed to spend each waking moment in his bedsit immersing himself in a reverie of occult vinyl teachings. He was fast becoming a blues disciple and possessed a religious-like fervour to spread the gospel of US roots music. The excitement on his face as he shared his latest vinyl goldmine finds with like-minded people like myself and the band was a joy to see. His obsessive love of the 1960s deep soul music of Muscle Shoals and Memphis was both instructive and helpful to me in my own developing mania for the genre and that in turn led to us recording the 'Give Out But Don't Give Up' album in Memphis a few years further down the line.

By this point in 1989 we were doing lots of E. At the Duchess of York in Leeds me and Innes chopped one up in the toilet before going on stage, snorted a half each and then went on. I was wearing black leather trousers, a black satin shirt, winklepickers, long hair. The crowd were going mental. It was great. There was no safety barrier, just kids who wanted to hear high-energy rock and roll. I felt incredible in the way you can only feel standing in front of a tight ass rock and roll band between two great guitar players on Les Pauls blasting through hundred-watt Marshall stacks. It's a godlike feeling that very few people will ever experience. Later Innes told me that he played two songs, getting really stuck into it, going mental, pulling shapes before he realised there was no sound coming out of his amp. He ran on stage so fucking high that he forgot to plug himself in. I think some kids shouted, 'You ain't plugged in, mate!' But they were great gigs on that summer 1989 tour.

We played a place called Princess Charlotte in Leicester and it was rammed, and these two guys were spitting at us throughout the whole gig, so I took the mic off the mic stand and fucking threw it at one of them. I had this technique where I could throw a mic and it would go flying, but I would let the cord go loose and whip the guy in the face, then pull it back. He went down so then I whipped his mate in the face. Throb threw his guitar down and him, my brother Graham, the Taft brothers and Throb all jumped in and kicked the fuck out of them. Then we resumed the gig, which was a stormer. Incidents like that always added a sense of danger and drama and edge to the performance.

Afterwards we always let kids come backstage and talk to us because we were into this punk idea where you should know your fans, which works up until you get big and then the bigger you get the crazier the fans and the weirder people get. But initially we would meet the fans because it was always nice to know who was buying our records and coming to see us. Some kids came back after the gig in Leicester and said, 'It was great what you did to those two guys, we know them, they're total Nazis.' According to them those Nazis always came and caused trouble at gigs. Like my old man says, 'You can't argue with a fascist.'

We had a booking agent called Mike Hinc who was a real character: dirty, greasy, matted hair stuck to his forehead, always smoking and sweating out the booze. Brilliant guy, a rock and roller of the old school. Mike was also agent for the Smiths. McGee had said to Hinc. 'Throw away the map, Mike, these guys just want to be on the road, they don't want to be at home, all they want to do is play rock and roll. Just get them as many gigs as you can at all the shitholes. They don't care where. They just want to play.' So he did and we just played everywhere and it was great.

In parallel to all that touring, we'd been getting into acid house.

# 20.

# Bless This Acid House

Brighton seemed to be full of beautiful blonde girls with amazing skin. We'd never seen anything like that in Glasgow, at least not where we grew up. Brighton's a university town and the town centre around the Lanes is like a small village. I hunted round the many record shops and vintage clothing stores for vinyl and cool threads and pretty soon faces became familiar. Every autumn there was fresh blood, because new kids arrived in town to study. If you went out to clubs, which I did, there were always new people.

The club scene was starting to get really interesting. There was an indie club called Sunshine Playroom run by a lovely guy called Sean Sullivan who was a massive Primals and Mary Chain fan. We'd go there for something to do on a Wednesday night. Then we decided to start our own club with our mate from Plymouth, James Williamson. We named the club SLUT and the poster, designed by James, was of Brian Jones wearing a Nazi uniform. It's a really great poster. It said 'Stay Sick, Turn Blue' on the top which was a phrase the Cramps used on the cover of their first single, 'Human Fly' on the Vengeance label. James added our favourite band names, song lyrics, artists, literary quotes, the Surrealists, Kenneth Anger, Buñuel and other radical filmmakers. We promoted gigs by Strawberry Switchblade, Felt, Loop and Weather Prophets because we were friends and fans of all those bands. The Scream had taken Loop on tour with us in 1987 during the *Sonic Flower Groove* days. That was a great tour. We loved Loop. Their single 'Spinning' is a total classic and Robert the singer and his then-girlfriend Becky and brother James Endeacott made a beautiful noise.

We made cassette tapes at SLUT, just like we had at Splash One, wonderful compilations of all our favourite rock and roll records on C-90 cassette tapes. The manager at the Escape was a guy called Rob Wheeler. He was originally from Nottingham and sometimes he would run club nights at different venues in town. When acid house started he was involved in that scene too and he had a small shop and clothing label called MAU MAU which was influenced by Duffer of St George. It was a small, tight-knit community of people. There was also a place called the Basement which was for Brighton Art School students on a Friday night and we played a Scream show there in the mid-eighties; a hot, sweaty subterranean hellhole where indie types went.

Josh Dean, who was driving our van when we crashed that day on the way to Manchester, was promoting exciting new US underground bands like Dinosaur Jr at the Escape. There was a good music scene developing in Brighton. I used to go to the Virgin Megastore on East Street almost daily. One day I went in and heard this track that sounded a lot like 'Velocity Girl'. I went over and asked the guy behind the counter, 'Who the fuck is this?'

'It's the Stone Roses,' he said. And then, 'They're doing a gig tomorrow night. I'm promoting it. D'you wanna come? I'll put you on the guest list.'

'Yeah,' I said. 'Alright, sounds interesting . . .'

I went to that gig with Innes and Karen and we thought the Roses were amazing. I'd never seen a frontman that confident in a band no one had ever heard of. They just *had it* and there were only forty people there, if that. They played four, maybe five songs, then Ian Brown said 'Right, we're off,' and that was it, which was a shame, because I thought they were brilliant. I think they'd played the Hacienda the night before to a sold-out adoring hometown Manchester crowd, but here in Brighton nobody knew who they were . . . yet.

The people we met in Brighton were lovely. I remember a guy called Nick Roughly who was this very handsome guy. He looked like Gerard Malanga with the leather trousers and the suede Levi jacket and the long sandy hair. Nick sang in a band on Creation called Blow Up and he had a lovely girlfriend called Tracy who was at the university. We used to always see Tracy out in the clubs and she really liked us. She was such a nice girl. One Saturday afternoon I ran into Tracy on the street and she said to me, there's this party tonight, an acid house party, it's worth going to. Innes came down that weekend. We actually went to try and buy speed more than anything. We just thought we'd give it a try.

The party was at a warehouse somewhere near Brighton train station and I remember the music was strange, unlike anything I had ever heard. They had some decks set up and we got there quite early. There weren't a lot of people there, but the people that were there and the guys on the decks looked like they came from the council estate. When you went to the indie club you'd never see anybody like this from that part of town. They were full of student kids who dressed like goths. If you went in the Zap Club it was Nick Cave doing a reading or Pussy Galore playing but it was the same thing: indie kids, alternative music fans. If you went to the Escape Club people would be wearing Comme des Garçons and designer clothes. A lot of it was influenced by reading *ID* and *The Face*, which was more an elitist thing. I remember thinking, *this is interesting*, because these guys looked more like football hooligans. That was 1988 when Karen started to buy acid house records.

The shift happened when McGee moved up to Manchester. We knew these girls up there that were friends of the band who'd been some of our earliest fans: Debbie, Tina, Lorraine and Sue. Jeff Barrett had been going to the Hacienda a lot because he was the press guy for Factory, the Mondays and New Order. McGee and Barrett were the guys proselytising for acid house. We were still really into Johnny Thunders, MC5, Stooges, the world of rock 'n' roll.

Barrett was taking journalists up there for acid nights when it was starting to kick off, and he got into the music early on. McGee moved up there and Tony Wilson found him a flat which belonged to one of the Factory Records board members, Alan Erasmus. McGee was pretty debauched at this point and he got into some naughty behaviour. He lived on Palatine Road, somewhere near the Factory offices. He was going to the Hacienda and getting on one. He loved the Mondays and he loved Factory. Debbie was taking him to these parties and he got totally immersed in acid house. McGee and Barrett began making tapes for us, all these records from Chicago and Detroit on twelve-inch import.

Throb, my brother and Martin Duffy had a shared flat in Hove, and one night they decided to throw a party. Felt had also moved to Brighton. Everybody was on speed and magic mushrooms that night. McGee came down from London with Barrett and they were both on E, but I didn't know that at the time. We were listening to a Johnny Thunders tape, and McGee or Barrett would take the tape out of the tape deck and then this weird disco 'music' would come on by bands like Ten City. People were going, what the fuck is this? Throb, when he wasn't upstairs in a debauch, would come down and put Thunders back on the stereo. Barrett and McGee would turn it off. This drama went on and on. Barrett was almost in tears, saying, 'Alan, Alan, they keep changing the music, they keep changing the music!' There was a build-up of tension because we were all on different drugs and into different music, like two parties going on at the same time. Throb's going, 'It's my fucking house, and we don't want to hear that fucking disco shit!'

At one point this mad kid, Simon Ashton, ran up and kicked McGee in the arse. When McGee turned around Ashton had disappeared. McGee lighted on Martin Duffy, who was innocent, and totally lost it, saying, 'You little fucking Brummie cunt.' He grabbed Duffy by the ears, and smashed his head off the wall. Duffy slid down the wall like in a Laurel and Hardy movie, all the way down to his boots, and collapsed on the carpet. Total slapstick.

I shouted at McGee, 'What are you fucking doing?' It was real violence, and I felt protective towards Duffy. He was quite a gentle soul.

'He fucking kicked me in the arse!'

'He never kicked you in the arse, it's fucking Ashton fucking kicked you in the arse!'

Upstairs, there was an orgy happening. Total mayhem. That was my introduction to acid house.

Later on, when we did E, I started to understand why Barrett and McGee were so freaked out that night. They were on a different plane. Your aural preferences on ecstasy are more set to the warm, rounded bass frequencies of acid house and electronic sounds; the *sturm und drang* of screaming, high-energy rock and roll guitars is more suited to a head full of amphetamine sulphate. Just as southern soul sounds great on smack, or weed is perfect for Jamaican reggae and dub. Different drugs for different sounds.

McGee took Karen and me to see Happy Mondays in early 1988, when they played at the Zap Club. McGee went backstage before the Mondays came on, came back out and said, 'Open your mouth.' He'd bought Es from Shaun Ryder, and threw one each down mine and Karen's throats.

I'd first seen the Mondays in 1987 on the night of the great storm when ancient trees fell and roofs were blown off houses, people killed and trains blown off tracks all over the country. The gig was in a basement underneath the Portland Club. Jeff Barrett put them on where they later had the Heavenly Social up near Regent's Park. Me and Throb went to check them out. We were living in hotels back then, never back home in Glasgow. We spent all our time in hotels in London, just having a good time. In between each song Bez continued dancing and I remember trying to work out what drug he was on because he never stopped. Is he on speed? Is he on coke? And Throb's going, I don't think he's on speed or coke. It must be some other new drug. It's not acid. What the fuck's that bloke's on? We should have just gone up and said, What are you on? Or asked Barrett.

A year later we were at the Zap Club and we took the holy sacrament with McGee. My first E was bought from the Happy Mondays. I think that's quite cool. I'm proud of that. However, I remember it not working.

I was still trying to find my voice as a lyricist. I knew what I *wanted* to write, but I needed to find *something* to write about. I knew I could write lyrics like 'I'm Losing More Than I'll Ever Have' and 'You're Just Too Dark to Care'; both were written from experience, *from* my life. But I had to live a bit more. Some of the songs on the second album, the high-energy rock songs, have really trashy lyrics because I wasn't sure how to write good rock lyrics yet. I put together words that sounded good but they didn't really mean anything. I was just filling up the space, not writing from my soul, just writing lyrics so the band could keep going. They weren't autobiographical, so they didn't have any meaning.

I remember asking Lawrence from Felt for some advice about it. He said, 'Why don't you write about speed. Why don't you write a song called "Speed Anthem", 'cause you're always taking speed.'

I had the urge and I had the calling, but I just hadn't worked out how to do it at that point. I was better at writing words for the ballads because they were quite tender and I could just open myself up for that kind of music. I hadn't quite worked out you had to write bluesy melodies for rock to work. I found it easy to write sixties pop melodies, and they were lovely but in conflict with the filthy riffs the boys were playing. In some cases the marriage of sugar and dirt does work, though. On 'Ivy Ivy Ivy', for example. I discovered later that if you start writing a bluesy melody you can write a meaner, darker lyric, it's an atmospheric thing created by the darker, sourer chords that you use for rock and blues. It's adult and it's pained; pop is more teenage: sweet, sugary and hopeful. Rock has an air of finality and violence about it, a hungry sexuality. I loved the way blues and soul writers wrote songs: simple, direct and honest, even if it was a song written to be a hit there was always a straightforward, brutal honesty in the music created by American working-class people, both Black and white. The country, soul and blues music that I loved affected me very much.

I was enraptured by artists such as Bobby 'Blue' Bland. His classic 'Two Steps from the Blues' album is a perfect example of elegant blues songwriting, musicianship and intense, restrained vocalising. Bland's phrasing is up there with Sinatra in my mind; both master storytellers of noir-pop-bed-chamber blues and adult existentialism. When Bobby sings, 'I know how it feels to be a stranger in a strange land', it feels like you are listening to the loneliest sound in the world. True blues from a troubled soul who's seen it all and suffered far too much. His voice is battered, weathered and weary. Bobby always sang songs of experience, his manliness unbowed and righteous in its defiance of an unfair, unkind and uncaring world. Have there ever been truer words sung than, 'Ain't no love in the heart of the city?' Check out Bobby Bland's 1974 pop soul classic and hear his majesty for yourself.

Then there was the great O.V. Wright whose voice burned and crackled with a carnal fire and brimstone world gone wrong conjuring up visions of fire and ice. His classic records are occult Mississippi Delta alchemical conjurings made under the guidance of the great producer, Willie Mitchell. Pain and lust are both sides of the same coin in O.V.'s Manichean world. His songs are all dark tales of diseased love, sex, sin and pleas for redemption. There is never resolution in these songs, just the facts. Blues as truth. Blues as a way of life; a resigned acceptance of a cold loveless world of pain and sorrow, with only the transient joy of illicit love stolen like a thief in the night. O.V. was a master of the craft. I wanted to learn the dark arts of that kind of songwriting. I hoped that someday I could emulate it.

At the time I was getting into *The Aesthetics of Rock* by Richard Meltzer. He was making a case for rock and roll in a classical and philosophical context, albeit with a dose of humour. I admired the way he understood how deep the counter-culture is and how poetic it can be. I felt that as well. He was elevating it to high art, which I believe it was.

The ballads on *Primal Scream* had good lyrics and were musically well-defined. They contain a specific atmosphere of darkness and longing. There's a raw sensitivity there that no one else was really doing in the underground music scene at that point. As for the rock tracks, the band are great on all of them: gonzo rock and roll as it should be played, with passion and total commitment, no irony, just ramalama balls-to-the-wall filthy fuck music. There was a period, however, when I felt like giving up. I had a meeting with Throb and McGee and told them how I felt; that I was struggling to write anything meaningful. Alan said to me, 'You've just got to tell your story. You're a natural lead singer and frontman, rock and roll is all you can do. You've got to keep doing it.' They believed in me.

At that point I was just trying to make the band work, still on the dole, struggling, and suffering from a slight depression as well. Karen worked at Barclays so I was always alone on weekdays, and I would go for walks around Brighton, ending up at the record shops. North Laine was amazing. It had half a dozen really good record shops and I'd visit them all then come back and sit by the old pier at dusk in winter, summer, spring or autumn, and just watch the sun go down. It always made me feel better, but I still didn't feel good inside myself. Something wasn't right. Maybe I was sad that the band wasn't happening and I wasn't going to be a rock star and would have to take a normal, straight job at some point. Being on the dole was eroding my soul. My dad was right all those years ago about being unemployed: 'A man has to have a purpose in life, something to get out of bed for in the morning.' I think I am quite melancholic by nature.

In those times no one really spoke about their feelings in the way in which they do nowadays. Today we have huge industries set up that profit from the idea that people suffer from a mental illness called 'depression'; from the big pharma corporations to therapists, there is plenty of money to be made from emotional misery. The culture I grew up in discouraged people, especially boys, from ever discussing their 'feelings'. You had to just accept whatever situation you were in and 'get on with it'. I am a strong believer in that ethos of self-help and stoicism. Indeed, my father is a great example of that. In 1983 he was given six months to live by the doctor unless he gave up smoking and drinking. So he just went cold turkey and never told anyone. On his own, no shrinks or treatment centres for him; a man of the old school brought up the hard way. I admire that. My malaise was a kind of melancholy which had emerged in my mid mid-teens and I am loath to describe it as 'depression'. It was a feeling that came and went from time to time and over the years I have observed that this change in my consciousness happened most whenever I went through long periods of creative inaction, as if the unused creative energy had somehow internalised itself in a melancholic feedback loop inside my body, and the effect it had always sunk me into inert states of uselessness and self-doubt. I wasn't always in a position to describe myself as 'creative', however, so I had no idea what was causing it.

I knew we had a unique spirit and great musical ability, but I was looking for the magic formula. I used to think about it all the time and I think it got me down. Not having any money didn't get me down, I was alright with that. I claimed the housing benefit and dole and I had some money from the Mary Chain left over. As long as I had enough money to occasionally buy some records, as long as I could keep feeding my music habit, I was happy. I was fine.

# 21.

# The Gospel According to Audrey Witherspoon

It was the summer of 1989 and I was in a pub on the Clerkenwell Road, across the road from Leather Lane, with Jeff Barrett. We weren't getting much press on the second album. No music journalists were into it in a big way and we weren't taken seriously by the weeklies. Barrett was a couple of beers in and he launched into this speech about the glory of Phil Spector's sixties Wall of Sound productions and the insane amount of emotion that Spector put into those records. He was almost in tears talking about it, really inspirational. It was the most emotional I'd ever seen him on a Wednesday afternoon. Then he started to talk about this acid house DJ and writer called Andrew Weatherall who wrote for this club fanzine called *Boy's Own*. Jeff showed me a copy of the fanzine and on the page where people were asked to list their favourite records of the moment this Weatherall fellow had picked 'All the ballads on the second Primal Scream album'. He was the only guy championing us. I felt touched that someone dug our music and I was intrigued. I knew I had to meet Andrew Weatherall.

In Brighton I'd been going to acid house nights. After the clubs shut at 2 a.m. someone would rig up a set of decks to a generator under the arches and out on the groynes, and everyone would just keep dancing on Es. The Escape would finish and everybody would still be E'd up, stood outside the Zap Club on the beach at two in the morning. No one wanting to go home yet, everyone still buzzing. Somebody would say, Oh, there's gonna be a party under the walkway by the arches here opposite the East Pier. Then you'd be waiting for something to happen, an interminable wait because you just wanted *more* house music and *more* dance action then somebody would say, There's gonna be a party at the groyne. It was just a quarter of a mile or so up from the East Pier, heading towards Hastings. Everyone was super friendly on ecstasy and my face was known as somebody on the scene; very few of these people knew that I was in a band. It was an underground scene: outlaw, illicit, occult and fun.

That summer Alan McGee moved into the flat directly above me on Regency Square. One night we went back to his to do more drugs after a party at the Zap Club. McGee said he'd been told that there was a big party somewhere out in the countryside where Andrew Weatherall was DJing. So in the early hours of the morning we found ourselves crammed into two taxis driving both wilfully and aimlessly out in the darklands of the East Sussex countryside looking for this mythical party where (our soon-to-be-guru) Andy Weatherall was DJing. The problem was we had no address or destination. Of course these were the days before mobile phones. All we had to go on was luck and willpower.

We bombed down mysterious country lanes and somebody would say, 'I can hear music, I can hear music, stop the car.' Everybody would pile out of the car excited, wandering out into the fields, but there'd be nothing there, just real country dark and a vast empty silence. After doing this a couple of times, we realised the music we were hearing was coming from the taxi driver's car radio. Everybody was so off their heads. Eventually as the dawn broke we found the party, stumbling up from the road through a field of long grass towards a small wooded glade of trees in the distance. Then as we made our way through the woods we were greeted by a vision of these huge, churchlike white tents. The new church: the church of acid house. We were like pilgrims on a psychedelic crusade to a holy shrine, a primeval invocation, a religious compulsion that couldn't be questioned. It was a desire beyond sex, a pagan summoning. As we were getting closer to the white tents we could hear the beats sucking us in. We were under the spell, ready for the dance, ready for the trance, and that's where Weatherall was DJing. That's where I first met him, in a field at six in the morning, off my fucking head on E.

Over the course of the summer of 1989 we really got into going to acid house clubs. Throb was a bit slower to pick up on it but Innes, Karen and myself were in there immediately. She was buying twelve-inch import records and hanging out with some people on the local scene. We had sort of split up that summer but were still sharing the flat which was sometimes difficult.

I remember going to Shoom when it was on Kensington High Street with Innes. Danny Rampling ran the club with his wife Jenny who did the door and it felt very exclusive. One of the first of many eye-opening things we saw as we entered Shoom was the vision of real-life pop star Mark Moore from S-Express surrounded by loads of really amazingly dressed, cool, glamorous girls. His scene just looked so goddamn glam, it was major. We loved S-Express. We thought those records were incredible.

I remember talking to this beautiful girl wearing a jacket made of peacock feathers and never before would I have sat down and started chatting to somebody like that, but on ecstasy all my inhibitions disappeared. The atmosphere in the club was of near-atomic levels of energy. It was sexual; not in an overt, sleazy, tacky mainstream way, but in the sense that people were expressing themselves freely with no sense of judgement or threat of violence or sexism and everyone was there for one reason: to dance to this incredible new contemporary electronic soul music in the infinite NOW. I remember feeling totally in the moment, like I was starring in a movie and everyone else was also a star in *their* own movie. Every brother and every sister was a star. That was one of the beautiful things about acid house: it was not hierarchical (that came later, with the overpaid, overhyped superstar DJs and super-clubs like Ministry of Sound and the mass-market capitalistic exploitation of the culture). I recall the feeling at Shoom as one of a celebration of life. Up until that time the music and scenes I'd been involved in, from punk to post-punk and rock and roll culture in general, were driven by anger, rage, nihilism and despair. I loved all that stuff because it's how I related to the world. I had a good healthy (or unhealthy) dose of negativism in my character. I loved music that spoke about heartbreak, struggle and pain and took a cynical view on human relationships and politics. My drug of choice was amphetamine sulphate – speed – which boosted my feelings of alienation and separateness. Ecstasy, however, was a different psychotropic trip. My life was changing and I didn't even know it.

The definitive hook-up happened when Weatherall reviewed the Scream for the *NME* Live pages writing under the pseudonym of Audrey Witherspoon, which is the name he used for his *Boy's Own* missives. It was commissioned by Helen Mead and we have Jeff Barrett to thank for this holiest of cosmic interventions because he came up with the idea (I don't think *NME* was in a hurry to review Primal Scream). Helen Mead and her boyfriend Jack Barron were recent converts to acid house. Jack had previously been into bands such as Einstürzende Neubauten, Sonic Youth, Swans, Nick Cave and the Bad Seeds, and the Jesus and Mary Chain. He'd since become a disciple of acid house and like a lot of us was getting into E in a big way. We would see Jack and Helen at McGee's acid house parties at Creation where we would hang with people like the guys from My Bloody Valentine.

McGee was buying ecstasy for us and throwing the parties. We were all on Mrs Thatcher's Enterprise Allowance Scheme. If you proved to the dole office that you had one thousand pounds in your bank account and came up with a fake business plan then you no longer had to sign on. This lasted for one year and it was very handy because it allowed us to go around the country on tour without the hassle of having to be back in Brighton at 10 a.m. on a wet Tuesday morning to sign on, which is just not practical when you finished a show in Hull at 2 a.m. the night before. We would take a train up from Brighton to London and get the Tube from Victoria to Bethnal Green then jump on a bus to Westgate Street E8 and climb the stairs at number 8 passing the Asian sweatshop on the other side of the wall on the way up to the Creation offices to be greeted by Alan, his eyes widened, a big smile on his face. 'Just open your mouth, Bob,' he said. 'Here you go. There's another one, save it for later.'

A small, tightly wound guy named Terry Chemical was always buzzing about. He carried himself with a paranoid air of malevolence, as if he was always just about to explode. I'd met him once before at the party outside Brighton where we'd met Weatherall a few weeks back. He thought I'd short-changed him in a drug deal. I hadn't, but he was so out of it that he'd forgotten I'd paid him the money a few hours earlier. McGee had to step in between us and vouch for my credibility. The last thing you want when flying on high-grade ecstasy is any fucking aggro. It made me wary of Terry. Later on we became great pals, that first misunderstanding completely forgotten. In the mid-nineties Terry and his then-girlfriend Lisa looked after me in his Kentish Town house, whenever I was out and about and worse for wear in London.

The Weatherall review in *NME* was titled 'Sex, Lies and Gaffer Tape'. He was into the band when we weren't fashionable. That year it was all Stone Roses, Pixies, Happy Mondays, Throwing Muses, the Wonder Stuff. Audrey gave us a good review: 'The songs. One sounded like T. Rex, one sounded like Gen X, one sounded like Big Star, one sounded like the Sex Pistols and one *was* the Sex Pistols.' There was a good photograph of me wearing a golden lurex shirt I'd bought from a high-street women's fashion store. I combined the shirt with black leather trousers. Exactly what I would wear to acid house clubs in the late eighties.

We were touring all over the UK throughout that summer. We played a lot up north and we'd take speed to do the gig and then drop Es afterwards for the ride home back to London, listening to house compilation tapes that Barrett, McGee or James Williamson had made for us: Inner City, Big Fun, Joe Smooth, Frankie Knuckles, Jamie Principle, Little Louis Vega, Sueño Latino, Derrick May, all the obvious classics. Frankie Knuckles' 'Tears' became an anthem for us all. It became a phrase to describe any experience or object that we found inspirational. 'That girl you got off with last night was tears.' 'Have you heard the latest Frankie Knuckles single? No? You should, it's total tears.' 'Weatherall's set at the Zap on Thursday was tears.' 'I've got some tears speed, d'ya want a line?'

We'd be E'd up on the motorway and sometimes we'd stop at a service station at five in the morning for a piss break and get the football out. We always took one in case an impulsive game was in the offing and we'd all be running around the empty car park in our leather trousers and Chelsea boot winklepickers, playing football E'd up. One time me and Throb ran across one of the glass bridges that join the service stations together on opposite sides of the motorway. It must have been about five or six in the morning, after daybreak. The sun had come up and we decided to have a race. As we were running it was like we were taking off, flying, high on ecstasy, speed and the joy and freedom of youth.

Some of these underground club records we were partying to started going overground and into the top twenty UK pop charts. These contemporary American soul records coming from US Midwest cities like Chicago and Detroit and British soul records as well, like Soul II Soul, felt like truly contemporary music: new, soulful, but electronic, completely different to this other scene that we inhabited, the dour indie scene. There was no comparison.

UK indie was self-satisfied, elitist and judgemental with too many rules and a Puritan aesthetic where anything glamorous or overtly sexual was viewed as highly suspect. Our move from the jangle-psych of *Sonic Flower Groove* to the greasy blues rock of our sophomore album was just too much of a leap of faith for some of our early followers to make. Although the sartorial choices of people on the scene were clothes mainly gathered from charity shops and jumble sales, the indie dandies were in short supply. There was always a feeling of miserableness in the air at indie gigs. The audience generally dressed in a drably utilitarian manner, whereas the acid scene was high-energy and full of beautiful, fashionable girls dressed in everything from high-fashion Commes and Bodymap to contemporary sportswear. People looked fresh and clean and everybody was friendlier because of the scene's holy sacrament drug, ecstasy. The indie scene was mostly drinking pints of lager which I could never get into. Pubs were never my scene. They weren't even taking drugs, just drinking. The two scenes were in complete opposition to each other. When we first started playing gigs it was to very small crowds in small venues all over the country and it felt new and exciting, but by the late eighties it had run out of energy. Indie was over as far as I was concerned.

Just before we got into acid house we went to see Spacemen 3. I heard their single 'Revolution' and I saw the video on Snub TV and thought it was great. They played at the Escape Club in Brighton so we all went to see them. Now, my overriding memory of that show was of loads of Spacemen fans just sat on the floor waiting for the band to come on, and when Spacemen 3 eventually started playing Jason and Sonic were both sitting on chairs as well. I'd read that these guys were Stooges and MC5 fanatics like ourselves, into high-energy rock and roll. I thought what is wrong with these twenty-year-old kids, teenage kids, eighteen-year-old kids, sitting on the floor cross-legged like doped-out hippies? We were all speeding, which didn't help the situation. We watched the whole gig, it was quite low-energy. I hadn't heard any of their music except 'Revolution' and later found out they were smackheads so it all made sense to me then. I remember kicking a couple of people sat on the floor when I was trying to get to the bar or the toilet: fucking get out the way, you cunt.

It really was a choice between sex and death, culturally speaking, between Eros and Thanatos. I chose sex. It was no contest at all. It was like inhabiting two different planets. It was a beautiful summer, as were the following summers of 1990 and 1991. I had a really great time as a young man at the end of my twenties, single and free with no responsibilities.

Although we'd had an acid house epiphany during 1989, things weren't really happening for the band, but the scene was exciting. It was futuristic. It was Now.

Some of the tracks we heard in the clubs were these long seven, eight-minute odysseys that were contemporary versions of the dub versions of reggae tunes we loved: sprawling, deconstructed, inventive, futuristic music. To be present when Andrew Weatherall first played a new track no one had ever heard before was like being initiated into an occult secret society. This was not music for straights, it was a truly underground happening and we were hip to the trip; modern psychedelia if you like. This new music conjured up visions of cities of the future, of pulsing technopolises. The club became a carnival of dark souls, shamanic dancing and ecstatic joy. Weatherall understood the power of music to weave spells on listeners' imaginations, to alter molecular structures. The body moves the heart which moves the head and kills the dread and brings us ever closer together. No one is a stranger on ecstasy. It's a chemical brother- and sisterhood. We all move to the same beat and dance our way out of this prison we call our bodies and society. Come together, brothers and sisters, come together as one.

When we weren't in the clubs we were still out on the road playing our high-energy rock and roll shows. We did a bunch of gigs that winter. Simultaneously the Madchester explosion was happening. The Stone Roses, Happy Mondays, Inspiral Carpets and 808 State had all broken country-wide and had singles in the Top 20. Suddenly indie bands were getting in the official pop charts and on *Top of the Pops* and having their records played on daytime radio. The Roses and Inspirals were both playing a modern version of sixties-influenced psych rock. The Mondays, though, were one-off originals. There's no precedent for them except maybe Can. There were a lot of great things happening in UK youth culture and we had a foot in each camp. We played our first gigs in Ireland that winter, a place I had always wanted to visit, and set off on a winter tour. We took Teenage Fanclub with us on the Scottish dates. I told McGee he should sign them because they were a really cool jamming band at this point, influenced by Crazy Horse as much as Alex Chilton, but he declined. He eventually saw the light in 1991 when they signed to Creation.

We were playing the music that we loved and lived for, speeding the whole fucking time. At least me and Innes were – Throb at that point couldn't afford coke, so I think he was speeding as well, but not the way me and Innes were. And we couldn't always afford the E, it was too expensive at twenty-five quid a hit; a week's dole money.

We played these gigs and there were only a couple of hundred people at each one, sometimes hardly any at all. I recall one show at JB's Dudley near Birmingham when there were twenty people, max. Two of those diehards were Tjinder Singh and Ben Ayres from Cornershop who told me years later they were there and it was a great show. At that point we were doing 'Cocksucker Blues' by the Stones, 'Up on the Roof' by Carole King and 'Lonesome

Town' by Ricky Nelson and the Cramps as the encores and playing all these ballads in amongst the main set of songs from the second album. We were a great rock and roll band on that tour, but no one was really listening. Nikki Sudden was supporting us solo on some of those dates and Dave Kusworth and the Bounty Hunters opened on some too. I loved Nikki and Dave's *Robespierre's Velvet Basement* album; a classic British rock and roll record. Those guys romanticised rock and roll even more than we did. True believers.

The last gig of the tour was in late December at Subterranea on Portobello Road, under the Westway. Ticket sales were not great. Around this time Nirvana were on their way up. They had released their first album *Bleach* on Sub-Pop, a label the UK press were really hyping along with the nascent Seattle scene. A couple of nights before our gig at Subterranea my friend Tim Tooher said to me, 'I've made all these flyers. I'm gonna go down to the Nirvana gig at the Astoria and hand them out, we need to get people to come and see the Scream. Maybe some of these grunge kids would like what you're doing.'

I said, 'OK, I'll go with you.' I thought maybe we could also go to the gig.

Tim and I stood outside the Astoria on a freezing Wednesday night handing out our flyers to completely disinterested Nirvana and Mudhoney fans, me in head to toe black leather biker jacket and jeans and Tim dressed like the River Phoenix character in *My Own Private Idaho*. Two rock and roll waifs. It was as cold as Margaret Thatcher's heart on the Charing Cross Road that evening so we gave up after half an hour and tried to get into the gig but couldn't because it was sold out. Shame.

We'd become close enough with Weatherall that he was starting to DJ at our gigs. Innes, myself, Throb and Toby all dropped E before going onstage that night at the Subterranea, which was not the best idea. We also did E at a gig in Islington Powerhouse that summer. We all came up at the exact same time and it was a bit of a mess. It took us to about halfway through the set to really get it together. Everything became softened on E, all my senses and cognitive abilities were out of alignment and time slowed right down. I couldn't find the beat properly and the music was slipping and sliding all over the place. On speed my senses were sharpened and I possessed an intensity of focus, my whole being totally locked into the hard rock rhythm of the band, the Godzilla-like power of the twin guitars matched the messianic feelings that speed gave me. Ecstasy was not a drug for playing rock and roll on: too soft, too loving.

No one from Creation came to the gig. No one. Not one single person was interested. We played 'Don't Believe a Word' by Thin Lizzy as an encore. Jeff Barrett was there, to his credit, and afterwards he came up to me and said, 'That Thin Lizzy cover was disgusting.'

I said, 'You don't like Thin Lizzy then?' I knew Barrett was never into blues-type rock music. He loved soul but he didn't like blues. And also it was the uncoolest thing in the world at that point, at the height of acid house and Madchester and years of the *NME* slagging off anything they termed to be 'rockist', a legacy of Paul Morley and all the Kid Creole and Scritti Politti and Prefab Sprout fans, to play a Thin Lizzy song. So I just thought, well that's just Barrett. I love him.

Then Weatherall came up to me with a warm smile on his face and said, 'I loved your version of "Don't Believe a Word". That was incredible.' His eyes lit up like they always did when he was excited and enthused about something.

I said, 'Oh, d'you like Thin Lizzy?'

'I got Phil Lynott's autograph ten days before he died,' he answered.

Fuck, I thought to myself. I love this guy. We're brothers. So that was the night.

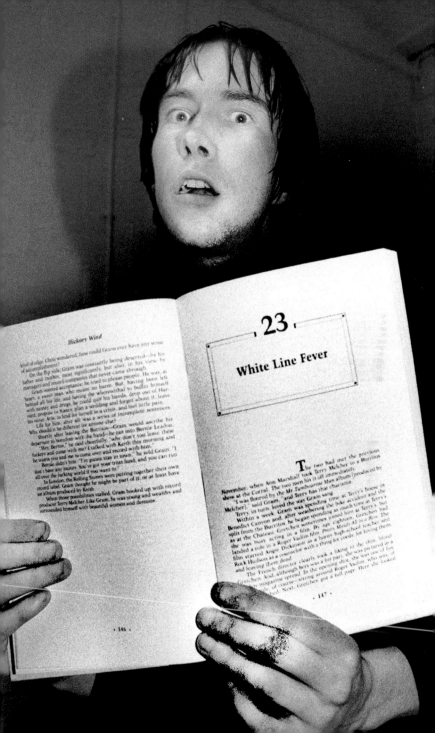

Psychic communion with Lord Sabre (Andrew Weatherall)

Innes and I showing respect to Her Majesty

Hijinks on the Screamadelica tour, 1991.
No lightweights need apply

The band and Denise Johnson on the way to Kinky Disco

Their Screamadelic Majesties

HMV Oxford Street, *Screamadelica* album signing, September 1991

The original painting by Paul Cannell, made for the single cover of 'Higher Than the Sun'

'Don't fight it, feel it'

Like kids in a
candy shop

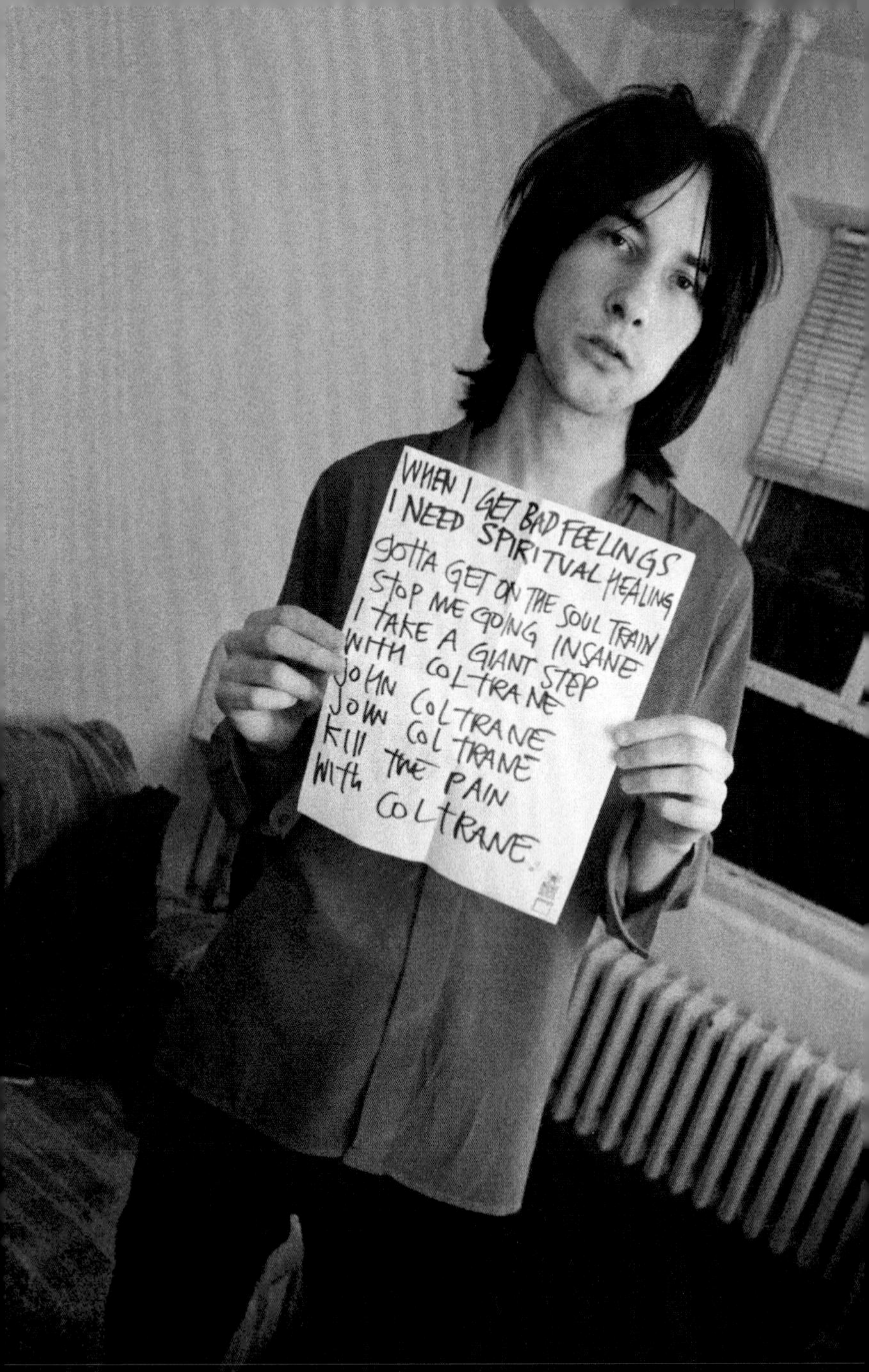
WHEN I GET BAD FEELINGS
I NEED SPIRITUAL HEALING
gotta GET ON THE SOUL TRAIN
STOP ME GOING INSANE
I TAKE A GIANT STEP
WITH COLTRANE
JOHN COLTRANE
JOHN COLTRANE
KILL THE PAIN
WITH COLTRANE.

# 22.
# Loaded in Walthamstow
# (Remix / *Remodel*)

Since the late seventies rap and hip-hop producers had been cutting up old records from the sixties and seventies and reconstructing them into new soundscapes which formed a sonic bed whereupon rappers could broadcast their truths to the world with ghetto beat poetry, making the new out of the old; like Jamaican dub this was total genius. This late twentieth-century art form was created originally at block parties in the Black and Latino districts of New York City using two turntables and a microphone: no bands, no musicians, no expensive, fancy studios, just hip taste and wild imaginations run riot. Sometimes they even plugged into the lampposts for electricity to power the parties taking place in post-apocalyptic city streets full of condemned tenements, a forgotten and despised people making real, vital and living art out of nothing. Fuck MOMA and all the rest of the safe, dead, bourgeois crap uptown: the true grease was happening on ghetto streets where African–American kids were listening to Kraftwerk and taking the German techno pioneers' synthesised nostalgic futurism even further into the future whilst poeticising and sexualising it. NYC radio stations began playing this new music and record companies duly followed, creating monster hits such as 'The Message' by Grandmaster Flash and the Furious Five or 'Planet Rock' by Afrika Bambaataa & the Soulsonic Force. When the Akai sampler arrived in 1988 it allowed music-makers to employ some of the cut-up techniques originated by the Bronx DJs combining live rock musicians into the mix.

The whole rap and hip-hop idea of cutting up music from the past to create the music of the future was collagist in intention but Burroughsian in practice; William Burroughs had made famous the cut-up technique he'd learned from the artist and writer Brion Gysin. Artists such as David Bowie experimented with the cut-up for writing lyrics, but *no one* had ever applied this technique to music in the way the OG rap people did and I'm not sure how down with Burroughs they actually were. They were poor, economically speaking, living in some of the most deprived, run-down and crime-ridden areas of the United States, but created their art and entertainment out of the unwanted junk of previous decades and in so doing gave birth to a new musical art form which now, forty years later, is the most successful musical genre on the planet.

The origination of rap music was a culturally heroic act. They say that necessity is the mother of invention; well, rap culture proves that one hundred per cent. There was more than a bit of the rap ethic and Burroughs 'cut-up' technique applied to some of the songs on *Screamadelica*: 'Loaded' and 'Slip Inside This House', for example, but again, this came about through us experimenting with the Akai S 1000 sampler and marvelling at the infinite creative choices it offered. Using dialogue from films was a favourite thing of ours to do back then. Indeed, we'd sampled Malcolm McDowell's voice from *A Clockwork Orange* on 'Spirea X' in 1986. I recorded that on a portable cassette player from a bootleg VHS video I had of the movie.

Jeff Barrett or Andrew Innes came up with the idea: Let's get Weatherall to remix 'I'm Losing More Than I'll Ever Have'. We had written a couple new songs for the upcoming European gigs but they were still 'works in progress' and not yet ready for recording. So McGee was going to release 'I'm Losing More Than I'll Ever Have' as a single, and Creation needed B sides.

At this point in time Weatherall had only ever worked on 'Hallelujah' for the Mondays alongside Paul Oakenfold and Steve Osborne and maybe an obscure twelve-inch by East India Trading Company. This, I think, was going to be the first time he'd actually worked alone in the studio. We persuaded him to say yes, and 'Loaded' was created at Bark studios in November 1989.

Weatherall did a first version which had a huge-sounding breakbeat under the original track. It was mainly instrumental, featuring loads of Innes's fantastic, funky, superfly wah-wah guitar. But to be honest it was shapeless and lacking in direction, a bit disappointing. It wasn't really going anywhere. I was expecting a miracle of sorts, looking forward to hearing him deconstruct our song, taking it somewhere new and unimaginable, so I was underwhelmed. McGee heard it and said to us, 'This isn't good enough to release, you've got to send him back in to the studio and do it again.' After all, McGee was paying the remixers' and studio's bills. So Weatherall had another attempt. The problem was he was showing too much respect for the song. It was mainly instrumental, although some of my original vocals were on there, with nothing much else added apart from a couple of funky rock breaks. He was still more or less sticking to the original arrangement. We still weren't into it but it showed promise. McGee sent him back in for the third and final time, and that's when Innes uttered the famous words to Weatherall: 'Stop fannying about. You've just got to fucking destroy it.'

I came up from Brighton on the train, bringing a bootleg VHS of the sixties exploitation biker flick *Wild Angels*, directed by Roger Corman and starring Peter Fonda and Nancy Sinatra. I had the soundtrack album too. It has a great cover illustration like the film poster; the band is Davie Allen and the Arrows who have a connection to the Chocolate Watchband. Innes brought along his

VHS recorder, driving all the way to Walthamstow from the Isle of Dogs. I also brought the Kim Fowley album *Outrageous* with that great deranged speech on it. We'd been using the track 'California Hayride' as an intro tape prior to us coming on stage. It was psychotically stirring stuff and got us in the mood to go into battle each night. We took *Outrageous* and the *Wild Angels* video and suggested to Weatherall that he put some dialogue on the track. We'd heard dialogue from films and Martin Luther King speeches used on acid house and BIG Audio Dynamite records and thought that it might be a fun thing to do. Weatherall knew what would work on the dancefloor, so it was his call. I also brought up a rare seventies funk album with a really great breakbeat in it and played that to Weatherall in case he thought it could be useful too, which he instantly dug. Innes stayed, I left, because I sensed Weatherall didn't want too many people from the band there getting in the way. Anyway, I had bought tickets months earlier to see Neil Young play an acoustic show at Hammersmith that night and left them to it. Sometime during that night of rock and roll necromancy the beautiful country soul cheating ballad 'I'm Losing More Than I'll Ever Have' transformed itself into the acid house dancefloor monster soon to be known across the world as 'Loaded'. Little did we know how it would change our lives.

When I heard the third mix I was shocked. Weatherall had based the track around a completely different breakbeat. On the previous two failed mixes he'd used a generic-sounding hard funk-rock breakbeat. It was too straight and didn't really swing. This time he used a monster Soul II Soul break which I thought he'd taken from 'Keep on Moving' or 'Back to Life'. It was actually sampled from an Italian bootleg mash-up of an Edie Brickell track 'What I Am' which swung like one of Pierrepoint's victims. Innes's main reason for having 'I'm Losing More' remixed was because we had recorded it to a drum machine so it was in perfect time, time-coded, which is necessary for remixing. We planned on adding percussion, conga drums, maracas, horns and strings and we knew Toby was not the best timekeeper, so we took no chances and played everything to the perfect machine rhythm then overdubbed Toby's drums later on. The track was also perfect for remixing because it had all these instruments to play around with plus Throb's acoustic blues slide guitar, Duffy's gospel piano and Henry's grooving bassline. The space with which the band played the end three-chord groove section of 'I'm Losing More' which Weatherall constructed 'Loaded' around was ready and waiting to be reimagined.

Weatherall had also tastefully and artfully chopped up the *Wild Angels* Peter Fonda dialogue and placed it at the very beginning of the track so the very first thing you hear is the concerned, paternalistic voice of a straight-A upstanding middle-aged conservative minister asking Peter Fonda, the dissolute leader of the Wild Angels outlaw motorcycle gang, 'Just what is it that you want to do?' Fonda replies with all the rebellious arrogance and ignorance of wasted youth, 'We wanna be free, to do what we wanna do, and we wanna get loaded, we wanna have a good time, and that's what we're gonna do, we're gonna have a party.'

They had a VHS video cassette set up along with a television in the studio which was DI'd (Direct Injection) into the mixing desk. Weatherall used an Akai S 1000 sampler to capture and cut up the *Wild Angels* dialogue. I didn't realise at the time but Seattle grunge band Mudhoney had used the exact same sample. I'd never heard any Mudhoney songs apart from 'Touch Me I'm Sick'. Jack Sargeant, a friend from Brighton, had given me a tape of some Sub-Pop stuff. It had 'Love Buzz' by Nirvana, and another Mudhoney track but not the Angels sample. I was into underground movies, Roger Corman American International pictures like *The Trip* and *Masque of the Red Death*. I liked all that trashy biker sixties stuff. That's where I heard it first.

'Loaded' was mixed in late November, a few weeks before Andy DJ'ed for us at the Subterranea gig. Our dressing room before the gig was filled with a gang of indie fangirls. Girls with

331

Wonder Stuff T-shirts on, but also real Primal Scream fans, saying to me very emotionally, 'Why is that man playing that horrible music? Please, please ask him to stop!'

I was on speed and I said, 'Get the fuck out of here! He's playing proper modern music. None of that fucking indie shit you've got on your T-shirt, that's proper modern music. If you don't like it, get the fuck out of here!'

I'm not comparing us to Dylan when he went electric, but when our fans heard the music that Weatherall was playing in the club before we hit the stage they were having these terrible reactions. It was very tribal. What was the problem?

When McGee heard the 'I'm Losing More' remix he said, 'This has to be the single! It's total genius.' The Weatherall mix had to be the A side because when people first heard 'Loaded' they instantly went mental for it. We'd never had a reaction like this to anything we'd recorded so far. Innes called me at home at about four or five in the morning and said, 'Bob, I've just been in Subterranea and Weatherall played the white label of "Loaded".' Weatherall was the only guy that had the record at this point. 'The whole place went fucking crazy!' He said the reaction was unbelievable. He was babbling with joy and excitement, telling me with pride that Kevin Rowland from Dexys and Mick Jones from the Clash – both guys that were heroes of ours – had approached him after the record finished to shake his hand. Word had spread around the club the record was by Primal Scream. Eventually he calmed down, became serious, and said, 'Bob, we might have a hit record on our hands here. It took the roof off, the whole place went mental.'

We were flying high on 'Loaded'. We'd made a great music video for it, filmed in a little studio near Battersea Roundabout, under the arches near the park gates and beautiful Chelsea Bridge. In the back of my mind, however, I was worried, because I knew that soon I'd have to sign off the Enterprise Allowance Scheme, which you could only be on for a year, and go back on the dole.

We set off on a short tour of Spain, France and Italy. Andrew's girlfriend at the time, Christine Wanless, worked in a laboratory. That summer of 1989 we would sit in Innes' flat with a huge jar of chloroform. We'd all be sitting with our heads sunk in the jar. The problem with chloroform is if you light a match there's an explosion. So on this tour, to alleviate the boredom, we took the chloroform with us in the van for the motorway journeys and guys were nodding out and shit. It's a soporific. We had a sound mixer named Ralph, a middle-aged goth, not a bad guy but boring as hell. One day Ralph blurted out, 'Enough is enough!' This was maybe three or four gigs into the tour and we were bombing down the French motorway on the way to Italy and Ralph said, 'Please let me out', in the middle of nowhere. So we just let him out. He was stood on the hard shoulder with his suitcase.

I shouted to him, 'Are you fucking serious?'

He replied, 'I don't want to be in a van full of guys doing chloroform, you're gonna blow the van up. You're all fucking psychopaths.'

Somebody, probably Innes or Throb, said, 'Hey Ralph, why don't you try some and chill out?' But he was adamant he wanted out and was leaving the tour. So we left him there. We completed the tour without a sound guy, and we never saw or heard from him again. I suppose Ralph was paranoid because there was always someone lighting a fag in the van.

The cavalry arrived in the shape of our mate from sunny Greenock, Taftie. Taft's real mission was to bring us a few ounces of speed, but on the way to Italy he dropped by the Creation offices to pick up the VHS of the 'Loaded' video for us to approve. Taft was one of our earliest fans. His brother George was a northern soul speed freak, still keeping on, still carrying the torch. Taft arrived with the speed, and with 'Loaded', the best video we'd made up to that point. To be fair, we'd only made three.

There was a little TV screen high up in the corner of the

minibus, above the passenger seats, with a VHS cassette recorder. We watched 'Loaded' again and again and I remember Throb saying to me, 'This video's gonna get you laid.' When we got back after the tour we all went to the Creation offices in Westgate Street and they showed the video on the big TV. All the girls from the company were watching it and Throb said with a knowing look, and that charming, devilish smile on his face, 'Watch that finger, girls.' He was referring to the part in the video when the camera zooms in on him playing slide guitar. It felt like the record was going to be a big success.

I missed the last gig in Barcelona on this tour. I had met a Spanish girl named Mar after the show in Valencia, and decided to hang out with her for a couple of days instead. You may think this is totally unprofessional, but we were playing gigs in Italy in huge tents with absolutely no one in them. We always put on a great show no matter how big the crowd was, but aside from the take-no-prisoners attitude we showed onstage, our lack of success was getting me down. It wasn't something I spoke about to the rest of the band. I didn't need to; the evidence was staring us straight in the face every night. The empty halls screamed *failure* and *the game is up*. The knowledge that I was about to sign on the dole again filled me with dread and depression. I couldn't see McGee financing another record or a future earning a living from this. I thought I was going to have to get a normal job.

I stayed with Mar for a couple of days, then I called Creation to ask if they could fly me home. I flew back to London and that very night went out to the Zap Club, got some drugs and just kept on it every night of the week.

Eventually I had to sign on and started to sink into depression, fearing the worst and unsure how the band could carry on.

Then, suddenly, they started putting the white labels of 'Loaded' out to clubs and DJs up and down the country. Word started coming back that the record was a huge club sensation. McGee was calling me up and giving me daily reports: 'Bob, I'm serious. This is going off big time. The record is kicking off. I think you might have a hit!' I was a bit overwhelmed. 'Loaded' was meant to be a B side, but it went out as a double A side with 'I'm Losing More'. It just spread like wildfire through the clubs and people were going crazy for it. I saw it for myself first hand in the Zap Club. It came on and the place went mental. Me and Throb stood at the side of the dancefloor going, 'Fuck's sake!' We'd never experienced anything like this in our lives; I hadn't even had it in the Mary Chain; that experience had been an underground, sub-cultural sensation. 'Loaded' was going to explode overground into the highest reaches of the Top 40 but also hit the archetypal indie-rock student audience. We already had some of them, but with 'Loaded' we were going to get the kids from council estates who were going to the raves in their drugged-up hundreds and thousands, and that was where the real energy flash of British youth culture was in 1990.

'Loaded' was single of the week everywhere when it was released. It was a phenomenon. It reached #16 in the UK singles charts, which is quite a feat for a small independent record label with hardly any cash competing against the corporate bankrolled majors.

We went on *Top of the Pops* for the first time with it, we were told to get to the BBC studio for 10 a.m. Now, none of us were early risers and we thought you just turned up and did your thing in the evening during the 7 p.m. weekly transmission, but no, at *TOTP* you had to do a whole day of run-throughs so they could get the camera angles right. We started early with the powders and booze so by the time of the final filming Innes, Throb, Toby and I were all on a concoction of ecstasy, speed, cocaine and whatever else there was knocking about. We figured if the song was titled 'Loaded' then we had to *be* loaded, even if it was a mime. We were artists and we took this performance very seriously.

All our lives had been building up to this moment. We'd all watched *TOTP* religiously every week since we were kids. If you check out the clip on YouTube you can see that Throb is dressed in a red teddy boy drape and black gambler's bow tie, leather trousers and cowboy boots, *very* Johnny Thunders. I was wearing a tight-fitting black leather trucker's jacket with a death's head badge on the upper left pocket, custom-made black leather pants, Chelsea winklepicker boots and pink and black plastic beads around my neck over a black T-shirt. The gorgeous Mark Gardner of Ride took Duffy's place on keys wearing a long-sleeved white 'Loaded' promo shirt with a psychedelic eye design that I'd copped from a book of psychedelic posters. Innes wore a blue embroidered kaftan that fit right in with acid fashions. After our performance I was so fucking high and there was no one from the company present to help us get home. I'd arranged to stay with a girlfriend over in Ladbroke Grove and I remember running through the labyrinthine BBC corridors trying to find a way out of the dystopian maze of the TV centre and running straight into a huge glass door. I didn't see it until it was too late. The Inspiral Carpets were standing on the other side of the door. I managed to get out and ran past them out into the freezing cold night, speeding across the road to White City Tube station. The glamour of rock and roll, eh?

Suddenly we were in *Smash Hits* and *NME* wanted to interview us again. We did an interview with Weatherall there and Innes brought along a couple of strips of dexys. Dexedrine tablets are wonderful pharmaceutical speed, a.k.a. the best drug in the world. We all took dexys to do the interview. Me and Weatherall had our picture taken and he pulled his hat down to cover his face. I think he was signing on the dole at the time as well so wanted to avoid recognition. Suddenly we had a hit record and we were getting interviewed on TV shows. It was wild. We were pop stars.

McGee announced that he would put us on a wage of eighty quid a week, which was a lot better than twenty-five quid a week or whatever I was getting from the dole. Then he decided we would have to make a follow-up single so we rented a rehearsal studio in Brighton in the Lanes and the whole band went in and jammed. After a couple of rehearsals we had the song 'Come Together'. I don't even think we demoed it. We told McGee we had a song, and he booked us a studio on trust.

Jam Studios was in Tollington Park Road in London, formerly a big Georgian villa that had been converted into a recording studio. It was previously known as Decca 4. We found out that Thin Lizzy had recorded their classic single 'The Rocker' there. We discovered the original quarter-inch tape boxes whilst rummaging and exploring in the basement. The Moody Blues and Caravan had cut some albums there too.

On the very first day of recording our drummer, Toby, arrived. 'Open your mouth,' he said.

I went, 'Why?'

'Open your mouth.' And he had a jar of pills.

'What are they?'

'Just open your fucking mouth.' So I did and he just threw these pills down us. Me, Throb and Innes. Then he took some himself.

'What are they, anyway?' I said.

He goes, 'That's what Keith Moon overdosed on the night he died.'*

We were all going, 'Yeah! Great!'

I can't recall how long it took for the drug to have an effect on us, but at some point all four of us collapsed. I was later told that Dick Green of Creation, McGee's partner, had called the studio to see how we were getting on with the recording, and spoke to Colin

---

* The drug was clomethiazole/heminevrin, which acts like a sedative, hypnotic, muscle relaxant and anticonvulsant.

Leggatt who was engineering the session. Dick said, 'How's it going?'

Leggatt said, 'Well, I don't know how to say this, but most of the band are in a coma.'

'What d'you mean, they're in a coma?'

'Well, Bob and Innes are on the floor, Throb's on the couch and Toby's just sprawled underneath the mixing desk.'

We hadn't even played a note yet.

Eventually we woke up. We were in Jam for about four days to record the track. This mate of ours, the Lord, who was a coke dealer in Brighton, came up for a visit. The Lord was a brilliant guy. A real character. He's currently doing twenty-five years because he got in with some heavy people and it got serious. The Lord was this charismatic working-class guy, good looking in a boyish, foppish way with wavy blond hair cut short, like a character out of *Brideshead Revisited*. He was really funny, super stylish, always dressed in a black Comme des Garçons suit and a crisp white shirt. When you went with him on a night out it was an adventure. He carried a big Adidas bag, and inside it he carried his 'personal'. 'Have some of this, Dick.' He called his mates Dick. 'Have some personal.' And he'd put this big Bowie knife into his bag and stick it up your nose. And it was the best feeling in the world. Amazing coke.

After we woke up from our coma we got to work and laid down a good take of the backing track with drums, guitars, piano, organ, bass, strings and horns and my vocals all recorded to our satisfaction. It was now time to record the gospel singers we had lined up. We were huge fans of Elvis's Chips Moman produced American Studios recordings and gospel pop stuff like the Staples Singers so we wanted to get some of that gospel action on our new track. We mentioned this to Creation and Fiona Clark who worked there gave us the number of a supremely talented singer, musician and arranger Nicky Brown. We spoke to Nicky on the phone and shared our ideas with him. He sounded like a good guy, and on the designated day, he came with four singers including himself. We were all a bit nervous because we'd never worked with a choir in this way. Nicky and his friends had all sung with both the London Community Gospel Choir and the Inspirational choir, the top two London outfits. That impressed us no end. They had never come into contact with the world of secular and commercial music before the session with us but Nicky was keen to make the connection. I'm glad he did. Despite our fuck-you rock and roll attitude, we all had huge respect for certain people and musicians not within our circle, and these people were all serious Christians. We wanted to make amazing music with their help, but we were initially reticent. The singers on 'Come Together' are Lawrence John, Faye Simpson, Sarah and Nicky Brown. The secret to their amazing sound was that they flipped the harmonies around so that the guys sang the high parts and the girls sang the lower parts. This was Nicky's idea and what a great one it was too.

Just before we were about to record the choir, our assistant manager Simon Stephens arrived with the Lord, and our favourite aristocrat led us into a side room where he gave us huge lines of 'personal'. Then we went out onto the studio floor and sang all our ideas to Nicky Brown and his choir of gospel singers. The coke had us all babbling at the same time with machine-gun intensity. God knows what the gospel singers must've made of us. With Nicky's help we stacked up the vocal tracks and harmonies so that the ten-piece choir sounded more like a thirty-piece choir. Each time the sound just got bigger and bigger, the sensation was emotionally overwhelming. It was godlike. It felt like we were in Phil Spector heaven, like that classic *Black Pearl* record by Sonny Charles and the Checkmates. What an inspirational single that was. Throb was amazing at counterpoint melodies and harmony. Such a talented guy. The beautiful top-line vocal on the Weatherall version of 'Come Together' is all Throb. He wrote that line – 'co-o-o-ome to-o-ge-ther as one'. A beautiful young Black woman called Faye Simpson who was only about twenty sang it.

She looked like Monie Love and had an amazing voice, so pure, so beautiful, so full of longing. We worked with Nicky and his entourage again a year later when we recorded 'Movin' On Up'.

When we finished recording 'Come Together' it sounded epic. We kind of based the arrangement on 'Darling Be Home Soon' by the Lovin' Spoonful. We had a string quartet come in and then we doubled them up like we did with the choir to create a bigger orchestral effect. Henry Olsen wrote the string parts with Throb. Apart from being a solid bassist, Henry was really great at writing string arrangements. Henry had originally come into our orbit through Toby. I believe 'H.' as he was known to us in the band lived downstairs from Toby in Stoke Newington. We had been recording some new songs for our second album, *Primal Scream*, at a little studio in Fulham owned by a lovely guy named Ian Shaw. We'd cut two songs, 'You're Just Too Dark to Care' and 'You're Just Dead Skin to Me'. We needed strings for 'Dead Skin' and Toby mentioned he knew a guy who could score strings. That's when we'd first met Henry. Somehow, maybe at Toby's insistence, Henry had become our bassist and recorded our sophomore album with us. H. also scored the strings on 'I'm Losing More Than I'll Ever Have'. I think Throb might have had a little bit of input on that one somewhere because he had such a great melodic sensibility. I recall them both intently discussing the arrangement up at Bark Studios, Walthamstow. H. was cool and a great asset to the band. His lead vocals on 'Inner Flight' are beautiful. He sings like a Church of England schoolboy chorister. His voice is so pure and soulful, uncorrupted almost, and this made a great contrast to the Dionysian sleaze of 'Loaded'. We had both the Apollonian and Dionysian principles at work in the band – wham-bam yin and yang!

# 23.
# Boy's Own Gang

Andrew Weatherall and his friends Terry Farley, Cymon Eckel and Steve Mayes all hailed from the Windsor area, just outside London. They had all been soul boys and fashion freaks in their teenage years (in Weatherall's case, a punk rocker) and had formed a club collective called *Boy's Own* after the irreverent fanzine they wrote and published. These guys were some of the first people to go to the clubs in Ibiza in 1986 and '87 and bring back the new sounds of Chicago House and the 'Balearic' ideal of playing any tune from any genre that sounds good on the dancefloor, promoted by original Amnesia Ibizan DJ Alfredo to the underground club scene in London.

Terry and Andrew were both DJs. Farley had a long history of clubbing, going all the way back to the seventies, before punk even. He was also a fan of Chelsea F.C. Style and music (and in Farley's case football) were their lodestars. The Boy's Own parties were the coolest in the south of England at that time. There were only ever a few hundred people there and the crowd was always cool – by that I don't mean those with fame, wealth and celebrity, none of that overground mainstream 'beautiful people' shit – but serious clubbers, music and fashion heads, people that were easy to strike up a conversation with. *Sussed* is the word I would use. The exclusivity of these parties wasn't one of privilege, they were pretty much working- and lower-middle class, but of being hip and knowledgeable about the scene and the latest great records released, or just being yourself, a character, and I met more than a few there. In a way, it was like a nineties version of how I imagine the early days of Modernism may have been. Guy Stevens DJing at the Scene and Ace Face Peter Meaden, leader of the top 100 Mod Faces in London. Cool young people into sharp threads and the latest US soul imports. Swap speed for ecstasy and Sue, Tamla and Stax records for Trax, DJ International and Carnaby Street, King's Road for Hyper Hyper, Ken Market, Browns, South Molton Street and you get the picture.

I can't say that I was totally immersed in the scene the way other people I knew were. I went to maybe three or four Boy's Own parties and the atmosphere was unlike any other. The people there had an egalitarian friendliness: openness and acceptance of differences was the vibe. I liked the way the Boy's Own crowd dressed too. It was all contemporary fashion, very clean and modern casual looks, and I thought it mattered that people had made an effort to dress up to go out. Brighton was still quite studenty. I wanted a bit of glamour, at least when I went out, and some of the Boy's Own crowd were into their clobber in a big way. I respected that. We connected immediately with Weatherall, maybe it was the rock and roll culture we shared that did it. We didn't have the same relationship with Terry Farley and I always found him a wee bit distant in a way, though in retrospect maybe he was shy. I mostly came into his orbit during the Boy's Own parties where he was either on the decks or hanging out with his mates. The man always had work to do.

At those Boy's Own dos it was clear that Farley was the guv'nor, or at least that's how it seemed to me, whereas I always had the feeling Weatherall was the perpetual outsider. He could be *of* a scene but he wouldn't allow a scene to ever completely define him. He was way too curious and smart for that. He had an ability to shapeshift. I guess I did too, and we recognised that in each other. If you were at a party and Farley and Weatherall were DJing you were guaranteed a fantastic night of the greatest music. They were both hip to the best new sounds from their years spent clubbing and record collecting. They both had serious taste in music.

After the success of 'Loaded' we were keen for Andrew to mix our next single 'Come Together'. The great thing about Weatherall was that he was not a rock producer. He wasn't recording the Pixies or Throwing Muses. He did not do an apprenticeship doing time working in the studio and working with loads of bands saying, This is how you do it, that's not how you do it. He didn't know the rules so he broke the rules. It was punk rock. We knew his approach was punk rock, in that he was consciously breaking down established barriers of what was perceived to be 'rock' or 'dance' music. His talent was in arrangement, collage. He would rearrange music in a way that was sometimes abstract. He had great imagination and a deep instinct for what worked in a song. He was an auteur, but a collaborative auteur. Andrew loved our band and he loved a good story. We understood that he got what we were about. What he did with our songs was incredible. It was like having a sixth member, like the Beatles had with George Martin or the Stones with Jimmy Millar. I'm not saying we were like the Beatles or the Stones but those are both good examples of the producer helping the band to new heights of creativity and ability, and quite possibly Weatherall was their equal. But to do that, you need good songs; without good songs you are nothing. We were starting to write some.

Weatherall had recently started working with a young engineer named Hugo Nicholson and this new creative relationship was to prove vital to all of our futures. Weatherall and Hugo's epic, mind-blowing, ten-minute mix of 'Come Together' took everything to another level. It was an acid house soul power anthem, a mantra of spiritual resistance, an electronic intifada, an analogue bubble bath for the mind and body, an ecstasy symphony, an interplanetary dub record, an anthem for bombed youth, a true testimonial.

McGee's instinct was we couldn't release two singles in a row that I didn't sing on, and I was in complete agreement with him.

There's a few 'oh yeah's and 'woo!'s throughout the track and a bit where I'm talking in the breakdown section quoting Robert Johnson's 'Terraplane Blues':

> *I'm gonna get deep down in your connections*
> *mash upon your little starter*

This had been an adlib of mine on the coda section of 'I'm Losing More' which Weatherall had cut up. Apart from that my main contribution was the *Wild Angels* sample and another mystery funk break that I'd brought in which features on the track. But McGee believed that if the band were to break big we needed a figurehead that people could identify them with. It couldn't be faceless, and I was that guy. He thought I should be a pop star.

McGee loved the recordings at Jam and then someone suggested we ask Terry Farley and Pete Heller to mix it as well. Terry and Pete had done a remix of 'Loaded' for us which had been well received in the clubs. I'm not sure how much studio experience Terry and Pete actually had at that point but that didn't bother us. We were totally into the idea of having DJs mix our music – we wanted our stuff to work on the dancefloor, so who better than the hippest DJs? Paul Oakenfold had come out of the same Ibiza–Alfredo–London acid scene as Weatherall and Farley and was having great success producing and remixing Happy Mondays with his great engineer Steve Osborne. The work that Oaky and Osborne did with Mondays was a big influence on our decision to work with DJs instead of 'rock producers'. We'd worked with enough of them to know they were all stuck in the past and we wanted to make the music of now and the future and leave them all behind. The acid scene around Boy's Own and Shoom was the best thing going. We'd grown up on dub and extended twelve-inch disco mix records and loved the way that the three-minute pop song you heard on the radio could be stretched to seven or eight minutes on the twelve-inch version (like 'Good Times' by Chic, still one of my all-time faves). We loved the instrumental sections where everything drops out, down to just bass and drums holding the groove and then the music is slowly reintroduced by sections of dubbed-out instrumental breaks just building, building, building back up to an orgasmic crescendo.

I always saw twelve-inch mixes as experimental pop music that could take you on a journey. Beattie and myself loved 'Death Disco (Megamix)' by PiL at the very same time that we were digging the 'Good Times' twelve-inch extended mix by Chic (indeed we attempted to combine the PiL attitude with the Chic song once when we'd covered 'Good Times' using PiL's Metal Box album canister as a drum and creating a Jah Wobble-style distorted dub bass sound to propel it) or 'Born for a Purpose / Reason for Living' by JA reggae great Doctor Alimantado, or early rap classic 'How We Gonna Make the Black Nation Rise?' by Brother D and Collective Effort.

The space afforded to the musicians and producers of such tracks allowed them to stretch out the song arrangement and play with the dynamic structure of the track, breaking free of conventionally arranged pop song structures whilst still working within them. This was commercial music with an avant-garde twist. You can hear the joy of these artists and producers finding new sonic frontiers using space and sound effects: the 'drop down' in a rhythm track to just bass and drums was such a relief to our young ears after years of the *sturm and drang* Wall of Sound screaming rock and roll guitars which we loved but had grown weary of, and pointed a way forward to where rock could reinvent itself using production techniques learned from listening to US disco twelve-inches and JA reggae dubs. The whole genre that later became known as 'post-punk' emerged from this consciousness. To my mind twelve-inch extended mix versions originated in the work of Jamaican dub masters, King Tubby, Lee Perry, Joe Gibbs and Errol Thomson productions where they would

345

sculpt and twist sounds, and stop time itself with deep-space funk and psychedelic re-imaginings of reggae vocal hits. Some of the greatest music ever to be heard was created by these guys. I wonder if the people at Philadelphia International – the geniuses Kenny Gamble and Leon Huff – were listening to the JA sound, because the extended version of 'For The Love of Money' by the O'Jays could've been produced at Joe Gibbs' or King Tubby's or the Black Ark. Or maybe the JA boys were listening to the Philly Sound and making their own 'versions'? Whichever way, it's all pure inspiration and produced some magnificent music.

Terry Farley and Pete Heller of Boy's Own Productions did their mix of 'Come Together', which was song-based, and Weatherall did his mix and that became a fucking massive hit. The Weatherall version was a hit in the clubs and the Farley version was a hit on Radio 1. I love Farley and Heller's version of 'Come Together'. It has all the love, yearning and optimism of those times in it. Terry and Pete were our rhythm section on that one and the band sound great too, Duffy's gospel piano and Innes's acoustic strum lay down a soft, warm, beautiful rhythm-bed for my vocal to float over. The mix has a dreamy, narcotic effect. The gospel boys and girls who introduce and close the record are both righteous and heavenly. Terry and Pete's beats are perfect. It always struck me as like a nineties version of 'Be Thankful for What You Got' by William DeVaughn, a pure summer soul sound, and the strings and horns gave it an emotional classicism. It's a fantastic pop record and I'm very proud of it. It was a SMASH HIT too. The patronage of guys like Terry Farley and Andrew Weatherall opened up a lot of doors for us; their blessing gave us credibility in the underground club scene and they were revolutionary sonic architects. Club DJs all over the country played our records because of the Boy's Own association.

In its first week of release 'Come Together' went straight in at #26 on the official UK singles charts. In the nineties singles were released on Mondays. You would get a midweek chart position on Wednesday, another on Friday and then sit by your radio on Sunday night waiting to hear it announced by the DJ on the BBC chart rundown. A much-coveted *TOTP* appearance depended on the chart position and the higher the position the more chance of getting on the show. McGee reckoned we would definitely get on *TOTP* because we had gone in so high. I was ecstatic. I went to bed Sunday night hardly able to sleep, too excited. Around 8 a.m. I got up out of bed, quickly went through to the living room and answered the phone hoping it was McGee with the good news. It was McGee, but he didn't have good news. I was shocked. I said, 'Why not? Our chart position is great, top thirty, new entry.'

'I've just spoken to our TV plugger Scott Piering. They've given the spot to the KLF, even though the KLF are behind you in the charts.'

'How the fuck does that work?'

'Piering says that he thinks with the level of radio play we're currently receiving "Come Together" will rise next week, so he says it's better to hold off because the BBC won't have you perform on the show two weeks in a row.'

Alan went on to say that Piering had agreed with the BBC to show our video over the closing credits of this week's show and that if 'Come Together' did rise higher in the chart then we would definitely get an appearance next week instead.

It all sounded weird and wrong to me, especially when he informed me that Scott Piering was secretly managing the KLF with Bill Drummond. We both knew we'd been royally screwed. The thing that hurt was we were paying Piering good money to get us onto shows like *TOTP* and he fucked us. He really did. He'd taken us for fools and totally stiffed us. I wanted revenge. The following week 'Come Together' stayed at #26 and KLF went up in the charts so we never got to perform it on *TOTP*. At the time it seemed like our whole future was dependent on the success of this record. We'd had a little taste, a glimmer of success and we loved it; not for the money (because there wasn't a lot about at that point), but because in order to live a creative life as artists, we needed another hit record to keep the band going financially. We had to keep up momentum after the massive success of 'Loaded'. It was a bitter lesson in the venal ways of the music business: Scott Piering had crawled and slid his way up the greasy pole to a position of being the 'go-to guy' for indie bands who were now getting mainstream radio airplay. He had originally made his name working at Rough Trade, building up a reputation as a 'nice guy' and making his music business contacts that way. But we learned a vital lesson from him: even the people from the so-called morally superior independent music world were out to exploit and screw you. We trusted Alan and Dick and that was it. We went back with McGee a long way, to the streets of Mount Florida and King's Park School. He was one of us, a Glasgow boy. Proper guy. Straight up.

A couple of months after 'Loaded' was a hit I decided to get my hair cut short in a Mod style. I was tired of having hair down to my shoulders. I based it on early sixties photos I had of Pete Townsend, Ray Davies and the Small Faces, with the fringe cut high and straight across the forehead in an ancient Roman style. The original Modernists copied the continental 'Roman cut' and I liked the severity of it: angular and violent. I could hide behind long hair but with this my face was all on show.

It was a statement of change, a new beginning. I wore a white cycling top with blue and yellow vertical stripes running down the side and white sixties Levis with black pointed Chelsea boots. I wanted a different look for every single and every video that we did. I'd been wearing black leather for a while and wanted a change. Something fresh and clean that chimed with the times.

I designed the look of every Primal Scream record sleeve from day one, either by myself or working closely with somebody like Julian House at Intro, Jim Lambie or Mathew Cooper. Sometimes Jim Lambie would create a stunning original artwork and that became the cover image: end of story. Perfect. It's always a collaboration, but I'm overseeing it, commenting, suggesting, watching over the whole process. I love it.

The one cover I never had any involvement with was 'Come Together'. At the time I had an idea to ask my good friend Lawrence from Felt to help, because he'd been doing some good stuff under the name Shanghai Packaging Company. At this point Felt had just split up and Lawrence had moved from Brighton to Sloane Street in Chelsea. His new flat was halfway between Chelsea and Knightsbridge near Cadogan Square.

One summer evening I got on the train from Brighton to London to meet him to talk about the artwork. He stayed at the very top of this mansion block, in what was basically a toilet at the very top of the building. Very *The Bed Sitting Room* – that sixties Spike Milligan film – or *Room at the Top*. Kitchen-sink drama vibes. I don't even remember if there was even a bed there, my guess was that he just stayed there so he could tell people he had a Chelsea address. He showed me these editions of Italian *Vogue* that he had been collecting, enthusing over a particular typesetting style this designer had been doing. 'I'll do it exactly like this,' he said. 'There won't be any photographs. It'll just be type.' And I thought, well that's quite cool. Very modern. Unexpected, from us. It's very Factory Records too, quite Peter Saville.

'Can you really do this?' I asked him.

He said he could.

I said, 'Yeah, OK then. Do it.'

We were gaining the confidence that success brings. We had decided to release 'Come Together' as a double A side with the Farley / Heller mix one side and Weatherall's mix on the other side, but before the single release we went to Japan on a short tour. We'd never been to Japan before and I got on the plane leaving Lawrence in charge of the design for the single. My first impression of Tokyo was of a high-tech city of the future. Very *Bladerunner*. Japan's economy was booming at that point and compared to the grey, run-down repressiveness of Thatcher's Britain it felt clean, modern and optimistic. We were made really welcome by the Japanese people we met, from the fans to the promotors, and everyone was super polite and friendly. The streets felt safe to walk around with no threat of violence, unlike the UK.

Whilst we were in Japan I received a fax from Creation showing Lawrence's sleeve design with the big cut-off-at-the-points star and the awful typeface all stuck together, everything looking like a mistake, artlessly done. I had a total freak-out and telephoned McGee in London. 'What the fuck is this?' I said. 'This looks fucking terrible. Tell you what, when I get back I'll design a new sleeve.'

'No,' McGee said, 'it's already at the printers. I'm pressing up a hundred thousand records. The pre-sales are massive. It's gonna be another hit. You're gonna have to go with this sleeve.'

'Pull the record,' I said.

But he wouldn't. I was beyond livid, embarrassed and ashamed that our new record, our second hit record, was about to come out with this abomination of a sleeve. I don't even think I saw it in colour at this point. It was just a black and white thing on a fax, but you could make out what the gist of the design was. When we got back I saw the colour proofs and I went even more ballistic. It looked all washed out. I had worked as a printer, of course, so knew what I was talking about. This looked like a run where there's too much water in the duct and not enough ink, weak and watery, insipid. It was shite.*

What I should have done was ask the actual Italian *Vogue* guy himself, or Peter Saville. It was a hard lesson to learn. I've been involved with every cover design since. If you want to do something properly, do it yourself, as they say.

---

* However, it *has* grown on me over the years. And I'm not just saying that because I know he's going to read this book – hi, Lawrence!

# 24.

# Hackney Paradise

Suddenly, we were pop stars. Not only in *NME* but also teen mags like *Smash Hits*, on the radio and TV. We didn't have anything to do except write songs, listen to music, go to clubs, buy clothes and take drugs. It was like we could finally live out our teenage fantasies. But the fantasy really was to make a great record. It wasn't just to get off with beautiful girls and get high all the time. Suddenly there was this confidence in the band because success does marvellous things for your self-esteem, ego and confidence. We always knew we were good, but suddenly we had a platform and credibility.

That summer McGee got me a publishing deal with EMI music. It was a good deal, which Throb and I did well out of. Innes had already signed away his future songwriting rights to a small company called Complete Music. It certainly wasn't a deal in favour of the artist and he couldn't get out of it, sadly. They had him tied to it for perpetuity.

Alan said he need an album's worth of songs from us and gave us a few thousand pounds advance so we could build a studio in Tudor Road, Hackney, which was just around the corner from the Creation offices in Westgate Street. All credit to Innes, whose idea it was. The studio was situated in a small industrial estate sat beside a large block of sixties brutalist council flats. We built a room within a room and Innes set up a little studio in there where we began writing the songs for *Screamadelica* over the beautiful summer into autumn and winter of 1990. These were the days when people didn't really want to go to Hackney. It wasn't 'hip' and it wasn't safe either. It was a dangerous area if you didn't know your way around.

Our set-up had a small control room area which had a keyboard in it, a small computer and an Akai S 1000 sampler. There was also a vocal booth, which had just enough room to stand up and sing in. There was a toilet out back near the car park and a storeroom. It was just somewhere we could go and write songs.

I was still living in Brighton and so was Throb but we'd come up about three or four days each week. Innes was living in the Isle of Dogs. I would stay in his spare room or with Douglas and Tim, just crash on people's couches. We'd go to the studio a few days a week and write songs, then when we got bored we'd nip over to the Creation offices and people like Sonic Boom would be there hanging out. He was friends with McGee and Laurence, the French girl who was our press officer. Laurence was the then-girlfriend of Jim Reid from the Mary Chain. I loved working with her. We would have blazing rows and shouting matches about some perceived slight or creative disagreement, both of us prone to emotionally violent outbursts. Twenty minutes later everything would be forgotten and we would be cool again. All very French. My brother Graham worked at Creation, running the warehouse. My ex-girlfriend Karen worked there too, with Innes's girlfriend Christine. It was a family affair, as Sly might say.

I'd been reading *Sweet Soul Music* by Peter Guralnick which describes the scene at Stax in Memphis in the sixties; how Isaac Hayes and David Porter would go into the ex-cinema where the Stax studio now stood and write hit songs. There were these great photographs of them both wearing elegant Gabicci sweaters and pork pie hats looking really suave, clean and cool. At this point I was wearing these great bottle-green cords which were original Levi deadstock from the late sixties which I'd bought from a kid named Greg Faye, who I found out about after reading a piece in *ID* magazine. He went to America and brought back these great original Lee trucker jackets and corduroy jeans. He sold his clothes from a room above his parents' pub in Fitzrovia. I bought a stunning pink Lee jacket from him. I had a good set of sixties tops and polo necks and I had just cut my hair short. I envisioned us as songwriters with our own studio to experiment in. My game plan was to write some more hit songs and get in the Top 40 charts. At that point we weren't even thinking about being a live band. Our job was to write enough good songs to make another album. I thought, we've got two hits, why don't we make it three then four. I became very hit-oriented, which is no bad thing.

That summer we wrote 'Damaged'. Throb, Innes and myself were jamming up in the spare room in Innes' flat which doubled as my sometime bedroom. We wrote the core of 'Damaged' and then we all went to see My Bloody Valentine play an amazing gig at ULU. We were all flying because we knew we'd written a great song. That same summer we wrote early versions of 'Don't Fight It Feel It' and 'Shine Like Stars' which was kind of funky to begin with. We'd sampled a breakbeat from 'Joy' by Isaac Hayes and Innes had put on a funky guitar part. Innes is such an instinctive, brilliant player, he's got the funk in him. It was a stab at a George McRae 'Rock You Baby' version. We loved seventies pop soul like George, The O'Jays, Delfonics, Chi-Lites, the Dramatics and the Temptations. The Philadelphia International productions by Kenny Gamble and Leon Huff and Thom Bell's magnificent orchestral arrangements were big influences too, as was Black Moses himself, Mr Isaac Hayes.

Our first two albums had been written on guitars and we were now working mostly on keyboards. Innes could play basic piano and so could Throb. Throb loved major sevenths, Carole King-style bittersweet chords. We called them sniff chords, like pure cocaine. There's no harshness or blues. It just softens the blow. It doesn't make you jerk back. Throb loved Carole King and Brian Wilson, he was a big softy at heart. The Beach Boys were also a huge influence on *Screamadelica*. We loved those unusual chord sequences Brian Wilson used with his heartbreaking melodicism. It hit you where it hurt. California Uber Alles, pure blue-eyed soul. Pocket symphonies for the kids. *Screamadelica* was a song-based record. Apart from 'Movin' On Up', 'Loaded' and 'Damaged' there were no guitar riffs on the album.

'Movin' On Up' was written in the Hackney studio. It was a gospel song originally that Innes and I had written together on the piano. We had the verse and chorus parts down and when we played it to Throb he had an idea and went to the piano and bashed out the middle eight 'My light shines on' section which also became the song's coda. We worked great as a team, the three of us. I loved working with those two. We knew it was a hit song, but we couldn't work out how to make it move; it was rooted to the floor, like a sad gospel ballad, funereal and at odds with the transcendent message of the lyrics. It needed to *fly* in order to hit people where we wanted to hit them. Then, one day Innes came in and said, 'I think I know the answer to the 'Movin' On Up' problem, and he played us the Bo Diddley rhythm on his acoustic guitar. Throb and I went, 'That's it! It's a rock song!'

The song was airborne at last, with a driving rhythm and hard rock propulsion, a forward motion. It was now high energy, an ecstatic call to arms and perfect single material. For the first time in our lives we had a studio, and the fruits of having that place were enormous. It was a place to go and hang out with mates, a place of creativity, and it gave us a focus that we wouldn't have had otherwise. Out in the world there were a lot of distractions. We were still young guys, with two hit records and a bit of money. Acid house was happening. Suddenly we had life chances and possibilities that were never open to us before. We all wanted to be recording artists and make good music. I was in record stores all the time, doing a lot of research into soul stuff, looking for breakbeats and arrangement ideas. We had a sampler in the studio and suddenly we didn't need to be this guitar band. We could write songs in other ways. We could go to McGee for a large recording budget and we could have gospel singers or strings or hire in exotic instruments. Let's get a harpsichord on 'Higher Than the Sun'. Let's get congas on 'Movin' on Up'. Let's get some strings on 'Come Together'. A harmonium on 'Shine Like Stars'. Suddenly we were thinking like guys that can make hit records and construct them orchestrally rather than just a five-piece kick-ass rock and roll guitar band. Our imaginations were feverish with new ideas. Technology can be liberating.

*Screamadelica*'s not just a pop record, neither is it solely a rock or dance record, it's all of those things and more. So we started thinking differently. There was no pressure on us to play gigs (we didn't have enough songs in the new style to play gigs anyway). Throughout that year, 1990, we just hunkered down and went to the studio and wrote songs. We also made new friends on the Brighton club scene with people who ran the various club nights, drug dealers and their hangers-on. We were doing a lot of E and staying up for days on that and coke. It went from everybody chipping in to buy a gram of coke to buying ounces of the stuff. At one point Throb was driving to London to buy ounces of coke to bring back to Brighton and selling it. I remember saying to him, 'You're in the charts, you're making money, you've got a future ahead of you. Why are you trying to be a cocaine dealer, you fucking idiot? if you go down, so does the band.' It was madness.

He drove up to London and back a few times in a car that he'd bought off some dodgy bloke in a club. I don't even think he had a driving licence at this point either. I told him he couldn't be in the band and be a coke dealer. Innes and myself talked him out of it, but when you went round to his flat on the Friday night, you were there till Monday morning. It was just carnage. And soon he got into freebasing as well. We all did. It was great fun, but we would do it at the weekend over at his flat with him and then go home and stop, whereas he would keep going. I don't know if heroin came in then or the next year, as in *really* came in. I'm not sure. But that's another story and not mine to tell.

Innes had gone on holiday in Ibiza with some friends from Manchester and through them he met a guy called Tony Martin. Tony worked the lights at the Hacienda and was also making music under the name of Hypnotone. Andrew really took to the possibilities available via the new sampling technology. His time spent in the studio with Weatherall and Tony Martin from Hypnotone had inspired him to learn for himself how to work the Akai S1000 sampler. He had acquired some primitive recording engineering skills through experimentation at his home studio in the Isle of Dogs using a Teac 4 track machine. Using this knowledge, Andrew set up the band's Hackney studio where we wrote and demo'd the new songs that would become *Screamadelica*. His wonderful pop-classicist chord sequences on songs such as 'Higher than the Sun' and 'Don't Fight It, Feel It' pushed the band's songs in new directions far away from the blues rock we'd become hung up on. Andrew's newly found fascination with synthesisers lent our latest songs a sci-fi modernity and otherworldly ambience. If Throb was an instinctive and unreconstructed Dionysian bluesy roots rocker then Andrew could be described in this period as an Apollonian pop-experimentalist with a studied professorial edge. I was the lyricist and melodicist and I stalked the territory somewhere between the two camps. The creative tension that stemmed from the combination of all three personalities whilst unified in songwriting and recording somehow metamorphosed into this other, more expansive, greater and more powerful entity. 'Creative Communism' would be a term for it, I guess.

Andrew and Tony remixed 'Come Together' which was released on twelve-inch. It was titled the 'hypnotonebrainmachine mix'.

It samples Brother J. C. Crawford from the MC5's *Kick Out The Jams* album proclaiming,

*I hear a lot of talk by a lot of honkies sitting on a pile of money about a high society, well. . . I say THIS IS THE HIGH SOCIETY!*

The chant of 'Think! Think! It ain't illegal yet!' from a Funkadelic seven-inch also made an appearance on there too. Working with Tony Martin gave Andrew some understanding of how the Akai S1000 sampler worked, knowledge which he was able to translate to our own album.

We had 'Don't Fight It, Feel It' written down and demoed with the piano chords and lyrics and even some Beatles-y guitar riffs too, but in my head I felt that it was out of my vocal range to sing. To my mind it had the potential to be a real soul belter, and I felt we should find a singer to do the song justice. I was already way into the idea of us being part of a songwriting and production company: Holland–Dozier–Holland and Gamble and Huff were our heroes. We had the songwriting down and Weatherall had the production side covered. We just needed the right singer.

That September, Innes informed us all that Hypnotone were playing a gig at the Solaris club on Gray's Inn Road. Solaris was run by two club faces, an Essex wideboy named Roscoe and his partner, a nice guy called Dave Mander. A saturnine girl named Pallas Citroen did the door. Pallas was Dave's girlfriend, lucky bastard. Everyone fancied Pallas. She looked as sultry as Sade but came from a council estate in Brighton. We became good friends. Pallas is super sharp and one of the funniest people I know. She's some girl. The main reason for Andrew's insistence that we attend the Solaris night was that there was a girl singing with Hypnotone that Tony had said we should check out. Andrew had asked if he knew any girl singers in Manchester because we were in need of a soul diva to sing 'Don't Fight It'. There weren't many people at the club that night but we discovered that the girl singing with Hypnotone had a big blues voice and she could hit all the notes. She was soulful too, and she had a presence. Her name was Denise Johnson.

After the gig we went over and introduced ourselves and congratulated her on her performance. In a matter of weeks she made her way down to EMI demo studios off Oxford Street to record her vocals on 'Don't Fight it, Feel It'. It was a fantastic session. Denise was easy to work with in the studio, open, positive and receptive to our ideas as well. I remember a lot of smiles and laughter. It might have been intimidating for some people to walk into our Scream scene cold like that, but Denise was pretty fearless and she sang her heart out. Her vocal on 'Don't Fight It' is stunning. It's hard to explain the feeling I had of hearing someone else sing a song that I had written (with Innes and Throb) to perfection. I sang on the demo we'd cut at our Hackney studio and it's alright, nothing great; it was a demo, a guide for potential vocalists to go by more than anything. But what Denise did with it was out of this world. After she'd completed the main song verses and chorus's vocal tracks Throb and I sang her our ad lib ideas, like the 'rama-lama-lama-fa-fa-fa gonna get high to the day I die' and the ever-rising 'can you feel it? can you feel it?' parts and Denise got stuck straight into those and sang a few ad lib ideas of her own too. We recorded a few tracks of completely improvised vocal takes so Weatherall had a lot of great stuff to work with on his magick mix.

We'd been listening to a lot of sixties and seventies Black American soul music. My deep soul collection was growing by the week and Innes had a pile of great Northern Soul compilation albums, mainly on the Kent label which had started finding and reissuing classic tracks. He was a 100 Club regular at Ady Crosdell's soul nights. I'd gone on a voyage of discovery reading about the great soul artists, producers, and most of all, songwriters. Black music was a place of social protest and righteous anger as well as a resource for the joy, pain and suffering caused by winners and losers in love. Eros and Thanatos were well represented in the

Black soul tradition. Blues people were the ultimate outsiders. Soul and country are both artforms created by working-class Americans, Black and white. There's a brutal honesty to the lyrics and the storytelling concerning everyday realities of personal struggle, heartbreak, romance, infidelity, and an ever-present acceptance of the harshness and unfairness of life which I am deeply attracted to. My dad would play Ray Charles and my mum, Hank Williams. I have it in me, a deep love of the blues.

A lot of the records we loved on the acid house scene had their roots in the soul and gospel tradition, tracks like 'Promised Land' by Joe Smooth for example. We realised that there was a direct lineage between Chicago and Detroit house music and the classic soul we loved. House was modern, contemporary soul. So, we set out to write a modern, electronic, soul classic, a dancefloor anthem, in 'Don't Fight It'. The camaraderie and democracy that we found in the clubs where everyone was kind and considerate and looking out for each other was surely a glimpse of a utopian here and now, a future dream-state scenario.

'Don't Fight It, Feel It' is about a kid on the dancefloor on ecstasy with their mates, the lights and music are perfect, everyone has come up on the drug at the same time, the whole club is peaking and is as one. It's about that perfect moment when everything coalesces and you are so happy to be alive you would do absolutely anything to keep that feeling forever. The clubs offered a place of refuge and worship, a much-needed place of escape for people who worked in dead-end soul-stealing jobs Monday to Friday, those who lived for the weekend when they could be free to really be who they wanted without some bastard ordering them around. People originally involved in the various underground dance and club scenes I've mentioned may have had many musical and style differences, but, and it's a big but, dressing up, going out with your mates and getting out of your head going dancing to fantastic music at the weekends can sometimes be the only real culture and freedom to be had in young working-class and middle-class lives before the onset of adulthood and responsibility and the life compromises that have to be made in order to become a 'grown-up'. The kids I met on the house scene were all gonna live the life they loved and loved the life they lived no matter what, and I loved them for that. My experiences on various dancefloors and afterparties during this period were some of the greatest, most transcendent, connected and soulful moments of my life and I wanted to celebrate that. That's why we wrote 'Don't Fight it, Feel It', for all the kids who felt the same as I did on those dancefloors.

Andrew Weatherall and Hugo Nicholson mixed 'Don't Fight it, Feel It' that autumn. There were three versions: two instrumental 'scat' mixes and a vocal mix. Everybody was astounded by it. Weatherall had a white label he was playing in the clubs and people would just go bananas. He was the only guy who had it. Wherever he played it, people were going fucking nuts for it. We said to McGee, you've got to release the single. It would've been our third single in 1990, but McGee thought it was too out there. In our heads we thought, this is just way ahead of everybody else. I had this mad delusional shit we were like George Clinton's Parliament-Funkadelic and it didn't matter who sang. I started getting into the Public Image idea that we were a production company, not a band. With hindsight, I think McGee was right, though.

We never had a contract with McGee because we were all into the Factory Records ethos. We had a profit share deal, fifty-fifty, which is how Factory had worked. We just thought that was the right, anarchist thing to do. Later on I discovered that kind of deal can also work against you, financially speaking, but that's OK.

One day McGee called me up and said, 'Sire wanna sign you. Seymour Stein wants to sign you for America.'

I didn't even ask how much money it was, I just went, let's

do it, because all the good English bands like the Bunnymen, the Smiths and the Cure were on Sire. But more importantly to me Sire had released all the records by Ramones, Richard Hell, Dead Boys and Talking Heads.

We were signed to Sire by the VP, Joe McEwan, who introduced us to this guy at Warners who had grown up in Austin in the sixties, a massive Thirteenth Floor Elevators fan called Bill Bentley. When he was sixteen years old in Austin he saw the Elevators play live and he said to Roky Erickson after a show, 'Roky, can you tell me what psychedelic music means?'

Roky said, 'Don't you know, man? It's where the pyramid meets the eye.'

In 1990 Roky was locked up for stealing mail. He wasn't opening it, he was just taking it, and that's a federal offence. Bill Bentley had an idea to help Roky: he asked bands that were fans of the Elevators like Jesus and Mary Chain, ZZ Top, REM, the Scream and some others to record Elevator tracks. We decided on 'Slip Inside This House', the opening track on *Easter Everywhere*, their second album, a nine-minute song over twelve verses. We cut it down to two verses and three bridges and rearranged the chorus, making it more concise. I had to do a cut-up of the song lyric but in a way that still made sense, a shorter version.

The day we had booked in the studio was a Saturday. I hadn't been feeling well, because I was taking so many drugs that summer and having such a good time that I'd run my immune system into the ground. The session was on a really hot day in August and I made it up from Brighton to the studio in London but felt so bad that eventually I collapsed as I was singing, straight onto the studio floor in a heap underneath the microphone with the headphones still strapped on my head. My freewheeling, dissolute lifestyle had finally caught up with me – here in a recording studio of all places, in front of the band – and I was in no fit state to do my job. I felt pathetic and small. What a loser I was. I'd let myself and the boys down.

Before my collapse I had managed to record a guide vocal but I was too weak to sing the song all the way through with any real power or conviction. I just couldn't sing it the way I wanted to so Throb did it instead. I gave Throb the new lyrics which I'd written out on a piece of paper the week before and I went back to Brighton with little men pounding the inside of my head with hammers and a nausea without end. My stomach retched until there was nothing left in it to throw up but still the fluorescent green bile dribbled out my lips from my sandpaper throat. I stayed in bed for two weeks after that, just soaking and sweating and puking it out.

Sire made a big twelve-inch EP / mini LP CD of all the mixes of 'Come Together' and 'Loaded' and they organised a month-long promo trip for me in America. I was tour-managed by a girl named Sandy who was Seymour's assistant, a beautiful Jewish New Yorker. At Sire you were surrounded by these really lovely, good-hearted, Jewish-American girls who all loved Seymour; he was like their dad or their uncle or something, it was very family-oriented. The guy who convinced Seymour to sign us was called Joe McEwan. In the sixties Joe went to university in Boston and became friends with Peter Guralnick. He also wrote for *Rolling Stone* in the seventies. He was a soul aficionado. In the sixties when all of his friends were into the white English rock bands who ruled in America he wasn't into white rock, he was into soul, and his buddy at college was Peter Wolf of the J. Geils Band, who had a blues and soul radio show. Joe was a soul man and a really good guy. I trusted him, he liked our band and he liked me. I think he saw that we were sincere and he responded to that with love and conviction. Joe also hosted a weekend radio show on a local station near his house devoted to sixties and seventies soul. He went by the nom de guerre 'Mr C'.

I was more than happy to go to the United States for a month's 'holiday', as I saw it; at home I was getting a bit down because

I was single spending a lot of time on my own, plus the band wasn't touring either, so I really relished the idea of a wee trip away from my subterranean Brighton lair. I needed to get out into the world and have an adventure. It would be the first time I'd been to the US since 1985 with the Mary Chain. This was five years later, November 1990.

It was a great trip. The schedule was to go from city to city: NYC, Boston, Toronto, Chicago, Detroit, Austin, San Diego, San Francisco, LA and be interviewed on big rock stations and college radio stations, go out for dinner with radio DJs, record store owners, local journalists and people who worked as sales staff for Warners in each territory. All the people I met on the trip were really cool, and seemed eager to listen to my tales of the acid house explosion in the UK that had coincided with the exciting new sounds of Stone Roses, Happy Mondays and the Scream.

You have to understand that what was happening in the UK at this point may as well have been happening on Mars as far as some of the people I met in the US were concerned. They had no idea about Chicago House or Detroit techno. In fact, at times, I felt like the British invasion bands of the sixties must have when they educated white Americans on the contemporary Black culture they had no knowledge of but that was happening in their cities, the main source of inspiration for the Beatles, Stones, Yardbirds, Them, etc. More than once I encountered the question, 'What kind of band are you? Dance? Rock? Alternative? Psychedelic?' The American need to compartmentalise music was anathema to me, but the interviewers were so used to a band having one signature sound that what we were doing spun them out. They were confused that 'Come Together' and 'Loaded' were made by the same band. I have to say I really enjoyed those moments.

When I wasn't working, being interviewed or in transit I went out vinyl-hunting in the many amazing record stores and bought loads of records and the *nouveauté du jour*, CDs. The record shops in the US were a vinyl junkie's dream scene. They seemed to be jam-packed full of every fucking record or rare seven-inch single I'd ever wanted. Rare shit that was hard to find and overpriced in London was cheap as chips over the pond; everything was on sale for just a few dollars. CDs were quite expensive in relation to vinyl , like $15 a pop, because the major gimmick was they were allegedly indestructible and contained a sound as clean and perfect as the artists had intended them to, as close to a high-quality studio reproduction as possible on a home stereo. Because of the hype millions of people began selling their original fifties, sixties and seventies vinyl which had been scratched and battered over the years and bought their lovingly curated album collections all over again on CD. For that very reason the secondhand shops were stacked with unwanted classics and guys like me just swept it up. I was in the right place at the right time. At the same time major record labels began repackaging their artists from the past onto the new, longer CD format where each disc ran for up to 70 minutes. I picked up classic compilations by artists such as Little Anthony and the Imperials, Tommy James and the Shondells, Gospel Greats, the Staple Singers, The Impressions and others. Sire paid for all of the records I bought on that trip and kindly flew them home to the UK for me.

There was also the small matter of shooting a promo video in LA for 'Slip Inside This House' which Weatherall had since mixed once again. It had been arranged that at the very end of my promotional trip across America the rest of band would be flown over and we would shoot a video in the desert. I had been up in San Francisco. Sandy went back to New York and I was met by another vice president of Sire, a guy called Howie Klein, the radio DJ who hosted the famous interview with Cook and Jones in San Francisco around the time of the Winterland gig where groupie girls were calling into the station live on air. He always had a handsome, clean-cut young boyfriend with him. He'd bring young guys to the gigs on the '94 tour with Depeche Mode and go, 'Hey Bobby, meet Steven', and there'd be this handsome twenty-one-year-old kid. 'He's fucked Tiffany, he's fucked Debbie Gibson *and* Tiffany!' Howie would chortle. And I'm thinking, yeah, and you're fucking him.

Anyway, Howie was a right laugh. He was in San Francisco during punk times, the Mabuhay Gardens and all that scene. I asked him about the SF punk band Crime who are one of my favourites and Howie started laughing at me. He couldn't believe that somebody would take Crime seriously. I was going, no, they're a brilliant band. I remember he took me to an S&M leather bar. I suspect he was basically trying to see if I was up for it. I was like, nah, I'm not into it, man, thanks. I remember him saying, you know all those guys, Jim Morrison and Mick Jagger, they all swung both ways in the sixties. He told me a great story about his friend at college sucking off Jim Morrison straight after a Doors concert. I just didn't fancy Howie at all. Not my type.

Anyway Howie flew me down to LA to do Rodney Bingenheimer's radio show. It turned out Rodney loved Primal Scream. He was a total anglophile and a legend, Rodney Bingenheimer: Kim Fowley, Joan Jett and the Runaways, the Stooges, the New York Dolls, Zeppelin all caroused at Rodney's English Disco. During a commercial break Rodney came out from his DJ booth to see me and said, 'Bobby! Oh my god, it's so great to have you here. It's great. I've got a surprise for you later. I want you to meet an old and dear friend of mine.' He said, 'Bobby Gillespie, David Cassidy. David, meet Bobby Gillespie of Primal Scream.' And it was David Cassidy of 'How Can I Be Sure' and 'Could it Be Forever' fame, one of the biggest pop stars in the world in the early seventies. Cassidy was every pre- and post-pubescent girl's wet dream for a few short years. The transience of fame incarnate. He was already a TV star on *The Partridge Family*, a beautiful-looking guy. But now, in the cold light of a nineties LA radio studio he'd lost those good looks that hung on a million teenage girls' bedroom walls and the glamour of youth had deserted him. He looked shot away.

'Pleased to meet you,' he said whilst looking straight through me. 'My new album's doing great.' He was obviously on the skids. He seemed sad. Poor guy. It's a mighty long way down, rock and roll.

David Cassidy disappeared into the Hollywood night. I was about to be interviewed by Rodney on the ROQ, and was thinking to myself, 'This is fucking major, man.' I was loving all the praise and flattery, with Rodney gushing as he played Scream tracks. Then Rodney said, 'Bobby, I've got another surprise for you,' and he called a number. 'Hey, hello? Arthur? Are you there?'

A voice on the other end of the telephone said, 'Yeah, I'm here.'

'Arthur, I've got Bobby Gillespie from Primal Scream here on the show, he wants to talk to you. OK guys, take it away . . .'

And suddenly I was talking to Arthur Lee live on the radio in LA, our number one rock misterioso, number one godhead. Apart from Syd Barrett he's the ultimate psychedelic cult hero, the reason we started our band. I was trying to hold onto my sanity at that moment.

At exactly the same time, unbeknownst to me Throb, Innes, Toby, Henry and Duffy were riding around LA in a white stretch limo with the radio on listening to Rodney's show, sniffing fine cocaine and drinking champagne. Throb heard me talking to Arthur Lee on the radio and he said that moment was like winning the fucking European Cup, like we'd arrived. They were driving up and down the strip whooping and hollering and having a fucking ball. After that, I was driven to the band's hotel where I met up with the guys and partied all night. The next morning Innes spotted something, a sign in the foyer. It turned out the hotel we were staying in was hosting a drug police convention. Pure Hunter S. Thompson. All of us in some room, high as the sky, looking out the window, paranoid, thinking just act normal, just act normal.

We stayed up all night, me and the boys, and then we were driven out at five in the morning to the Mojave Desert to shoot the video for 'Slip Inside This House'. Us uninitiated British mugs thought it was going to be really hot because it was the desert, so no one took coats. I was dressed in a long-sleeved T-shirt for fuck's sake, and of course out in the desert in November it's freezing at sunrise. On the way out there we listened to 'Stairway to Heaven'. I was so happy. I looked at Throb and Innes and everybody else thinking, this is fucking amazing. We were heading out into the Californian desert, with the sun coming up, Zeppelin playing. A few months ago we were signing on and now here we were in California, dreaming. Whenever I hear 'Stairway' and Robert Plant sings, 'There's a feeling I get when I look to the West', I'm back in that bus with the boys on our way to the Mojave Desert.

On the same trip I befriended this girl called Darcy who was so intelligent I kind of fell in love with her. Unrequited, I may add. She was the video commissioner for Warners. Big job. She commissioned the videos and would line up the directors for the band. It was her job to put the band together with the right directors and editors. She'd worked on fucking 'Love in an Elevator'. After the video shoot we were in LA for a few more days doing interviews, and Darcy called me up and asked what I was doing that evening. She invited me to see Neil Young and Crazy Horse making a video that night in the backyard of a Mexican restaurant. Sure enough when I got to the restaurant there was Neil and the Horse up on a small stage, doing the video for 'Country Home' on the *Ragged Glory* album. It was amazing. And they were playing live. They had the playback on, but they were playing live through amplifiers as well on low volume. During a break in shooting Darcy introduced me to Billy Talbot, the Crazy Horse bassist. I think Billy's real reason for coming over our way was to hit on Darcy. I was flying high on crystal meth; we were fucking out of it the whole time we were there. I told Billy that

I loved the Crazy Horse album and I loved Danny Whitten and he started saying 'Oh Danny, man, he was such a beautiful guy.' He started singing 'I Don't Want to Talk About It'. It was beautiful. I said to him, I wish you would play 'Barstool Blues'. He goes, 'I would love to do it, man, but we've got to make the video.' And he looked straight into my eyes and started singing:

*If I could hold on to just one thought*
*For long enough to know. . .*
*And then I joined in.*
*Why my mind is moving so fast*
*And the conversation is slow. . .*

It was brilliant. Talbot was such a soulful little guy. I could see why Neil Young needed the Horse so much. No other band he played with could touch them for soul and sincere rock and roll feeling. The restaurant garden was so small that I could literally touch Neil Young's feet. There were ten people in the 'audience', one of whom was me. I wish I'd spoken to Neil. Darcy told me the next day that Neil had said to her, 'Was that the guy from Jesus and the Mary Chain?'

These guys were my heroes. That's what 1990 was. It was a magical year. Everything and anything was possible.

When I finally returned home to my dark basement flat in Brighton I was shaken by some kind of a change in the atmosphere. I was heavily jetlagged and probably still coming down off the drugs I'd taken in LA, but I noticed that something wasn't right. It felt like I'd been burgled. Something was missing. I walked through the flat to the kitchen and bedroom at the rear, and stuff was missing from there too. I went back through to the living room and sat on the arm of the couch and looked around once more, then it hit me. All of Karen's belongings had gone.

She'd never told me outright that it was over between us, but I knew in my heart that it was. We were both emotionally inarticulate. Nothing was discussed, it was all dark moods and emotional withdrawal. The first signs had been her physical detachment. I would put my arm around her as we fell asleep and she would move away to the other side of the bed. I knew that you couldn't force someone into being in love with you. I understood. She was young, beautiful, in her early twenties and wanted a taste of what else was out there. It hurt all the same. She'd moved up to London with her new boyfriend Grant Fleming. I was happy for her. My way of dealing with the break-up had been losing myself in endless touring and then the success of 'Loaded' and 'Come Together' happened. I was young, free and single and enjoying the fruits of pop stardom. I hadn't really stopped to grieve the death of our relationship properly; instead I buried my feelings in sex and drugs and rock and roll. Fuck the pain away, as Peaches sang. I told myself that I was fine and didn't really feel too bad about losing Karen, but I was deluded. I took many lovers, none serious though. I was kidding myself that I was happy this way. I had a promiscuous side to my character and maybe I was trying to fill a hole that could never be filled, like addiction I suppose. I wondered to myself sometimes what I was hoping to find. All those one-night stands seemed like fun at the time, but then the next morning the alcohol and drugs had worn off and I found myself in some cold, strange room with a student girl whose name I didn't know, having to make awkward conversation, and excuses. I always had an urgent need to split the scene. I wanted to have fun without commitment and it was OK for a while.

The merry-go-round had stopped for a moment and here I was alone in our half-empty flat, and although we weren't going out with each other anymore, and we were both seeing other people, it was only when all her stuff had gone that I finally realised it was truly over. The feeling of her absence hit me hard. I howled. I fell on the carpet, sobbing heavily, crumpled up, shivering like a tramp on the street.

# 25.

# The Children of Marx and McLaren

Alan McGee was really clever when he told us not to play any gigs, just write songs. At that point McGee was on top of the world. In reality he was our manager, I spoke to him every other day and we discussed 'career' strategy, gossiped and bitched about boys' stuff. Alan was always jetting off somewhere to do new licensing deals for Creation and taking a lot of coke along the way to keep him up and alert to do business and then party afterwards. He had women everywhere. Suddenly, Seymour Stein was signing the Valentines, Ride and the Scream to Sire and through this major-label validation Alan was achieving music industry respect and was about to become a major player. The main thing we got wrong was that we should have had a strong American manager; that was a fucking disaster, because we had nobody to represent us in America, ever, and we've paid for that to this day. We never did enough work over there, and the record company were never watched closely or truly communicated with. You need somebody working the record company and the radio stations and TV. It's a major job. McGee was pretty naïve in a lot of ways, but we trusted him to take care of the business and leave us to do the music.

The advantages to be had from having someone as driven and self-assured as Alan McGee overseeing your career are ones of complete artistic freedom and the sure knowledge that whatever happens to your fortunes they will have your back. When you've spent your mid to late teenage years together and had a lot of shared experiences it forges an unshakeable, gang-like bond of 'us against the world'. Throb, Innes and myself all loved McGee and believed he had our best interests at heart. No other record label boss on the planet, except maybe Tony Wilson, would have put up with our crazed antics and madcap schemes. McGee was along on the helter-skelter ride, right beside us all the way, because he had the safety of knowing that his partner at Creation, Dick Green, would do his utmost to keep it together, balancing the books so to speak. Something which was nigh-on impossible under the circumstances for a financially strapped independent record label. Like us in the Scream, Alan and Dick had big dreams and were ready to sacrifice all they owned (not much at this point) for the glory of the label. Indeed, there is a legendary story that Dick remortgaged his house to further finance the ongoing recordings of My Bloody Valentine's 'Loveless' album. Now *that* is commitment to the cause. Remember, at this point in time neither McGee or Dick and Creation had had any serious chart action. The JAMC hits had come after they had left Creation and signed to WEA. McGee once described this late eighties period as one where they were constantly 'robbing Peter to pay Paul'. Dick would hold off on payments to record distributors and recording studios whilst McGee was hopping on planes to Europe and the US to secure advance monies for various Creation album releases with foreign distribution companies. That's why he released so many compilation albums around then.

We trusted Alan and Dick and no one else would have given a band like us so many chances with so few sales or critical approval. I guess the combined force of our friendship and personalities sealed the deal. Alan may have signed bands such as House of Love to labels like Phonogram making himself a pile of money and praiseworthy music press columns, but he couldn't hang out with them because he had nothing in common with a dead zone like Guy Chadwick. Instead he always came back to us, because we were from the same swamp. The streets of working-class Glasgow. We were all punk rockers with Himalaya-sized chips on our shoulders and our aggression could not be hidden or contained. I'd watched Alan as he transformed from the quiet and gentle-mannered music fan I'd first met and hung out with in Mount Florida through the punk years of 1976, '77 and '78 into the enthusiastic, idealistic young fanzine-editor guy who ran a Psychedelic Club above a pub in Fitzrovia, then into the cocksure Malcolm McLaren-esque manager of the Jesus and Mary Chain. He was now styling himself as 'the President of Pop', a live-wired, ginger-haired explosion of opinions and energy; always ready with a quote glorifying his latest signing or malevolently putting down a rival band or label. McGee was a fabulist in the best sense. His self-belief at this point was intoxicating. I was so happy that we'd given him two huge hit records at last to back up his claims about our creative potency. We'd both been mocked for years by certain critics but now it was our turn to take possession of the destiny of rock and roll, and we both knew that we would wield that dream-weapon appropriately; a chance we'd been waiting for all our lives.

During the winter of 1990 Innes was splitting up with his girlfriend Christine and spending a lot of time away from the Isle of Dogs flat they shared. Christine, when drunk, could be very cruel and abusive. I'd witnessed her drunken Geordie rages a few times and the mild-mannered Andrew who hates confrontation had had enough of that humiliating crap. Andrew emotionally withdrew and finally escaped, which worked out well for the band because he ended up sleeping and working in the Hackney studio.

One night me and Innes went out to a club night at Dingwalls. The club was called Flying, and it was run by an acid house wideboy called Charlie Chester. We were excited because that night Boy George was playing the club, performing a Club PA of 'After the Love Has Gone' by Jesus Loves You, a really good single on George's More Protein label. We'd made it and 'Everything Begins With an E' by M. C. Kinky singles of the week in *NME* when we hosted the singles page. We slagged everybody else off. Boy George was really charismatic, a genuine star, and his performance that night was brilliant. He commanded the small stage as though he was playing an arena. I had a quarter ounce of speed in my jacket pocket and was feeling real good. After the club we went back to the studio, and Innes and I slept top to tail in sleeping bags in the vocal booth, which was the warmest place available. There was no heating. I didn't get much sleep that night, speeding away in my sleeping bag.

We did quite a few nights like that, staying up, trying to write songs, encouraging each other in the shared discovery of our new-found creativity. It was a great time; very pure and idealistic. This arrangement built genuine camaraderie because it felt like it was us against the world. The Hackney studio served as a bunker, providing the emotional warmth of inter-band solidarity. It also worked as a creative shelter where we could hide from the outside world whilst writing our 'masterpiece'. The brotherly bonds that had been forged over the last couple of years of road work between Innes, Robert and myself were only strengthened as a result of the hermetically joyous experience of writing songs and living inside that little studio on Tudor Road, Hackney E8.

I was still going to a lot of clubs, doing Es and staying up for days on end. My life in 1990 consisted of listening to music, working on the album, going to record stores and scouting the shops for interesting vintage clothes. I wanted to become a good songwriter so I listened to the masters; sixties and seventies soul songwriters, checking out the productions and song arrangements, which musicians played on specific records. I listened to a lot of country soul guys, like Dan Penn, Donnie Fritts and Kris Kristofferson. Grown-up, adult songwriters. Serious guys with a life story. Literary songwriting. Songs of experience. Our early work was mostly songs of innocence. I wanted to write songs of experience, so I had to live some. There was also a bit of Brian Wilson, mainly in the chordal work and melody. Innes and Robert were both great at writing lovely chord sequences on keyboards. I was a primitive guitar guy, but my thing was writing top-line melody because that came easy to me. Gimme a great chord sequence and I'm away. It was clear that the forthcoming record would not be a rock album. It was a singer-songwriter album. That's what *Screamadelica* is really. It has a reputation for being a dance album, but there's only maybe half the songs on the record you can dance to. It's got a bit of everything, many moods, that's what makes it an interesting album.

I was making Weatherall tapes of stuff that he'd never heard, like Dion, Donnie Fritts and Dennis Wilson, and he was sending back over music that he liked. The tracks he was sending over weren't dance or electronic apart from a couple of Chris & Cosey tracks. There was ex-Pop Group guitarist Gareth Sager's band, Head, odd post-punk things like singer-songwriter Lucinda Williams and Guy Stevens-era Mott the Hoople. He was heavily into ballads.

When Weatherall was asked if he considered acid house to be 'political', his answer was that it wasn't, but that in being criminalised by the government and police it became so. It's very similar to my take which is that acid house didn't mean to be political, but it *was* political in the context of the times, because it was a reaction against Thatcher's assertion that 'There's no such thing as society.' She was atomising society with her Friedrich Hayek and Milton Friedman-inspired neoliberal credo of individualism, whereas acid house was about inclusivity, communitarianism. There was an attitude of, 'You alright, mate?' People were looking out for each other.

Thatcherism was all about the individual whereas acid house was about everybody. I think it was subversive for many reasons but that was certainly one of them. Weatherall was smart. When he made that mix of 'Come Together' he saw what was happening with acid house and he knew that this was a time for young people to *actually* come together. It was a rebellious, seditious thing. They were arresting people for having parties, criminalising it. It's probably worse now to live under austerity as a young person than it was under Thatcher because even then you could still go and claim dole and housing benefit and jobs might have been better paid as well. There was no zero-hours. So in many ways we're in a worse place than we were. If she could have brought austerity in, she would have fucking done it, but I think they were too scared to do so back then because people were still fairly militant. Acid house made a difference.

The late eighties had been a depressing time. We'd had a decade of Thatcherism and it had felt like we were living in a dystopia. The sudden explosion of acid house revolutionised British youth culture. It was an inspiring time to be young and alive and pure magic that we bonded with Andrew during this period. Like punk rock, acid house was a revolutionary scene which inspired countless people to become DJs, club promoters, visual artists, remixers, producers, singers, musicians, artists. It was out of this scene that *Screamadelica* was born. To me, acid house culture was a joyful celebration of underground resistance; not with guns, bullets and bombs, but with love, drugs, great music, sex and righteous youthful energy. Countless friendships were forged on dancefloors all over the country in small towns and big cities between 1988 and 1991. Acid house was a cultural revolution that somehow managed to unlock vast reserves of creativity in people who, until that point hadn't even realised that they could be creative beings. People like Andrew Weatherall went from low-paid temporary jobs as a youth building sets for fucking *Sooty and Sweep* and a sales boy in a King's Road fashion store, to working on a building site as a bricklayer, to becoming a major record producer producing the hippest records, to someone whose talents were sought by the biggest band in the world at that point, U2. He turned them down.

Or take our dear friend and future collaborator David Holmes. David was working as a hairdresser in a Belfast salon until he was inspired by Weatherall to start his own club night, Sugar Sweet. Holmes had brought Andrew over to DJ in Belfast. At the afterparty Weatherall told the enthused young Holmes that he should give DJing a try as well. Andrew put David in touch with other cool, up-and-coming DJs and through that patronage and support David was able to bring the best DJs spinning new music over to Belfast to kick off the Northern Irish house scene.

These wonderful things would not have happened without acid house, which, like punk, inspired you to 'do it yourself'. It was a liberating time and that's why songs like 'Don't Fight it, Feel it' and 'Higher Than the Sun' capture the utopian spirit of those days in the acid underground. Both songs are hedonistic anthems, and they *were* hedonistic times. A lot of people discovered their creativity through acid house, whether that be making posters for the raves, DJing, making little films or T-shirts. It was truly egalitarian and they became remixers, producers or even artists themselves making music. The technology had developed to the point where anybody could buy samplers and start ripping old records and make new records out of it. It's exactly the same thing: making the future out of the past. We were obviously very inspired by that and I think it was a radical moment, at least creatively. Black people and white people, gays and straights together in the clubs, the beginnings of some of the best things about modern-day Britain happened during those times, multicul-turalism for one. Football hooligans were getting on one, taking Es, and at matches the violence started to disappear.

Acid house *did* make a difference.

We would never have had hit records without acid house. *Screamadelica* would have never happened without acid house. The band would not have had its thirty-year career without acid house.

I think the punk thing has been overdone now. It's disgusting what's happened to that because ninety-nine per cent of people have missed the fucking point. Punk wasn't just about music. Punk was about being autonomous, creating a new life for yourself. Doing it for yourself, not in a neoliberal way, but in a creative way, and that's what McLaren's whole lesson was. The lesson of 1968 and 1977 and 1989 was to make your own revolution. *You* can make a difference in *your* life and maybe other people's lives, but *you* have got to be the creator. Don't be a spectator, be a creator – that's what the message of punk was, and, to me, that's also the legacy of acid house. Don't be a spectator, be a creator. To me, that's powerful. I see these guys on TV punk documentaries and in reissue magazines like *Mojo*, and they all say the same thing, recycling the same old shit about how punk rock was a street-level reaction to the excesses of sixties and seventies dinosaur bands who'd gotten so big and wealthy, removed from their fans, like Eric Clapton, Rod Stewart, the Stones, ELP, Genesis, Led Zeppelin, Pink Floyd and their Flying fucking Pigs. It was only *partly* a reaction to that; rock and roll *had* lost touch with its original roots of high-energy fun, flash and rebellion and become bloated and decadent, yes, but it wasn't just about rock and roll. You had to believe in the ruins. That's what McLaren said (paraphrasing legendary Spanish anarchist Buenaventura Durruti), you must destroy to create. I love all that shit.

Weatherall was, like us, a disciple of McLaren and Rotten. In the sixties, Jean-Luc Godard described the bourgeois Maoist students in Paris 1968 as 'the children of Marx and Coca-Cola'. Well I'd describe my generation as the children of Marx and McLaren. My dad is a Marxist (albeit a Marxist who saw Gene Vincent *and* Eddie Cochran play together at the Glasgow Empire in 1960, on the tour where Eddie died in that fatal car crash) and so, somewhere between that background, growing up in a house full of radical politics and my deep attraction and addiction to the rock-and-roll glamour and subversive glory of the Sex Pistols lies my creative and political consciousness. My artistic and political consciousness are merged I suppose, a hybrid. I wouldn't call myself a Marxist, I'm a Socialist, but there's definitely more than a strain of it in me. I also believe that the tenets of Marxism and Christianity have a lot in common. A shared belief in treating your fellow man and woman with love and compassion and respect, a shared morality and belief that a better world is possible. I was starting to understand the potential power for transformative change and agency in rock and roll as well. I felt the power of this during my punk days. I left a lot of punk shows as a teenager completely energised and full of new courage to dream and be creative, to be *me*. Rock and roll gave me the courage to be myself no matter what else was going on in my community at work or college or on the streets where I lived. It helped give me a code for living. Awakened my consciousness. A sense of what was cool and what was not. Punk and post-punk was my first cultural revolution. It gave me a belief system and was also a religion of sorts, a cause.

I was a loner kid used to solitude when Glasgow City Council decided to demolish Springburn, wipe out my community and clear the streets of kids. On my own since age nine, living in my head, looking for connection, punk gave me a reason for living, and acid house did the same. Those were great times to be young alright. Acid house changed the culture of music. I'd been witness to many indie gigs and most of them were really fucking miserable. At gigs the energy in the room was always on the stage, always with the band. When I'd seen Status Quo, the Clash or Lizzy the kids were as much part of the show as the band, everyone dressed in chains, razorblades, plastic and leather (or in Quo's case double denim), pogoing and headbanging, proper high-energy rock and roll fun. At these shows there was still the split between the performer and the audience; the spectator society, non-participatory entertainment. I loved the first few Mary Chain riot shows because the audience were breaking through the Fourth Wall, the imaginary, invisible barrier that separates actors from audience. Everyone left the theatre with the experience that *they* had been part of the show, participants, not just mere spectators; with acid house, the DJ and the audience were as one, both on the same level. When the DJ played the right records or a sequence of the right records, everybody was on the same ecstatic level. That's what was revolutionary about it. You needed other people to attain that state of transcendence. You needed to be in a room full of other people on ecstasy. Everybody's heartbeat sequenced to the bass drum, like a mantra; it was pagan. A tribalistic, mass shamanic experience. Like sex, it's more fun with other people.

I also loved the fact that the music press didn't get it. There was this insurgency happening in music in England and they missed it. They fucking missed it. A couple of people got it, and they became mad acid disciples, but ninety-nine per cent of them missed it. They weren't hip enough to get it. They were just Straights with no counter-culture nous.

There were so many great new records being released each week in 1991, it was almost impossible to keep up. Innes had a lot of the good ones. McGee had a great collection, as did Barrett, and James Williamson had got deep into it from hanging out with McGee so much in 1989. I just liked going to hear Weatherall playing, that satisfied my interest because you could never keep up with it however hard you tried. There were all these little record shops springing up everywhere to meet the demand for the new music. I was going to buy records from Black Market in Soho, next to where the Duffer was in D'Arblay Street. I'd go in there and buy records like *Tears* by Frankie Knuckles, but to be honest it always felt a bit intimidating; that place was seriously happening, the vibe in those days was intense with focused fanaticism. The young DJs from the Boy's Own scene Rocky and Diesel were selling twelve-inch imports from a shop in Kensington Market, and I bought Richie Haven's 'Back to My Roots' from them. They were good guys, totally on it. Whilst in Ken Market I'd go check out the latest designs on display at Fiona Cartlidge's Sign of the Times store. That place was always buzzing as well, a real hub of the London club scene. Fiona would sell stuff made by new young designers and she was always so positive and enthusiastic. Her parties were legendary. There was one in Kensal Rise I went to with Mark Moore of S-Express; everyone dressed up, looking really glam. Beautiful girls, gay boys, fabulous times. There was definitely an updated neo-Mod element to the acid house scene which I observed.

A huge record on the scene was 'Why Did You Do It' by seventies Brit funk-rock band Stretch. When I first heard it I thought it was the Happy Mondays – same sleazy urban groove, same leering vocal, same hard-hitting truthful in-yer-face street-poetry lyrics. In fact, there is a Monday's song with the exact same attitude of confrontational accusatory poet-speak, 'Loose Fit'. I always wondered if the Mondays had heard the Stretch song; Oakenfold certainly had. 'Talent borrows, genius steals' as Oscar Wilde said. Nice one, lads.

Whilst in London I'd go to the Trocadero, a shopping centre which was built into Piccadilly Circus station. There was a really cool shop there called Rich and Strange which was run by the guys in the acid jazz band the Sandals. I bought some amazing original sixties green-lensed fly-eye sunglasses just like the ones worn by Peter Fonda in *Easy Rider*, and a great pair of seventies Lee navy-blue corduroy bootcuts, they looked fantastic with a pair of jodhpur boots from Robot in the King's Road and my black leather Trucker jacket cut like a Levi one. A handsome and charismatic guy by the name of Wildcat Will worked there. Wildcat had the whole Fonda *Easy Rider* motorcycle-outlaw look down perfectly. Sometimes he looked like a North Beach poet in black polo neck and beads. There never seemed to be anyone manning the till because they were all hanging out in the back room playing bongo drums and flutes and getting stoned all day. Making money wasn't a priority to those guys, they were true bohemians, counter-cultural outlaws.

In those days I'd come up from Brighton, disembark at Victoria and get the Tube straight to Oxford Circus. Up the escalator, through the ticket barrier onto the concourse, turn right and Tower records was right in front of you. Tower had an 'oldies' section which was amazing. They had racks of sixties and seventies American and British hit singles for £1.50 each. Brand-new re-pressings of Stax, Atlantic, Tamla, Philadelphia International, you name it, they had everything there. Amazing collection. I'd go there and pick up a load of the classic seven-inch soul singles I was looking for.

On my little trips around these shops I couldn't help but notice there was a buzz, a scene, an energy, a positivity, a sense of purpose that something new and exciting was happening in London and around the country. We were on the scene, and now, of the scene. Our link to Weatherall, Farley and Boy's Own gave us credibility. I was living in the moment, savouring it. I really felt alive in those days, making new connections.

## 26.

# The Underground Goes Overground

That summer the Stone Roses had announced they were going to play at a place called Spike Island. They had not long ago released their new single 'One Love', not so much a song, more a Santanaesque guitar jam with a utopian lyric whispered in a threatening manner by Ian Brown. I dug the twelve-inch version where ace guitarist John Squire really cut wild and loose over the funky liquid groove laid down by their incredible rhythm section of bassist Mani and drummer Reni. The video was great too, with the band performing in front of a wall of fire. Ian Brown looks at his very best here, all razor cheekbones and implicit threat. 'One Love' was the follow-up to their classic 'Fools Gold' which had to be *the* rock single of 1989, maybe an equal tie with 'Hallelujah' by Happy Mondays and 'Blues from a Gun' by the Jesus and Mary Chain. Some people were disappointed with 'One Love', feeling it not as good as 'Fools Gold'. I was into it but I wondered how they were going to follow up such a classic single.

I thought the Roses and the Mondays were great bands and I was inspired by them both. Without them kicking the doors down we would have had no radio play or TV exposure. Also, their success had created a huge audience of fresh teenage heads who were ready and primed for the new Primal Scream sound. I was always interested in what both bands were doing and whenever they released a great new track it spurred us on to do something great too. It was great to have other contemporary artists in the UK to feel kinship and affinity with. We were all roughly the same age and inspired by the energy of acid house. I first met Mani, future Primal Scream bassist, at the Hacienda on a mad acid house night. He was very complimentary about the Scream especially our single, 'Ivy Ivy Ivy', and I never forgot that.

I travelled up to Spike Island with a girl I was seeing and our new booking agent Alex Nightingale and Karen, who I was still good friends with. We first ran into Alex in the Zap Club the year before. He hassled McGee for a job in the music business and Alan put him in touch with Mike Hinc. Alex worked there for a few months then left to start his own EC1 agency, representing his first artist, the Orb. McGee moved us from Hinc to Nightingale. The bus we had all paid ten pounds to get on was actually organised by ON-U Sound, Adrian Sherwood's label. We stopped in East London to pick up Sherwood himself, and then the bus stopped again just round the corner from Sherwood's house and on walked Jah Wobble. I shit myself. I couldn't speak. I'd learned to play bass copying this guy; he was a hero to me. You don't realise how much the likes of the Clash, PiL, the Pistols, Weller and Siouxsie were like real gods to me. I couldn't work out why Wobble was on the bus, but later found out that ON-U sound act African Head Charge were playing at Spike Island and Wobble was in the ON-U stars line up that day, with Sherwood doing the sound out front.

The gig was weird. The PA wasn't loud enough to properly hear the band and the wind kept blowing the sound around. The thing I remember most is the way the Roses appeared onstage, coming on one at a time. The vast crowd high on Madchester mania and whatever else they'd ingested went fucking mental. It was a moment alright. The Roses represented something to that audience, they gave off a swaggering, arrogant attitude with just the right amount of mystery, a blank screen for their fans to project all their longings, fears and fantasies onto. Their lyrics could mean nothing and everything at the same time; read into them what you will. The band were attituded to the max. Ian Brown was the perfect frontman, with androgynous, wolflike looks, wearing the baggy designer fashions for the time, and in John Squire they had a guitar hero for the modern age, steeped in classicism but able to wrench soulful emotions from his six-string razor. The rhythm section of Mani and Reni was the best in the country, no contest; funked-out psychedelic masters, those two. What I'd give to have a rhythm machine like that. But that story comes later. . . The atmosphere in the crowd was fantastic and there was a great sense of expectation. I felt a tectonic generational shift happening. This was the nineties and these teenagers and twenty-somethings had *their* own bands playing *their* music. It felt fresh, new and exciting. Everyone was on one, tripping on acid or spliffed out. A new order was coming into being. Here's to the eternal Now. As the Roses sang,

*The past is yours but the future's mine*
*You're all out of time*

After the band had finished their set – there was no encore, the Roses never did them – I walked through the crowd with my date and almost stood on Karen who was laid out on the grass on her back, eyes wide open with a look of childish wonder and enlarged pupils like big black UFOs. I told her that the show was finished and we had to make our way back to the bus to Brighton. I asked Karen what she thought of the show, and she replied very sincerely, 'Oh Bobby, the fireworks were GREAT!' She'd lain on the ground for the whole gig, totally bombed on ecstasy.

I walked through the backstage area on the way back to the bus and saw Squire and Brown standing with Shaun Ryder. I looked to see if Mani was there, but I couldn't see him. I figured, they'd played to thirty thousand people and probably needed some space. I remember they looked pleased with themselves. This gig was a really big deal for the time. I'd seen these guys just a year before and they were playing to twenty-five people in the Escape Club in Brighton and now they had thirty thousand fans worshipping them. That was inspiring and I thought, if they can do it, so can we. I have to give credit to the Roses, Spike Island was an ambitious gig. Up until that point bands from the independent scene had mainly played concert halls and theatre venues, nothing of this size and magnitude. I could see what they were doing. They were more interested in 'happenings' than normal concert tours. Spike Island was their attempt at a Monterey Pop or Woodstock for the nineties. I admired their ambition.

Noel Gallagher saw me walking through the crowd that day. He was a roadie for the Inspirals. Noel said I looked like Joey Ramone. I think I had a striped T-shirt or a sixties shirt with one of my dad's old nylon polo necks. A turquoise one that I used to wear in the Mary Chain with ripped jeans. And the shoes I wore would have been suede Robot shoes from the King's Road, almost teddy boy shoes but with a Doc Marten sole.

The Roses were obviously a force for good whereas the Mondays were sleazy and dangerous, the yin to the Roses' yang. Although the Tories were still in power, it felt like young people finally had this exciting new music scene and a beautiful drug that was bringing people together with positive energy and creativity everywhere you looked. Possibilities seemed to be opening up, there was a crack in the sky and a light shining through it. A culture shift was happening, and we were part of it.

At this point Innes shared a flat with Alex Nightingale in Hackney. It was an old primary school that had been converted into flats. Very eighties. I knew Nightingale from going to the clubs in Brighton. We became friends and he'd come back to my flat and we'd get wasted.

Alex Nightingale was a strangely charismatic kid. Always alone, it seemed, and causing a scene. There was a real anger there mixed with tenderness and I related to that. He had the good looks of a young David Hemmings, blue-eyed, blond hair, but softer features. Once we'd dug beneath the Brighton working-class street-junkie persona he used as a protective shield, we found that he was really an English middle-class public school-boy in possession of a dark and malevolent sense of humour very much like that of the band. We clicked immediately. When the clubs closed someone always found somewhere to have an afterparty till God knows what hour. When Nightingale was at these parties he was always holding court, telling stories and making people laugh. He was chemically involved, shall we say, and always had a bottle of Jack Daniels on his person. As a youth he'd followed Psychedelic Furs and New Order around on tour obsessively. His mother was BBC Radio 1 DJ Annie Nightingale, so Alex had grown up with rock stars such as Pete Townsend and Keith Moon hanging out at his mum's house; Annie was friends with all the sixties rock aristocracy. Alex regaled us with tales of decadent seventies rock excess, and we all sat rapt. He was a great raconteur. The flat Alex shared with Innes would be the centre of activity and drama over the period of writing and recording *Screamadelica*. I would now stay with them when I was up in London working in the Tudor Road studio. The only problem with staying at the Innes–Nightingale flat was that it was sometimes hard to get any sleep: there was always some kind of party or scene going on there. Sex and drugs and rock and roll central.

We continued our work at the little studio in Hackney, writing more songs. We wrote the skeleton of 'Inner Flight' with the keyboard chords and the flute melody and spaced-out electronic textural sounds. I knew that it had to be an instrumental and I'd been obsessed by a track called 'Think' from the *Super Fly* soundtrack. I'd listened to it endlessly on the plane journey coming back from Japan on my newly purchased CD Walkman and thought it might be a good idea if we wrote an instrumental track in the same vein. I decided not to write lyrics for this one, to let the music speak for itself. When we felt we had enough songs written we decided to book some studio time to finish off the album. We already had 'Come Together', 'Loaded', 'Slip Inside This House' and 'Don't Fight it Feel It'. We just needed to record the other five new songs we had written since last summer and then we had an album.

The *Screamadelica* sessions took place over a period of three or four weeks at Jam studio on Tollington Park Road where we had cut 'Come Together'. We liked the vibe there. It was myself, Throb, Innes, Duffy, Toby and Henry. No one else. I remember having to take speed to sing 'Higher Than the Sun', just to give me the courage because I knew it was a very special song. I had worked really hard on the lyrics. This was exactly what I wanted to say at this point in time about my life. I had delusions of grandeur thinking that so long as I sang this song well, it didn't matter if I died because this would be my testimony. I'd read that in 1967 Arthur Lee had been haunted by premonitions of his death and felt that 'Forever Changes' was going to be his last words to the world. It was a big deal for me to sing this song, it was an important one. In those days I didn't have a lot of confidence as a vocalist, because of the bad experience I'd had recording the first album. After that I was always a bit apprehensive about singing in the studio.

I wrote 'I'm Coming Down' on acoustic guitar in my basement flat in Brighton. When I played it to Innes and Robert; Innes wasn't sure, but Throb loved it. Andrew thought it needed a different type of arrangement: basically keyboards, drum machines and electronics. He was right about that. Over that month in Jam we recorded 'Shine Like Stars', 'Movin' On Up',' Inner Flight', 'Damaged' and 'Higher Than the Sun'.

We got the same gospel singers in for 'Movin' On Up' as we had used on 'Come Together'. We recorded them live harmonising, then double-tracked the harmonies to make it sound stronger, and stacking more harmonies on top, stacking them up so it sounded like a full choir. That was fun. When we heard those soul-powered gospel voices lifting the chorus of 'Movin' On Up', blasting through the huge Jam studio speakers, it felt godlike. We were all in in gospel punk heaven, shivers and goosebumps right down to our souls.

We recorded 'Damaged' live on the studio floor in two or three takes with Henry Olsen on double bass, Throb on acoustic, Innes on electric, Duffy on country soul piano and Toby using brushes. We laid it down with the right amount of gentle power and tasteful licks. All the new songs on the album were written on piano or keyboards, not guitar, apart from 'Damaged'. We'd stopped writing bluesy riffs. Even 'Movin' On Up', which every-one thinks is this guitar song, was written on piano.

A lot of work went into the harmonies on 'Inner Flight'. Henry sings like a choirboy on that. He had a really good sense of harmony and it sounds like the Beach Boys if they had taken ecstasy instead of pot and transcendental meditation.

For the duration of the recording I would sometimes stay at Tim Tooher's flat overlooking the railway tracks up at Willesden Junction, in North West London. It was ridiculously noisy. Tim and I would go head to tail in his bed, a single mattress laid on the bare floorboards of his tiny bedsit overlooking the busy tracks below. Each night I'd come back from the studio super excited and buzzing and we'd sit up chatting, playing records and then finally crash in the early hours. Next morning I'd wake up and have some cornflakes and a cup of tea. I would always play 'We've Got to Have Peace' by Curtis Mayfield which put me in an inspirational mood before I left for the studio.

Halfway through the sessions our recording engineer, Colin Leggett, quit on us. He said, 'I really can't wait to mix this stuff,' and when I told him that he wasn't mixing it he quit. So we finished on our own, recording guitar overdubs and my lead vocals with the studio tape op boy, the assistant engineer (basically the teenage kid that's was just starting learning his trade in the studio). I don't remember much about the sessions themselves but I do recall Martin Duffy dropping acid when we were recording 'Inner Flight'. He was tripped right out of his head, on a totally different planet, stood on top of the sofa in the control room beside the mixing desk. He was shouting, 'I'm pissing on the sky! I'm pissing on the sky!' It was brilliant, just like a proper album session should be. Thankfully no one was collapsing at these sessions like we had when recording 'Come Together'.

Alex Nightingale represented Alex Paterson as a DJ. Alex had DJ'ed at Paul Oakenfold's club night Spectrum at Heaven on Villiers Street where he played what people called 'ambient' music, otherworldly drifting soundscapes. Clubbers who needed a break from the non-stop Chicago house acid beats of the main room where Oaky played would go to the 'chill out' room to be soothed by Paterson's selection of beatless, drifting ambient music mixed with bird sounds and whatever else he fancied dropping into the mix. Paterson's ambient record collection went perfectly with the post-rush whoosh of an ecstasy peak: the calming, soothing sounds made the listener feel safe and cocooned in a womblike, protective sonic warmth.

Alex had released a fantastic twelve-inch single which he'd made with Martin Glover (Youth) and Jimmy Cauty (later of the KLF) titled 'A Huge Ever Growing Pulsating Brain That Rules from the Centre of the Ultraworld', which at eighteen minutes and forty-nine seconds is really an ambient progressive rock track. Alex would play this track constantly and it piqued Innes's interest. Nightingale suggested to Innes that Primal Scream ask the Orb to mix some of our new music.

Andrew had met Alex Paterson a couple of years before at Spectrum. Paterson was of Scottish descent and very easy to get on with. Innes suggested the idea to me. For the 'Higher Than the Sun' mixes Paterson worked with an outrageously talented young engineer called Kris Weston, known to us as Thrash. The Orb gave us about fifteen little sections of song mixes, some vocal, others instrumental, some with drums, some without. It was like a Burroughs 'cut-up' of our song, and as it was, it made no sense, just various unrelated sections of sound and vocal dubs. Innes managed to splice the vital parts of them together to make both a seven-inch single radio edit which ran at 3.36 minutes and a twelve-inch single version at 6.43 minutes.

At the same time Weatherall and Hugo Nicholson had taken on 'Higher' and Weatherall had suggested to us that he would like to bring in Jah Wobble to play bass on it. We were ecstatic. The Wobble mix was released as 'Higher Than the Sun (A Dub Symphony in Two Parts)' on a separate twelve-inch with 'Higher Than the Orb' on the B side. Everyone was so blown away by the latest mixes that we all agreed 'Higher' should be released as the next single. McGee absolutely loved it. He said, 'I'm going to release it as a single. It's not gonna be a hit, but it's a statement. The statement is *We're better than everybody else*'. I loved that about Alan. It wasn't an arrogance but a need to push things, to put a rocket up the arse of the music scene. It's an important record. I remember at the time doing interviews saying shit like '"Higher Than the Sun" is the most important record since "Anarchy in the UK".' I meant it as well.

'Higher Than the Sun' was single of the week in *NME* and *Melody Maker*. I don't think it got many radio plays, but that wasn't the point. It's a hymn to the transformative powers of psychotropic drugs, written from the solipsistic point of view of a drug user. The inner flight of the contemplative junkie lost in daydreams and ecstatic visions. The all-powerful feeling of grandiose potency that envelops the user. I loved to be in this state of transitory perfection. When on certain drugs I felt like the lyrics to 'Big Black Car' by Big Star:

*Nothing can hurt me*
*nothing can touch me*

The demon of nihilism is awoken in certain people after prolonged drug use. I was one of them. Sometimes I felt so good I didn't care if I died. 'Higher' is a song that elevates the transitory beauty of a chemically altered consciousness above everything else. It has no morality. It just is.

The thing about Andrew Weatherall and Alex Paterson was that they were both 'non-musicians'. This was appealing to our punk instincts. Weatherall wasn't trying to make 'hit records', that never entered his mind, he just wanted to make thrilling music that worked on the dancefloor; be it a high-energy stomper single release or a gentle, more ballad-style album track, he would mess with the arrangement, breaking it down to almost nothing, sparing only the purest essential components of the song before reconstructing it again. In his mixes, time was elastic – something to be pulled this way and that – mirroring a psychedelic drug experience in which time slows down and then speeds up again, a sensory experience where nothing is real and nothing is unreal.

Weatherall's skill at arranging music was both visceral and avant-garde. His autodidactic worldview gave him a freedom of thought which, when mixed with the counter-cultural ideas that stoked his already fervent imagination, placed him firmly outside the 'academy'. He was an outsider artist in a way; happiest out on the margins, doing his own thing because he could be more free out there. He was never interested in the mainstream, and like ourselves, music was a portal for him to escape the straight life. No one else could have thought of (de)constructing tracks like he did, rearranging our melodies and music into abstract pop. Hugo Nicholson deserves credit here too, because some of Weatherall's best work was done in collaboration with Hugo. They were a proper team. Andrew had the vision and Hugo the technical studio skills needed to realise Andrew's ideas. Hugo had some good ideas of his own too. They just killed it every single time.

Andrew and Hugo really did become our extra band members on *Screamadelica*, and in the case of 'Higher Than the Sun' so did Alex Paterson and Thrash. We had the songs and the music but those guys had an understanding of both what worked on the contemporary dancefloor *and* how to misuse the new studio technology and bend it to their will. Both Weatherall and Paterson had dabbled in occult practices during their youth and understood the power of the will – when you set your mind to achieving something and you focus your deep spiritual energy and psychic powers then magical things can happen – but you have to be tuned in to certain frequencies within yourself, the universe and others in order to do so. It takes years of psychic training and spiritual work to arrive at this point and not everyone has the stamina or strength of will to get there. Weatherall definitely channelled shamanic energies and understood magical transmissions. That's why he was such a good producer. He had it down. Both Weatherall and Paterson were children of the counter-culture, and had also been inextricably tuned into the seismic vibrations of British youth culture of which they were both disciples and initiates. True believers.

From glam rock to soul boys through to punk and post-punk and now acid house, they both had a history of being close to the energy source. The new studio technology of samplers allowed people like Andrew and Alex the power to exercise their imaginations in a way that was previously impossible. Neither of them were what could be termed 'musical'; neither played an instrument or wrote conventional songs (at that point), but through sheer will, spiritual power and hip music taste they helped us create a new wave of sonic exploration married to a pop sensibility. Suddenly, you could be jamming on your guitar to Clyde Stubblefield (James Brown's Funky Drummer) along with a sample of a seventy-piece orchestra playing Wagner's Ring

Cycle mixed in with gamelan flutes, West African percussion and raga sitars from India and this would create a beautiful bed of layered sound over which one could place a psychedelic pop song. To create music like that before would have cost hundreds of thousands of pounds in studio bills, travel fares and musician fees; now, with the Akai S1000 sampler, it was all at your fingertips, either in your bedroom or a studio. The only limit was the imagination, and between ourselves, Weatherall and the Orb, we had that in bundles.

The last track to be mixed on *Screamadelica* was 'Shine Like Stars'. Everything else was done but I can't remember the sequence of the mixes. There were times when McGee would say to Weatherall, 'I think you could do better,' and send him back into the studio. McGee was diligent. I remember Creation calling me up and telling me not to go to the studio. The tape op engineer kid had turned up for work that morning and all the gear had gone. It turned out the studio owner Chris Stainton had done a runner. He had disappeared and taken the mixing desk with him along with some of our tapes. I was pleased about that because I wasn't sure about the arrangement of 'Shine Like Stars' we'd recorded. I thought it was wrong even though I loved the song. The Orb and Weatherall had mixed it and we didn't like that either.

I'd been listening to *The Marble Index* a lot and had become obsessed with that record. So I suggested we try it with Duffy playing the harmonium. We went to Eden Studios and recorded it there. We added some samples and Indian-style tabla percussion and sampled some Indonesian gamelan music from an album that Innes owned. There *may* have been a sample from *The Marble Index* on that song as a tribute to Nico. There were some Star Trek noises on there too. Weatherall had been away DJing in Ibiza. When he came back he did a perfect mix of 'Shine Like Stars'.

I wrote those lyrics about the times when I would come to bed late at night and Karen would be asleep and I would think about how beautiful she looked, how fragile she was as she slept. No defences, no attitude, just calm, gentle and vulnerable. I wanted to protect her from the violence and corruption of the world. I enjoyed watching Karen out on the dancefloor. She could sometimes be socially nervous, lacking in confidence. I'm not sure that she held herself in high esteem. When Karen had had a few drinks she could lose herself, inhibitions falling away, and be victorious and full of the transcendental power transmitted by the music. Music fills the heart with courage and a deep sense of connection. It has the power to connect all the damaged souls. It's a form of spiritual healing. As the great Nina Simone sang on 'Save Me',

*the ones that hurt really feel the most*
*crying together from coast to coast*

For 'Shine Like Stars' I wrote about watching Karen lose her inhibitions, about the power of music.

*I watch you dance you look so happy*
*lost in a moment of abandon,*
*you're set free*

That song is a hymn to the transcendent, ecstatic power of music to release us from our earthly chains and set us free, catching a glimpse of the eternal Now. Music can connect us to our own souls. We have become too disconnected from who we really are because of all the existential pain we carry. We have to separate ourselves from the very core of our being to get through the day. Music is a place of deep spirituality; a place for holy communion with ourselves and other members of the tribe and Karen's vulnerability whilst sleeping inspired the song. Her normal defences were down and I could see her as she really was.

'Movin' On Up' is a song about struggle and redemption. At various times in our lives we may find ourselves lost in a wilderness of our own making. Reaching out and asking another person for help can be a difficult but ultimately liberating experience. It's hard to make it through this world alone. 'Everybody needs somebody', as the song goes. We have a deep need to believe in somebody or something and we need faith in another human being that we can trust. Without love and trust we are nothing. But love and trust need to be earned.

Everyone will feel alone and helpless at some point in their lives and some find it very difficult to reach out and ask for help. This can be pride, arrogance, inability to communicate, insecurity, low self-esteem or sheer bloody-mindedness. But solitude and exile can be a good thing. 'Movin' On Up' was written as a universal song of courage in the face of adversity. A song that acknowledges the empowerment that the experience of personal struggle can give a person. A song that admits wrongdoing, failure and spiritual confusion yet takes responsibility and confronts demons head on. It was written as a commercial pop-gospel song. We wanted to lift people. I believe that inside all of us are vast reserves of power; it's only when we're seriously tested do we realise our true strength. We are spiritual beings with unlimited capacity for love and creativity. We build defences to keep the world and other humans at bay, to present a tough front to the world, but really we are full of fear and mistrust. Maybe 'Movin' On Up' is a hymn for all the desolate, lost, angry, confused, self-hating people of the world. I should know because I was one of them. It's a hymn to the transcendent, healing, life affirming power of community I found in rock and roll and acid house.

We'd asked to work with Jimmy Miller on 'Movin' On Up' and 'Damaged' because we loved his work with the Stones on that run of classic albums Jimmy produced: *Beggars Banquet, Let It Bleed, Sticky Fingers, Exile on Main St* and *Goats Head Soup*. Keith said he was the best he's ever worked with. He was seen in the corporate nineties music business as a burnout, and he wasn't getting much work. It was easy to track him down. When we found him he was living in London and eager to work. The 'Movin" mix was getting done at Eden Studios, over in Chiswick. I went down with Weatherall to check out the scene. We were both excited to meet the great man.

When we got to the studio and introduced ourselves Jimmy told this joke. 'How can you tell when a woman comes?'

Somebody said, 'I don't know.'

Jimmy replied, 'Who cares!'

All these guys working in the studio started laughing. Me and Weatherall looked at each other. It was embarrassing. Weatherall just walked out of the control room, and I followed. He said to me, 'I'm leaving.' He was really upset. 'I don't care how many great records the guy's made, but putting down women like that, no fucking way.' We asked Weatherall if he'd like a go at mixing 'Movin' On Up' and he said, 'Give us a tape of the track and I'll see what I think.' I heard back from Creation that he wasn't into mixing the song. Next time I saw him out I asked why.

'It's a bit too *Stars on Sunday* for me,' he said, referencing a tacky religious programme of the time. Cheeky cunt.

There was a problem with the Eden mix of 'Movin' On Up', I can't remember what it was exactly. Jimmy had to go back to the United States and mix it (and 'Damaged') over there. Innes was given the job of going over to supervise the mix. On the way back to Brighton from the aborted 'Higher Than the Sun' video shoot Alan McGee had arrived with a cassette tape. It was a tape of Jimmy Miller's master mixes of 'Damaged' and 'Movin' On Up' and I remember sitting with Innes and Throb and playing it on his car stereo system. Maybe it was Throb's write-off Saab or his Sweeney-style grey Ford Granada: a seventies UK version of US muscle cars, it was a beast. We used to ride around in it blasting the theme tune of the Brit TV cop show *The Sweeney*. We whacked 'Movin' On Up' loud through the stereo and as soon as it started we were just like, fucking hell! We'd recorded everything back at Jam in London, with the gospel singers, the guitars, the conga, Duffy's piano, the kitchen sink. . . Jimmy had taken the congas and hand-claps out and kept the bass, my vocals, gospel singers, Innes's acoustic, Throb's slide and lead, Duffy's piano and stripped it down, building up a new rhythm track around a pulsing bass drum and surrounded it with some new percussion. It just sounded so clear, powerful and beautiful. He'd cut some of Throb's guitar riffs into two parts so they would answer my vocals instead of cutting across them all the time. Throb was a master guitarist but he had a propensity to play over absolutely everything like one huge guitar solo from start to finish. Jimmy edited Throb's stellar axe work in such a way that suddenly all this space was created and the song could breathe and move and had dynamics. Jimmy Miller gave us this incredible mix. It sounded as good as anything that our heroes had ever made.

We knew at that point that we had a motherfucker of an opening song for our album: a 'Safe European Home' or 'Janie Jones', yes, that good. When Weatherall had mixed 'Shine Like Stars', we all knew that it would be the last song on the album, but we still didn't have the first song. And now we were jubilant. 'Movin' On Up' was gonna open the album. It's a classic opening track. 'Damaged' was a classic as well, a proper brokenhearted country soul ballad; a true blues for all the damaged sons and daughters, healing music for the soul. Andrew told me that Jimmy had decided to place Toby's drums way down in the mix because he was out of time in places and there was a messy re-entry before the coda section. We all performed great on that one: Duffy's wonderful, bluesy, country southern soul licks, Henry's stand-up acoustic bass, full of space with cosmos-sized holes that allow the song to breathe, Throb's Celtic-soul acoustic guitar picking and Innes's Steve Cropper Stax stabbing rhythm chops and the stinging shared (by Henry and Innes) lead guitar solo all contributed to a golden-sounding recording cut live on the studio floor at Jam. All I had to do was croon my words, a tale of the transient joys of young love, of romantic fire gone out too young and too soon. 'Damaged' is an existential blues of nostalgic sorrow. Everyone can relate to that. You could hardly hear the drums on it. Jimmy put the bass up in the mix to give a percussive illusion and mixed the drummer right out. Sonic alchemy. Jimmy was a genius. A rock and roll genius. I got to know him better a bit later when we worked on the *Give Out* album, and despite getting off to an embarrassing start with the bad joke at Eden, he was lovely man.

Jimmy told me that the first record he ever produced was by George Clinton and the Parliaments. They both told me the same story independently of each other. So I felt a wee bit like we were convergent in this, part of a chain, a link between the music that George and Jimmy had created and we were carrying on the tradition, bringing new energy and with Weatherall's help through modern technology, updating it and keeping it alive at the same time. I just loved all that stuff.

That summer of 1991 we released two singles: 'Higher Than the Sun' released on 22 June (my birthday), reached #40 in the charts for two weeks and then dropped out. 'Don't Fight It, Feel It', released on 24 August, reached #41 and also dropped out after two weeks. Neither was a Top 20 or Top 30 hit like 'Loaded' or 'Come Together'. With 'Higher' we achieved critical acclaim, though, and 'Don't Fight It, Feel It' became an underground club sensation, Weatherall's finest, maybe. It's a mind-blower even to this day, powered by a dark sexuality and hedonistic nihilism:

*I live just for today*
*Don't care about tomorrow*

That's the way we lived our lives back then.

I became obsessed with chart positions and mainstream success. From growing up with punk and post-punk culture I realised the media was a channel for change. If we were on TV looking, dressing and acting a certain way, playing a certain kind of experimental pop music then any kid out there who felt alone or different or alienated might feel less alone. Coming along to our shows or listening to our records might inspire them to be creative themselves.

# 27.

# Let It Scream(adelica)

We decided to go on a short seven-date tour, starting in Birmingham. Andrew Weatherall and the Orb were the tour DJs and de facto support band. We all packed into a little minibus and rode up to the Birmingham Institute listening to this compilation tape I'd made and 'Honaloochie Boogie' by Mott the Hoople came on. Everybody was singing along. Weatherall looked over to me and quoted Ian Hunter's lyrics:

*Now my hair gets longer as the beat gets stronger*
*Wanna tell Chuck Berry my news*

All our mates were there and we were setting off on an adventure. It was fucking amazing. Finally, we were on our way. Innes and I were on an evangelical acid house trip. We marched into the Creation offices in Westgate Street and went to see McGee at his desk. I said, 'Alan, we have an idea. Innes is a qualified chemist, he has a chemistry degree from university. He also has the recipe for MDMA. Will you front the money so he can buy the chemicals in large amounts and rent us a cottage in the countryside where he can make ecstasy so that we can hand out tabs for free to every kid who comes to see us on the tour?' We loved ecstasy so much we wanted to turn on the whole world.

'We'll all go to prison,' McGee said, with regret. 'The party will be great, but we'll all go down. Sorry, boys, the answer is no.' And that was that.

On the tour we had the venues opened and licensed till two in the morning. Alex Paterson would DJ first, the doors opened at nine. The Scream would go on after Alex's set and then Weatherall would DJ until closing time after the Scream set. We would get coked up to go on stage, do the gig and then all drop ecstasy and get out on the dancefloor with the audience and groove to Weatherall's set. We stayed in a motel in Birmingham, like the Crossroads Motel, and just fucking partied all night. Douglas and Tim Tooher came on the tour with video cameras. I walked into Throb's room at four in the morning and Douglas was lying on his back on the bed holding his video camera pointing up to the ceiling and Tim was lying face down on the other bed holding his video camera, with the video camera aimed at the floor. I thought, that's not gonna be much of a film.

I went to Weatherall's room the next day and he was a bit done in so after that he decided to go solo and fly to every gig. The manager on the tour was a guy called Ivor who had tour-managed the House of Love, a speed freak as well. It was such a druggy tour. The next night was the Hacienda. I walked up the steps to my room at the guest house we were staying in, with Nightingale behind me, and as I turned and looked over my shoulder I saw him do a somersault, backwards down a steep flight of stairs, all the way down to the bottom. I ran down to the bottom and he was having an epileptic fit. When he came to, he was taken to hospital so he missed the gig.

Weatherall's engineer Hugo Nicholson became part of the touring party, playing drum loops live. We were playing some of the songs to a pre-recorded rhythm backing track and we still had Toby in the band, but he would only play drums on a couple of songs and the rest was a drum machine and samples, with Hugo playing along to the rhythm track, adding loops, sound effects and dubbing. It was great. So he became a member of the live touring band with Toby playing percussion. We brought Denise Johnson along too. Denise was a great foil for me live. It was like having two centre forwards with the Lizzy-esque twin guitar attack of Throb and Innes, Duffy's genius country soul piano, Henry holding down the bass to a solid and steady rhythm and Toby, a great spirited rock and roll drummer with a soulful attitude who played like he meant it. Denise and Hugo both brought something new and fantastic to the party and we were ready to take on the world. I loved that eight-piece band.

With the backing tapes we sounded like we could be a big band. Suddenly there was this clarity and you heard the power of these musicians, world-class players, all of them. The Hacienda gig on 23 July was crazy. It was a big deal for us to headline the Hacienda, because we were such Factory fanatics, and Weatherall was too. It felt like we'd made it. It was a very special night for us and we played great. Whenever anything bad happened, like the equipment going down, it always brought out the best in the band because we thrived on adversity. There's an interview from that gig by the Stud Brothers for *Melody Maker* which is wild. It ran with great photographs by Tom Sheehan. Tom Sheehan brought up the Gram Parsons biography by Ben Fong-Torres. I opened it up and was reading it, coked out my brains, and *White Line Fever* was one of the chapter titles. I looked like a vampire.

Noel Gallagher told me he was there and he loved it when our equipment broke down and we went into 'Dark End of the Street', just me, Throb and Innes. Gallagher said his mate turned to him and said, 'What the fuck's going on? What the fuck are they doing?' And Noel said to his mate, 'They're making history here. Just you fucking watch. Something special's happening right now.' Noel knew.

The rest of the tour I don't remember so much. I don't think we helped ourselves with the drugs. I remember Glasgow Plaza Ballroom: eighteen hundred people going mental. We walked on stage and it was like we'd won the World Cup Final. The last time we'd played in Glasgow at the Tech College in 1989 people were booing and shouting abuse. And then in 1991 we walked on the stage and all the hands were in the air as though we'd won the cup. It was insane. Of course we all took E after the gig to dance to Weatherall. It was just debauchery. We were backstage at the Plaza with our mums. I was having an argument with my mum, Douglas filming it all, and when she realised what was happening she punched Doug in the face. Innes was trying to get his mum to drop an E.

At the gig in Nottingham, I had to play most of the set sitting on the floor because I was just fucked. It wasn't a great gig. We just kind of limped through. We'd hammered it too hard. I offer my apologies to anyone who paid money to see that.


We had to drive overnight from Bristol straight after the show back to London to do the soundcheck at nine in the morning or something horrific, before the shops opened in Leicester Square Empire Ballroom. We were all wasted from the night before, all still flying like motherfuckers.

Two weeks earlier, when we were rehearsing for the tour we had Jah Wobble come to the rehearsal room up in Caledonian Road and he jammed with Innes, Duffy, and Throb on 'Higher Than the Sun', over the gigantic breakbeat. The idea was that when we played Leicester Square Wobble was going to join us for an extended freak-out version with him on bass. I wish I'd taped that jam. It was incredible. When we played with Wobble it sounded like we could be a big band. Suddenly there was this space and clarity. That was like a dream come true for us as PiL fans. We had that to look forward to at the end of the tour.

After the soundcheck the bass player, Henry, came up to me looking really serious and said, 'Can I speak to you, Bob? I don't want Jah Wobble to play tonight.'

I was shocked. 'What d'you mean, man? It sounded fantastic. He's only coming on for "Higher Than the Sun".'

I don't know if he said *If he plays I won't play*. I can't remember. But he said, 'I don't think he should play. *I'm* the bass player in Primal Scream.' Pathetic shit like that.

I climbed up the stairs from the darkened subterranean ballroom out into the bright summer morning sunlight in Leicester Square and told the boys the news.

'Fuck,' they said. 'What we gonna do? You don't wanna upset H., you know. He's the bassist in the band.'

I said to Simon Stevens, our assistant, 'Look, it's still early in the morning. Can you call Wobble and just tell him it's not gonna happen tonight?' What I should have said to Henry was, 'It's fucking happening, mate, and if you don't like it this is your last gig.' But he'd been with us when times weren't so good and now times were good I tended to think that would be a bit hard-hearted. It was the end of a debauched tour and I was frazzled. In the end we decided, OK, maybe we don't want to split the band up.

After the tour finished I got a message from Nightingale that Wobble wanted to speak to me. I wanted to apologise for our shit and rude behaviour but before I spoke to Wobble I had to speak to his manager, a former member of the Leighton Buzzards. I had to suffer the indignity of this fucking guy's untutored verbiage of insults before he would give me Wobble's phone number. Wobble was courteous, polite and very cool. He said to me that we shouldn't treat other players the way we had treated him and I wholeheartedly agreed. I explained the situation that we were in on the morning of the Empire show and admitted we were in the wrong and that I was so sorry. He gave me forgiveness and that meant a lot. He was an idol of mine, Innes and Throb too. I felt much better after talking to him. He'd been one of my earliest musical influences and we had a connection. There was a line from PiL to *Screamadelica*. I felt we had picked up the baton.

We all went to get some much-needed sleep for the important gig later that night. On the way to the hotel I went to Daddy Kool, the reggae shop in Berwick Street in Soho and bought an original seven-inch of Tapper Zukie's radical classic 'New Star', then I had a nap. The gig was a massive success. There were a few stage invasions. Mal from Cabaret Voltaire was in the dressing room afterwards. I was just blown away by him being there. He was like, 'What a fucking great gig!' This guy's one of our heroes. All the acid kids that we'd met in clubs came down dressed up in their stylish fashions, and the gig was a sell-out. Afterwards everybody was partying. Our very own street-level version of 'High Society', a carnivalesque atmosphere of narcotic reverie and joyous abandon. We had a transvestite called Graham who followed us around then. I first met Graham on the Soho acid house scene through amazing girls we hung out with, Sidonie and Ruth. He became close friends with my mother and used to visit her in Glasgow.

A couple of days after the Empire Ballroom show I got a phone call from McGee saying, 'We need an album cover.' I was still on a heavy drug comedown from the tour. Earlier that year I'd seen this artwork on the 'Phobia' single by Flowered Up and I asked Jeff Barrett, whose Heavenly label had released the record, about it. He told me the artist was Paul Cannell. Barrett told me Paul had also done some stuff for Manic Street Preachers, but to my mind it was just sub-Jamie Reid. But the 'Phobia' cover had a drawing of a really angst-ridden, angry, paranoid, freaky little creature on it which looked like a more autobiographical artwork. I was immediately drawn to this.

Jeff set up a meeting between me and Paul Cannell. I told him, 'Look, I want you to paint our singles covers and what I'm gonna do is give you a title. I'm not gonna let you hear the song. I just want you to paint from the title.'

He was like, 'I wanna hear the song!'

I said, 'No, you can't hear the song.' Because I thought if he heard the song and he heard the lyrics it might be too represent-ative and too literal.

The first one he did was for 'Higher Than the Sun'. I went out to where he lived in East London, Forest Gate or somewhere. I looked at the painting and I liked what Cannell had done very much, it was nothing like 'Phobia' which is a one-line pencil drawing, a scrawled-up ball of paranoid energy. This painting was full of colour and abstract shapes, you could read what you wanted into it just the way I approached writing lyrics. It reminded me of the paintings my parents had on the wall of our flat in Springburn in the sixties. It had a wonderful positive energy radiating from it but also a darkness too. I asked Grant Fleming to come along to photograph it. Grant worked in the Creation offices in the dance department, he was close with Oakenfold and Weatherall, a former teenage tour manager for Sham 69, mates with the Cockney Rejects and a West Ham fanatic. Grant was great fun to have around in the touring party and has taken some fantastic photos of us on tour and at video shoots.

I would direct Grant to photograph certain sections of the painting that interested me and then I would work with this graphics guy who had a computer, and I would say, 'Take that section of the painting, OK, let's crop it here, and there, OK, that's the front cover.' And then I'd take another section of the painting and that would be used as the back cover. Using that process we made the sleeve designs for 'Higher Than the Sun' and the remix. That's the first time the *Screamadelica* sun appears. It's kind of a greyish, mauve-coloured sun, nowhere near the famous red, black, yellow and blue album image. This one is more saturnine and ominous. We also pulled out the sun image to use as the labels for both 'Higher' singles, printed with the sun in black and yellow on a blue background. Then we repeated the process with the 'Don't Fight It, Feel It' single and the remix by Graham Massey of 808 State. I chose the images from Paul's painting, a junked-out acid house phantasmagoria full of images of melted minds and frightened, tortured birds in flight, a visual representation of the assassination of imagination, or the explosion of imagination enabled by psychotropic drugs. It has that duality, yin and yang.

I asked Paul what his working methods were. I was fascinated how this soulful and highly sensitive working-class guy with no formal art school training could conjure these visions from his subconscious into being. He told me he would take magic mushrooms and shoot up smack to get him in the mood for painting these psychedelic tableaus, much in the same way we would take amphetamines or cocaine to get us in the aggressive mindset to do battle onstage.

Paul Cannell was an amazing artist. He risked his life to make his art. He was an all or nothing kind of guy. I once walked around Primrose Hill with him in the late nineties. His observations of the world around him were incredible and he really did have an artist's vision. He saw things in places invisible to ninety-nine per cent of people. He saw art everywhere and I learned a lot that day. He was a one-off and his band Crawl were cool too. I gave Paul my silver shirt that I had worn in the 'Movin' On Up' video cos he saw Kurt Cobain wear a similar one in the 'Heart Shaped Box' video. He loved Kurt, a fellow artist who documented existential pain and had a fondness for opiates. Both too sensitive for this world. Paul had the misfortune of being born into the working class; had he grown up in Richmond rather than Forest Gate things may have turned out different. Class defines and destroys us in this country. The cunts at the top are laughing at as all because they've set up the system in such a clever way. Over two thousand years of hierarchal power wielded by the unholy matrimony between the twin evils of royalty and the Church conjoined by the bastard aristocracy and the newly moneyed merchant class. Scum upon scum upon scum: a plague on all their houses. They set up the class system of wealth and labour extraction and had us all fighting and blaming each other, or 'the other', the Catholic, the Jew, the Muslim, the Hindu, the foreigner, the Black man or woman or homosexual for generations of poor wages and working and living conditions and unequal life chances that the lower orders have had to endure. Centuries of exploitation.

Nowadays they continue to divide, rule and conquer us successfully. We're all mainlining tech-fascist algorithmic mind control and it's being zapped 24/7 into our skulls via smartphones or tablets. We are dazzled and distracted by the neverending, imbecilic, empty spectacle of celebrity 'culture'. People thought *Big Brother* was a new kind of cruel entertainment shot in real time, but it was really a prophecy of the near future. All life is now a simulacrum of life; as J. G. Ballard said, 'nothing is real and nothing is unreal'. We meekly submit to the moral deprivations wrought by predatory neoliberal capitalist rogue economics and we bow down to the sinister demonic visions of twenty-first century far-right politicians who sell us the only available employment deal left in town: zero-hours 'contracts', chattel slavery dressed up as 'freedom of choice'; we abandon all hope.

Paul Cannell was a self-taught painter, an autodidact, never went to art school or had any encouragement to be a creative person. He found his own frame of reference in the streets of the area he grew up in and art books from the public library which he devoured. The pained, abstract images torn from his subconscious mind came at a price. Paul OD'd on heroin in the summer of 2005 in his parents' house. It wasn't the first time; some say it was suicide. Cannell was special and gifted, one of the best humans I ever met.

We sat around in the office talking about cover art for the forth-coming album. I hadn't asked Paul to do a new painting for this, there was so much day-to-day rock and roll madness. McGee pointed to a red and white 'dealer' poster for 'Higher Than the Sun' which was tacked up on the wall above his desk – someone (Grant Fleming later told me it was Mark Dennis) had taken the sun image and solarised all the colour and painterly detail out of it – and said, 'That's the cover, that sun. Use that image, Bob.' I took this idea down to the graphics guy in Putney and we played around with it on his computer programme. Eventually we settled on the famous blue-faced sun with black and white eyes and exploding yellow rays against an all-red background. We cropped the sun rays at the top and bottom of the frame to achieve intensity of focus. It looked fantastic.

For the back sleeve we laid out the song titles in large type across the width of the sleeve in a style that referenced *Changesonebowie*, Bowie's classic Greatest Hits album I'd owned as a teenager. Super stylish and modern, so unlike anything else at the time. Then for the gatefold I looked through the transparencies of band photos we had and I took that photograph from the 'Don't Fight It, Feel It' video that Grant Fleming had taken of Throb all in white playing a huge sitar, me sitting cross-legged in black polo and wraparound shades 'playing' violin, Innes clapping and Stephanie Ansell sitting on the harpsichord playing a flute. I wanted it to be like a classic underground rock album. A portal into a mysterious otherworld. I deliberately put no writing on the cover. There are no musician credits. There's no band name or album title on the front cover. The songwriting credits and the production credits are on the labels and I had as little info on it as possible, so it would look mysterious, like a Factory record or a Zeppelin record, so that it was all about the music. I didn't want anything to spoil Cannell's wonderful 'damaged' sun. I liked the fact it inverted the acid house smiley logo.

At this point we were all having a great time, all the things we had dreamed about as teenagers were becoming reality. I also thought, this is not gonna last. At some point there will be a reckoning. The damaged sun was also a damaged son. It was a darker, more cynical version. It was a burned-out sun. As night follows day we were soon to become 'damaged sons' ourselves. But that was in the post. Not yet. We were still having too much fun. Later, in 2010, the Royal Mail would put Cannell's *Screamadelica* sun on an official UK stamp alongside *Let It Bleed* by Rolling Stones, *Led Zep 4*, *London Calling* by the Clash, *Ziggy Stardust* by David Bowie. I'd like to think that Cannel the anarchist punk would have loved seeing his artwork adorned with HRH Queen Elizabeth's head embossed in gold beside it. Quite ironic. He'd be happy to see his album cover alongside some of the all-time classics of rock and roll.

*Screamadelica* was born but it didn't yet have its title. One night after we'd been out raving, probably at Kinky Disco, all Friday and Saturday nights, we crashed out at dawn, Sunday morning coming down, debris and party mess everywhere. That afternoon round at Nightingale's flat we were sitting about just shooting the shit. Someone said, 'We need something as good as Funkadelic's *One Nation Under a Groove*.'

Somebody else said, 'Yeah, like "screamadelic".'

Then someone else said, 'Screamadelica'.

We went, yeah, that's it. Genius. Alex Nightingale always says it was him who thought of it, but then, he would. *Success has many fathers, failure none*. Innes sequenced the album. We knew that it would start with 'Movin' On Up' and end with 'Shine Like Stars' but what about all the tracks in between? They were a mixed bunch with no real musical association, all different instrumentation and moods. Innes has said he sequenced it in such a way that it would be the soundtrack to a kid going out on the weekend.

> The defiant rock and roll of 'Movin' On Up'
> blasting out whilst you get all dressed up and
> ready to go out and face the world
> 'Slip Inside This House' as you venture out into the night
> the unknown before you
> the thrill of adventure

*'Don't Fight It' plays in in the club as you hit the dancefloor and*
    *drop*
        *your E    so that it's 'Higher Than the Sun' as you come up*
               *peaking on the drug and everything*
               *becomes psychedelicised*
*followed by     the dreamscape of 'Inner Flight' as your spirit*
*glides on the transcendent*
   *effects of psychotropic euphoria that morph into the ecstatic*
               *drug-induced*
                       *feelings of empathy*
                         *solidarity and*
          *utopian visions of universal brotherly love that is*
                 *'Come Together' and you drop*
                      *another E*
*for the gonzoid funk rock of 'Loaded'*
   *before sinking into the comedown       crash*
   *and melancholy*
           *contemplation of 'Damaged' and*
              *'I'm Coming Down' after you've*
     *stumbled home and are curled up in bed*
*on your own in a cold, grey room*
*the bedsit blues*
*the glamour, clamour*
*colour and noise of the club*
            *a distant memory now*
*voices in the radiators*
*the guilt-ridden*
*self-loathing*
*paranoiac ice-cold electronica of the dub symphony in two parts is*
*a hell without end*
*your head and heart full of dread and paranoid thoughts*
*body shivering, bones aching, panel-beaters beating inside your*
*skull as malevolent demons emerge from the subconscious, please*
*stop! please stop! until*

> *– redemption –     the trip finally ends in light*
> *your soul bathing in the sea-shanty, womblike*
> *warmth of 'Shine Like Stars'*

Whatever the intention, it sounded right to me, the album had peaks and troughs just like a drug trip. You could chart your night out through this album.

We were releasing an original-sounding album in the vein of *Metal Box* by PiL and *Tago Mago* by CAN. They were *the* two lodestar experimental pop albums for me. An underground rock record. I didn't know if it was going to be a hit, but I was thinking, if we never make another record, it doesn't matter. This is a statement. This is the fucking best record in the world right now. This is the best band. And I know Nirvana was happening at the same time, but I didn't really take notice of them then – later on with *In Utero* I would – I was too wrapped up in our stuff to be interested in anything else at that point, obsessively so. *Screamadelica* and *Nevermind* were released on the same day, 23 September 1991.

For some people, that's the day the nineties really began.

# Image Credits

## Plate Section Images

*Section One*

Glasgow's own Yuri Gagarin. Author's personal collection.

With Dad, May Day 1962. Author's personal collection.

With Mum and Graham, Ardrossan, July 1967. Author's personal collection.

35 Palermo Street, 1967. Author's personal collection.

'Bobby does a Beatles', 1963. Author's personal collection.

Aged 16 in my bedroom. Author's personal collection.

1970s fashion. Author's personal collection.

'Boy about Town', Strathclyde University, 1979. Les Cook.

On the road with Altered Images and Siouxsie and the Banshees, 1980. Author's personal collection.

Drumming for Altered Images, Middlesbrough Rock Garden, 1980. Author's personal collection.

With Alan McGee, Mount Florida, 1980. Author's personal collection.

Playing bass with the The Wake, Henry Wood Hall, Glasgow, 1982. Billy Thomson.

First ever Primal Scream photo session, 1984. Karen Parker.

Moody bastard. Karen Parker.

First Primal Scream gig, The Venue, Glasgow, 12th October 1984. Karen Parker.

Uncaptioned, Primal Scream. Lawrence Watson.

Uncaptioned, Jesus and Mary Chain. Mike Laye.

Jesus and Mary Chain on *The Old Grey Whistle Test*, 1985. Luke Hayes.

Drumming. Luke Hayes.

Throwing drums. Alastair Inge, Camera Press London.

Second album tour. Luke Hayes.

## Image Credits

Andrew Innes. Luke Hayes.

Throb. Luke Hayes.

*Section Two*

Uncaptioned, Bobby with book. Tom Sheehan.

With Andrew Weatherall. Grant Fleming.

Showing respect to Her Majesty with Innes. Grant Fleming.

Hijinks on the Screamadelica tour, 1991. Grant Fleming (left) and Tom Sheehan (right).

Primal Scream and Denise Johnson on the way to Kinky Disco. Grant Fleming.

Their Screamadelic Majesties. Grant Fleming.

Uncaptioned, Bobby singing. Grant Fleming.

Screamadelica album signing, HMV Oxford Street, September 1991. Getty Images/Mick Hutson.

'Higher than the Sun', painting by Paul Cannel, with thanks to Dick Green.

'Don't fight it, feel it'. Getty Images/Kevin Cummins.

Like kids in a candy shop. Andrew Catlin.

Uncaptioned, Bobby with lyrics. Grant Fleming.

### In-text images

p. ii Author's personal collection.

p. 1 Author's personal collection.

p. 2 Nick Hedges.

p. 73 Author's personal collection.

p. 74 Author's personal collection.

p. 145 Mike Laye.

p. 146 Luke Hayes.

p. 271 Grant Fleming.

p. 272 Andrew Catlin.

pp. 413–18 Posters supplied via author's personal collection.

p. 419 Poster by Gordon Dawson @creamguillotine.

pp. 420–22 Posters supplied via author's personal collection.

# Acknowledgements

Thank you ...

To Robert and Wilma Gillespie for preparing me for the struggle.

To Katy, Wolf, Lux and Graham, for love and support.

Gerry McElhone and Sean O'Hagan for encouragement.

Lee Brackstone for asking me to write the book in the first place.

Ellie Freedman for listening and patience.

# ALTERED IMAGES
# ALTERED IMAGES

## LIVE AT-

# THE WAKE
# PRIMAL SCREAM
## Tuesday 2 Nov. 1982     8 pm
## Henry Wood Hall · SNO Centre
## Claremont St. (off Berkeley St.)

**advance tickets £1.50**
*available from Virgin, Listen & Primitive Records
or pay at the door*

A CREATION
ARTIFACT
NIGHT

Which side will you be on?

THE JESUS
& MARY CHAIN

BIFF BANG POW!

OCHRE 5.

PRIMAL SCREAM

LATE BAR. 9 till 2 a.m. £1·50 PUNK ROCK DISCO

THE VENUE. THURSDAY 11th OCTOBER.

Primal Scream
The Original –
Mixed Up Kid
Garage/Punk Rock Disco
at
Lucifers
22 Jamaica St.
Sunday 24th Feb
Price:£2·00

FRIDAY, APRIL 5
A GOOD FRIDAY CELEBRATION...
FROM ENGLAND
THE FIRST AMERICAN APPEARANCE OF
JESUS AND MARY CHAIN
SHOW STARTS AT 1:30AM
DJ: ANITA SARKO
DANCETERIA
30 W 21ST
COMP FOR TWO
THIS INVITE CANNOT BE SOLD OR TRANSFERRED
ADMISSION SUBJECT TO DOOR SELECTION
ON CONGO BILL, MIDNITE
STH PARTY

A SPLASH 1 HAPPENING

# PRIMAL SCREAM

## THE SOUP DRAGONS

Only a wrist is seen, with cuts

PSYCHEDELIC PUNK ROCK SOUNDTRACK

SUN.14 JULY 46 WEST GEORGE ST. £2.00

The story of a son who murders his mother's boyfriend.

Each kiss runs for 100feet, naked.Thry walk each other on the bed, with a boy friend and a dog.

Two Children live in a closet.It exists with dialouge with a former boy friend.

Ondinde sitsin the Judges seat,Ivy on the floor someone seems to raping her.Ultra Violet climbs onto the Judges table.A party of people crowd into the room.Rene Richard is a Russian Prince. The sound is very noisy.

A woman,supposedly dead,lies on a table.A number of people come in and place photographs on her body.Rene Richard makes nasty and sacrilegous remarks.At the end the 'dead' woman gets up. Ondine comes in,talks and lays down on the table

An eternal triangle as the hustler challenges the neighbour to try and take away a boy sunbathing on the beach.She fails.The second reel takes place in the bathroom.

FAC 51 THE HAÇIENDA

TUESDAY 23 JULY

# PRIMAL SCREAM

DJs

ANDREW WEATHERALL

THE ORB

AND SPECIAL GUESTS

9PM TILL 2AM £7 ADVANCE TICKETS AVAILABLE FROM PICCADILLY BOX OFFICE & THE HAÇIENDA